THE **COMPLETE IDIOT'S GUIDE®** TO

Motorcycles

Fourth Edition

by the Editors of Motorcyclist™ magazine with Darwin Holmstrom and Simon Green

ALPHA

A member of Penguin Group (USA) Inc.

This book is dedicated to the memory of Aaron Creamer, the only true friend I've ever lost to motorcycling, and one of the best young flat-track racers ever to don a steel shoe. Rest in Peace number 64.

ALPHA BOOKS

Published by the Penguin Group

Penguin Group (USA) Inc., 375 Hudson Street, New York, New York 10014, USA

Penguin Group (Canada), 90 Eglinton Avenue East, Suite 700, Toronto, Ontario M4P 2Y3, Canada (a division of Pearson Penguin Canada Inc.)

Penguin Books Ltd., 80 Strand, London WC2R 0RL, England

Penguin Ireland, 25 St. Stephen's Green, Dublin 2, Ireland (a division of Penguin Books Ltd.)

Penguin Group (Australia), 250 Camberwell Road, Camberwell, Victoria 3124, Australia (a division of Pearson Australia Group Pty. Ltd.)

Penguin Books India Pvt. Ltd., 11 Community Centre, Panchsheel Park, New Delhi—110 017, India

Penguin Group (NZ), 67 Apollo Drive, Rosedale, North Shore, Auckland 1311, New Zealand (a division of Pearson New Zealand Ltd.)

Penguin Books (South Africa) (Pty.) Ltd., 24 Sturdee Avenue, Rosebank, Johannesburg 2196, South Africa

Penguin Books Ltd., Registered Offices: 80 Strand, London WC2R 0RL, England

International Standard Book Number: 978-1-59257-704-0
Library of Congress Catalog Card Number: 2007932653

10 09   8 7 6 5 4 3

Interpretation of the printing code: The rightmost number of the first series of numbers is the year of the book's printing; the rightmost number of the second series of numbers is the number of the book's printing. For example, a printing code of 08-1 shows that the first printing occurred in 2008.

Printed in the United States of America

Note: This publication contains the opinions and ideas of its authors. It is intended to provide helpful and informative material on the subject matter covered. It is sold with the understanding that the authors and publisher are not engaged in rendering professional services in the book. If the reader requires personal assistance or advice, a competent professional should be consulted.

The authors and publisher specifically disclaim any responsibility for any liability, loss, or risk, personal or otherwise, which is incurred as a consequence, directly or indirectly, of the use and application of any of the contents of this book.

Most Alpha books are available at special quantity discounts for bulk purchases for sales promotions, premiums, fund-raising, or educational use. Special books, or book excerpts, can also be created to fit specific needs.

For details, write: Special Markets, Alpha Books, 375 Hudson Street, New York, NY 10014.

Publisher: *Marie Butler-Knight*
Editorial Director/Acquiring Editor: *Mike Sanders*
Managing Editor: *Billy Fields*
Development Editor: *Ginny Bess Munroe*
Senior Production Editor: *Janette Lynn*
Copy Editor: *Jennifer Connolly*

Cartoonist: *Steve Barr*
Cover Designer: *Rebecca Harmon*
Book Designer: *Trina Wurst*
Indexer: *Tonya Heard*
Layout: *Chad Dressler*
Proofreader: *John Etchison*

Contents at a Glance

Contents

Foreword

I have these really vivid visual images of bikes from when I was very young. I remember when I was about 5 years old, my aunt was going with a guy who had a bike. He came over to the house with his Harley. It had the two-tone tinted windshield like they had in the '50s, and on the bottom part of the windshield there was a sticker of a girl in a two-piece bathing suit. And I remember my mother going, "Get away from there!" And I said, "I'm not looking at the girl, I'm looking at the bike." And she said, "I know what you're looking at. Get out of there." "I'm not, I want to look at the bike." So I remember my mother having a huge fit over this pornographic motorcycle!

The first bike I ever got was a Honda 350 back in 1971. I bought it from a Harley-Davidson dealer in Everett, Massachusetts. I remember I went down and just bought it. You didn't have to have a license in those days. You didn't even have to know how to ride. You bought a motorcycle like you bought an air rifle. The salesman said, "Hey, okay, good luck," and you were off.

I remember getting on the freeway, not knowing what I was doing. I turned my head to see if a car was coming, and my glasses blew off. So now I'm on something I've never ridden, in the rain, with no helmet, of course, and I can't see. But I still remember thinking, "This is fun!"

Another time I was on that bike, still not very familiar with it, I got caught in some rain grooves. The tires just wanted to follow the grooves, you know? I thought, "How do I get out of this?" I remember just sailing past my exit and thinking that maybe I'd run out of gas or something. I had no idea what to do. That's why I think training is important. Back then, I learned by *almost* having accidents.

Riders today shouldn't have to learn the way I did. My advice to newcomers to motorcycling is this:

- Take a motorcycle safety course. That's the first thing.

- Lie down on the ground and have a friend put the bike gently on top of you. (Just kidding, folks—don't try this at home.) Okay, now magnify that feeling by a thousand because that's what it's like when you fall off a bike. Everybody falls off at some point, and you have to be willing to accept that.

- Never take the bike when you're in a hurry because that's when you'll have an accident. If work is 10 minutes away and I got up an hour early, I'll take the bike. If work is 10 minutes away and I've got to be there in 10 minutes, I'll take the car.

The motorcycling world is different now than when I got started. It's less cohesive than it used to be. The simplest poll to take is to ride down the street and wave, and see how many riders wave back. I'm probably the last generation of guys who wave at everybody. Owning a motorcycle used to be a lifestyle. Now it's more a lifestyle accessory, like a cell phone or a fanny pack.

Today people have a lot more money to spend, and they're not learning how to ride. I'm amazed at the number of people who just don't know how to ride. It's like you just buy this rocket ship that you sit on. But you have to prepare for motorcycling like it's a sport—because it is.

The editors at *Motorcyclist*™, Darwin Holmstrom, and Simon Green have pulled together a lot of great advice and information on the sport of motorcycling. As both an idiot and a motorcyclist, I found this book very helpful.

—Jay Leno

Motorcycle enthusiast, comedian, and host of *The Tonight Show*

Introduction

The motorcycle world is hard to understand from the outside. Most non-motorcycle people are hesitant to join in because everybody knows that motorcycling is dangerous. I'm guessing that buying this book means you're on the outside, wondering whether to enter. Well come on in; things probably aren't what they seem.

I remember being on the outside myself. I can cast my mind back to being a kid at my grandpa's house in England, and being hypnotized by his motorcycles. My dad drove a car, and all that was to me, was paint, wheels, and seats. His dad was different, though—he rode bikes, and to my baby blues they were freaky things. They looked so complex when you got up close with their weird pipes and levers, exposed engines covered in elaborate fins, shiny metal here, dull metal there. It all looked so functional, so raw, so focused.

Back then I was too young to realize what a true motorcyclist my grandfather was. He spent his entire career working at Norton Motorcycles, one of the most famous manufacturers of the day. This meant that bikes were more than just a mode of transport to him, they were his life. When the inevitable happened and I wanted to ride, too, I was immediately told "no" by my father. Motorcycles were too dangerous.

That all seems like a long time ago now; I've been inside the motorcycle industry for most of my life. Currently I spend more time writing about bikes than riding them, but for a long time it was the opposite. Obviously I defied my dad and got a license, but later I took it one stage further and became a full-time motorcycle instructor. For five years I introduced others to motorcycling, and I did it in Britain, where licensing often requires five full days of intensive training.

The point is that I spent all of those years watching new riders just like you come walking through the door, and most of them had similar concerns to my father. It would always take some time to alleviate those concerns and gain their trust, but I'm proud to say that I always did. It was one of the most satisfying experiences of my life to watch them walk out of the same door, license in hand, knowing they were as safe as possible and that they really "got it."

This book has been designed to achieve the same end result as the training school, to turn you from a hesitant new rider into a fully informed motorcyclist. Somebody who not only understands the potential dangers of motorcycling, but gets how to dramatically reduce those risks.

That's the trick, really; every new rider has to accept motorcycling for what it is. We choose to ride an exposed piece of machinery in a world filled with other road users, people with wildly varying levels of skill. Smart motorcyclists understand those dangers and do everything possible to minimize them. True motorcyclists understand the need to ride defensively, and they get how vital it is to protect their bodies with the right bike gear. For this kind of motorcyclist, it's a surprisingly safe sport.

There are the other kind, too, the arrogant kind you'll see in summer dressed like they're tanning while riding their bike. By reading this book, you've already separated yourself from that herd, which is good because if you enter this world, you can't do it by half measures.

If you can walk the line between having fun and knowing when to take it seriously, the motorcycle world's enormous community will embrace you. They're a great bunch of diverse people, who all subconsciously respect each other's commitment to being a true motorcyclist. Don't be surprised if you meet some lifelong friends along the way: my wife, best man, my closest friends, in fact nearly all of my friends are people that I initially met just because we all ride motorcycles.

For those of us that understand the risks and are always prepared, bike riding is one of the most exhilarating experiences in existence. To be "at one" with such an ergonomically designed machine, defying gravity through twists and turns, and effortlessly accelerating away from everything else on the road with just a drop of your wrist, is quite simply addictive.

So yes, motorcycling can be dangerous, *in the wrong hands*, and that's what it comes down to. You've already got off to a great start by taking it seriously enough to buy an informative book, so I don't have to worry about you. Just take it all in, respect your bike, and I'll see you out on the road someday.

How to Use This Book

This book follows a linear, step-by-step structure and takes you through the entire motorcycle experience from start to finish. The book is structured this way to help you minimize the risks associated with motorcycling, to help make your entry into the sport safe and enjoyable.

I've divided the book into five parts, each designed to take you to a new level of enjoyment in a safe, orderly fashion.

Part 1, "Biker Basics," sets the stage for the adventure you are about to embark on, providing a general overview of why we ride, the history of motorcycling, and the types of bikes available.

Part 2, "So You Want to Buy a Bike?" helps you identify what type of motorcycle you need and teaches you how to buy your first motorcycle. You get detailed discussions about the parts of a motorcycle and, more important, how those parts relate to you, the rider.

Part 3, "On the Road," is probably the most important part of this book. It helps you actually get out and ride. This is where you put your knowledge to the test, where theory translates into reality.

Part 4, "Living with a Motorcycle," condenses the entire spectrum of the motorcycle-ownership experience into chapters that cover maintenance, repair, customization, and collecting.

Part 5, "The Motorcycling Community," provides an overview of the world you are getting into. When you buy a motorcycle, you are not just buying an object; you're investing in a lifestyle. This part discusses the many places in which you'll meet fellow motorcycle enthusiasts, including motorcycle clubs, races, and rallies.

I've also included four appendixes that you'll find useful. Appendix A lists all the new bikes for sale in the United States, along with the bikes that are best suited for beginners and the bikes I believe are best buys. Appendix B features a comprehensive list of used bikes that make ideal first motorcycles. Appendix C highlights useful motorcycle-related resources, and Appendix D is a glossary of the terms you'll encounter in this book.

Extras

Throughout this book you'll find tips and information that will help you ride better and safer without looking like a dork in the process. This information is highlighted in sidebars:

Motorcycology

Tips and inside information providing insights into safe, enjoyable motorcycling.

Motorcycle Moments

Anecdotes of historical and personal moments in the history of motorcycling.

Steer Clear

Advice on practices and hazards to avoid if you want to keep the shiny side up, which means not falling down.

Cycle Babble

Definitions of technical motorcycling terms that pop up throughout the book.

A Note About the Fourth Edition

There's been a lot going on recently in the motorcycle world. After years of keeping a low profile, motorcycling suddenly got a lot of exposure in the form of several television shows. The theme was consistent throughout all of these programs: the chopper—more specifically, building custom choppers from scratch, with the shows' format being either a judged competition, or a soap opera filled with drama, mystery, and suspense (or filled with none of the above, depending on your perspective).

At the exact same time, another segment within the motorcycle community experienced a dramatic growth: stunt riding. Young guys were taking ultralight sportbikes and abusing their abundant power, making them do things they were never designed for. The poor bikes.

What this all means is that a whole bunch of new riders have joined the motorcycling community since this book was last published. From the mainstream came the people with a newfound love for choppers, and from the underground came another crowd, riding sportbikes just like the ones used and abused by the stunt people they'd been following.

It already looks like the televised chopper scene is dropping off in popularity and the stunt scene was always too antisocial to thrive, but the good news is that all of the new riders have stuck around. In fact, the growth seems to have just begun; sportbike diehards are already developing a new subculture, radically customizing their bikes in ways that make all of the original choppers look tame. In a new twist, these sportbikes are all set to go mainstream, with their own television show just starting to air.

Some of the new riders from the chopper scene have evolved, too, trading in their bikes for something more practical, sometimes trading in for something less practical. Either way, motorcycling is growing, and growing fast.

This is great news for everyone. More people riding bikes means more money coming into the industry, and that means more choice for bike riders, everywhere. From a wider selection of new bike models to a more comprehensive array of bike gear, from new magazines to a bigger choice of bike events, there is more of everything and it's all catering to us.

This guide has been constantly evolving since the first issue. In this fourth edition I've included some more riding advice, added new sections to cover the changing world of motorcycling, and I've increased the size of the color section. I even altered the concept of this color section; it now features "recommended buys" from every major category of bike you may be considering.

In short, this book should still be the most thorough introduction to motorcycling available. So whatever brought you into the motorcycle world, welcome—I'm glad you're here.

Acknowledgments

I would like to thank all the people who helped with this book. Judy and Dan Kennedy at Whitehorse Press have been incredibly helpful, providing me with much information at the exact moment I needed it. It's as if they read my mind at times. I found their excellent book *The Motorcycling Safety Foundation's Guide to Motorcycling Excellence* to be the single most useful resource I used in writing this book. Whitehorse's *Street Smart* video series also proved to be an essential source of information.

I would also like to thank the Motorcycle Safety Foundation in the United States and the Driving Standards Agency in the United Kingdom, partly because without the groundbreaking work they have done in the field of motorcycle safety, this book could not have been written, and partly because of all the lives they have saved.

I received a great deal of last-minute help getting items I needed for photo shoots from several people and companies, especially Ron Harper at Chase Harper, Ann Willey at National Cycle, and Ken Hendren at Vanson. Over the years, I have used products from all three companies, which is why I chose them for the photos—I know they are of the highest quality. It was nice to discover that the folks making those products are of the same high quality.

I want to thank the photographers who supplied me with last-minute photography: Brian J. Nelson and Timothy Remus.

I'd like to thank all the motorcycle journalists who inspired me to not only ride, but to write about my experiences. The work of Aaron Frank, Warren Pole, Grant Leonard, Cook Neilson, Dan Walsh, Mick Philips, Alan Seeley, Art Friedman, Kevin Cameron, Peter Egan, David Edwards, Greg McQuide, Andrew Trevitt, Matthew Miles, Mark Hoyer, Kent Kunitsugu, Don Canet, and countless others helped me get through many long winters in the Northern Plains. I'd like to give a special thanks to those journalists who write about safety issues, writers such as David Hough and Lawrence Grodsky. Not only have they helped me learn what I needed to know to write this book, but they also may have saved my life a time or two.

I'd also like to thank my wife, Jessica, whose support (not to mention encouragement and patience) helped make this book possible.

I'd especially like to thank *Motorcyclist*™ editors Mitch Boehm and Aaron Frank, who connected me with this project.

Trademarks

All terms mentioned in this book that are known to be or are suspected of being trademarks or service marks have been appropriately capitalized. Alpha Books and Penguin Group (USA) Inc. cannot attest to the accuracy of this information. Use of a term in this book should not be regarded as affecting the validity of any trademark or service mark.

Part 1

Biker Basics

Congratulations! As a beginning biker, you are about to embark on an adventure that will change your life. No other hobby will affect you at such a fundamental level as motorcycling. It will start subtly: at work, you'll find yourself daydreaming about going for a ride while you stare at the gibberish on your computer screen; in meetings, you'll look right through your boss and instead see the road outside the window. In your mind, you'll be riding on that road. Before you know it, you'll have a pet name for your motorcycle, which, of course, you'll tattoo on some hidden part of your body.

In other words, you will become a biker.

You are about to enter the community of motorcyclists. In this part of the book, you'll learn about that community, its history, and all it has to offer you—including an introduction to the joys of motorcycling.

Chapter 1

The Motorcycle Mystique

In This Chapter

- ◆ Why motorcyclists love to ride
- ◆ Motorcycles as "chicken soup" for "your soul"
- ◆ The cultural impact of motorcycles
- ◆ How motorcycle films have shaped generations of motorcyclists
- ◆ The advantages of owning a motorcycle

Perhaps one word best sums up the appeal of motorcycles: *fun*. Fun is what I had the first time I rode my neighbor's minibike nearly three decades ago. It's what I had this morning when I took my bike out for a ride.

But it's a complex fun, composed of many facets. Part of the pleasure of riding comes from the freedom and mobility the machine gives you. The exhilaration you feel as you power effortlessly up to cruising speed provides a portion of the fun. Part of your enjoyment comes from developing your riding skills—your ability to control the beast.

In this chapter, I show you why motorcycle riding can be such a rewarding, exhilarating, and liberating experience.

The Thrill of the Open Road

The sun creeps over the treetops, its warm rays driving the chill from your limbs as you open the garage door and wheel your motorcycle out onto the driveway. You prop up the bike and check to make certain everything is okay, which it will be because you take good care of your machine. You don your helmet and jacket and pull on your gloves, and then start your engine. The beast jumps to life and then settles into a patient, powerful idle. You look over the bike one last time, and then mount up and ride away. Now the fun begins.

At about the same time, your neighbor, co-worker, friend, or family member is unloading his—or her—dirtbike at a local off-road park. He goes through the same rituals, giving the machine a thorough preflight inspection, donning protective gear, and then mounting up, snicking the machine into gear, and riding away. Now the fun begins.

You take it easy at first, waiting for your tires to warm. You shift through the gears, feeling the satisfying mesh of the cogs, and breathe in the cool, clean morning air. The vibration through the handlebars and footpegs feels reassuring, making you aware of your machine's mechanical presence.

As you ease out onto the practice track, looking for oncoming riders, you do a warm-up lap. With each lap, you increase your speed, getting air over the jumps. The bike responds perfectly to every weight shift, to every control input.

As your tires warm, you start accelerating harder through each curve. You snake through a series of S-curves, settling into a rhythm among you, the road, and your bike, engaged in a dance as elegant as any ballet. This is what it's all about.

As your muscles warm, you start riding harder, hitting the triple section perfectly, and taking inside lines where others are taking the longer, slower outside one. You and your bike find the track's rhythm, one that's less of a ballet and more of a break dance. This is what it's all about.

It doesn't matter whether you're riding a cutting-edge sportbike, a heavyweight cruiser, a big touring bike, or a powerful but agile dirtbike; the thrill of the ride is what draws you out again and again. Whatever emotional baggage you may have accumulated, you leave behind on the open road. When you're participating in a dance with your bike and the road, it doesn't matter that your boss is a pointy-headed sociopath, that your spouse shouts at you, or that your kids act like juvenile delinquents. There's no room for such worries on a bike because the activity at hand requires your total, undivided attention.

Bikes Are Beautiful

Most of us find motorcycles themselves gratifying—objects of art with an innate beauty that fills some need within us.

Motorcyclists tend to be *gearheads.* We love looking at our motorcycles almost as much as we love riding them. (In fact, some folks seem to be more enamored with viewing their machines than they are with riding them; legions of people trailer their motorcycles to different events around the country instead of riding them.)

Motorcycles possess a functional beauty, more so than any other motorized vehicle. The reason is simple; there just isn't room on a bike for anything unnecessary. You'll be seeing all kinds of beautiful bikes throughout this book, but for starters check out this Ducati 916. It epitomizes modern motorcycle design; the bike was initially created to be a lean, fast race winner, yet it's still widely regarded as one of the coolest looking street machines ever made.

Cycle Babble

While it's not exactly a technical term, often you will hear the word **gearhead** used when describing a motorcyclist. Gearhead refers to a person with a strong interest in all things mechanical.

Ducati's Superbikes, such as this 916, feature highly tuned engines, race-bred chassis and gorgeous bodywork enveloping the mechanics. The 916 epitomizes the purpose-driven beauty found on a modern motorcycle.

(Photo courtesy of Ducati USA)

It's hard to believe now, but when Ducati unveiled this bike in 1993 it had a completely groundbreaking style, though much of its design was primarily functional. Its exhaust pipes were tucked under the seat for high-speed streamlining, and the back wheel was completely exposed on one side to aid in super-quick wheel changes during a race. Ducati immediately put the bike to work in the World Superbike Championships and in its first season, it won. The 916 and its descendants won a total of eight world championships, and elements of its design are still being copied, by everyone from large-scale manufacturers to custom builders creating one-off show bikes.

The exotic superbike is just one type of drool-inducing motorcycle; some folks dig the old school V-Twin look. Harley-Davidson—the kings of the V-Twin have been selling everything they can make for many years, and to many eyes their products have been elevated to near art status. To most cruiser aficionados, the only thing better than a Harley is one of the customized machines of such chopper builders as Arlen Ness and Dave Perewitz. These bikes often resemble metallic sculptures more than motorcycles. A visit to any custom-bike show can take on the trappings of a visit to a museum.

All of this provides a good example of how important the look of a motorcycle is. That's as true of a Yamaha, Triumph, Laverda, or BMW as it is of a Harley or a Ducati. Motorcyclists love the way bikes look, and for every bike, there is someone who loves its appearance.

I learned this the hard way. A while back, in an article on motorcycle style, I poked fun at a bike that was generally accepted as being one of the uglier machines to have been produced during the past 20 years. I wrote that these motorcycles were probably very nice bikes, but they were so butt-ugly that no one ever found out because no one would be seen on one. I thought this was a fair assessment, since the bike had been a sales disaster.

Motorcycology

The demise of an entire motorcycle company can partly be traced to its producing one motorcycle that the public found visually unappealing. BSA attempted to enter the modern motorcycle market by producing a three-cylinder motorcycle, the BSA Rocket 3. The bike showed promise, but its styling, created by an industrial design firm with no experience in the motorcycle market, received such a dismal public reception that the resulting low sales caused BSA to implode.

Fair or not, at least one reader took issue with my critique and wrote in suggesting that my head was deeply embedded in a place that defied all laws of physics. The man owned one such "ugly motorcycle," and it had given him more than 100,000 miles of enjoyment. I felt bad about that situation, not because the reader questioned my hygienic habits and insulted my ancestors, but because I had belittled a motorcycle that obviously meant a great deal to him.

The Tao of Two Wheels

Some time ago, a colleague of mine, a reporter who covered religious topics at a newspaper, asked me why I didn't go to church. I told her I did go to church every day I went out riding my motorcycle.

For many motorcyclists, the ceremony of going for a ride provides the same spiritual sustenance other people find through the ceremonies conducted by organized religions. The similarities are striking. We wear our leathers and riding suits as vestments, we have a prescribed ritual for starting our engines, and our favorite roads compose our liturgy.

The very nature of riding a motorcycle forces the rider into a spiritual state. Think of it this way: most religious systems encourage some form of meditative technique. Christians have prayer. Some Native Americans meditate inside sweat lodges, and Eastern spiritual systems advocate elaborate chanting techniques. All these methods have as their common general goal the transcendence of the self or ego in order to get in touch with some greater force.

Motorcycling forces riders to transcend their egos—to empty themselves and exist in the world around them. The consequences of not being totally aware of their actions and environment, of becoming distracted by the baggage of their everyday lives, are too great. When you're out in the world on a bike, you must be completely in the moment, completely aware of your surroundings, or you may find yourself meeting your concept of God earlier than you might have hoped.

But when everything is working, when you and your bike are totally in sync and the road rushing under your feet feels like an extension of your body—at those times, you get in touch with divinity.

Biker Chic

Not all that long ago, motorcycles were considered the domain of leather-clad hoodlums—guys you didn't want your daughter to be seen with. But that stereotype has always been inaccurate, and most people now realize that.

Motorcycling began to gain social acceptance in the 1960s, when the Japanese began exporting small, unintimidating motorcycles to the United States, but only in recent years has motorcycling been elevated to the status of high fashion.

Celebrities have always ridden motorcycles. Clark Gable terrorized Los Angeles on his Ariel Square Four. Marlon Brando used his own personal motorcycle in the film *The Wild One*. James Dean rode bikes from the time he was in high school. Steve McQueen's real-life racing antics made the jump scene in *The Great Escape* look feeble.

But these were Hollywood's bad boys—sexy rebels who knew no fear. You wouldn't find a nice woman like Donna Reed or a respectable fellow like Jimmy Stewart straddling a motorcycle.

Sometime during the 1980s, that changed. This shift in our collective perception began slowly. Photos of celebrity CEO Malcolm Forbes touring the world on his Harley-Davidson appeared in mainstream magazines, and Juan Carlos, the King of Spain, could be found touring his domain on a Harley. And, of course, Hollywood's latest string of bad boys—people such as Mickey Rourke, Sylvester Stallone, Bruce Willis, and Arnold Schwarzenegger—came out of the closet and proclaimed themselves bikers.

But it didn't stop there. Nice, respectable folks such as Jay Leno and Mary Hart let the world know they were motorcyclists. Country boy Lyle Lovett began appearing on magazine covers aboard his hot-rod Ducati. Rosie O'Donnell seldom appeared in the tabloids without her Suzuki Intruder. Ewen "Obi-Wan" McGregor took months off from his lucrative film career to take the trip-of-a-lifetime adventure tour. Mark-Paul Gosselaar of *NYPD Blue* likes to ride motocross. And Anthony Quinn's son Francesco has been riding since the tender age of four.

Now motorcycles are must-have fashion accessories for celebrities and celebrity wannabes, much like nipple rings were *de rigueur* for Seattle grunge rockers in the early 1990s.

The Art of Motorcycles

Although the motorcycle-as-nipple-ring is a fairly recent development, bikes have always had a strong influence on popular culture. In turn, popular culture has played a strong role in developing the motorcycle community.

The appeal of motorcycles to actors is no coincidence. Because riding a bike is a high-profile activity, motorcycles have always been an excellent method for studios to showcase and draw attention to their stars.

The history of motorcycles in film is as old as the history of motion pictures itself. Motorcycles appeared in some of the earliest silent films, including *Mabel at the Wheel* (1914), in which Charlie Chaplin drops Mabel off the back of his motorcycle and into a mud puddle.

Films about motorcycle riders appeared early on, including in *No Limit* (1935), in which English actor George Formby played a motorcycle-riding hero battling a gang of biker toughs.

While motorcycles played many roles in Hollywood films, the medium of film played an even more influential role in shaping motorcycle culture. As motorcycle films became more popular, increasing numbers of riders tried to emulate their screen heroes. When Marlon Brando portrayed Johnny in *The Wild One*, he portrayed a very atypical motorcyclist. After a generation of bikers grew up with Brando's Johnny as a role model, though, the image of the leather-clad, motorcycle-riding hood, while still an aberration, became much more common.

Because of the influence of films, portrayals of motorcyclists became self-fulfilling prophecies. The myriad outlaw-biker B-movies Hollywood cranked out during the 1960s and 1970s spawned a subculture of motorcyclists who modeled themselves on the bikers in those films. When Peter Fonda portrayed the philosophical Wyatt in *Easy Rider*, he gave birth to the real-life hippie poet-biker stereotype. When Arnold Schwarzenegger came back as promised in *Terminator 2: Judgment Day*, he did so on a Harley Fat Boy. Soon a Harley and a cigar were the macho man's must-have accessories of the 1990s.

From Wild Ones to Biker Boyz

For many years films like *The Wild One* and *Easy Rider* seemed to mark the beginning and end of Hollywood's most influential period on motorcycling. Even now they're two of the most important motorcycle films ever made and classics that every bike rider should see.

The Wild One became the archetypal biker flick because it was the first to portray the unique breed of bikers that sprang up in post–World War II America.

This film initiated a decades-long period of mistrust between motorcyclists and the general public. Johnny and his buddies seem pretty tame by today's standards; compared to bikers portrayed in later flicks, they're about as nice a bunch of boys as you'll ever meet. But back in 1953, Johnny represented the antichrist to Middle America.

Motorcycology _____

The event that inspired the film *The Wild One,* the so-called Hollister Invasion, was actually more of a nonevent. On the Fourth of July of 1947, about 3,500 motor-cyclists rode to Hollister, California (a town of about 4,500), to attend a race meeting. Another 500 or so riders showed up just to have a little fun. A few of these bikers got a bit out of hand, and by noon the next day, 29 of them had been cited for drunkenness, indecent exposure, and traffic violations. Unfortunately newspapers ran hyperbolic tales of anarchy and debauchery as thousands of bikers ran amuck, and *Life* magazine printed an infamous photo of a beer-guzzling rider stretched out on his cus-tomized Harley amid a pile of beer bottles. (The photo was staged by the *Life* photogra-pher.) The myth of the outlaw biker was born.

The Wild One gave birth to a new genre: the biker B-movie. In the 1950s and 1960s, Hollywood cranked out a pile of low-budget biker flicks. Each of these films tried to outdo the others in portraying the wild outlaw biker. *Easy Rider,* starring Peter Fonda, Dennis Hopper, and Jack Nicholson (in his first major film role), finally shattered that stereotype. Directed by Dennis Hopper, the movie changed everything. No lon-ger was the antihero biker a confused Neanderthal, mindlessly lashing out at what-ever got in his way. Instead, *Easy Rider* presented the biker as a sensitive, thoughtful enigma.

With the film Easy Rider, *actors Dennis Hopper and Peter Fonda turned the Hol-lywood biker image upside down.*

(Photo courtesy of Motorcyclist™ magazine)

Fast forward to the current day, and after years of silence on the biker movie front, it's happening all over again. Hollywood has realized that the bike world has been rejuvenated with younger riders and new attitudes, and they've started putting out movies like *Torque* and *Biker Boyz*. Do these new flicks finally improve the bike riders' image? Yeah right, apparently we're still trouble with a capital T!

Motorcycle Moments

Although Peter Fonda was an accomplished motorcyclist before he filmed *Easy Rider*, co-star Dennis Hopper was anything but. Before he made the film, Hopper's motorcycle experience was confined to a scooter he had owned in the 1950s—and he had crashed that machine in a rather spectacular fashion. After finishing the film, Hopper admitted to having been scared silly by his Harley.

Easy Rider: The Convenience of Bikes

Given the influence motorcycles have had on film and on our general culture, it's easy to argue the more esoteric appeal of motorcycling, but the sport has some practical benefits as well.

The relatively low price of motorcycles makes them attractive as practical transportation. While prices have risen dramatically during the past couple of decades, for the most part, bikes are still much less expensive than cars. You can buy a motorcycle in "like-new" condition in the $3,000 price range. For that money, you can pick up a bike that will deliver years or even decades of trouble-free transportation. Try finding a car for the same amount that isn't ready for the crusher.

In congested urban areas, the small size and mobility of a motorcycle provide real advantages over a car. An experienced rider can zip through traffic, and in places where the practice is legal (such as California), you can ride between lanes on the freeways (a practice known as *lane splitting*).

And with a motorcycle, you will never have to worry about a parking spot. You can always find a space to back into because you'll require only a fraction of the space a car requires.

Another practical benefit of motorcycles is their fuel efficiency. Even the biggest touring bike or fastest sportbike gets as many miles to the gallon as most econo-cars, and when ridden prudently, a smaller

Cycle Babble

Lane splitting (or filtering) refers to the practice of riding between lanes of traffic on a freeway. While this practice may sound dangerous, studies indicate that it might actually be safer than idling along in a traffic jam.

motorcycle can go for a couple of weeks without visiting the gas pump. The student training bikes, from a motorcycle school at which I taught, managed a frugal 80mpg.

If global climate change is caused by the burning of fossil fuels, as the majority of scientists believe, then we may soon be facing the prospect of dramatically increased fuel prices. In a world filled with gridlocked cities, the fuel and space-efficient nature of motorcycles could create a new boom of motorcycles as a serious form of transportation. This has been the case for several years in Europe, where many people have completely given up on owning a car.

The Least You Need to Know

- You get from motorcycling what you put into it.

- Like meditation, motorcycling requires your undivided attention.

- Biker flicks have shaped motorcycle culture as much as motorcycle culture has shaped biker flicks.

- Motorcycles can be practical as well as fun.

Chapter 2

A Brief History of Bikes

In This Chapter

♦ How motorcycling developed from cheap transportation into a passionate hobby

♦ The myth of the outlaw biker

♦ How the baby boomers changed the face of motorcycling

♦ Harley-Davidson's role in today's motorcycle market

Motorcycling offers more pleasure than any other activity a person can engage in (well, okay, not *any* other activity, but almost). It also extracts a high penalty for making mistakes. If you're going to be a motorcyclist, you'll need as much knowledge as you can get to survive out there, and a solid understanding of the history of the sport is part of that knowledge.

But knowing how we got here from there serves as an ego boost as well. Motorcyclists are gearheads, people with an almost unnatural attraction to things mechanical. Like every other group, we have our inside secrets, status symbols that tell whether a person is a hardcore rider or just another dork with a motorcycle. Few of these clues scream "Dork!" as loudly as a rider poorly versed in the history of motorcycles. In this chapter, I'll give you the inside info you'll need to become a true motorcyclist.

Humble Beginnings

Almost as soon as the modern bicycle appeared toward the end of the nineteenth century, some inspired individual (my hero) decided to strap an internal-combustion motor to the contraption. By the turn of the century, a variety of motorized bicycles were available to the general public.

The motorized-bicycle experiments of two young men, William S. Harley and Arthur Davidson, proved to be more influential to American motorcycling than all the rest combined.

The pair realized their experiments had commercial potential, and along with Arthur's brothers, Walter and William, they formed the Harley-Davidson Motor Company in 1903 to manufacture motorized bicycles. From this humble beginning sprang the longest continuously running motorcycle-manufacturing firm in the world, affectionately known as The Motor Company.

But Mr. Harley and the Davidson boys weren't the only people conducting such experiments.

 Motorcycle Moments _____

Gottlieb Daimler, the German inventor who produced the first functional four-stroke engine, may well have created the first gasoline-powered motorcycle. After his early experiments using an engine to power a four-wheeled horseless carriage produced less than satisfactory results (probably due to the whopping 0.5 horsepower the motor cranked out), Daimler built his *Einspur,* or single-tracked test vehicle, in 1885. Although crude, this vehicle incorporated many features still found on motorcycles today, such as a cradle frame and twist-grip controls on the handlebars.

In 1902, one year before the formation of The Motor Company, a German engineer named Maurice (Mauritz) Johann Schulte designed a motorcycle, the first to be produced by Triumph Cycle Co., Ltd., of England. This machine was still very much a motorized bicycle with a Belgian-produced engine fitted to its frame.

The early years of the twentieth century saw hundreds of similar companies form. The low power output of the engines available at the time made them better suited to power small, two-wheeled vehicles than larger, carriage-type machines, and motorcycles thrived as forms of personal transportation. Plus, cars were still too expensive for most people to own; motorcycles were cheaper and more plentiful.

Like all technology of that time, motorcycle development proceeded at a frantic pace. Soon the early motorized bicycles were supplanted by machines designed from the start to be operated by some form of engine. By the end of World War I, most of the technical innovations we see today had been tried with varying degrees of success. Because other technologies, such as metallurgy—the study of metals—hadn't kept pace with such innovations, by the 1920s, motorcycle designers had settled on relatively simple designs. The brilliant ideas of those early designers proved to be ahead of their time, and many would have to wait until the 1970s or 1980s to finally find acceptance.

Although the sport of motorcycling thrived initially, the same technological advances that drove its success led to the first of the sport's many crises. As internal-combustion engines became more powerful and efficient, they became more practical as power sources for horseless carriages. And with the advent of affordable automobiles such as Henry Ford's Model T in 1913, average people could afford to buy cars. Clearly, it was easier to haul the entire family to church in an automobile; you could only haul three or four family members on a motorcycle, and then only if it was equipped with a *sidecar*. By the end of World War I, many of the companies manufacturing motorcycles had either gone out of business or switched to the manufacture of some other product. Motorcycles might have become extinct except for some clever marketing moves on the part of the remaining manufacturers.

Motorcycling survived by positioning itself as a sport, a leisure activity, rather than trying to compete with automobiles as practical transportation. The move made sense. People had been racing motorcycles all along; promoting riding in general as a sport was a logical extension of that activity.

This market positioning helped motorcycling survive its second great crisis: the Great Depression. This worldwide economic disaster finished off many of the remaining motorcycle-manufacturing firms that had survived the advent of the inexpensive, reliable automobile, and, again, those companies that survived did so by promoting motorcycling as a sport.

Cycle Babble

Sidecars are small carriages attached to the side of a motorcycle to provide extra carrying capacity and extra stability in low-speed, low-traction conditions. Sidecars usually consist of a tubelike cockpit area resting on a frame that attaches to the motorcycle on one side and is held aloft by a wheel on the opposite side.

The Wild Ones: The Outlaws' Conveyance

Motorcycling in America entered the modern era following World War II. Important technological advances had been made before the war, but most people were too busy struggling to survive the Depression to pay much attention.

World War II changed all that. After the war, a lot of restless people came back from Europe and Asia, people not content to go back to the way things were. They could afford transportation, and they had an elaborate new highway system to explore. Many of them decided to explore those new roads via motorcycles.

As you saw in the previous chapter, the film *The Wild One* played an important role in the formation of the postwar motorcycling community. It was a difficult time for many Americans. We'd won the war, but afterward, nothing seemed quite the same. To the general public, Johnny, Marlon Brando's character in the film, represented everything that was wrong with the country. Like Communism, the stereotype of the outlaw biker became a focal point for their fears.

When Marlon Brando roared into small-town America in The Wild One, *he used his own motorcycle, a 650cc Triumph Thunderbird very much like this 1953 example.*

(Photo © 1998 Timothy Remus)

But not everyone feared Johnny. Some people wanted more out of life than the latest automatic appliances in the kitchen and a new Plymouth sedan parked in the driveway. For them, Johnny represented an escape from the mind-numbing conformity of McCarthy-era America. In Johnny, Brando created a role model for these disaffected young people—a figure who jelled in America's psyche as the archetypal outlaw biker.

The Japanese Invasion

Throughout the 1950s, motorcycling remained the domain of extreme gearheads and onepercenters (outlaws). Nice people didn't ride a bike. Nice people didn't even associate with those who did ride, whether they were upstanding members of the American Motorcycle Association (AMA) or hardcore outlaws.

The reason for this involved more than just the perceived danger of the sport or of motorcyclists' outlaw image. There were practical reasons for the marginality of motorcycling as well.

Part of the problem was that the machines themselves demanded a great deal from their owners. The technological advancements of motorcycling hadn't kept pace with those of automobiles. By the 1950s, cars were relatively reliable, easily maintained devices, and the experience of owning one wasn't all that different than it is today.

Bikes were another story.

The reason only gearheads owned motorcycles back then was that you *had* to be a gearhead to own one. There was nothing easy about riding a bike. Even starting the beast was a traumatic experience in those pre-electric-start days. Glance at the starting procedure of a mid-1950s Triumph as outlined in its owner's manual, and you'll be instructed to tickle carburetors (Ooh Missus), retard the spark (an instruction, not an insult), and align the piston according to the phase of the moon. Once you'd accomplished all this, it was time to *kick-start* the bike. If your bike was in a good mood that day, it would start without backfiring and smashing your ankle into hundreds of tiny bone shards (now that would ruin a Monday morning).

Cycle Babble

Kick-starting is a method of starting up a bike engine on a machine with no starter motor. A lever sticks out of the side of the engine, which you "kick." In reality this translates into putting all of the momentum you can gather throughout your whole body and directing it down toward your foot in a massive lunge. Mind you don't kick over that shiny bike by accident!

And all this just to *start* the bike. Keeping it running was just as difficult. Riders who put a lot of miles on their machines knew the inner workings of their bikes intimately. They saw them frequently, sometimes even when they hadn't intended to: more than one rider saw pistons, valves, and connecting rods flying from their engines as they exploded like oily grenades just below their baby-making equipment.

You Meet the Nicest People on a Honda

Part of the reason for the stagnation in motorcycle design at this time was lack of competition. The Indian Motorcycle Company (the first American motorcycle company, preceding Harley-Davidson by two years) had quit building motorcycles by the mid-1950s; even before it gave up the ghost, it had long ceased being competitive with Harley-Davidson. The British manufacturers had to keep up with only one another, and as long as none of them raised the stakes too high, none of them had to try too hard. There were interesting developments taking place in other European countries, but those countries were still in such turmoil from the war that manufacturers there concentrated on producing cheap transportation for their own people and weren't interested in exporting motorcycles to the rest of the world.

That was soon to change. In only a few years, these complacent manufacturers found themselves up against some very serious competition from a most unlikely source: Japan.

Like Italy and Germany, Japan was in ruins following World War II. Japan's manufacturing infrastructure had been even more severely devastated. After the war, Japan had to start from scratch. The Japanese rose to the challenge, and rather than rebuilding the past, they looked to the future for their inspiration.

 Motorcycle Moments

> While most early Japanese motorcycles were small bikes, the bikes manufactured by the Rikuo Company were big exceptions. That company manufactured large V-twin Harley-Davidson replicas, built under a licensing agreement with The Motor Company. Soon Rikuo was improving on the Harley design, introducing telescopic forks in 1948, a year before Harley introduced the innovation. This was followed by the introduction of a foot-operated gearshift (Harley still used a cumbersome, hand-operated system) and automatic spark advance (for easier starting). By this time, Rikuo believed it had modified its design to the point that it no longer had to pay for the license agreement. Harley disagreed and made its displeasure known to the Japanese government, which, in turn, withdrew its orders for police bikes from Rikuo, forcing the company out of business.

As in European countries, Japan's postwar motorcycle industry emerged to service society's need for cheap transportation. That industry had a humble beginning, with many manufacturers building clones of bikes from other countries.

Americans had little use for the more or less overgrown mopeds coming out of Japan, nor did any other country for quite a few years. But by the late 1950s, Japanese motorcycles began to make their way into Europe and then into the United States. By this time, Japanese bikes had evolved into distinctive, original machines with innovations that made riders take note. These were elegant, reliable, nimble, and fast bikes—and cheap, to boot.

The innovation people most took note of was the inclusion of electric starters on many of these machines. No longer did riders need the legs of mules to kick-start their bikes; they simply pushed a button and rode off.

Unlike other manufacturers, the Japanese realized the sales potential of motorcycles that were convenient to use, and no Japanese company capitalized on convenience as a selling point as well as Honda. In an ad campaign designed to highlight the utility of its machines, Honda set the sport of motorcycling on the path toward respectability.

Motorcycology

Before becoming a manufacturer of motorcycles, Soichiro Honda, the founder of Honda, operated a series of businesses that were less than successful. In fact, he once described his life as "Nothing but mistakes, a series of failures, a series of regrets." But he credited those failures for his success. "Success can be achieved only through repeated failure and introspection. In fact, success represents one percent of your work and results from the 99 percent that is called failure."

That campaign was the famous "You meet the nicest people on a Honda" series of ads, and it single-handedly undid much of the damage done to the image of motorcycling by films such as *The Wild One*. The ads, which featured "normal" people doing non-outlaw-type things on Honda motorcycles, appeared in 1961 and were so effective that they made the sport of motorcycling seem acceptable to society as a whole. The ads had such a powerful effect that for years afterward, the word *Honda* became synonymous with small motorcycles, much like the name *Xerox* is used as a verb meaning "to photocopy."

The Japanese Hit the Big Time

Because the Japanese were producing only small motorcycles and not "real" bikes, the other major manufacturers didn't consider them a serious threat and paid little attention to them. That proved to be a mistake—a fatal mistake for many of the more marginal manufacturers—because the Japanese were deadly serious.

This Honda ad proved so effective at getting people to buy motorcycles that it's still studied in advertising classes today.

(Photo courtesy of Vreeke and Associates)

As the 1960s progressed, the bikes coming from Japan increased in size and capabilities, but the other manufacturers still paid them little heed. By 1965, when Honda introduced its CB450 Super Sport, the competition had wised up. This bike, known as the Black Bomber for its racy black bodywork, handled like a European machine and could outrun a stock Harley-Davidson with more than twice its engine displacement.

Finally, Japan's competitors realized what they were up against and found the motivation to respond to the threat. The British manufacturers BSA and Triumph began to jointly develop a large-displacement multicylinder machine in an attempt to preserve their advantage in sporting bikes, and Harley grafted an electric starter onto its big-twin engine in an attempt to provide Japanese-style convenience.

Both these projects proved to be too little too late. By the time the British unveiled their triples, which were flawed machines with styling only a mother or designer could love, Honda had unveiled its big gun: the four-cylinder CB750 Four.

It's impossible to overstate the impact this bike had on the motorcycling world.

What Honda did by introducing the CB750 was the equivalent of a car company producing a high-quality sports car equal to or better than the best machines produced by Porsche or Mercedes, and then selling it for the price of a Kia. Here was a machine capable of outrunning any mass-produced motorcycle on the road and able to do so all day long without any mechanical problems. Plus, people could afford it.

Perhaps the most significant motorcycle in history, the 1969 Honda CB750 Four changed the face of motor-cycling.

(Photo courtesy of Vreeke and Associates)

Given the success of the big Honda, it was only a matter of time before other Japanese manufacturers followed suit and produced big bikes of their own. Kawasaki jumped into the four-cylinder arena with its mighty Z1, and after a couple of false starts, Suzuki also joined the fray, followed by Yamaha.

These big-bore motorcycles devastated the competition. For the British, hampered by management unable to let go of pre–World War II motorcycle designs, the competition proved to be too much. Harley-Davidson managed to survive, partly due to the fanatical loyalty of its customers, but entered into a long period of decline. For a while in the 1970s, it looked like the Japanese would be the only people left in the motorcycling business.

Baby Boomers on (Two) Wheels

The success of the Japanese manufacturers in the United States provides one of history's best examples of being in the right place at the right time. The Japanese caught a wave caused by the baby boom generation, and this massive influx of young people provided the fuel to propel the Japanese invasion.

Although some restless individuals returning from the war spent their newfound wealth on motorcycles and raising hell, most used that money to pursue the American dream—a dream that included raising a family. And raise families they did, prolifically, creating a new generation so large that their whims would dictate trends for the rest of their lives and shape our culture for generations to come. The impact of the so-called baby boom generation will be felt long after the last baby boomer has moved on to that great salvage yard in the sky.

The Boomer Boom

Just as the first small Japanese motorcycles began to appear on the West Coast, the first wave of baby boomers was getting its collective driver's license. It didn't take an advanced degree in economics to see the profit potential of providing these kids, products of unprecedented affluence, with fun, affordable, and reliable motorcycles.

The maturation of the Japanese motorcycle industry mirrors the maturation of the baby boom generation. As these kids grew in size, so grew the Japanese bikes. By the 1970s, most baby boomers were entering adulthood. They roamed farther, rode faster, and were physically larger than when Mr. Honda started importing his small Super Cub and Dream motorcycles into the country. They no longer needed small, inexpensive motorcycles to ride to football practice or down to the beach. What they needed were full-size motorcycles with enough power to satisfy their adventurous spirits, bikes comfortable enough for cross-country trips. And the Japanese were happy to oblige.

Motorcycology

While the Italians produced mechanically brilliant motorcycles during the 1960s and 1970s, cosmetically they left much to be desired. The bikes were beautiful from a distance, but upon closer inspection, the quality of paint and bodywork was abysmal. One well-known example of this was *Cycle* magazine's 1974 Ducati 750SS test bike, which came with an actual fly embedded in the fiberglass of the fuel tank, perfecto—a free fossil!

By this time, these young people had become accustomed to the convenience and reliability of Japanese motorcycles. Harley-Davidsons of the 1970s were only incrementally improved over those built during the 1930s. Compounding these problems, American Machine and Foundry (AMF), Harley's parent company at that time, was more interested in turning a quick buck than in doing long-term development. Even Willie G. Davidson, a direct descendant of one of the company's founders, Arthur Davidson, admits that their bikes suffered quality-control problems during this period as a result of AMF's desire to get as many bikes as possible to the market.

Problems were even worse over in England. During the 1950s and 1960s, the British bike industry was mostly run by the same people who had brought the industry to prominence in the 1930s and 1940s. These people tended to oppose even the slightest change, often ignoring the specific requests of their American distributors.

The result was that the British motorcycle industry was in complete disarray and unable to cash in on the demographic trends taking place in the United States. It couldn't even develop a reliable electric-starting system that didn't explode through the engine cases on every ninth or tenth starting attempt.

For the bulk of this massive new generation of Americans, British or American motorcycles were not an option. The German firm BMW produced spectacular bikes that were as reliable and convenient as Japanese machines, but they cost more and weren't as widely marketed in the United States. The Italians also produced motorcycles that were in many ways equal to or superior to the Japanese bikes, but these, too, came at a premium price. Add to this the peculiar Italian penchant for designing and developing spectacular machinery but then showing near-total disinterest in producing or marketing those same bikes, and the Italians were an even smaller blip than the Germans on the radar of most motorcyclists. For most riders, the only real option was to buy Japanese.

The Bust

Whenever something is going well, those profiting from it convince themselves that it will go well forever. That's just human nature. The Japanese manufacturers imagined that their lock on the American motorcycle market was secure. But they were wrong.

In hindsight, it makes sense. As the baby boomers grew older, many of them lost interest in the adventuresome activities they engaged in during their youth. Even if they were still interested in pursuing sports such as motorcycling, their lives were changing in ways that limited the available time they had to do so. After they graduated from college, their careers began demanding ever-increasing amounts of their time. And when they started families, those families cut into both the free time they had to ride and the amount of cash available to spend on adult toys such as motorcycles.

You would think the motorcycle manufacturers would have seen this trend coming, but they didn't. By the time the tail end of the baby boom generation entered the workforce in the early to mid-1980s, a time when the manufacturers could have logically expected a market downturn, the Japanese had increased production to record levels. And when the bust hit, American distributors found themselves with warehouses filled with unsold Japanese motorcycles.

Throughout most of the 1980s, the American distributors concentrated on eliminating this surplus, selling three-, four-, and even five-year-old carryover bikes at a fraction of their original cost. The cost of carrying these machines for nearly half a decade drove many dealers out of business, and the lost profits from having to sell the motorcycles below cost almost bankrupted at least one of the Japanese manufacturers.

Manufacturers are still feeling the effects of this debacle. Those few people who had bought motorcycles at list price during the early 1980s were not too pleased to come back to trade those machines a year or two down the road and see the exact same bikes sitting on showroom floors priced at less than half of what they had paid. Not only was this insulting, but it made it extraordinarily difficult for them to sell their own used bikes.

Motorcycle Moments

While the 1980s surplus of unsold motorcycles proved an expensive mistake for the sellers of those bikes, bargain hunters had a field day. In 1985, I purchased a brand-new carryover 1982 Yamaha Seca 650, a bike that listed for $3,200 new in 1982, for $1,399 right out of the crate. Many riders still use those bargain bikes on a daily basis, racking up hundreds of thousands of miles on them.

The Risen Hog: The Resurrected Motorcycle Market

Once again, the future of the sport of motorcycling appeared uncertain, but help was coming. The cavalry was on its way, but this time it had chosen a most unlikely mount: Harley-Davidson motorcycles.

In 1981, a group of 13 senior Harley-Davidson executives purchased Harley-Davidson from owners AMF. Work commenced on a new engine, and the introduction of that engine, known as the Evolution, opened up an entirely new market for Harley-Davidson.

Before 1981, Harleys were still motorcycles of the old school, meaning that to own one, you had to have the mechanical acumen to overhaul the beast on the side of the road in the middle of the night with nothing but a Zippo lighter, an adjustable wrench, and an intimate familiarity with the motorcycle's internals to guide you. Harleys just were not practical, reliable machines for the majority of riders.

The Evolution, or Evo, engine ended that sorry state of affairs and proved to be a reliable, long-life engine. For the first time, an owner didn't have to be a grease monkey to ride a Harley.

Harley's image as an unreliable Stone Age artifact prevented the new machine from gaining immediate marketplace acceptance. To get a bit of breathing room, Harley petitioned the Reagan administration to impose a temporary tariff on imported motorcycles with engine displacements over 700cc.

In the end, Harley's successful comeback proved to be a blessing for everyone and contributed much to the rebounding of the industry as a whole. So successful was the new Evo engine that Harley asked the federal government to remove the tariff a year before it was originally scheduled to be lifted. By the early 1990s, Harley was selling every motorcycle it could make, with people waiting months and even years to be able to purchase one. By the summer of 2001, Harley surpassed Honda in total United States sales for the first time since the 1960s.

As you saw in Chapter 1, Harley's newfound success permeated every aspect of American culture. Soon you could buy everything from official Harley-Davidson underwear to Harley-Davidson toilet-seat covers and Harley-Davidson cigarettes.

Ironically, the one thing that was tough to find was an actual Harley-Davidson motorcycle. Weary of the quality-control problems it had during the AMF days, Harley was careful not to expand its production beyond its capabilities.

As Harley's increasing popularity fueled a new interest in motorcycles, the lack of available Harley-Davidsons created a vacuum. Once again, the Japanese stepped up to fill this vacuum.

And once again, the baby boomers were the driving force behind this new interest in motorcycling. These were the same people who had bought all those little Hondas in the 1960s, who had terrorized the highways on thundering Kawasakis in the 1970s, and who had spent the 1980s raising kids and making money.

Now their kids were grown up, and they once again found themselves with some free time and money on their hands. They missed the fun they used to have on their motorcycles, so they got back into the sport.

For some time, motorcycling's popularity has been increasing. Sales for the four Japanese manufacturers—Honda, Yamaha, Kawasaki, and Suzuki—have been on the rise since 1992, Harley-Davidson sells every bike it can build, and the European manufacturers are experiencing unprecedented popularity in the United States.

BMW, Ducati, and Moto-Guzzi are a larger part of the American market than they ever were in the past. Triumph began producing bikes in 1991, after being out of action for nearly a decade. Even MZ, an Eastern European manufacturer, has begun importing bikes to the United States.

We even have some homegrown competition for Harley-Davidson, for the first time since the first demise of Indian. Polaris, an American manufacturer of snowmobiles and all-terrain vehicles, introduced a large cruiser-type bike called the Victory in 1998 and offers an eight-model lineup for 2007.

Today's motorcyclists can select from a larger variety of motorcycles than ever before, and every one of these motorcycles provides levels of reliability and performance that were unimaginable 30 years ago. There has never been a better time to be a motorcyclist.

The Least You Need to Know

- Motorcycles have been around nearly as long as the modern safety bicycle.

- The Japanese took the sport of motorcycling to new heights of popularity with their small, unintimidating, reliable, and fun machines.

- The fate of motorcycling since World War II has mirrored the fate of the baby boom generation.

- The rebirth of Harley-Davidson following the introduction of the Evolution engine proved so strong that it helped pull the entire motorcycle industry out of an economic slump.

- Today's motorcycle buyers have more choices than at any other time since the first part of the twentieth century.

Street Squid or Dirt Donk? Types of Motorcycles

In This Chapter

◆ Doing it in the dirt: types of dirtbikes and dual-sport bikes

◆ Which street standards are endangered species

◆ Cruisers: the ultimate American bikes

◆ Touring machines

Back in the olden days, one bike pretty much served every purpose. You could buy a BSA Gold Star, for example, and use it as everyday transportation on public roads. That bike could be adapted to dirt use, too—just remove the front fender, change the tires, and bolt on a higher pipe. And should you want to go racing, with a little work on the engine, your Gold Star could be competitive on any track in the world.

Now, though, there's not only a bewildering choice of bikes for a new rider, there's also an overwhelming amount of peer pressure. If your buddies ride Harleys they'll burn your ears off if you tell them you want a Honda. If your friends all tear it up on sportbikes, they'll give you a million reasons not to ride a cruiser. Just like when you were growing up, you'll have to take your own road.

Split Personalities: Dual-Sports

Many riders want to travel off the beaten path, but at the same time, they need a motorcycle they can legally drive on public roads to get to that unbeaten path. Motorcycle manufacturers have long recognized this need; that's why they make *dual-sports.*

Cycle Babble

Dual-sport motorcycles (sometimes called *dual-purpose* bikes) are street-legal motorcycles with varying degrees of off-road capabilities.

Each of the big-four Japanese companies, as well as several European firms, manufacture some form of dual-sport. Some examples are as follows:

♦ Honda makes the XR650R, maybe the most off-road-worthy of all the big dual-sports, almost certainly the best off-road dual-sport currently coming out of Japan.

♦ Kawasaki builds its KLR650, a good lightweight street-oriented bike.

♦ Splitting the difference is Suzuki's DR650SE, which is generally a better street-bike than the Honda and a better dirtbike than the Kawasaki.

♦ BMW's main entry in the dual-sport market is its gigantic R1200GS. But BMW also builds the terrific G650X.

♦ KTM, an Austrian manufacturer best known for their off-road racing success, makes the 640 Adventure, a great (but pricey) entry into this category.

♦ Aprilia, an Italian firm, offers its ETV1000 Caponard, with a glorious 998 V-twin engine but an advertised dry weight of 474 pounds. That's almost 100 pounds lighter than the BMW GS—almost 100 pounds heavier than the KTM.

♦ Triumph's dual-sport entry is the 1050 Tiger. Unlike most of the twin-cylinder competition, the Tiger utilizes a silky smooth transverse three-cylinder engine, and again big means heavy.

A big engine in a dual-sport will mean a big bike, and a big bike can weigh a lot. If you're off-road and you drop it, you'll start to hate picking up that big bike pretty quickly. So when you're buying a dual-sport you should try to decide what your ratio is going to be for on-road riding versus off-road riding. If you're into doing more roadwork, then buy a bigger bike; if you prefer the idea of exploring unpaved roads, then buy a smaller, lighter one, or maybe even go for a more focused road-legal dirt-bike.

Any of the bikes listed will make an ideal first motorcycle. In addition to having vary-ing degrees of dirt-worthiness, each makes a very nimble and forgiving streetbike. They're all fantastic city bikes. Their easy handling makes them excellent bikes for a learner, but their all-around capability means a rider won't outgrow them after learn-ing to ride. (If you want to check out these and other dual-sports, see Appendix A.)

The only drawback these bikes have is that they're tall machines. Part of the reason they work so well both on and off the road is that they have long-travel suspensions, which place the seat high off the pavement. While this lets riders see traffic, it also presents some challenges for those with shorter inseams. A word to the wise: test-ride one; the height isn't for everybody.

There's another type of dual-sport: the *leviathan.* These are large-displacement machines based on streetbikes. In a way, they're throwbacks to earlier times, when a single machine was used for all purposes.

BMW introduced the first of the leviathans in 1980, when it brought out the R80GS, an 800cc twin-cylinder bike with high fenders and upswept exhaust pipes. This versatile bike proved popular, especially in Europe, but it might have remained an anomaly had it not been for one event: the Dakar Rally.

The Dakar Rally (previously called the Paris Dakar Rally) is an off-road endurance race across thousands of miles of desert

> **Cycle Babble**
>
> The term **leviathan** origi-nally referred to a biblical sea monster but has come to mean something of immense size and power, a good description of these big, multicylinder dual-sports, which can weigh almost twice as much as the largest single-cylinder dual-sports.

along the west coast of Africa, and it is here the leviathans really shine. The event's popularity generated the production of Dakar-style replicas from most of the major motorcycle manufacturers.

These were bikes like the original R80GS: basically streetbikes with a bit of off-road equipment, but with bodywork resembling the Dakar racer—bikes such as the Ducati/Cagiva Elefant and Triumph Tiger. Honda has long made its V-twin Africa Twin 750, and Yamaha produced its own Dakar-style bike, the 750 V-twin Super Ténéré, but these were never imported into the United States.

Most single-cylinder dual-sports have modest off-road capabilities, but these levia-thans are best suited to graded dirt roads; they are just too heavy for true off-road work. You'd be certifiable to take them up a mountain trail, for instance. But these big buggers make really good streetbikes, in part because of their long-travel (therefore comfortable) suspension, lofty visibility, and nimble handling. If you're a tall rider, you could do a lot worse than to buy one. If you're of shorter stature, a good tip is to slide your butt almost off the edge of your seat just before stopping. This can help you find good foot contact with the floor.

Cycle Babble

Super-Motards are lightweight dirtbikes fitted with road-race wheels and tires. They're raced all around Europe and now stateside, too. Several bike companies have started to make a sanitized version for public sale.

Finally, there's a new kid on the dual-sport block: the *super-motard*. Super-motards (also known as Super-Moto) were created as a halfway house between a true off-road race bike and a street bike. The result is a smaller and lighter machine that looks like a dirtbike fitted with road-going wheels. You'll notice I say wheels and not just tires. Motards (a common abbreviation) don't run on the typical tall off-road-type wheels; they wear much shorter and wider road-going wheels—complete with super-sticky road-racing tires and road-based gearing.

Motards have their own race series, which predictably takes place half on paved sections and half on dirt; the series attracts professional riders from both sides of the coin. Go to a race and watch the Supercross stars banging arms with the big-name roadracing pros. It's a riot to watch.

Believe me, Motards are about as much fun as you can have on two wheels, they're forgiving motorcycles, which you can throw around with wild abandon—all the while feeling like a race hero. I highly recommend one as a second bike.

Suzuki was one of the first manufacturers to launch a European-style Super-Motard for sale stateside. This DR-Z400SM is about as much fun as you can have on two wheels while staying legal!

(Photo courtesy Suzuki USA)

Cruisers: The All-American Bikes

Choppers, customs, cruisers—whichever term you use, you are referring to a distinctly American style of motorcycle. The American landscape, both social and geographical, shaped this style of motorcycle into its present form.

Many of the restless soldiers returning from Europe and Asia after World War II chose to explore the United States on motorcycles, but the motorcycles that were widely available didn't suit them. Outlaw bikers called the big Harley-Davidson touring bikes of that time "garbage wagons" because they considered all the accessories and extras mounted on them garbage. In fact, Bylaw Number 11 of the original Hell's Angels charter states, "An Angel cannot wear the colors (club insignia) while riding on a garbage wagon." The first thing most outlaws did was chop off all superfluous parts, which to them was anything that didn't help the bike go faster: fenders, lights, front brakes, whatever. Hence the term *chopper.*

Choppers came to symbolize the outlaw motorcycle contingent, the infamous one-percenters. By the 1960s, these bikes had evolved into radical machines far removed from the intent of the original customized bikes, which was improved straight-line performance. Anyone seeking outright performance rode a Japanese or British bike. Harley had long since given up the pretense of producing sporting motorcycles.

Cycle Babble

A **chopper** once referred to a custom motorcycle that had all superfluous parts "chopped" off in order to make the bike faster. Today it refers to a type of custom bike that usually has an extended fork, no rear suspension, and high handlebars.

People rode Harleys to look cool, and nothing looked cooler than a Harley chopper. The extended forks and modified frames of these motorcycles made them nearly impossible to ride, but the owners didn't seem to mind. Riding a motorcycle with unsafe handling characteristics seemed to be another way of letting society know the rider didn't care if he or she lived or died.

Over the years, such machines gained in popularity—even as they declined in practicality—but manufacturers seemed not to notice. It wasn't until the 1970s, after decades of watching American riders customize their bikes, that the manufacturers got into the act and began offering custom-styled bikes.

The birth of the factory custom can in large part be attributed to one man: Willie G. Davidson. Willie G., as he is known, worked in Harley's styling department, but he was also an avid motorcyclist who knew what people were doing to their bikes.

One popular customizing technique was to take the fork off of a Sportster and graft it onto a stripped-down Big Twin frame, so Willie G. did just that at the factory. The result was the original Super Glide.

Choppers sure are cool look-ing, but they can be a pain in the butt to ride, literally. It can also take a grocery store–sized parking lot to turn one around with their extra long wheelbase.

(Photo courtesy of Simon Green)

The Super Glide model, offered in 1971, wasn't a screaming success, due in part to a funky boatlike rear fender (known as the *Night Train* fender). The next year, Harley gave the bike a more conventional rear fender and sold thousands of Super Glides.

Harley wasn't the only company working on a custom-styled bike. The British manu-facturer Norton also developed a cruiser in the early 1970s. Unfortunately, its cruiser, the ungainly High Rider, was based on Norton's hot-selling Commando sportbike and the odd marriage wasn't well received. The bike only contributed to the compa-ny's eventual demise.

Kawasaki was the first Japanese company to test the factory-chopper waters, intro-ducing its KZ900LTD in 1976. The bike featured pull-back buckhorn handlebars, a teardrop-shape gas tank, a seat with a pronounced step between the rider and pas-senger portions, and a liberal dousing of chrome plating. These bikes forced the rider into a backward-leaning riding position (raising unbridled hell with his or her lower back), but otherwise, they were still functional, useful machines.

As the decade progressed, the Japanese stuck to this formula. This approach had a limited future; the real future of cruisers was being forged elsewhere, by Willie G.

Two of Willie G.'s creations, in particular, proved to be the models for today's cruisers: the Low Rider, introduced in 1977, and the Wide Glide of 1980. Study these bikes, and you'll see elements of every cruiser now produced. The bobbed fender of the Wide Glide can be found on cruisers from Honda, Suzuki, and Kawasaki. The kicked-out front end and sculpted fenders of the Low Rider hint at the shape of Yamaha's Road Stars. These two bikes are arguably the most influential factory customs of all time.

What of the Japanese? As the 1980s progressed, Japanese manufacturers got closer and closer to building motorcycles that looked like Harley-Davidsons. But they have taken cruiser styling in new directions, too. Honda now builds its Valkyrie, a massive six-cylinder cruiser. Yamaha's Royal Star looks as much like a classic Indian motorcycle as it does a Harley-Davidson. (See Appendix A to get a good look at these bikes.)

This segment of the market has thrived for many years, and for good reason: cruisers are easy bikes to live with. Many of them are nearly maintenance free. To many people they look good and, when outfitted with a windshield, are comfortable out on the road. They may not handle as well as sportbikes, or haul as much gear as touring bikes, but in many ways, they fulfill the role of a standard, all-around motorcycle. Many riders don't ride a motorcycle to get from point A to point B as quickly as possible. They just like to ride. If that describes you, you might be cruiser material.

Power Cruisers

An interesting thing happened as the twentieth century wound to a close. People began demanding more performance from all types of motorcycles. Sportbikes began to increase in popularity, and not just among younger riders. Longtime riders and those who had returned to the sport after an extended absence from riding began to appreciate the tremendous performance offered by modern sportbikes. Even cruiser buyers began wanting more power and better handling. In response, manufacturers resurrected the "power cruiser" category.

The original batch of power cruisers in the early 1980s tended to be multicylinder machines, usually V-fours. Honda started this trend with its Magnas, and Suzuki joined in with its ill-fated Madura series. Yamaha's V-four power cruiser proved so popular that the mighty V-Max is still with us in the twenty-first century. Kawasaki also got in the act, but it used an inline-four engine to power the Eliminator series, its combatant in the 1980s power cruiser wars. Today's crop of power cruisers uses

V-twin engines almost exclusively. Honda brought out the original member of the current class with its mighty VTX1800, which cranks out more than 100 horsepower at the rear wheel. But Honda breaks with V-twin conformity with its six-cylinder Valkyrie and show-stopping Valkyrie Rune. Yamaha and Kawasaki also jumped on the power cruiser bandwagon. Yamaha chose to go the low-tech route, using the air-cooled pushrod engine from its Road Star series to power its Road Star Warrior power cruiser. In a turn of events that hasn't occurred since the introduction of the Knucklehead in 1936, Harley now ranks among the undisputed technological leaders in this class. The liquid-cooled V-Rod engine cranks out 109 horsepower at the rear wheel. Triumph, on the other hand, wants to trump everyone with its 2.3-liter three-cylinder Rocket III.

Harley's Wide Glide was one of the most influential cruisers ever built. Just about every cruiser now being produced displays some elements of Wide Glide styling.

(Photo courtesy of Motorcyclist™ magazine)

Sportbikes

If you aren't the easy-rider type, or just find the stereotypical cruiser-riders image unattractive, then you might be interested in something with a little more sporting capability. Well, you are definitely in the right place at the right time: the range of sporting motorcycles available has never been better.

Sportbikes are designed to handle well at high speeds. When British bikes began to appear in the United States in appreciable numbers following World War II, it became obvious that while Harleys may be faster in a straight line, the British models could run circles around a Harley when the road began to wind. This gave the British a reputation as the producers of the original sporting motorcycles. The British managed to maintain this reputation until the early 1970s with bikes such as the awesome Norton 850 Commando and Triumph T160 Trident.

When the Japanese began producing large four-cylinder motorcycles, these became the new leaders in straight-line performance. The term *Universal Japanese Motorcycles (UJM)* was coined to describe them.

While they were wicked fast, most UJMs of the 1970s didn't handle all that well, mostly because of inferior suspension components and flimsy frames. They outhandled Harleys (which tended to be about as nimble as a freight train), but they couldn't keep up with a properly functioning Norton Commando.

Cycle Babble

During the 1970s, the Japanese became so identified with four-cylinder, standard-style motorcycles that the term **Universal Japanese Motorcycle (UJM)** was coined to describe them.

The real breakthrough in the development of sportbikes from Japan was Honda's 750cc Interceptor, introduced for the 1983 model year. With its revolutionary V-four engine, this bike was Japan's best purpose-built sporting motorcycle yet.

The Interceptor revolutionized sportbikes. It started off a technology war between the Japanese manufacturers that continues to this day. Kawasaki brought out its original 900 Ninja, a bike in many ways as groundbreaking as the Interceptor. Yamaha introduced its five-valve FZ750, a bike so influential that Ferrari adopted some of its technology for its cars. And Suzuki blew the world away by introducing its GSX-R series, the first generation of the true modern sportbikes, bikes that are little more than racers with headlights.

The Italians are another prominent force in the sportbike scene. When they started building large-displacement sportbikes in the 1970s, such as Moto Guzzi's V7 Sport and Ducati's 750SS, the Italians raised the ceiling on riders' expectations from their machines. While they weren't initially exported in numbers large enough to become a real presence in the United States market, recently they've become a benchmark for performance bikes. In fact, America has since become Ducati's number-one export market.

Today's sportbikes have a wider appeal than ever before. You can participate in *track days*, which is arguably what they do best. You can use a sportbike as a potentially super-fast modern road machine (watch out, though, or you'll be mourning the loss of your driver's license), or you can use it as the basis for a custom bike as innovative

Cycle Babble

Track days are organized riding events held at a racetrack. Professional instructors will teach you how to ride either your own bike or a rental bike, and speed around a racetrack in relative safety.

and wild looking as any chopper ever created. Because there are now so many niche scenes, the sportbike world is experiencing unprecedented growth.

Pure-Dirt

The motorcycles manufactured for purely off-road use today tend toward the extreme end of the motorcycle spectrum. These are machines such as the screaming race bikes leaping through the air in arenas around the country during Supercross races. True off-road bikes fall into two distinct categories, two-stroke or four-stroke.

Two-Strokes: The Screamers

Two-stroke *dirtbikes* usually don't make good beginner bikes. In fact, many of them are intended strictly as racing machines. With some two-stroke engines you have to mix oil into your gas before you fill your tank, which is a messy, time-consuming process (and inconvenient if you find yourself miles from home without a can in which to mix fuel). More civilized models will feature a separate reservoir for the two-stroke oil, almost like a smaller second gas tank. The advantage to this setup is the bike mixes the oil and gas on its own.

Cycle Babble

Dirtbikes are machines intended for off-road use and aren't legal to ride on public roads. Sometimes the term **pure-dirt** is used to distinguish a dirtbike from a dual-sport motorcycle.

Adding to this inconvenience is the fact that due to their emissions and noisy nature, many two-stroke motorcycles aren't even legal to ride on public roads. This means you'll have to transport the machine from your garage to the place you intend to ride in a pickup truck or a trailer.

Finally, two-strokes tend to have extremely abrupt power delivery, unleashing a whole bunch of horsepower in a trouser-soiling instant. When the engine is at lower rpm's the bike feels powerless, once it hits a certain point, the acceleration is suddenly overwhelming. This is great for racing, but unwelcome for a novice. Often you'll end up on your butt as the lightweight bike flips you off the back. That's not to say they can't be a lot of fun—but they're better off in experienced hands.

Four-Strokes: The New Power Elites

Alternatives to two-stroke racing dirtbikes are available for those who want to do serious off-road riding: four-stroke trailbikes.

First we must clear up a big misconception: four-stroke power, the same type of motor you'll find in any car or truck, never went out of style. However, until recently, these bikes have been disadvantaged by weight and starting, compared to the two-strokes. Today's four-stroke pure-dirt bikes start just as easily, produce a smoother and more useable power, and, in some cases, weigh less than their two-stroke siblings. Case in point: the 450cc four-strokes now produce horsepower numbers in the realm of the old race-ready two-stroke 500s—in a less violent manner, while weighing the same.

The big breakthrough was when the high-performance production four-strokes got their weight under 250 pounds. This wrapped the smooth power into a lightweight, easy-to-start package that really pushed the four-stroke ahead of the two-strokes. Honda has long been a proponent of such motorcycles, and its CR-F series offers a terrific alternative to two-strokes. However, Honda is not alone—there's also Yamaha with its YZ-F bikes, Kawasaki with its KLX-Rs, and Suzuki has had its tough DR-Zs for many years.

Before we move on, bear in mind that while any pure-dirt motorcycle (four-stroke or two) won't usually be legal to drive on public roads (they'll often be missing necessary electrical equipment, such as lights, turn signals, and horns), it can be possible to make them road-legal, but that can be missing the point—it's not really what these specialist bikes are all about.

Street Standards: A Renaissance

Because the British and Japanese motorcycles were so influential to motorcyclists who entered the sport in the 1960s and 1970s, the look of these bikes became imprinted in our psyches as the way a motorcycle should look.

These were pretty basic bikes: back then, function dictated form. The gas tank sat above the engine to allow the gas to run down into the carburetors. The need to place the engine between the two wheels, and the way the human body bends, pretty much dictated the placement of the rest of the parts.

As motorcycles became more specialized in the 1980s, the look of motorcycles changed. Motorcyclists were so excited by new developments that we didn't realize we were losing something in the process. Then one day in the late 1980s, we realized that the basic bike no longer existed. Motorcyclists began complaining about this situation, and soon the Japanese designed bikes that embodied the virtues of those older models.

Unfortunately, while the inclusion of the older styling features contributed to a retro look for these new machines, it also detracted from their overall versatility. Suzuki and Kawasaki were the first to come to the market with standard motorcycles. Kawasaki's entrance into this new/old market segment was the Zephyr 550, a good-looking four-cylinder UJM-type bike introduced for the 1990 model year. It sold well in Europe, but not in the United States. Very few of these machines found their way to the public highways, and they were soon dropped from Kawasaki's lineup.

The VX800, Suzuki's entrant that the same year, did slightly better in the market. It was a competent, full-size machine that fulfilled the promise of the versatile standard. But it was never a sales dynamo and was imported to U.S. shores for only four years.

Neither Kawasaki nor Suzuki gave up on the concept of standard bikes after the lukewarm reception of their initial efforts. Kawasaki imported increasingly larger Zephyrs, but they came with increasingly larger price tags. None of the Zephyr series offered anything a rider couldn't find in a used GPz900 Ninja—and for a fraction of the Zephyr's price.

Honda was the first Japanese manufacturer to find relative success in the standard bike market, with its Nighthawk 750. Here was a bike that offered the versatility UJMs were known for and looked okay doing it. Perhaps the factor that contributed most to the bike's success was its low price. In this case, you really did get your money's worth.

While the Nighthawk was the first modern Japanese standard to hold its own in the marketplace, it never set any kind of sales records. Looking back, all of these bikes mixed the *naked bike* look with a subtle touch of the cruiser, which was pretty odd considering that many riders of the 1960s and 1970s bought naked British and Japanese bikes to set themselves apart from the cruiser crowd. Luckily, a couple of manufacturers rethought the concept.

First, Yamaha introduced the Seca II XJ600. At first glance, this nimble, fun bike might not be considered a standard, since it included a small, frame-mounted *fairing*, but in retrospect maybe that was the point.

The riders were finally happy; the fairing actually added to the bike's practicality. It seemed that being *naked* wasn't a prerequisite for a standard. Suzuki also realized this and brought out its Bandit series. These bikes are comfortable motorcycles that incorporate some of the best technology available, a useful fairing, and a reasonable price.

The success of the Bandit finally spawned a resurgence in the standard motorcycle. Suzuki still make the Bandit 1250 plus the newer SV650 and SV1000. Their SV models are so good you can actually race them competitively!

Cycle Babble

The devices mounted at the front of a motorcycle to protect the rider from the elements are called **fairings**. These range from simple Plexiglas shields mounted to the handlebars, to complex, encompassing body panels that enshroud the entire front half of the bike. Bikes without any type of fairing are known as **naked bikes**.

Currently, the standard bike category has a more exciting selection of models to choose from than any other, partly because there aren't really any rules. Every manufacturer has taken a slightly different direction with their contributions. Some companies like Honda make bikes that are essentially their sportbikes without the plastic bodywork: check out the 919 and 599 Hornet series. Kawasaki makes the ultimate throwback bike; with tongue placed firmly in cheek, they re-used the name of their original (and iconic) naked streetbike, the super-cool Z1000. If you wanna sound like you know your stuff, refer to it simply as the Zee One.

Kawasaki couldn't get the sales it needed with the Zephyr, but they seem to have hit the sweet spot with a cool new version of their legendary Z1000.

(Photo courtesy of Kawasaki USA)

Then there are those Italians again. You can choose from the stunning Ducati Monster, featuring the most beautiful gas tank I've ever had the fortune to stretch my body over. Rival Aprilia makes the manic Tuono, and MV Agusta has blown everyone away with the avant-garde and super-expensive Brutale.

Finally, in an almost perfect circle, Triumph is back in the big standard streetbike game. Back in the 1960s the ultimate streetbike was the Triumph Bonneville; it's the bike the Japanese copied, and the bike that stole enough Harley sales to keep

Willie G. awake at night. It was the pesky little motorcycle that just did everything right, and looked so hot doing it. After a few years out of business it's so appropriate that Triumph is back in this category with its radical three-cylinder engine Speed Triple and a fun new version of the original Bonneville.

The fierce competition in this category indicates that there is a really strong market for standard-style streetbikes. If you're a fan of these types of bikes (there's no doubt that I am), and you like to be different, then this is a pretty cool time to be a motorcyclist.

The Ultimate Behemoths: Touring Bikes

Another category of specialized motorcycle to appear over the last several decades is the purpose-built *touring bike*, a bike equipped for longer rides on the road.

 Cycle Babble

A **touring bike** is a bike equipped for longer rides, with fairings and lockable saddlebags. While early bikers looked on motorcycles equipped for touring with scorn, calling them *garbage wagons,* over time they began to see their appeal. They began to refer to garbage wagons as *baggers* and finally *dressers,* the term many Harley riders use today.

Harley started this trend by offering a fairing and luggage as optional equipment on its Electra Glide back in the 1960s, but other companies were slow to pick up on the trend.

In the late 1970s, BMW introduced its first factory dresser, the R100RT, a bike that met with market success.

Honda had been producing a bike specifically for touring: the Gold Wing. In time, Honda began offering fairings and luggage as accessories, but these were still add-on parts, equipment for which the machines hadn't been specifically designed.

Other companies offered touring packages for their standard bikes, too, but there's a problem with this approach: accessories affect the handling of a machine, often adversely. Large fairings and luggage can really make a bike get squirrelly.

So Honda took up the challenge, producing its 1980 GL1100 Gold Wing Interstate, Japan's first turn-key touring bike designed from the ground up to have an integrated fairing and luggage.

Of course, the other Japanese manufacturers responded with purpose-built touring rigs of their own, but it seemed as if every effort they made only sent Honda back to the drawing board with a vengeance. This one-upmanship led to the Gold Wing GL1200 in 1984. This bike set new standards in function and comfort. The Gold Wing 1500, a six-cylinder behemoth introduced in 1988, blew away even its predecessor. The Gold Wing proved to be such a perfect touring machine that the other Japanese manufacturers simply gave up trying to compete in that market segment.

The success of the Gold Wing meant that the ultimate behemoth class of touring bikes saw relatively little change for more than a decade, but eventually things began moving on the touring front again. All it took was a little competition, this time from BMW. In 1999, BMW introduced its K1200LT, and for the first time in more than 10 years, Honda's mighty six-cylinder Gold Wing began losing magazine comparison tests against its heavy-touring market competition. Honda responded by introducing the 1832cc Gold Wing, a bike that was much better in every way than its predecessor. Likewise, BMW has kept upping the ante with its K1200LT.

Not all segments of the touring market went into suspended animation while the Gold Wing waited patiently for a challenger to its throne. There were some exciting developments in other types of touring motorcycles, such as the *sport-touring* segment of the market. Sport-tourers combine the comfort and carrying capacity of a touring bike with the handling and excitement of a sportbike. You can think of these machines as sportbikes with larger fairings and hard, lockable luggage.

Cycle Babble

Sport-tourers are hybrids, combining the performance of sportbikes with the practicality of tourers. To many, they're the best of both worlds.

This class existed for a long time without having a proper name. In fact, almost every BMW built in the last quarter of the century falls into this group.

Although the term sport-touring *is fairly new, BMW has been building such bikes for decades.*

Kawasaki produced the first purpose-built Japanese sport-tourer with its Concours, introduced in 1986. Honda followed suit, bringing out its ST1100 in 1991. Over on the other side of the world, manufacturers such as Aprilia, Ducati, and Triumph also offer BMW competition in the sport-touring arena.

These bikes represent a compromise, giving up a bit of sporting capability to the smaller, more agile sportbikes, while sacrificing some luggage-carrying capability when compared to the ultimate behemoths. It seems a compromise many riders are willing to make. If you like to crank up the throttle in corners and cover huge expanses of geography in a single sitting, but you don't need to carry everything you own with you on a trip, these bikes may be a good compromise for you, too.

Manufacturers have also developed the touring cruiser, another subcategory of the touring bike. The touring-cruiser bikes combine the looks of cruisers with the functionality of touring bikes. With their windshields and hard luggage, they are more comfortable and convenient than cruisers, yet they retain the American look that makes cruisers so popular. Yamaha's Royal Star Venture and Victory's Kingpin Tour are two of the larger and more recent entries in this class. A bit down the food chain in overall bulk (but not overall capability) is Kawasaki's Vulcan Nomad. And, of course, Harley has many entries in this category because it invented the category.

The Least You Need to Know

- Dual-sport motorcycles make excellent all-around bikes, especially for beginners.

- Cruiser styling reflects the unique tastes and needs of traditional American motorcyclists.

- Sportbikes are high-performance motorcycles designed to go fast and handle well. They usually have full-coverage bodywork and crouched riding positions, although there are some exceptions.

- Pure-dirt bikes look like dual-sports but are designed strictly for off-road use— and many are illegal to ride on the street.

- Standard-style motorcycles are characterized by comfortable riding positions and minimal bodywork.

- Touring bikes are usually large motorcycles with fairings; hard, lockable luggage; and other touring amenities.

Part 2

So You Want to Buy a Bike?

Now comes the most exciting part of your entire adventure: getting your first bike. It's fun just to go out and look at it, and admire its combination of form and function. You'll soon be able to visualize its details, the curves in its bodywork, and the way it smells when you park it after a ride on a warm summer day. The machine will become a part of you.

But your first bike will be as demanding as it is exciting. To keep your bike in the condition you brought it home in, you'll need to have a basic understanding of its mechanical nature. And just buying a bike in the first place can be a traumatic event. As with any form of commerce, people sell motorcycles to make money, and if you walk into a dealership unprepared, you will be their cash cow.

In this part of the book, you'll learn what kind of bike is right for you, what that bike is made of, how different bikes work, how to buy your first motorcycle without getting ripped off, and what extra gear you'll need after you buy the bike.

Chapter 4

Choosing the Right Bike

In This Chapter

- ◆ Deciding which type of motorcycle best meets your needs
- ◆ Why a smaller bike may be a good choice
- ◆ New bike or used bike? How to decide
- ◆ The hidden costs of motorcycling

You are about to enter into a relationship with a mechanical object unlike any you have had before. Owning a motorcycle is a much more intimate experience than owning a car or pickup truck, perhaps because you meld into the machine when you ride, your body encasing the mechanical heart of the bike. You become part of the machine. You ride just inches away from the engine, the source of your bike's power, and you feel and hear the internal-combustion event more directly than is possible in an enclosed vehicle.

And you control the direction in which you travel with your body, leading the bike down the road with your own subtle movements just as you would lead a dance partner. This provides a much more immediate experience than sitting inside a glass bubble, turning a steering wheel vaguely connected to some invisible mechanism.

Given the nature of this intimate relationship, it is vital that you choose the right partner. With the dizzying array of motorcycles available, choosing that partner might seem daunting at this stage, but it's really not as confusing as it might seem. You don't have to know every detail of every bike ever made; you only need to know yourself and your own needs.

What Do You Want to Do?

Before you select a type of bike, you first need to determine what kind of riding you want to do (as discussed in Chapter 3). If you have no interest in riding on public roads and you just want a bike to ride through the swamps and forests, you should probably consider getting a strictly off-road dirtbike.

But you will probably want something you can ride on the road. Riding off-road is great fun, but by getting a bike that isn't street-legal, you cut off a lot of your future options. Unless you already have friends who are into serious off-road riding, you'll probably want a machine you can legally ride to the local hangout to visit old friends and make new ones.

Or maybe you don't give a rip about riding off-road. You might have visions of riding through corners on a high-performance sportbike, leaning over so far your knees skim the surface of the asphalt. Or perhaps you envision yourself making epic road trips aboard the biggest touring rig available. Maybe you dream of conquering the jungles on a dual-sport machine.

On the other hand, you may not even know what you want out of a bike just yet.

Whether you know exactly what you want out of the sport or you're still trying to figure that out, it's best to keep your options open. Just because you want to see the world doesn't mean you have to buy an ultimate-behemoth luxo-tourer. And just because you want to be the next speed racer doesn't mean you have to buy the bike that won at Daytona this year.

Although bikes have grown increasingly specialized over the last 15 years, they remain remarkably versatile machines.

Any bike can be a tourer if you take it on a trip. I've put 1,000-mile days on a hard-edged sportbike. I've traveled the entire United States on a big V-twin cruiser. My wife once rode a 500cc thumper from the Canadian border to Mexico and back.

And in the right hands, any bike can be a sportbike. While riding an 18-year-old, 650cc Japanese bike, I've shown my tail to testosterone-crazed squids (sportbike riders with more enthusiasm than talent) on the latest sporting hardware. And while riding a modern sportbike, I've been embarrassed on a twisty road by an old dude on a Harley that was older than I was.

While any bike can be used for nearly any purpose, there is a reason certain types of motorcycles are used for certain tasks more frequently than others. I still suffer from wrist problems from touring on a sportbike, and my wife bought a larger bike within weeks of returning from her trip on the thumper. And that guy who smoked me on his old Harley would probably love riding a modern sportbike, if he ever tried one.

Choosing a Versatile Motorcycle

You might think you know what you want to do before you start riding, but after you've been at it a while, you might discover an interest in an entirely different form of riding. You might get a Harley Sportster thinking you'll use it only to ride to the lake on the weekends, for example, and then develop an itch to ride to the farthest corners of North America.

That's why it's a good idea to get as versatile a motorcycle as possible for your first bike. As I said in Chapter 3, the big dual-sports are about as versatile as a bike can get. They can handle unpaved roads and worse, and they can be set up for touring.

However, you might not be interested in this type of bike. You might be turned off by the looks of the machine. Another disadvantage of the dual-sport bikes is their height: they are tall machines. While sitting up high is an advantage because it lets you see over traffic (and, more important, helps other drivers see you), it presents some challenges to those with shorter inseams. To fit on one, you need to be of at least average height, or you may find these bikes a bit of a handful in stop-and-go traffic.

Honda's XR650L is a good example of a dual-sport. These bikes are about as tough and durable as they come, making them willing and able both on-road and off.

(Photo courtesy of Honda USA)

If dual-sports aren't your thing, that doesn't mean you're out of luck. There are many versatile pure-street bikes to choose from, too.

Browse the buying guide to new bikes in Appendix A to learn more about the many types of dual-sport or pure-street bikes that might be right for you.

Getting a Good Fit

A big factor in versatility is comfort. If you are comfortable on a bike, you can ride it harder and farther. And different bodies fit on different bikes. You can't really tell by looking at it if a bike is going to fit you, either. For example, I fit nicely on Yamaha's YZF600R and could ride one from coast to coast without needing wrist surgery. But Honda's CBR600F3 puts my hands to sleep within minutes. Yet a new rider would be hard-pressed to see a noticeable difference between the two bikes if they were parked side by side, and many other riders find the Honda just as comfortable as the Yamaha.

Motorcycle *ergonomics*—the science of designing motorcycles that conform to the human body—receives a lot of attention in the motorcycling press these days. Ergonomic considerations influence all aspects of motorcycle design, from the riding position to the placement of the controls, which, in turn, contribute to the overall versatility of a motorcycle. The better a motorcycle fits you, the more comfortable you will be. The more comfortable you are, the more useful your motorcycle will be, though be aware, things change at speed.

Cycle Babble

The science of **ergonomics**, or human engineering, is used to design devices (including everything from cars to chairs) that conform to the human body. Ergonomics is a prime consideration when designing motorcycles; the idea is to provide maximum efficiency while keeping operator fatigue to a minimum.

That cruiser which feels so comfortable while stationary, with your legs pointed forward and your body dead upright, will be very different at 70 mph with the windblast catching your exposed body like a sailboat. The flip side is that a sportbike, which puts the weight of your whole upper body on your wrists at low speeds, will support your body weight at high speeds. That's why a test ride is so important. I talk more about trying out and buying bikes in Chapter 7.

Starting Out Small

Probably the most common mistake new riders make when choosing their first bike is buying a bike that's way too large for them. All of the best riders I know worked their way up in size, only getting rid of a bike when they were actually riding it to its full potential. The people I know who just learned to ride and went straight out and bought a 1000cc sportbike, well let's be brutally honest, they're terrifying! They're often a danger to other riders.

I discuss the basics of riding in Chapter 10, but it's important to explain a little about how motorcycles work here so you'll understand this point. Just like bicycles, motorcycles are unstable vehicles: if you don't hold them up, they'll fall over, though unlike a bicycle they're very heavy to pick up. When you ride, your bike is held up by its own inertia, as well as by the gyroscopic and centrifugal forces of its spinning wheels.

But any time your motorcycle is not traveling in a perfectly straight line, its weight shifts around in a manner you may be totally unused to. When traveling, a motorcycle doesn't follow its front wheels around a corner like a car does; instead, the bike leans around corners, rotating around a central axis, much like an airplane.

Because of this, you don't steer a motorcycle the way you drive a car. Instead, you *countersteer* it, using the handlebar to lever the motorcycle into a lean and initiate a turn.

Cycle Babble _____

Countersteering is the only way a bike will go around a corner above 10 or 15 mph. For a right-hand corner, push the handlebars away from you very slightly with your right hand. The bike will go right, even though this actually steers the bike left (hence the term *countersteer*). For a left-hand corner, push the handlebars with your left hand.

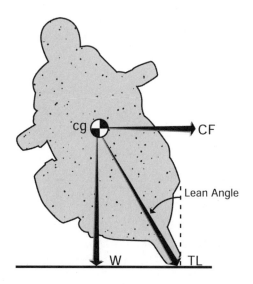

Instead of turning like a car, motorcycles lean into a turn, rotating on the machine's central axis like an airplane.

The point I'm trying to make here is that, on the road, motorcycles move around a lot in weird ways. This takes some getting used to, even on a lightweight motorcycle. On a heavier bike, this can be so disconcerting that it scares a new rider into never learning to steer the motorcycle properly.

The people who seem to run into the most trouble are those who choose a heavy-weight cruiser, a big touring motorcycle, or a liter class sportbike for their first bike. It's comparable to having a Lamborghini Diablo or a Mack truck as your first car.

Perhaps it's a Freudian thing, but size seems to be some sort of a status symbol for cruiser riders. As a popular T-shirt slogan says, "Size does matter." Unfortunately, for a new rider, it matters in a negative way.

For one thing, the heavy weight makes the motorcycle tend to ride in a straight line, even when you attempt to negotiate a turn. The more bike weight you have, the more you have to wrestle the machine through every turn. In addition, excessive weight can be especially problematic in cruisers because of certain handling characteristics common to the breed. Because of the steering geometry required to give cruisers their chopper-like look, they tend not to be the best-handling bikes on the road. To many novice riders, the bikes feel as if they are going to flop over.

Trying to master a large touring bike is usually a mistake for a novice. I've seen the enthusiasm of a lot of new riders nipped in the bud after they bought an ultimate behemoth-type touring bike before they were ready. When you get in over your head on one of these machines, their heavy weight is going to hurt you. When things start to go wrong on an 800-pound motorcycle, they go wrong fast.

In the worst-case scenario, selecting a motorcycle that's too large can ruin your enthusiasm for the sport and get you seriously hurt; by contrast, if you select one that is too small, you may outgrow the bike sooner, but you'll hone your riding skills much faster.

Starting Out Slow

New sportbike riders tend not to have weight-related problems because sportbikes generally are light, maneuverable motorcycles.

Although they are not physically large machines, the problem with sportbikes has to do with power—specifically, the fact that they might have too much of it for a novice rider. Grab a handful of throttle on one of the larger machines, and you'll be traveling more than 100 mph before your brain even has a chance to register your change in speed. The slowest of these bikes can be overwhelmingly quick. Before you buy one for your first bike, you should honestly assess your self-control and your riding ability. These bikes, which are often little more than race machines made road legal, present a challenge for even the most experienced rider

Best Bets for New Bikers

The trick is to find the right compromise: a bike small and safe enough to learn to ride, but competent enough to keep up with you as your skills grow. There are machines in each bike category that fulfill these requirements. As I mentioned earlier, any of the dual-sports makes a great first bike if you physically fit it and like its style. And most of the standard-style motorcycles are easy to learn to ride, and you can live with them for a very long time. Most of these bikes have high sporting capabilities, too, if you find yourself drawn to sportbikes.

The middleweight cruiser class teems with good choices for a first bike if your taste runs toward custom-style motorcycles. Just about any of the 500cc to 800cc cruisers are bikes you will enjoy riding for a long time.

If you're adamant about getting a Harley-Davidson for your first bike, you've got choices there, too, although the Big Twins are physically large bikes and will probably be uncomfortable for most novice riders. They also cost as much as most new cars.

But Harley makes its Sportster series for people looking for a bike smaller than a Big Twin. These attractive motorcycles represent good values for the money. And because Harley addressed the Sportster's biggest problem—vibration—for 2004, the Sportster has become an excellent choice for the beginning rider.

If you hanker to see the world on your bike, you're in luck, even if you're a beginner. Any bike that fits you and has enough power to keep up with traffic can be outfitted for touring. You can tour on a dual-sport, standard, cruiser, or sporty bike; you don't need an ultimate behemoth. Don't get me wrong: the big touring bikes are fantastic machines. I've owned one myself and used it more than any other bike. These bikes are just too heavy for a novice rider.

Harley's ultimate behemoth, the CVO Screamin' Eagle Electra Glide ($33,495), shown here, dwarfs Harley's entry-level bike, the 883 Sportster ($6,495), shown below.

New or Used?

When you've selected a type of motorcycle, you need to decide whether you want to buy a new bike or a used one.

Price is probably the prime determining factor in this decision. If money is no object, you can just waltz into a dealership and buy any bike that strikes your fancy. But most of us have to make prudent decisions when it comes to expenditures, especially when it comes to spending money on recreational activities such as motorcycling. If you're on a budget, buying a used bike can be a wise decision.

We will go into the details of buying a used bike in Chapter 7. In general, though, modern motorcycles are pretty tough to destroy. One exception to this rule is sport-bikes: there's been a trend for younger guys to *stunt ride* on sportbikes. They are in effect buying their bike to destroy it, so at all costs steer clear of buying a bike that's previously been used for stunt riding. Once they've finished with them, these bikes are usually just fit for the garbage can.

Generally, though, most lightly used bikes are in fairly good condition. This is especially true of motorcycles that appeal to more mature riders, such as touring bikes, cruisers, and standards. Dual-sports are usually in fair condition, unless the owner has attempted to do serious off-road riding on them.

One disadvantage of buying a used bike is that you are never quite certain what you are getting. Another disadvantage of buying used is that you don't usually get a warranty. I show you how to minimize your risks in Chapter 7.

Motorcycology

We won't discuss buying used off-road motorcycles because these are primarily race bikes, or bikes that have been ridden by expert riders under extremely stressful conditions. If you choose to purchase a used off-road motorcycle, you should be prepared to entirely rebuild it.

Cycle Babble

Stunt riding is common with younger riders who are often new to motorcycling. They will use their bikes to pull tricks like wheelies, often causing a lot of damage to their motorcycle and themselves. It has been made popular by the underground video scene.

But given the reliable nature of modern bikes, these disadvantages are fairly insignificant. The advantage of buying used is that used bikes are less expensive than new ones. This is especially true of Japanese motorcycles, which historically have had fairly poor resale value. For example, Kawasaki's 2007 Ninja 500R retails for $5,049. At that price, the little Ninja represents one of the best values in motorcycling. Nice, clean, used models can be found for as little as $1,500 to $2,000. These bikes may be 10 years old or more, but they are the same basic motorcycle as the new model.

Harley-Davidsons used to prove the exception. A few years back people had to wait months to buy new Harleys, so the used market went insane. I once saw a 1998 Sportster 1200 Custom, a bike that listed for $8,700, advertised in a newspaper for $13,000. A premium of $4,300 is quite a price to pay for being impatient. Fortunately for buyers (and unfortunately for those looking to turn a quick buck), that climate has changed. Already you can find new Harleys sitting for sale on showroom floors, a situation unheard of a few years ago. When supply and demand equalize, only a fool would pay more for a used bike than a new bike.

While buying a used bike may make the most sense from a pure dollars-and-cents point of view, buying a new bike has its advantages, too. When you buy a new bike, you get a warranty. While the odds of a modern bike breaking down are slim, it does happen, and when it does, that warranty is nice to have.

Another benefit of buying a new bike is that it can be easier to finance. Often the dealer will be able to finance the machine, saving you the hassle of procuring your own loan. And many manufacturers offer attractive low-interest financing packages.

Buying a new bike frees you from some of the worries of buying a used bike. Knowing the machine's complete history has certain benefits. When you are a bike's only owner, you can break it in properly yourself, and you know the bike has been properly maintained.

Plus, there's the intangible benefit of riding a brand-new motorcycle. There's nothing quite like the feeling of riding away from a dealership on your brand-new bike.

The Costs of Cycling

The most obvious (and largest) cost of motorcycling is the cost of the bike itself. New streetbikes range from a low of around $3,000 for a Kawasaki Ninja 250R to a high of $29,999 for an MV Agusta F4 Senna. Most new bikes fall into the range of $7,000 to $15,000.

Used-bike prices can vary even more than new-bike prices. I tell you where to find price references for specific bikes in Chapter 7, but expect to spend at least $2,500 to $5,000 for a good used motorcycle (unless you're a skilled bargain hunter).

No matter what type of bike you buy, or whether you buy new or used, you will find some unexpected costs. Some of these costs, such as buying insurance, will become apparent soon after you write the check for the bike. Others, such as the cost of basic maintenance, will rear their ugly heads only after you've racked up a few miles.

These costs aren't obvious to a new rider, and a little knowledge ahead of time can influence your choice of a bike. As you will learn, that choice will, in turn, influence those hidden costs.

Insurance Costs

Some insurance companies simply will not insure a motorcycle. Those that do usually use a completely arbitrary method of determining insurance premiums based on engine displacement. Basically, the smaller your engine is, the lower your insurance costs are likely to be, and any bodywork will add to your premium. This may seem logical to someone who knows absolutely nothing about bikes, but once you understand more about engines (which I discuss in Chapter 6), you'll realize that engine size means little.

But that's the way things are, so it's a good idea to take insurance costs into account when selecting a motorcycle. Check insurance prices in your area before buying a bike. Rates for the same bike from the same company can double from one location to the next. For example, my wife, who has a spotless driving record, paid about $260 per year for full-coverage insurance on her Honda ST1100 when she lived in North Dakota. When she moved to Minneapolis, her insurance premiums (using the same policy) doubled, shooting up to nearly $600 per year.

Maintenance Costs

Even less obvious than insurance costs are maintenance costs. While modern bikes don't require an annual overhaul like many older models do, they still require more maintenance than most cars. This is partly because motorcycles are so technologically advanced.

Motorcycle designers have to use sophisticated mechanisms to get a relatively small motorcycle engine to generate so much power. Thus, these engines require more routine maintenance than less highly stressed engines. Add in the other procedures your bike will require, such as carburetion adjustments and chain and tire replacements (which I discuss in Chapter 17), and you can expect to fork out some serious cash for tune-ups over the years.

And if you don't do your own basic maintenance and instead take your bike in for things such as oil and tire changes, you can add a significant amount to your overall total. But there are some things you can do to minimize these expenses. The less you abuse your motorcycle in general, the less money you will have to spend maintaining it.

The Least You Need to Know

- The perfect bike for one rider may be ill suited for the next rider.

- When choosing a bike, consider the type of riding you want to do, the versatility of the bike, and the comfort of the bike.

- While a big bike might impress your buddies, it may also seriously hamper your growth as a skilled motorcyclist.

- There are valid reasons for choosing to buy either a new bike or a used bike. Used bikes are generally cheaper than new bikes and can be in good enough condition to ride. However, new bikes often come with financing and warranties, and are in perfect condition when you buy them.

- Different types and sizes of motorcycles have different hidden costs, such as the cost of insurance and the cost of maintenance.

5

Anatomy of a Motorcycle

In This Chapter

- ◆ Understanding the mechanical bits that make your bike tick
- ◆ How the top and bottom ends of the engine make your motorcycle go
- ◆ How the carburetor and induction system work
- ◆ The importance of the frame, wheels, and tires
- ◆ The uses of bodywork

Many riders love motorcycles for their elegant lines, disrupted by the least possible number of mechanical components. Yet the simple appearance of the motorcycle belies a complex mechanical system—or, rather, set of systems.

In *Zen and the Art of Motorcycle Maintenance*, author Robert M. Persig writes that it is a mistake to see the motorcycle as simply a collection of parts. Rather, he describes motorcycles as a collection of ideas, and he describes working on bikes as "working on concepts." He writes, "That's all a motorcycle is, a system of concepts worked out in steel."

To get a complete understanding of a motorcycle, you'll need a little mechanical background, a basic understanding of Persig's "system of concepts." In this chapter, I give you a guided tour of the inner workings of a bike.

The Nature of the Beast

Motorcycles are mechanical devices. Bikes that have tried to hide their mechanical nature have usually failed to win over the motorcycling public. Philip Vincent, founder of the Vincent-HRD motorcycle company, discovered this in 1954 when he tried to sell versions of his magnificent Vincent motorcycles cloaked in fiberglass bodywork. The failure of the Black Prince and Black Knight helped seal Vincent's fate, and the last Vincent motorcycle was constructed at Vincent's Stevenage factory in 1955.

Subsequent fully enclosed motorcycles have fared little better than the Vincent. Ducati marketed a fully enclosed series of bikes, the Paso's and 907 I.E., in the late 1980s and early 1990s, but these never set motorcycle buyers on fire. As a result, Ducati now offers several models with small half-fairings (the devices mounted at the front of a motorcycle to protect the rider from the elements) or no fairings at all, to better showcase its engines. Honda tested the market for shrink-wrapped bikes when it introduced the Pacific Coast in 1989. This model did so poorly that it was withdrawn from the market; it was such a competent all-around motorcycle, though, that it rose from the dead and returned to production.

Other designers learned from the lack of success of these bikes, and newer designs, such as the wave of sporting twins from Japan, highlight rather than hide their engines. Motorcyclists appreciate a bike's mechanical nature, and any biker worth his or her leather jacket is well versed in the anatomy of a motorcycle.

Meeting the Motor

The motor seems a logical place to start when dissecting a bike. After all, motorcycles are named for their engines. The engine, more than anything else, gives a motorcycle its character and personality. Looks may stir you to buy a bike, but the characteristics of the engine keep you riding it year after year. As Philip Vincent said, "Motorcycles are supposed to be ridden, and one cannot see the model when one is riding it."

In the next chapter, you'll examine the different types of engines and how the type of engine and its state of tune affect the character of the motorcycle. In this chapter, you just focus on the different parts of the engine and what each one does.

The engine proper is usually divided into two parts: the lower portion, called the *bottom end*, which includes the parts that transmit power to the rear wheel; and the upper portion, called the *top end*, which is where the internal-combustion process takes place. The engine also includes a system to introduce an air-fuel charge into the chambers where combustion takes place. This is called the *induction system* and consists of either a carburetor or carburetors, or fuel injectors. It works in conjunction with a series of valves that are part of the engine's top end.

Cycle Babble

The **bottom end** of a bike refers to the bottom part of the engine, where the crankshaft and (usually) the transmission reside. The **top end** refers to the upper part of the engine, which contains the pistons, cylinders, and valve gear. The **induction system** consists of the apparatus that mixes an air-and-fuel charge that goes into the combustion chamber, located in the top end.

The Belly of the Beast: The Bottom End

I like to compare motorcycle components to the human body, to make it easier to envision. The bottom end is the entrails of a bike. This is where all the commotion in the engine is converted into forward motion.

The two clamshell-like metal halves that surround the bottom end are called cases. All motorcycle engine bottom ends contain at least one crankshaft (on certain designs, two crankshafts occupy the space within the engine cases, but these are rare, especially in the United States).

The crankshaft is connected via connecting rods to the pistons, which are the slugs moving up and down within the cylinders (the hollow shafts in the top end inside which internal combustion occurs). The connecting rods attach to the crankshaft on eccentric journals (sections of the crankshaft offset from the crank's longitudinal centerline), and their up-and-down movement is converted into a circular motion through the design of these journals.

As you'll see in the next chapter, the design of the crankshaft does much to give the engine its character. For example, design of the crankshaft and the engine's firing order give Harley-Davidsons their characteristic rumbling sound (it's what also contributes to Harley engines vibrating like washing machines with unbalanced loads).

The Transmission

On most modern motorcycles, the circular motion created by the crankshaft setup is transmitted to the transmission through a series of gears or by a chain.

For all practical purposes, you can think of the transmission of a modern motorcycle as part of the bottom end. The crankshaft and the gearset usually reside inside the same cavity within the cases. This is called a *unitized transmission*. Since the 1950s and 1960s, it has been a part of just about every motorcycle engine designed.

One notable exception is Harley-Davidson, the only company still manufacturing motorcycles that use separate engines and transmissions, connected by a *primary drive*. The primary, as it is called, consists of a sprocket attached to the crankshaft that rides outside the engine cases in a case of its own (called the primary case). This case is connected to the transmission, which is located behind the engine via a primary chain.

Harley's primary drive system presents added maintenance chores: the primary chain must be periodically adjusted, a rather difficult process that creates more opportunities for things to go wrong. The exposed components are also more vulnerable to damage than components protected within the cases. No one knows for certain why Harley continues to use this archaic setup, but if I had to guess, I'd say it's purely for looks.

The transmission is an integral part of the bottom end on most motorcycles, but it is really a separate system. *Manual transmission* design varies from bike to bike, but most share some basic characteristics. Each transmission contains a gearset, which, as you might have guessed from the name, is a set of gears. Designers use complex mathematical equations between the diameter of these gears and a variety of other parts on the motorcycle to give a bike certain characteristics.

These gears are engaged by shifting a lever with your left foot, which moves *shifting forks* inside the transmission, which, in turn, move the gears within. If you have any trouble with the transmission, odds are it will involve those forks.

Cycle Babble

A **unitized transmission** (often referred to as a "unit transmission") is a transmission that is an integral part of the engine's bottom end.

A **primary drive** is a drive chain, belt, or gears connecting the engine's crankshaft to its transmission.

A **manual transmission** is a device consisting of a set of gears (the gearset) that enable an operator to get up to speed. All motorcycles now being produced have manual transmissions. In a motorcycle, the gears within the gearset are moved around with devices called **shifting forks**.

Harley-Davidson is the last major manufacturer still using an external primary drive on its motorcycle engines.

(Photo © 1998 Darwin Holmstrom)

Valve Clatter: The Top End

The top end of a motorcycle is where the internal-combustion process takes place. The top end consists of the pistons, the cylinder block, and the head, which contains the valve train. As mentioned earlier, pistons are metal slugs that move up and down in the cylinders. The energy created by burning the air-fuel charge (a mixture of gasoline and air) acts on the tops of the pistons (known as the crowns) to make your bike move. Pistons are both simple and complex devices, but for the sake of this discussion, I'll stick with this simple definition.

The cylinder block is a rather simple device, too: a hunk of aluminum with holes bored through it, inside which the pistons move up and down. This hunk serves two purposes:

1. It channels the pistons' energy and forces them to move up and down (rather than flying all over the place, which would not help make your motorcycle move).

2. It dissipates the intense heat created by the burning air-fuel charge and the friction caused by the motion of the pistons. This is done by some sort of coolant circulating throughout the block, by cooling oil being sprayed on the hot spots on the piston, or by air flowing over the outside of the block (the reason for the fins visible on your engine). Usually, some combination of the three methods effectively cools the engine.

The *valve train* is the most convoluted and confusing system in the top end. It consists of a cam, which is a rod with eccentric lobes on it that opens the valves. Valves are devices consisting of metal stems with flat disks on one end. They ride in metal tubes, called valve guides, and open and close at precise moments to let air-fuel charges into the *combustion chambers* and to let the waste gases created during the combustion process exit.

There are two basic types of valve trains: overhead cam systems and pushrod systems. Each system has several varieties, but they all share some common traits.

Most modern bikes use overhead cams. In this type of valve train, the cams are located above the valves and act on them through a system of rocker arms, or the cam lobe acts directly on the valve. Rocker arms are metal levers that rotate on a small shaft like an upside-down teeter-totter; the cam lobes push one side of the rocker up, causing the other side of the rocker to push the valves down, opening them.

The pushrod system has cams located below the combustion chambers, usually in the engine cases, that act on pushrods—long, metal rods connected to the rocker arms located above the valves. This is hardly a dead technology. These days, Harley-Davidson, Buell, Yamaha, Kawasaki, and Moto Guzzi all still use this traditional method of valve actuation in some of their engines. BMW uses a hybrid cam-in-head system, which locates the cam in the cylinder head but below the valves. BMW's system uses short pushrods to open the valves.

Overhead cams have a more positive action (less slop in the system) and allow the engine to operate at a higher rate of *revolutions per minute* (rpm) than can pushrod engines. The term *rpm* refers to the number of times a crankshaft spins around each minute. Being able to run at higher rpm means an engine will put out more overall power.

Cycle Babble

The head sits atop the cylinder block and houses the **valve train,** the system of valves that let the air-fuel charges in and let the exhaust gases out. The area at the top of the cylinder where the air-fuel charge burns and pushes the pistons down is called the **combustion chamber.**

Revolutions per minute (rpm) refers to the number of times the crankshaft spins per minute, essentially how fast an engine can spin. Often the term *revs* is used, especially in conversation.

One advantage of Harley's—and some Japanese cruisers'—pushrod system is easy maintenance. Harleys use hydraulically adjusted tappets (small metal slugs between the cams and the pushrods) that eliminate the need for periodic valve adjustments. Some overhead-cam designs also use hydraulic-valve adjustments, but most require periodic manual adjustments.

Harley-Davidson is one of several motorcycle manufacturers still using a pushrod-operated valve system.

(Photo © 1998 Darwin Holmstrom)

In a surprising move, Yamaha chose a pushrod-operated overhead valve system for its entry into the big-inch V-twin cruiser class, the Road Star. This was the first time a new Japanese motorcycle engine had used pushrods in some time. But this seemingly antiquated system hasn't hurt the Road Star's popularity one bit.

To Inject or Not to Inject? Induction Systems

Since Gottlieb Daimler constructed the first gasoline-powered motorcycle back in 1885, motorcycles have had *carburetors*—complex devices that mix gas and air into the fuel charge, which is then sucked into the combustion chamber. Carburetors—or carbs, as they are often called—rely on suction to deliver the air-fuel charge to the combustion chamber. Although modern carbs are remarkably efficient devices, they share many similarities with the crude device old Gottlieb bolted onto his half-horsepower engine way back when.

Today most motorcycles have one carburetor for each cylinder, with a few exceptions.

The carburetor's century-long supremacy as the ultimate form of motorcycle induction system has been challenged in the last decade by *fuel injection*. Fuel injection refers to a system that forces the fuel charge into the intake port with an electronic pump.

Cycle Babble

Fuel-injection systems inject an accurate amount of fuel into each of the engine's cylinders. Fuel injection works independently of vacuum differences between atmospheric pressure and that in the combustion chamber.

The first reliable motorcycle fuel-injection system appeared on the 1980 Kawasaki Z-1 Classic. Since then, every other manufacturer has been working to fit fuel injection on every model they offer.

With the universal acceptance of fuel injection in the automotive world, it might seem odd that motorcycles have been slower to adopt the technology. Fuel injection offers certain benefits, such as greater control over the ratio of the air-fuel charge and less dependence on atmospheric conditions. But the problem is usually a matter of cost, as in what the customer will pay for the privilege of the technology. The cost of development time to fit fuel injection throughout a model lineup isn't cheap; even so, more bikes are using such systems. Modern technology has finally made fuel injection a viable option on motorcycles.

The Clutch

One of the major obstacles designers of early motorcycles faced was creating a system for engaging and disengaging the power transmitted to the back wheel. This wasn't a problem as long as you were moving, but once you decided to stop, it quickly became important.

Most early motorcycles used a leather belt to transmit power from the engine to the rear wheel! This belt connected directly to the crankshaft. To give the rider some control over the flow of power, a pulley mounted on a lever was used to tighten the belt.

Unsurprisingly, this system proved to be only marginally effective, even on the underpowered machines of the time, and it soon became clear that a better system was needed. That system was the *clutch*. The clutch is a series of spring-loaded plates that, when pressed together, transmit power from the crankshaft to the transmission.

Early clutches were operated by a foot pedal, like on an automobile, with levers mounted to the gas tank to shift gears in the transmission. It's still sometimes fitted on custom choppers as an old-school engineering touch.

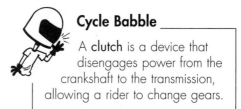

When the British began exporting motorcycles to the United States with hand-operated clutches and foot-operated shifters, stateside riders soon realized the benefits of such an ergonomic system, forcing Harley-Davidson to adopt hand clutches and foot shifts for its motorcycles.

Nearly every full-size motorcycle built since World War I uses a clutch, with a couple of oddball exceptions. Honda experimented with a clutchless, or automatic, transmission on its CB750A Hondamatic in the mid-1970s, and Moto Guzzi marketed an automatic bike at about the same time. Neither was a sales success. Unless you run across an example of one of these rare bikes, you should probably resign yourself to the fact that it's time to learn to use a clutch and a manual gearbox.

Rotating the Rubber: Drive Systems

You now have a fair idea about what all that commotion taking place down below your legs is all about, but really, it means nothing if you have no way of transmitting that commotion to the back wheel of your bike.

As with many other aspects of motorcycle technology, the three final-drive systems most commonly used today—chain, shaft, and belt—had all been tried before the European squabbling that started World War I got out of hand.

In Chains

In the early years of the sport, the crude belt system mentioned earlier was employed, but by the end of World War I, most manufacturers had settled on a *chain final-drive system* (although a few opted for drive shafts). The simplicity and ease of repair of a chain-driven system made it a logical choice back then.

In this system, a sprocket mounted to an output shaft in the transmission is

Motorcycology

Although they're messy, the chain lubes and solvents now available are much cleaner and easier to use than ever before. While we may get some oil on our boot, the motorcycle pioneers were covered in the nasty, sticky stuff.

connected to a sprocket attached to the rear wheel of the motorcycle by the drive chain. Although such a setup requires periodic maintenance (the chain gradually stretches, so the rear wheel needs to be adjusted to take up the slack), the benefits of this system make it popular to this day.

Unlike shafts (discussed in the next section), chains smoothly absorb much of the impact created during acceleration (which is the main reason they elongate over time). Shafts, which are much more rigid than chains, feed that energy back into the frame, causing vertical motions some riders notice. These motions are called shaft jacking, and while it's not a serious problem in most real-world riding conditions, it can detract from a bike's handling.

Probably the biggest drawback of chain drives is that they are messy. Besides needing to be adjusted, they need to be lubricated on a regular basis. The solutions used to do this are sometimes sticky and greasy.

Getting the Shaft

Shaft final-drives do affect handling: they transmit the energy a chain absorbs directly to the *chassis* (the combined frame and suspension), causing the rear of the motorcycle to move up when it should move down, and vice versa. Still, shaft drives are popular because they are so convenient and low-maintenance, especially when traveling. It's hard enough packing a motorcycle for an extended trip without having to put cans of lube in your duffel bag next to your shirts and underwear. Because of this, the most popular touring and sport-touring bikes have shaft drives.

Cycle Babble

Shaft final-drive systems transmit the power to the rear wheel via a drive shaft. Think of them as a shorter version of the drive shaft from a car. The **chassis** refers to the combined frame and suspension on a motorcycle.

A couple of clever companies (BMW and Moto Guzzi) have all but eliminated the antics associated with shaft systems by using creative rear-suspension geometry. By arranging suspension components in a parallelogram-type position, the rear suspensions on these bikes feed the shaft-jacking motion into the frame along a horizontal axis rather than a vertical axis, converting the up-and-down motion into a forward-and-backward motion. The rider hardly notices this sort of movement.

Whereas clever designers can overcome the shaft's acrobatics, another drawback of shaft systems cannot be overcome so easily: their weight. Shaft drives are heavy, and that weight is unsprung, meaning that it is not supported by the suspension. Unsprung weight tends to work a bike's suspension harder and decreases the bike's ability to change directions.

The drawbacks of both shaft and chain systems led some companies to explore an old alternative: belt drives.

Belt It Out

Although belt drives were abandoned early on, by the beginning of the 1980s advances in materials (now rubber belts are reinforced with steel thread) had once again made them a viable alternative. Harley-Davidson was the first to reintroduce the concept, equipping special-edition bikes (such as its original Sturgis model) with both primary- and final-drive belts. The primary belt system never caught on, but the final-drive belt did, and today every Harley and Buell made comes standard with such a belt.

Kawasaki also experimented with belts on some of its small-displacement bikes.

The advantages of *belt final-drive systems* over chains are that belts are much cleaner, requiring neither messy lube nor cleaning solvents. While they do need periodic adjustments, they need such attention less frequently than chains.

The advantage of a belt system over a shaft is that belts, like chains, do not transmit unwanted motion into the chassis. They also do not come with the unsprung weight penalty of a shaft system.

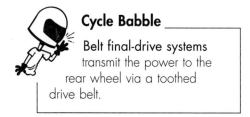

Cycle Babble

Belt final-drive systems transmit the power to the rear wheel via a toothed drive belt.

The disadvantages of belt systems, at least in the case of Harley-Davidson's application, is that accurate adjustment is critical and they are true buggers to replace when they do go bad, especially on the Big Twins. Except for certain models, most Big Twins require that you partially disassemble the frame in order to replace a belt. And to replace a belt on all Big Twins, you must remove the primary drive and clutch assembly, which is no small job.

This disadvantage has been negated on many of the newer bikes using belts. Victory uses a removable subframe to ease belt replacement, as does the Buell Firebolt. Such convenient features make a belt drive increasingly attractive. Even BMW uses a belt on its F650CS Single.

Putting It All Together

The frame, suspension, wheels, and tires on a motorcycle are basically the things that hold a bike together and keep it from falling down. In the past, that was pretty much all they did, but modern designers use them for much more.

The frames on early motorcycles were just a collection of tubes holding all the parts together. In the 1970s, however, designers began to realize that the stiffness of the frame affected overall handling characteristics and began experimenting with stiffer designs.

Motorcycle frames looked more or less the same from the time Harley and the Davidson boys built their first motorcycle until the mid-1980s. As a result of developments over the past 15 years, the twin-spar aluminum frames found on most modern sportbikes resemble the single- or double-cradle designs of the past about as much as an F-117 fighter jet resembles the Wright brothers' Flyer.

Suspension—which refers to the combination of forks, shocks, and, to a degree, tires—also has come a long way over the same time period. Just having a suspension was quite an innovation at one time. Early bikes relied on sprung girder forks up front and a soft saddle in back. It wasn't until the 1940s and 1950s that most motorcycle manufacturers began offering the hydraulic front forks and swinging-arm rear suspensions we now accept as the industry standard.

Once accepted, this setup became engraved in stone. It didn't change for the better part of 30 years.

During the 1970s, dirtbike manufacturers developed a variation of the swinging-arm rear suspension that used a single shock (Monoshock), and that system found its way onto streetbikes in the 1980s. The advantage of these systems is that they allow the wheel to travel farther up and down when the bike strikes a bump or other surface irregularity before the shock reaches the end of its travel and transmits a jarring thump to the rider. By incorporating variable-rate linkage into such a system, designers have introduced even more suspension travel into the shocks. This type of system is the most common in use today.

Cruisers usually use the older dual-shock setup because it gives these bikes the retro look cruiser buyers want. The ride quality on some cruisers tends to be a bit harsh because they often forfeit wheel travel to get a low seat height.

A few manufacturers have attempted to market alternatives to the hydraulic fork front suspension, most notably Bimota, with its Tesi model, and Yamaha, with its GTS. Neither bike has sold well, however.

BMW has produced the most successful alternate front suspension, the Telelever system. This replaces the shock-absorption function of a conventional hydraulic fork with a shock absorber located behind the steering head. This clever system solves many of the chassis-dynamic problems associated with a traditional fork, but I believe that part of its success can be attributed to the fact that it still looks like a traditional fork.

Wheels and tires have also seen a surge of development since the early 1970s. The first technological advancement was the advent of cast wheels in the 1970s. These allowed bikes to use automotive-type tubeless tires, which provide a tremendous safety advantage because they are less likely to blow out than a tube-type tire. If you have ever had a tire blow out on a car, you know you don't want it to happen to you when you're riding a bike as it will only leave one functioning wheel, not three.

Tires themselves have come a long way, too. Today's touring tires can last 10,000 to 15,000 miles. And today's radial street tires provide phenomenal grip, though at the expense of high mileage. A super-*sticky* tire can be worn out in 3,000 miles.

Cycle Babble

Sticky is a term used to describe sporting tires that provide incredible grip.

What all this means is that you have access to motorcycles that ride better, handle better, last longer, and are safer than anything a motorcyclist could have imagined possible just a few years ago.

It's Electric

The system least likely to cause trouble in your motorcycle is the electrical system. But if you do encounter an electrical failure of some sort, it will most likely occur early in the bike's life, well within the warranty period.

The function of the electrical system is to …

- ◆ Provide current to the ignition to burn the fuel charge.
- ◆ Power all the electrical devices on your bike, such as the headlight.

The electrical system consists of a battery, some form of electrical-generation device, and an ignition system to provide spark to the combustion chamber. I discuss this system in greater detail in Chapter 16.

Bodywork

Bodywork, a major component on most motorcycles today, didn't even exist on most motorcycles 20 years ago. For the first 95 years of motorcycling, bodywork just meant some sort of container mounted to the frame to store the gasoline.

The Europeans deserve much of the credit (or blame, depending on your own preferences) for making bodywork such a pervasive part of motorcycle design. BMW, Moto Guzzi, and Ducati all marketed motorcycles with fairings in the 1970s. (As you learned in Chapter 3, fairings are the devices mounted at the front of a motorcycle to protect the rider from the elements.) By the end of the 1970s, the Japanese manufacturers were starting to do the same.

The only really surprising thing about this development was that it took the manufacturers so long to get in on the act. Perhaps the manufacturers were still haunted by the relative failure of the Vincent enclosed motorcycles discussed at the beginning of this chapter.

As the 1980s progressed, bodywork became more encompassing. Soon many streetbikes came with not only fairings, but also *cowlings* that covered the engine. These items were designed to integrate with the rear portions of the bike, resulting in clean-looking bikes that have no visible engine components, creating an almost automotive appearance. Cowlings can protect you from the heat coming off the engine, and also help to shield you from rain working its way up through the nooks and crannies of a regular fairing.

Cycle Babble

A **cowling** is a piece of bodywork that covers the engine area.

As long as the bike still looks like a motorcycle, riders appreciate such bodywork, as well as the additional weather protection it provides.

Like everything, though, those benefits come at a price. As I mentioned in Chapter 4, the price of bodywork is higher insurance premiums and higher repair costs. Even routine maintenance becomes more expensive on a bike that must have its bodywork removed.

Yamaha's YZF-R1 features such attractive bodywork that at first glance, some observers mistake it for an Italian motorcycle.

(Photo courtesy Yamaha USA)

The Least You Need to Know

◆ The engine gives a motorcycle its character and personality.

◆ The bottom end of the engine is where all the commotion in the engine is converted into forward motion.

◆ The top end of the engine is where the internal-combustion process takes place.

◆ The drive systems used today are chain, shaft, and belt.

◆ Bodywork, such as fairings and cowlings, helps protect motorcycle riders from the elements.

Chapter 6

Start Your Engines

In This Chapter

- Why different types of engines give motorcycles different characteristics
- The difference between two-stroke and four-stroke engines
- The types of four-stroke engines: singles, V-twins, and more

In the previous chapter, you took an in-depth technical look at the parts of a motorcycle. Now you're going to venture into a more esoteric, subjective area: the engine, the soul of a motorcycle.

You might wince at this bit of anthropomorphism, thinking a motorcycle has as much of a soul as a toaster or an electric screwdriver. But motorcyclists who have ridden for a while know the truth: motorcycles possess a distinct, essential spirit, and while the word *soul* doesn't exactly describe it, it comes closer than any other word in the English language. If bikes don't have souls, someone forgot to tell that to my motorcycles.

A variety of characteristics give each bike its unique identity, but none so clearly defines a bike's personality as its engine. And each type of engine has different characteristics, which is why certain types are used for specific motorcycles.

Many of the internal differences that give an engine its character are technical details beyond the scope of this book. But knowing the basic types of engines and what you can expect from each will help you select the bike best suited for you.

Engineering

All engine types get their characteristics from a combination of *horsepower* and *torque*. While closely related, horsepower and torque are not the same thing: each is a measure of a different characteristic of an engine's power. Their relationship is complex, but Dan Keenen of Dynojet Research, a company that builds machines used to measure horsepower and torque, explains it in a way even I can understand. Keenen describes horsepower as a measure of how fast you can go, and torque as a measure of an engine's snap, or how fast it can get to its maximum speed.

In the real world, torque is usually more usable than prodigious amounts of peak horsepower. The benefits of lots of horsepower tend to be most apparent at speeds well beyond what local law-enforcement officials will allow; you can use torque at speeds that won't land you in jail.

Two basic types of motorcycle engines are in use today: the two-stroke and the four-stroke. Over the following pages, you'll look at each one.

Cycle Babble

Horsepower is a measure of an engine's strength. It is called horsepower because it was originally calculated by measuring how much weight a horse could lift in a certain period of time. Torque is a twisting force, and in a motorcycle, it is a measure of the leverage the engine exerts on the rear wheel.

The Four-Stroke

Anyone who has ever added oil to a car has experience with *four-stroke engines;* the vast majority of road-going vehicles ever to turn a wheel on streets in the United States have four-stroke engines.

Cycle Babble

The four-stroke engine is sometimes called the *Otto cycle,* in honor of its inventor, Nikolaus August Otto. It's called a four-stroke because the piston makes four strokes, or movements along the length of the cylinder, per cycle.

The four-stroke gets its name from the number of strokes the piston makes during each power cycle (each series of events that produces power). The piston first moves down, drawing in the air-fuel charge (intake stroke) and then moves up (compression stroke), at which time the air-fuel charge ignites and burns, pushing the piston down (power stroke). The fourth stroke occurs when the piston moves back up, forcing out the burned gases (exhaust stroke).

The Single

The single, so called because it only has one piston and cylinder, is the most basic of engines—it once powered most motorcycles on the road. In the old days, motorcycles were such problematic beasts that the general philosophy held that the fewer moving parts you had, the less chance there was that those parts would break. If there was a way of having zero-cylinder motorcycles, without having to pedal, they'd have done it.

As designs and materials advanced, along with production techniques, manufacturers were able to create ever more complex motorcycles, with two, three, four, six, and even eight cylinders. Generally, the more cylinders you have, the smoother the engine runs. But with a counterbalancer (weights inside the engine) to cancel out some of the vibration, plus rubber motor-mounts, today's big singles will no longer blur your vision as they vibrate you off your seat.

Buell's Blast represents a modern interpretation of the sporting single-cylinder motorcycle, once the most common type of bike.

(Photo courtesy of Motorcyclist™ magazine)

The primary drawback of single-cylinder engines, though, is that they don't make a lot of horsepower, which has contributed to their waning popularity.

But singles have advantages, too. Because they have few parts, they tend to be light powerplants (engines), which is why they are so popular in dirt bikes and the big dual-sports. And although they might not generate a lot of power, they still provide satisfying amounts of grunty torque.

Suppose you are riding a BMW F650CS single. Beside you, your companion rides a Suzuki GSX-R600, a four-cylinder bike that makes more than twice as much horsepower as your Beemer, but roughly the same torque. You pass the city limits, and the speed limit rises to 65. Say, for the sake of argument, that you're both running at roughly 2,500 rpm. You both whack open the throttle at the same time. You'll pull away first—even though the Suzuki has twice as much horsepower—because at 2,500 rpm you have about 34 pound-feet of torque available to you, while the Suzuki has only about 22 pound-feet of torque available (torque, the force the engine exerts on the rear wheel, is measured in pound-feet).

Of course, within a few seconds, the Suzuki will have rocketed away from you when all that horsepower kicks in, but by then you are both going faster than the powers that be will allow anyway. And if the Suzuki rider drops the shifter down a few gears, she will have left you behind from the moment you hit the throttle. Either way, she will have accelerated to go-to-jail speeds quicker than you can process the sound of the sirens on Officer Bob's police cruiser as he begins a high-speed pursuit.

The point of this hypothetical scenario is that while single-cylinder bikes offer less overall power than multicylinder bikes, the power they do offer is often more usable in the real world, a world populated by traffic lights, stray dogs, pedestrians, senior citizens, and law-enforcement officials. The same is true of many twin-cylinder motorcycles.

The V-Twin

The *V-twin* design found widespread support even in the early days of motorcycle development, largely because it fit the shape of the bicycle-style frames used on motorcycles at the time.

Cycle Babble

A **V-twin** engine is a two-cylinder engine with its cylinders splayed out in a V shape.

By 1907, Harley and those Davidson boys displayed a prototype V-twin engine for their motorcycles. When Englishman Philip Vincent decided to add another cylinder to his Comet and create the first Rapide, the two cylinders together formed a traditional V. And when the Japanese got serious about building American-style cruisers, their engine of choice was the V-twin, too.

Modern manufacturers build V-twin motorcycles for a variety of reasons; some are practical and objective, while others, such as tradition and style, are purely subjective.

V-twin engines vary widely in their characteristics. Some designs, such as Harley-Davidson's 45-degree big V-twins, vibrate excessively. But Harley has taken the Twin Cam 88/88B Big Twin engines and either rubber-mounted them (touring and Dyna Glide models) or fitted them with counterbalancers (Softail series). Likewise, Harley rubber-mounted its 883/1200 Evolution engines in its Sportsters.

Other V-twin cruisers use narrow-angle V engines but also use some sort of system for reducing vibration. Honda uses a staggered crankshaft, which fools the engine into thinking the V angle is a wider 90 degrees. Other manufacturers, such as Kawasaki, use heavy counterbalancers.

One characteristic common to most V-twin engines (and all successful ones) is ample torque, especially in the larger models. Riders of high-revving sportbikes often comment on the lack of peak horsepower that V-twin bikes usually display, but they're missing the point. While V-twins usually give away a lot of power up at the top of the rpm band (which, in the real world, means at triple-digit speeds), they make up for it by offering tremendous usable power at lower rpm.

On a cruiser with a large V-twin engine, you can probably forget about riding all day at 145 mph, but when you whack open the throttle at lower speeds (such as the 65 to 70 mph you'll usually find yourself riding), you are rewarded with satisfying thrust that sets you back in the saddle.

The Boxer

In 1923, Max Friz, an engineer working for BMW, built a motorcycle engine, the R32. It was a 500cc *opposed twin*, using basic principles still in use today. This engine earned the nickname Boxer because the pistons thrust outward, away from each other, like fists.

This wasn't the first opposed engine, but Friz's execution was unique, and the effectiveness of his design makes BMW's Boxer engines popular to this day. By opposing each other, the pistons cancel out primary vibration, creating a remarkably smooth twin-cylinder engine. And by locating the pistons on the side of the engine, Friz placed them in the cooling airstream, lead-

Cycle Babble

Opposed twins (two-cylinder engines with the pistons opposing each other) are called *Boxers* because the pistons look like fists flying away from each other.

ing to a cool-running—and, thus, long-lasting—engine. It's not uncommon to find BMWs with 200,000 or more miles showing on the odometer.

The success of Friz's design wasn't lost on manufacturers from other countries. During World War II, Harley-Davidson used his Boxer design for a military motorcycle; in 1941, Ural began manufacturing a Beemer clone in Russia. Harley ditched this idea soon after World War II, but Ural is still at it.

Many people find that the Boxer design offers an ideal compromise between twin-cylinder torque and multicylinder smoothness. Like the V-twin, a Boxer's primary characteristic is abundant torque rather than massive peak horsepower. This torque is usually found a bit higher in the rpm range than a V-twin's, but it still comes on early enough to be useful in the real world. In return, Boxers tend to have more top speed than V-twins. Combine that with the engine design's inherent smoothness and the result is Boxer riders who can cruise for extended periods at elevated speeds.

Edward Turner's Speed Twin

In 1927, a young man in Britain named Edward Turner, working alone in his own shop, designed and built a 350cc single-cylinder motorcycle. The British motorcycle industry took note of this achievement, and he soon landed a job designing bikes. By 1936, he'd worked his way up to general manager and chief designer at Triumph Engineering Co.

In July 1937, Turner introduced the 500cc Speed Twin, which featured a 27-horsepower *parallel-twin engine* that formed the basis of most Triumph motorcycle engines well into the 1980s. This engine, and its imitators from companies such as BSA and Norton, became the powerplant of choice for sporting motorcycles for decades to come.

Cycle Babble

A **parallel-twin engine** is a two-cylinder engine with its cylinders placed side by side in an upright position. From the side it can be mistaken for a single-cylinder engine.

Because of the design of its crankshaft, along with certain dynamic problems inherent in the parallel-twin design, these engines vibrated much more than a Boxer engine, but they vibrated less than a V-twin. Plus, they were light and powerful for their day. Their compact size enabled engineers to create compact motorcycles that could run circles around the big Harleys and Indians of that era, and the power output of a 650 nearly equaled that of the big V-twins, which displaced as much as 1200cc. For a long time, it was the most commonly used sportbike engine.

Although the parallel twin has long since ceased being the powerplant of choice for superbikes, the design still has enough appeal to keep it in production. Modern versions, with redesigned crankshafts and counterbalancers to tame vibration, power a variety of midsize bikes from manufacturers such as Suzuki and Kawasaki. Kawasaki produces parallel twins in both cruiser and sportbike form. These motorcycles make ideal first bikes. I'm especially fond of Kawasaki's EX500/Ninja 500 series; these are comfortable, good-handling, nimble motorcycles with enough power to keep a rider amused for decades.

The British Triple

Eventually, the British responded to the Japanese invasion and introduced a new engine design, the *inline-triple*. In many respects, this was just a parallel twin with an extra cylinder grafted on, but it featured some unique characteristics—notably, its compactness. British twins gained their reputation for being fine-handling motorcycles in large part because their compact engines allowed designers to tuck everything in, leaving very few hard parts to scrape the pavement during high-speed antics. With the triples, designers went to great lengths to retain that compactness.

Although promising, these bikes initially had too many problems to save the British motorcycle industry. Anyone who wants to learn how not to conduct business would do well to study the development of the T150 Triumph Trident and BSA Rocket 3. A design firm with no experience in motorcycles was hired to style the bikes, resulting in bizarre-looking machines. Mechanically, the new bikes also failed. Although the engines were powerful, they proved unreliable in service, victims of underdevelopment.

After the appearance of the new bikes was universally rejected by motorcycle buyers, Triumph successfully restyled the Trident (BSA had gone out of business by that time) and gradually worked out the mechanical bugs, but it was just too late. By then, Honda had already introduced its CB750 *inline-four*-cylinder bike and, in doing so, effectively stripped the British of any influence in the motorcycle market.

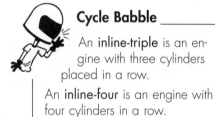

Cycle Babble

An **inline-triple** is an engine with three cylinders placed in a row.

An **inline-four** is an engine with four cylinders in a row.

Honda CB750: A Four for the Masses

The effect Honda's CB750 Four had on the motorcycling world can be compared to the effect the introduction of Microsoft's Windows operating platform had on the personal computer industry. Sure, the old DOS system retained a few die-hard adherents, as did the British motorcycle industry, but just as the vast majority of computer users prefer Windows to DOS, the vast majority of the motorcycling public wanted inline-four-cylinder bikes.

Although twin-cylinder bikes have experienced a resurgence in popularity in the past several years, most riders still want four-cylinder motorcycles, which makes sense: the benefits of four-cylinder bikes can't be denied.

The primary benefits of a four-cylinder engine in a motorcycle are smoothness and a capability to run at higher rpm than a comparable twin. Sportbike fours generally are tuned to make their power higher up in the powerband than twins, and they produce less torque at lower rpm. All but the most highly tuned fours make adequate torque down low. Some inline-fours aimed at a more general audience, such as Suzuki's 1200S Bandit, make more torque than many twins.

A strike against four-cylinder motorcycles in the past was that the engines were rather bulky, although designers have since rectified this situation. For example, most manufacturers of inline-fours have moved ancillary items—water pumps, starter motors, and alternators, for example—to make the engine narrower. They've also stacked the transmission shafts to reduce the engine's length.

Still, inline-four engines remain more complex than twins and singles. More parts mean more expensive maintenance.

Odds are, you'll end up with a four-cylinder engine, not because it's better (or worse) than any other type, but because it is such a common design. This is especially true if you buy a used bike.

Honda's groundbreaking CB750, introduced in 1969, was perhaps the most influential motorcycle in history.

(Photo courtesy of Vreeke and Associates)

The Inline-Six

For a few years in the mid-1970s and early 1980s, a handful of manufacturers fooled around with *inline-six-cylinder* motorcycle engines. The parallel twin had grown to a triple, then the in-line fours were the same thing with yet another cylinder tacked on, so a six probably seemed logical. But these proved to be oddities, footnotes in the motorcycle history books. The odds of you stumbling across one of these beasties by chance are slim (unlike the bikes themselves, which are as wide as a Peterbilt), and now most of these machines are the property of collectors.

The Italian company Benelli produced a 750cc six-cylinder bike, but like many old Italian bikes, this is one you'll probably see only in pictures. More common were the big sixes produced by Honda and Kawasaki. These were functional motorcycles, but both were victims of their own excess. The width and weight of those six-cylinders just proved to be too much, so handling suffered horribly. And if four-cylinder engines are complex to maintain, then sixes can be absolute nightmares.

Cycle Babble

An **inline-six-cylinder** engine is an engine with six cylinders in a row.

The V-Fours

When Honda introduced its water-cooled *V-four engine* bikes for the 1982 model year, pundits predicted the demise of the inline-four. It seemed reasonable at the time. These engines have exceptional power characteristics, providing good torque figures and more than adequate horsepower. Plus, they are one of the smoothest engine designs in existence.

This engine design became something of a standard—powering a variety of sportbikes, cruisers, and touring bikes—but it never came close to replacing the inline-four. That was probably due to the expense of manufacturing such a complex engine design rather than any inherent flaws with the concept. In service, these have proven to be remarkably reliable motorcycles.

If you are in the market for a used motorcycle, a bike with a V-four engine is a safe bet. These bikes have been nearly indestructible.

Cycle Babble

A **V-four engine** is an engine of four cylinders arranged in a V-shape configuration, with two cylinders on each side of the V.

The Gold Wing

The engine Honda uses in its Gold Wing touring bikes is unique—it doesn't really fit into any other category. The only thing comparable to the four-cylinder version is the engine Subaru uses in its cars. This is a flat, Boxer-type engine, with four or six liquid-cooled cylinders instead of two air-cooled cylinders, like BMW uses. The flat-four- and flat-six-cylinder engines used in Honda's Gold Wings are called flat because their cylinders are arranged in a flat, opposing configuration.

When Honda introduced its Gold Wing in 1975, it created a new class of motorcycle: the luxury tourer.

(Photo courtesy of Simon Green)

These are the smoothest engines used in motorcycles, period, and are a major part of the Gold Wing's appeal to the touring crowd. They also have a fairly centralized mass, which makes the entire motorcycle easier to maneuver. I've seen Gold Wing riders whip their bikes around as if they were riding sportbikes instead of ultimate behemoths weighing almost twice what the average sportbike weighs.

The L-Twin

Italian manufacturers have developed a unique take on the V-twin concept. By widening the angle of the V to 90 degrees (changing the shape from a V to an L, thus giving the configuration its name), they have created a smoother, more balanced twin-cylinder engine. Ducati's engines, which are longitudinal (they are positioned lengthwise in the frame), most obviously display the L configuration. Moto Guzzi's engines, which are transverse (arranged crosswise in the frame), are also angled at 90 degrees. These are incredibly well-designed engines, as proven by their multiple successes on the world racing circuit.

The Two-Stroke

The other common type of motorcycle engine is the *two-stroke;* we briefly touched on it earlier. It's called two-stroke because its cycle consists of only two strokes (yes, really): the piston moves down, drawing in the air-fuel charge, and then moves up, at which point the charge ignites, forcing the piston back down and starting the process all over again. To provide lubrication for such an engine, oil must be mixed in with the fuel charge. This is what gives some two-strokes their characteristic smoky exhaust.

While this type of combustion cycle creates a high-revving, powerful little motor, it does so at a price: air pollution. And that is the reason Environmental Protection Agency standards essentially banished two-strokes from U.S. roads. Today two-strokes are found mainly on off-road bikes and Grand Prix racing bikes in the 125cc and 250cc classes. But two-strokes aren't secure even there; off-road four-strokes have made serious inroads on what was previously exclusively two-stroke territory.

Cycle Babble

Two-stroke engines are named so because their power cycles consist of just two movements, or strokes. The piston moves down, drawing in the air-fuel charge, and then up, combusting the charge.

Motorcycology

In the mid-1980s, Yamaha managed to get a two-stroke streetbike past the sensitive noses of the EPA, with the help of a catalytic converter. The RZ350 was a superb little sportbike. It could really be made into a road-burner with a little work and an aftermarket pipe, but this eliminated the catalytic converter and made the bike illegal to ride on most public roads.

The Stroker Age: The Japanese Two-Strokes

With the exception of Honda, Japanese manufacturers originally invaded the United States market with small two-stroke motorcycles.

Japanese two-strokes ranged from small 50cc mopeds to Suzuki's GT750 and Kawasaki's infamous three-cylinder 750cc H2. Although some of these bikes continued in production until the late 1970s, it was already clear that increasingly stringent air-quality rules would make two-strokes extinct, at least in the United States. Other than Yamaha, which continued to develop its popular RD series throughout the decade, most manufacturers quit developing two-strokes for the U.S. market, other than for scooters and bikes such as Aprilia's RS50 repli-racer.

Many of us grew up riding these fast, lightweight, cheap machines, and our memories of them are probably clouded by all the fun we had on them (and perhaps all that exhaust smoke has damaged our memories). Two-strokes are still out there, although they become tougher to find every year.

Even if you can find one intact, they tend not to be practical motorcycles. They generate a lot of power for their size, but that power usually comes on suddenly at the very top of the rpm range. I've found it takes a special type of lunatic to make good use of a two-stroke, a somewhat crazed motorcyclist who rides with the throttle wide open and controls speed with the shifter. Every ride, even a simple trip to the local convenience store, is a Grand Prix event for these folks. While you may be just the sort of lunatic I'm describing, this is not the best way to learn to ride.

The Least You Need to Know

- ◆ The engine is where you'll find a motorcycle's soul.

- ◆ The combination of torque and peak horsepower shapes an engine's personality.

- ◆ The shape and design of an engine contribute to its power-delivery characteristics.

- ◆ Four-stroke engines have broader ranges of power than two-stroke engines and make better bikes for beginners. The number of cylinders also influences power-delivery characteristics.

- ◆ Two-strokes tend to have power-delivery characteristics best suited for experienced, slightly insane motorcyclists.

Chapter 7

Buying Your First Bike

In This Chapter

- ◆ Where to find a bike
- ◆ What to look for in a bike
- ◆ What's it worth?
- ◆ Wheeling and dealing

By now, you're so familiar with the workings of engines that you can tell a Kawasaki from a Suzuki just by the sound. And you know exactly what kind of bike you want. What's next? Getting your first bike. The time has come to lose your moto-virginity.

Like your first lover, you will remember your first bike as long as you live. Although you will always enjoy the freedom motorcycling brings you, nothing quite compares to the heady exhilaration of those first rides. At this point, the best way to ensure that those rides are as pleasurable as possible is to get a good, dependable motorcycle.

Where to Buy Your Bike

Shopping for a motorcycle differs from shopping for a car in every aspect. For the most part, cars are appliances, like washing machines (some even look like them) which are bought and sold by staid, sensible people.

Motorcycology _____

Finding a good motorcycle shop is a challenge in itself, but if you find a truly great one, you may have found a fun place to hang out, drink coffee, and absorb moto-culture. A good dealer knows that hardcore motorcyclists tend to spend every cent they have on bikes and accessories, and will go to great lengths to make you feel at home in his or her shop.

Motorcycles are expressions of passion, and the people buying and selling them tend to be passionate people, some are just plain nuts. (Should you doubt this, ask yourself when you last saw someone covered with Chevrolet tattoos, wearing a T-shirt stating he'd rather see his sister in a brothel than his brother in a Toyota.)

Just finding a motorcycle differs from finding a car. You can find motorcycles in several places, some obvious and others less so.

Dealerships

The most obvious—and perhaps the easiest—place to find a bike is at a dealership. If you're buying a new bike, you'll have no choice but to buy from a dealer. But even if you're buying used, buying from a reputable shop can be the best way to get your first bike.

Physically locating a motorcycle dealership can present a challenge if you're not familiar with the area you're living in. People selling motorcycles don't have the kind of cash flow car dealers have, so usually you won't find motorcycle shops amid the endless car lots, strip malls, and office buildings in the sprawl suburban America has become. Motorcycle dealerships can be hidden in out-of-the-way locations where leases are lower. Check the Yellow Pages under "Motorcycles" to find dealers and repair shops in your area.

Choosing a Dealer

Not all dealerships are created equal. The quality of the staff makes or breaks a shop.

When you're buying your first motorcycle, it's tough to know whether you are being taken advantage of. My first experience with a dealer turned out badly. I wanted to buy a 100cc Kawasaki dirtbike, but my father distrusted Japanese products (this was the early 1970s in rural Minnesota), so he took me to a shop selling American-made minibikes. He liked the minibikes because they were powered by snowmobile engines, which he believed to have been built right there in Minnesota. Actually, these engines were manufactured in Japan and were wholly unsuited for summertime operation. The second day I owned the bike, I seized a piston.

The dealer fully expected us to be back the next day; he knew these bikes were unfit, but he had a plan. He traded me the trashed minibike for a new 80cc Yamaha motorcycle. It ended up costing about 20 percent more than the 100cc Kawasaki would have cost, but it was either that or keep the blown-up minibike.

If that wasn't bad enough, the dealer lied to me about the model year of the bike. I was too naïve to know where to check the date of manufacture (see bullets below) and ended up buying a two-year-old carryover motorcycle for more than the price of a new one.

But I was only 11 years old, and I didn't have this book. Here are some tips to keep this from happening to you:

♦ Learn as much about the motorcycle as possible. Check the buying guides to new (Appendix A) and used (Appendix B) bikes to see if it's listed there. Go to the library and read back issues of motorcycle magazines that have tested the bike.

♦ Make sure your salesperson knows motorcycles. Ask good questions. By the answers, you can tell whether the person is uninformed, unscrupulous, or both. (See Chapter 8 for examples of questions you should ask.)

♦ Check the mileage on the odometer against the mileage on the title, and check the model year on the title against the date of manufacture on the frame, usually located on a plate riveted to either the steering head or the lower frame tube or beam. If something's not kosher, chances are, neither is the shop selling the bike.

Buying a motorcycle from a salesperson who knows bikes and whom you can trust can be fun, the beginning of a productive relationship. But getting ripped off can poison you for life. Generally, you're more likely to have a bad experience at a shop where motorcycles are just a sideline, such as a car dealership that also carries a line of bikes, or a dealership devoted primarily to snowmobiles, watercraft, or some other type of recreational vehicle and just carries motorcycles because its franchise requires it. Your best bet is to find a shop that lives and breathes motorcycles.

But like any generalization, there are exceptions. The best salesperson I've ever dealt with worked at a Chrysler shop that carried Honda motorcycles. If you can find just one person at a shop who knows and cares about motorcycles, that's good enough.

The date of manufacture is usually stamped either on the steering head or on the frame of a motorcycle.

(Photos © 1998 Darwin Holmstrom)

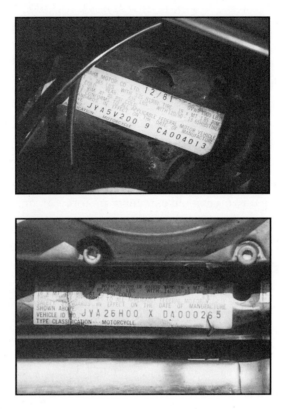

How's Their Service Department?

Finding the right dealership with a salesperson you trust means little if the mechanic working in the service department is a lazy, clumsy fool.

This is more of an issue when buying a new bike under warranty than it is when buying a used bike. With a used motorcycle, if you get a good deal, you can always take it to a mechanic you trust somewhere else. When you buy new, you may be forced to go back to the same dealership for warranty work; many shops balk at covering warranty work on motorcycles bought at other dealerships.

An unskilled mechanic actually wrecked the top end on one of my bikes once. This was at a shop where I'd developed a relationship with one of the salespeople, a nice guy and a dedicated motorcyclist. I made the mistake of assuming that the personnel in the service department were as competent as my friend in sales.

I was leaving on a solo motorcycle trip to the Ozark Mountains in a couple of days, so I brought my motorcycle in for a complete tune-up. I wanted to make certain my bike was running well.

When I picked up my bike, it wouldn't idle. In fact, it never idled again. The mechanic, who I later learned had been hired because his father owned the shop, had over-tightened the valves. Before I left the parking lot, I'd bent a valve stem. You guessed it, that's not good.

I was still somewhat of a novice and didn't know what had happened. I took the bike back to the service department, and even though they knew exactly what they had done, they blamed the problem on dirt in the carburetors. They kept the bike over-night to clean the carbs, but there was nothing they could do, short of a valve job.

Shops like this usually develop reputations in the motorcycling community. Within two years of trashing my bike, this shop went out of business.

So how can you find out which shops offer reliable service? Wherever motorcyclists hang out, they talk about mechanical things. And they love to gossip. If you can find a coffee shop, a bike night, or a bar where motorcyclists congregate, ask them about the reputation of a shop's service department. If several people agree on a shop to avoid, avoid it. If you have no local hangout, check with independent repair shops. These are often staffed by mechanics who cut their teeth in local dealerships and who usually know the scoop on other shops.

The Classified Ads

The other obvious place to hunt for a used bike is in the classifieds section of a news-paper. I enjoy this form of shopping because it puts me in direct contact with the local motorcycling community. When I go to look at bikes I've found in classified ads, I meet all kinds of motorcyclists, from people who bought a bike on a whim years ago but never rode it much, to hardcore riders who are moving on to a different bike.

Shopping the classifieds requires you to bring even more knowledge to the transaction than buying from a dealership. The range of conditions you will find classi-fied bikes in varies as widely as the personalities of the owners selling them. Even the most unscrupulous dealer fears lawsuits enough to make certain the wheels are correctly bolted on. (At least, they usually do—I once tested a bike that handled so squirrelly, I stopped and discovered the dealer had mounted the wheel backward!)

You never know what to expect on a machine you found through the want ads. Frames can be bent from accident damage. Chain alignment may be wonky from adjustment by cruel people who should be banned from owning a wrench. Seats may be attached with duct tape. Remember, your life depends on the condition of your machine, and any one of these conditions, as well as a host of other possible problems, could have you hanging out with the other roadkill.

Many people will let you test-ride a bike, but check it out carefully to make certain it's safe before taking it on the road. Some people will want the money up front before even allowing a test ride. Before judging them too harshly, would you let a total stranger ride your pride and joy? What if they were a novice? Later in this chapter, I'll show you what to look for when you examine a bike.

Motorcycology

Another source of motorcycle ads are the newsprint magazines that contain nothing but photos of vehicles that are for sale. In many metropolitan areas, these magazines either have large motorcycle sections or are entirely devoted to recreational vehicles. While it's possible to find good buys through such magazines, more often than not, you'll find yourself chasing down overpriced bikes in much worse condition than they appear in the photos. Still, these magazines are worth checking out. If nothing else, they're fun to read.

When buying a bike from a private party, obtaining a clear title is absolutely critical. As with buying from a dealer, make certain the information on the title matches the information on the bike. This is especially important on motorcycles with high theft rates, such as Harley-Davidsons, but it's important with all bikes. A friend of mine once replaced the frame on his Suzuki after a crash without changing the title to reflect that change. One morning, he went out to the street to find that his motorcycle had been carted off by the police. They wouldn't release the bike to him because of the irregular title. He ended up forfeiting the bike because it would have cost him more to get it back than it was worth.

If you buy a motorcycle that turns out to be stolen, you will not only lose the bike, but you may well end up in legal trouble for receiving stolen merchandise. Generally, this is a problem only when buying from private parties, but dealerships have sold stolen motorcycles, too. One clue that something may be less than above board is if the bike has a replacement title from another state.

Buying a motorcycle through the classifieds requires you to bring more to the table yourself, but it's often worth the effort. Private sellers don't have to build the overhead costs of running a dealership into the price, so you have a better chance of getting a bargain. The best advice I've got is to take a friend (or trusted mechanic) who does know what to look for, then thank them with a beer later or a meal on the way home.

I read the classified motorcycle ads every day, even though I'm usually not in the market to buy a bike. I find it's a good way to keep up on the motorcycle market, as well as the motorcycling community. I like to see who's selling what and how much they're asking. Sometimes I find even more information than I expected. My all-time favorite ad, written by a guy selling his Harley Electra Glide, ended with the following phrase: "She caught me cheating, and now it's the big D for me: make offer."

Bulletin Boards

If you are lucky enough to have a local hangout for motorcyclists, chances are, there's a bulletin board there with ads and snapshots of bikes pinned on three deep. (If you don't have such a place, you will probably find a similar bulletin board at the shop of an independent mechanic.)

These bulletin boards contain some of the best deals available. Usually, the seller knows what he has and what it's worth, and is offering the bike at a fair price.

My all-time best motorcycle buy, a Suzuki GS650G, came off of one such board. I went to look at the bike, not expecting to buy it because I had only $500 to spend, and the bike appeared to be in pristine condition—which it was (and still is).

The young man selling it was asking $800—a fair price, given the condition of the bike. When I told him I had only $500, he was ready to take it on the spot. I told him the bike was worth more and to think it over and call me the next day if he still wanted to sell it.

The next day he called, and I found myself the proud owner of what turned out to be one of the most reliable and rugged motorcycles I've ever owned.

Motorcycle Clubs

Motorcycle clubs are another rich source of used motorcycles. Members of clubs tend to buy and sell a lot of motorcycles. They trade bikes the way some kids trade baseball cards and comic books.

Again, check with other motorcyclists at local hangouts and shops to find out what kind of clubs operate in your community. I discuss clubs at greater length in Chapter 19, but for now, I want to point out the advantages of clubs when shopping for a motorcycle.

Members of motorcycle clubs tend to be longtime motorcyclists, people who love to talk about bikes, sometimes too much! But be patient as you can learn a great deal about every subject in this book from these people and they are an especially valuable resource when it comes to buying motorcycles.

The bikes these folks sell tend to gravitate toward the higher end of the price scale, usually with good cause. The following is a list of reasons a motorcycle bought from a club member will likely be worth the money:

- ◆ Club members' bikes are usually in excellent condition. They take pride in their equipment, partly because they know their fellow members will judge them by the quality of their bikes, and partly because they bond with their machines even more closely than a "normal" motorcyclist (if there is such a thing) does. They treat their bikes like members of the family; that's why they joined a club.

- ◆ People in clubs have enough motorcycle savvy to buy bikes that are worth something, motorcycles with decent resale value.

- ◆ They know the value of their machines and usually won't ask more than they're worth, if for no other reason than that other club members will doubt their intelligence if they get greedy.

- ◆ Motorcycle clubs are an especially tight subcommunity within the general motorcycling community. If one club member ripped off another club member, he or she would be ostracized from the group.

Garages

An astounding number of perfectly good motorcycles rest in people's garages. As pointed out in Chapter 2, Japanese manufacturers sold shiploads of motorcycles in the 1980s. A lot of these bikes eventually found their way to corners of garages, where they've sat unlicensed for years.

Finding bikes this way can be problematic. For starters, if you snoop around in people's garages, you could find yourself staring down the wrong end of a shotgun. The best way to find out about these lost treasures is through word of mouth, which, in itself, presents a problem. These bikes aren't at the forefront of their owners' consciousness. Owners don't spend much time thinking about these machines and probably spend even less time talking about them.

If you do see a bike sitting in someone's garage, the trick is to figure out (a) whose garage it is and (b) how to tell the owner you're interested in the bike without letting him or her know that you regularly peep through people's open garage doors.

Steer Clear

Even if you get a good price on a garage bike, it might not be worth the trouble. Sitting idle causes problems, such as dried seals: when rubber seals in the engine and suspension sit without fluids for an extended time, they dry and crack, causing leaks and a host of other problems. Unless you're prepared to undertake major mechanical repairs, make certain a bike has been stored properly and that most of the fluids stay inside the engine.

Once you've cleared that hurdle, the trick is to negotiate a price. Most likely, such owners have no idea what the real value of their bikes are, so you never know how much they will ask for them. The owner could throw out a number that is ridiculously low or high, or else guess something in the ballpark of reality.

If it's low, I go for it without regret. The owner has no use for the bike, other than as a place to store stuff on. I consider it my duty to liberate the neglected machine and make it a productive member of the motorcycling community. And I don't worry that I'm ripping the owners off. Obviously, they don't need the money, or they would have sold the bike long ago.

If the number is ridiculously high, my advice is to walk away. The owner believes that price to be the bike's true value, and if you try to barter, the person will probably be insulted.

The Internet

Although you might be a novice to motorcycles, I'm going to assume that you are not unaware of computers or the Internet, or of the Net's value in finding things to buy, such as motorcycles. Some of the following websites make prime hunting grounds for the bike of your dreams:

- www.ebaymotors.com

- www.cycletrader.com

- www.powersportsnetwork.com

But be advised that there are a ridiculous number of scam artists on the web who will fleece the unwary as part of a day's work. Here are a few tips: avoid buying long-distance; be wary of complicated deals; likewise, be wary of large down payments to hold the merchandise; and insist on a face-to-face sale. Finally, remember this: if a deal seems too good to be true, it almost certainly is.

The web can also be a prime research source if you're somewhat undecided about which motorcycle is right for you. *Motorcyclist* and *Motorcycle Cruiser* magazines both have archives of past road tests on their websites—www.motorcyclistonline.com and www.motorcyclecruiser.com, respectively—so you can get the editors' lowdown on bikes you're considering.

What to Look For

Buying a used motorcycle seems something of a crapshoot to the uninitiated. Judging a dependable bike from a pile of junk may appear difficult to the first-time buyer, but a couple of basic motorcycle characteristics make it easier than you might think.

First, motorcycles have nothing to hide. If a frame has been repaired, you will see welds or cracks in the paint. If the bike leaks fluids, those fluids will ooze out before your eyes.

Second, there's just not that much to a motorcycle. Compared to cars, they are relatively simple devices.

Further simplifying the buying process is the fact that what you need to check is limited to just a few basic items; luckily, you won't need to worry about all the parts of a motorcycle covered in Chapter 5 (at least on Japanese bikes—European and American machines present a few more challenges).

The things to look for when buying can be broken down into two broad categories: condition and completeness.

Critical: Condition

You need to ascertain the mechanical and cosmetic condition of a motorcycle before you make an offer.

Judging a bike's cosmetic condition is easy: just ask yourself how it looks. By looking at the bodywork and such items as mirrors, turn signals, and mufflers, and examining those items for scratches, dents, and other deformities, you can usually tell whether a bike is in good shape. Pay particular attention to the outside edges of those items, the edges likely to contact pavement in even the most minor tip-over.

Usually you will find some evidence of a tip-over, even if it's just microscopic scratches. Finding a machine that hasn't fallen over at least once is rare. If the scratches are so minor they are difficult to see, you needn't worry. Often they can be minimized with some chrome polish and some elbow grease. (Be aware, however, that a dealer will also find these scratches if you someday decide to trade in the bike.)

Even if you find more major evidence of a low-speed spill, that shouldn't dissuade you from buying the bike; just reflect the costs of cosmetic restoration in your offer. Often the owner will have already taken such things into consideration when setting a price.

With any kind of accident damage on a motorcycle it's essential to check the frame alignment. First, make sure the front wheel is steered dead ahead; then, kneeling on the floor directly behind the bike, look at how the front and back wheels align. Do the same thing kneeling in front of the bike, too. If they don't appear to be straight in relation to each other, it's easier to go on to the next bike.

Motorcycology _____

Some motorcycles have built-in odd noises. Suzuki's two-valve GS series, for example, had a cam-chain guide that allowed the chain to slap while idling at low speeds. This causes no damage whatsoever, but the mechanical knocking sound has caused many unnecessary top-end rebuilds because owners didn't know about the defect and thought something was wrong.

When purchasing European or American motorcycles, there are a few other things to watch for. Cosmetically, Harleys will more often than not be immaculate as Harley owners typically spend more time than most cleaning their bikes, but you need to check things such as the belt-drive system (discussed in Chapter 5). Fraying or missing belt teeth indicate future problems that are expensive to correct.

The level of finish on older European bikes tends to be lower than that of Japanese motorcycles, and corrosion can be a problem. This is especially true of Italian bikes, but it can be a problem even on BMWs. For example, BMW didn't apply a clear finish to exposed aluminum on items such as the fork legs. While this finish tends to yellow with exposure to sunlight, giving the forks on older Japanese motorcycles a dingy appearance, it protects the metal from corrosion. This corrosion becomes more pronounced in coastal areas because of the salt in sea air. It's also a problem for machines used during the winter because of the salt placed on roads in snowy climes.

The outside condition of a bike can help give clues to the condition of internal parts. If a bike looks good and runs well (if it starts easily when both cold and hot, if it idles smoothly without making horrible noises, and if it accelerates adequately for a bike of its size), odds are, it's okay inside. The owner has more than likely lavished as much care on the motorcycle's internals as he or she has on the bike's appearance.

Motorcycology

If you have a high degree of mechanical skill, as well as access to tools and a decent workshop, rebuilding bikes that have been crashed can be an inexpensive way to get a decent motorcycle. But be forewarned: This is not an undertaking for mechanical novices.

I once went shopping for a Harley-Davidson with a friend of mine who was looking for an Electra Glide. At one dealership, we found two of them. Both bikes were the same model year, both were similarly equipped, and both had around 57,000 miles on them. The price on each bike was identical. One bike was black, and the other a hideous dusty-rose color. My friend was partial to black motorcycles.

Unfortunately, the black one was in much worse shape cosmetically. It had spent much of its life sitting outside in the elements, judging by the corrosion on the engine and other aluminum parts. This was a red flag to me: if the previous owner had taken such abysmal care of the outside of the bike, what sort of care had he given the inside?

I advised my friend to buy the rose-colored bike, if he was determined to buy either. But he bought the black one with the pitted aluminum.

The bike was nothing but trouble, right from the start. He'd had it less than a week when the clutch went out and left him stranded on the freeway. The next week, the drive belt went out. After we fixed that, he started having trouble with the carburetor. We took it apart and discovered that someone had tried to repair it using what looked like rubber cement.

My friend had that bike for several years, and he never did get it to run right, even after he overhauled the engine. He spent so much money fixing the thing that he could have painted the rose-colored bike several times over.

Completeness

Along with the condition of a bike, make certain that all the pieces are there. Items such as missing side covers or other body panels can cost as much as a cheap motorcycle.

Check a motorcycle to make certain it has the following items:

- Side covers, the plastic covers that cover components located behind the engine, under the seat, can often break and come off the motorcycle. They are very expensive (and, in some cases, impossible) to replace.

♦ Emblems and insignias are often glued or screwed to the tank or side cover. They are also difficult to find for older motorcycles.

♦ If a bike has an aftermarket fairing, make certain that all the original lighting and turn-signal brackets and components come with the bike. If you decide to restore the motorcycle to its original condition, you'll need these pieces; on some bikes, they can cost as much as the motorcycle itself.

Steer Clear _____

Before upping your offer because the seller assures you that a bike has had a recent tune-up, make sure that he or she can provide documented proof that the tune-up has been performed.

♦ Fenders will probably be an issue only if someone has tried to build a chopper out of a motorcycle. Generally, such bikes make poor candidates for restoration and should be avoided.

Be especially concerned with completeness when buying an older motorcycle. You may find items such as side covers and seat covers unavailable for an older bike. These parts usually can be found with a little legwork. (I discuss alternative sources for parts, such as salvage yards, in Chapter 17.) Just because a bike isn't complete is no reason to reject it outright: just reflect the potential cost of replacing parts in your offer.

Some motorcycles, like this classic Honda, are obviously not complete. Unfortunately, it's not always this easy to spot when something is missing. Make sure you know exactly what you're getting, or not, as the case may be.

(Photo courtesy of Simon Green)

What's It Worth?

You've found the bike of your dreams. It's mechanically and cosmetically perfect, and you already have visions of roaming the highways on it. Now you have to figure out how much the bike is worth.

There's not much to negotiating the price of a new bike. Your best bet is to call every dealer within reasonable driving distance (remember, you will probably have to return to that dealer for warranty work) and find out what each one is charging for the model you're interested in. Once you have the best price, you might want to go to the nearest dealer you trust and give them an opportunity to match it. Even if they can't match it exactly, if they can even come close, it might be worth a few extra dollars to buy from someone you trust who is located nearby.

When shopping for a new motorcycle, you can save a lot of money by remaining flexible about which make and model to buy. Say you've decided to purchase a midsize cruiser, such as Kawasaki's Vulcan 800 Classic. While searching for such a bike, you find a decade-old Honda 800 Shadow in mint condition at one third the price of the Kawasaki. While the Kawasaki is a fine motorcycle, the Shadow is capable of providing every bit as much enjoyment, and with its shaft drive and hydraulically adjusted valves, the Honda will save you hundreds of dollars per year in maintenance costs over the Kawasaki. You can pocket the money saved and use it to finance a cross-country motorcycle trip.

You can also save a lot of money by watching for carryover models. While shopping for the best deal on a Honda 750 Shadow, you might run across a brand-new last year's model Kawasaki 800 Vulcan for $1,500 less. In this case, maintenance costs will be roughly equal because both bikes have manually adjusted valves and chain drives; if you keep an open mind that will be an extra $1,500 in your pocket.

Buying a used bike is where the process most diverges from buying a car. Because motorcycle prices can fluctuate widely from region to region, depending on how large a market an area has, accurate price guides are difficult to compile.

Further complicating the creation of useful price guides is the wide variation in the condition of each motorcycle. One seller's Yamaha 1100 Special can be in mint condition at 60,000 miles, while the next guy's can be a hunk of junk at 10,000 miles.

When deciding how much a bike is worth, a guidebook's value assessment is only part of the equation. In addition to things such as condition and completeness, you have to look at routine wear and tear. Keeping a motorcycle in tip-top running condition is an expensive proposition. A bike with a fresh tune-up is definitely worth more than a bike that needs a tune-up.

Another item that increases a bike's value is fresh tires. You should be able to tell by looking whether the tires have low miles: check the depth of the tread at the edges of the tire compared to the depth of the tread at the center. A good pair of sticky tires can run you over $500, with mounting and balancing, so factor that into your price determination.

On the other hand, new tires of low quality actually detract from the value of a bike, at least in my personal equation. If a bike has a pair of bargain-brand tires, I have to decide whether to ride on tires that I consider undesirable or to toss out a nearly new set of tires and spend $300 on another pair. If a bike is wearing a pair of budget-brand tires, I automatically deduct $250 from my offer.

It's a good idea to speak with as many other owners of a certain model as you can before making a purchase (here again, belonging to a club can be beneficial). Also check any service bulletins that may have been issued to your dealer on a certain model before buying that model.

These rough guidelines may help, but in the end, it's just going to be you and the seller. The entire process may boil down to how badly you want to buy the bike or how much the owner wants to sell it. One thing I can guarantee: if you buy the motorcycle that's right for you, one or two years from now, as you're riding down the road enjoying your machine, you will not be thinking, *Damn, I paid too much for this thing.*

Making the Deal

Now comes the most crucial (and most nerve-wracking) part of the entire process: negotiating the deal. You've decided what the motorcycle is worth to you, and the seller knows what the bike is worth to him or her. Now the two of you have to see if those figures jibe.

For me, negotiating the price of a motorcycle isn't the same as negotiating the price of anything else. People have more of an emotional attachment to motorcycles than they do to other goods: you're buying someone's passion. Whereas I have no moral qualms telling someone they're insane if they think a car or a radio is worth a ridiculous sum of money, I'll politely decline purchasing a motorcycle if the owner has an unrealistic opinion of its value. Its emotional value to that person may be such that the bike actually is worth the price to the owner (but not to many other human beings).

In such situations, you'll have to use your own judgment of the seller. If he or she seems reasonable, bring out the source you're using to arrive at your price and explain that their price is a bit steep. If the seller seems like a lunatic (and they're out there), extricate yourself from the situation as quickly as possible.

On the other hand, if the price is in the ballpark, I'll haggle until I get it in my acceptable window. If I can't, I'll usually leave them my number. It's amazing how many people will call you back: once given the lure of real money, it's generally a buyer's market.

In the end, this is a decision only you can make. I've provided you with the basics, but when you're face to face with the seller, trying to make a decision that will affect your life for years to come, you have to be the final judge.

The Least You Need to Know

- The quality of a dealership and of its service department is almost as important as the quality of the motorcycle itself.

- Clubs are a great source of motorcycles and information about motorcycles.

- Before taking a motorcycle out for a test ride, inspect it as if your life depends on it—because it does.

- Be flexible when choosing a motorcycle.

Chapter **8**

Insider Tips on Buying a Bike

In This Chapter

- ◆ Keeping your maintenance costs down by selecting a low-maintenance bike
- ◆ Getting the best price from a dealership
- ◆ Financing a bike at the lowest interest rate
- ◆ Saving money on insurance

In Chapter 7, I told you how to buy your first bike. Now let me give you a few hints on other costs and responsibilities associated with buying a motorcycle, such as maintaining, financing, and insuring that bike. I'll also give you advice on trading bikes and some more tips on getting the best prices.

The purchase price of a motorcycle is just the tip of the iceberg when it comes to expenses you'll incur when owning a bike. Maintenance will be a huge expense, but I'm going to give you some hints on how to minimize that expense.

A smart shopper can also minimize the costs of financing and insuring a bike. I'm going to show you some ways to save money when you finance and insure a bike. I'm also going to offer some tips on trading in a bike, if you ever decide to do so.

Minimizing Maintenance Costs

Your choice of a bike can determine how much maintenance you'll need to do. Sometimes engineers design motorcycles with certain high-maintenance features to increase the performance of a bike. More often than not, though, features that make a motorcycle easier (and cheaper) to maintain are excluded just to save production costs.

If you're after extremely high performance, you'll have to accept the fact that you'll have to spend more money on maintenance. But if you're willing to accept a slightly lower level of performance, you can look for certain features and practice certain riding habits that will help you keep maintenance costs down.

Three elements, in particular, will affect your maintenance costs: the shaft drive, the centerstand, and the valves. (See Chapters 16 and 17 for a description of these parts.)

Getting Shafted

Select a bike with a shaft drive. As you'll see in Chapters 16 and 17, chain maintenance is the most frequent procedure you'll need to perform on your bike. It's also the dirtiest.

Sporty bikes will usually have a chain because chains tend to disrupt handling less than shafts. If you want such a bike, you'll usually have to accept a chain as part of the package. But there has been a trend in recent years to use chains on types of bikes that, by nature, aren't the best in handling, such as midsize cruisers. This is purely a cost-cutting measure on the part of the manufacturers.

If you want to buy a midsize Japanese cruiser, my advice is to get an older, used one because these usually have shaft drives.

Another option is to select a bike with a belt-drive system. These can be a good compromise between the handling benefits of a chain and the maintenance benefits of a shaft. Belt-drive systems, such as the one used by Harley-Davidson, require less maintenance than chains, but only slightly more than shafts. The main drawback of Harley's belt-drive system is that fixing one can be expensive.

Getting Centered: The Benefits of a Centerstand

Make certain that your bike comes equipped with a centerstand. All Japanese bikes used to come with centerstands—it was one of the things that set them apart from Harley-Davidsons, which have never been equipped with modern centerstands.

In the 1980s, Japanese manufacturers began excluding centerstands from ultra-high-performance sportbikes because the designs of the exhaust systems used on those bikes prohibited the mounting of centerstands and also because centerstands hindered cornering clearance.

But in the past few years, manufacturers have also begun excluding them from bikes that already have limited cornering clearance, such as cruisers. This is another cost-cutting measure. Combine the lack of a centerstand with a chain drive, and I guarantee that you will create new expletives while maintaining your bike. Understand, though, that the reality of modern motorcycling is that many owners purchase after-market service stands. (Service stands generally support one end of the bike or the other, and are separate from the motorcycle. Centerstands bolt to the motorcycle's frame.) These days, it's simply the price of being a motorcyclist.

Hydraulically Adjusted Valves

One of the costliest aspects of maintaining a motorcycle is adjusting the amount the valves move up and down.

This is a crucial and expensive (therefore, often neglected) part of motorcycle maintenance. On most modern motorcycles, valve adjustment is too complex a job for an inexperienced mechanic to tackle alone. Most riders take their bikes into shops to have the procedure performed.

If the motorcycle has any bodywork that the mechanic has to remove to gain access to the valves, or if the motorcycle is constructed in a way that requires the mechanic to go to heroic lengths to gain access to the valves, labor costs will be even higher.

Fortunately, modern metallurgy and manufacturing techniques mean that valve adjustments on new motorcycles don't have to be done nearly as often as on old bikes. Keep that in mind when you're trying to choose between an older bike and a brand-new one.

There is another way to avoid this expensive bit of maintenance. Back in the early 1980s, Honda introduced several motorcycle models that had overhead-cam engines with hydraulically adjusted valves. Suzuki and Kawasaki followed suit, introducing cruisers with similar systems. All new Harleys come with hydraulically adjusted valves. Such systems completely eliminate the costs of valve adjustments.

Getting the Best Deal

To get the best deal on a bike, you're best off dealing directly with a sales manager. As I said in Chapter 7, call all the dealerships within the distance you are willing to drive (both to buy the bike and to get it serviced), and have the sales manager quote you an *out-the-door price*. This will be the amount you'll actually pay and will include all hidden costs, such as taxes, licenses, and other fees.

Cycle Babble

The **out-the-door price** is the amount you'll actually pay for a bike, factoring in all hidden costs such as taxes, licenses, and other miscellaneous fees.

If the manager beats around the bush and won't give you a straight out-the-door price, he or she could be planning to stick you with some hidden costs. This may give you some insight into how the dealer will handle any warranty work or other issues that might come up later, so you might want to shop elsewhere if the dealer is evasive.

You might already know that you'll find the best buys on bikes in the off season—in the fall and winter. What you might not know is that you'll find the very best buys on the last Saturday of a month because, at that time, dealers are anxious to meet their monthly sales quotas.

To Your Credit: Financing

Most people don't have the cash on hand to buy a new motorcycle, so many people are forced to finance bikes. The interest paid in finance charges can represent a significant amount of the overall cost of owning a motorcycle, so before you even go looking for a bike, you should arrange the lowest-priced financing you can find.

First, call at least three banks to get the following information:

♦ The interest rates for unsecured personal loans with payments spread out over both a 36-month period and a 48-month period.

♦ The same information about a loan if it is secured by the title to your bike.

♦ The monthly payment for a $10,000 loan in each instance.

You use the amount of $10,000 so that you can calculate your payments based on the amount you borrow. For example, if a bank quotes you a monthly payment of $320 for an unsecured, 36-month loan of $10,000, you can divide $320 by 10, and you'll know that you're being charged $32 a month for every $1,000 you borrow. If you borrow $4,000 to buy a Kawasaki 500 Ninja, just multiply 32 by 4 to learn what your monthly payments will be. Here are a few more tips on how to make it easier to finance your new bike at a dealership—and more:

♦ Have personal information ready and in order. The dealer or loan officer will want to see a payroll check stub, will want to know how long you've been at the job, and will pull your credit report. You should also get a credit report on your own to make sure everything is accurate.

♦ Even if you have less than stellar credit, you might be able to get financing. What a dealer/loan officer wants to see is that you've got a good, solid job to handle your outstanding debt.

♦ Make the biggest down payment you can afford. It will significantly reduce your monthly loan payments. A good starting point is 25 percent.

♦ Know that there are alternatives to getting a loan from the dealership. For instance, check out financing the bike through motorcycle-manufacturer lending institutions. Or check the independents, such as Household Retail Services, Inc., used by many dealers. And don't forget resources on the web. Check out www. bestloandeals.com, www.cyclebytel.com, www.motorcyclelender.com, and www.123motorcycleloans.com on the Internet.

Getting Insured

Most states require you to at least have liability insurance before you can operate a vehicle on public roads. If you finance your bike and use its title as security, you need to have full coverage. Full coverage isn't a bad idea anyway if your bike is worth a significant amount of money, but be prepared: full-coverage insurance on a bike is expensive, especially if you live in a major metropolitan area. However, you can do some things to minimize your expenses.

As I said in Chapter 4, most companies base insurance rates on several factors, such as the type of bike, the size of its engine, and the amount of expensive bodywork on the bike. They also take your driving record into account.

There's nothing you can do about your driving history (you can't change the past), but you can minimize your insurance costs by choosing a bike that is under 600cc and has minimal bodywork. The list of new bikes under 600cc without plastic fairings is short:

Aprilia RXV or SXV 4.5 and 5.5

Honda Rebel

Honda Nighthawk

Honda VLX Shadow

Honda 599 Hornet

Kawasaki Eliminator 125

Kawasaki KLX250S

Kawasaki Vulcan 500 LTD

MZ RT125/RT125 SM

Suzuki DRZ400S and SM

Suzuki GZ250

Yamaha FZ6 Fazer

Yamaha Virago 250

Yamaha XT225

Yamaha TW200

The list of used bikes that meet this criteria isn't much longer. In addition to used models of the bikes in the preceding list, it includes a few more choices:

Honda CB650SC/CB700SC Nighthawk

Honda FT500/VT500 Ascot

Honda VF500C V30 Magna

Honda VT500/VT600/VT700 Shadow

Honda XL350R/XL500R/XL600R

Kawasaki EN450 454 LTD/EN500 Vulcan 500

Kawasaki KLR600

Kawasaki KZ550/KZ550 LTD/KZ550 Spectre

Kawasaki ZL600 Eliminator

Kawasaki ZR550 Zephyr

KTM 400/XCe

Suzuki DR350SE

Suzuki GS550E/L

Suzuki GSF400 Bandit

Triumph Speed Four

Yamaha XJ550 Seca/Maxim (although some Secas came with a small bikini fairing)

Yamaha XT550/XT600

Yamaha YX600 Radian

All these bikes will work as a first bike. Some will work better than others, and some will be better buys than others (see Appendixes A and B for lists of which are the best first bikes and which are the best buys). All will be relatively inexpensive to insure, especially the older, less expensive models.

Another trick for getting lower rates on your full-coverage insurance is to get a policy with a high deductible. Purchasing a policy with a $500 deductible instead of a $250 deductible means that you'll pay the first $500 to repair the bike if something happens to it. This might seem like a lot of money to shell out in case of an accident, but it won't take you long to save that much on your premiums.

Besides, if you do file a claim, almost every company will raise your rates an exorbitant amount (probably by as much as you'll spend just to fix the bike yourself if you have a higher deductible). If you do make a claim, most of the time, you will pay for it one way or another. Usually, it costs less to fix it yourself in the long run.

Trading Bikes

If your first bike isn't what you had hoped, or if you're ready to move up to a different bike, you may face the decision of whether to trade it in at the dealership to get money toward your new bike.

Usually, you will get more money selling your bike straight out. In a couple of cases, I've made more by trading a bike, but the vast majority of times I've traded, I've lost money. In both cases where I came out ahead, I had an unusual motorcycle—one the dealer already had a buyer lined up for. If I had been able to find such a buyer on my own, I would have made more money than I did when I traded.

The only advantage of trading is convenience. When trading bikes, convenience is usually expensive. You will almost always get more money selling your old bike yourself, and you will always get a better price if you buy your new bike without a trade.

The Least You Need to Know

- You'll save a lot of money over time by choosing a low-maintenance motorcycle.

- Make certain you know the out-the-door price before buying a bike.

- Interest can be a significant part of the overall cost of buying a bike, so shop around.

- In the long run, you can save a lot of money on insurance by having a policy with a fairly high deductible.

Getting the Gear

In This Chapter

- ◆ The facts of helmet use
- ◆ Which type of helmet provides the most protection
- ◆ Essential protective gear
- ◆ Gear that will help you beat the elements
- ◆ Where to find the best deals on accessories

There's no doubt that many motorcyclists live for a therapeutic solo ride on the open road, soaking up riding in its simplest form. Others, however, have a different set of priorities: they just like to be seen by as big a crowd as possible.

Whatever camp you fall into, you'll need gear, lots of gear. Well, you're in luck—there is enough gear discussed in this chapter to make us the envy of scuba divers. While some of the items in the chapter are optional, maybe even frivolous, others are absolutely essential.

Helmets: Keeping What You've Already Got

Have you ever banged your head on a doorway, or the edge of a desk? Did it hurt? It did? Okay, what speed were you traveling at when you hit that doorpost? Walking pace, huh? Do you want to find out how much it would hurt at 7 mph (twice as fast as walking pace)? Okay then, run down the street and aim the top of your head at a good solid post (not really, I'm just trying to remind you about pain). Am I making the point well enough? Can you imagine the pain at 35 mph?

Here's another twist on it. Have you ever been hit in the face by a little piece of debris while riding a bicycle? What about getting a fly in your eye? Fancy that happening at 70 mph? Do you think it'd be okay, or would you get permanent damage? Are you really willing to find out?

Just in case you're one of those people that don't feel pain, I'll give you another reason. Have you ever been in a convertible car at speed, trying to hold a cell phone conversation? It's impossible, right? Way too loud. Well, again, use your imagination and remove the car's windshield; you already know it won't be any quieter. Finally, for authenticity, we can add the noise of your own motorcycle engine. I wonder how long it will be before you're lying in bed at night with your ears ringing.

Maybe for now we'll assume that you don't feel pain, you have skin like tanned leather, and your ears are immune to constant loud noise … pardon? Let's consider accidental impact, or road abrasion. Almost all of us fell off a bicycle as a kid. I remember bailing, then getting up and crying my eyes out with my knees bleeding and my head throbbing. I would guess it happened at 15 mph. I don't know about you, but I don't ever want to hit the ground at 45 mph, or 75 mph, without a helmet. I can't imagine what would happen to my skull, or to my brain.

Maybe the guy saying you don't need a helmet doesn't have a brain worth protecting. It's a logical conclusion. I'm sorry to be so blunt on this one, but look at what we're dealing with. If you've got a brain, you protect it with a helmet. Period.

How Helmets Are Made

Helmets help keep the contents of your head on the inside rather than the outside by using four basic components in their construction:

- **The outer shell.** The outside of a helmet can be constructed of fiberglass, *polycarbonate* or *TriComposite* material. Either way, it spreads the energy from an impact across a wide area, reducing the chances of head injury in the exact spot where the impact occurred.

◆ **The impact-absorbing lining.** This is sandwiched between the outer shell and the comfort padding and is usually made of a dense layer of expanded polystyrene. It crumples to absorb the impact.

◆ **The comfort padding.** This innermost layer of soft foam and cloth conforms to your head and is primarily responsible for how comfortable the helmet is.

Cycle Babble

Polycarbonate is a posh word for plastic, the cheapest outer-shell material used in helmet production. Whereas **TriComposite** is a mix of three woven materials: Kevlar, carbon fiber, and fiberglass. This mix creates the most expensive outer shell for a motorcycle helmet.

◆ **The retention system.** This consists of the strap—connected to the bottom of the helmet—that goes under your chin and holds the thing on your melon.

Helmets come in a variety of styles, from small, bowl-shape half-helmets that may protect your brainstem (if they manage to stay in place) to sleek, fully enclosed helmets that protect everything above your neck. In between are the three-quarter, or open-face helmets, which cover most of your head but leave your face unprotected. These give much better cranial protection than half-helmets, but if your face contacts the pavement at speed, an open-face helmet will provide you with a one-way ticket on the ugly train.

Neither half-helmets nor open-face helmets offer the comfort or protection full-face helmets provide by shielding the wearer from the elements. Whichever type of helmet you choose, the important thing is to wear it. It is the single most crucial piece of motorcycle gear.

This helmet from Davida is one of only a few open faces offering serious protection and good soundproofing.

(Photo courtesy of Davida Helmets)

Choosing the Right Helmet

The main considerations in choosing the right helmet for your head are fit, fit, and umm, oh yeah, fit. It's so important I've given "fit" its own section. Though first, here are some other things worth knowing.

Helmets come in a variety of styles and prices. You can probably still find a $10 helmet, if it's what you think your head's worth, but good helmets run up to $700.

Why do some helmets cost more than others? There are a variety of reasons. The material used in the outer shell will make a big difference. Polycarbonate helmets are the cheapest, and have been known to spread the impact, then bounce as they pop back into shape. Fiberglass helmets cost more but they absorb impacts more efficiently by crumpling. TriComposite helmets use an expensive mix of materials that spread the impact extremely efficiently, and weigh very little.

Paint schemes add to the price of a helmet; expect to pay more for a helmet with graphics than for a solid-color helmet. (If the paint scheme replicates the helmet of a top racer, expect to pay even more.) Wearing a brightly colored helmet isn't a bad idea, though; at least the car drivers will see you.

Another factor in helmet price is ventilation system. A good helmet will channel air all around your noggin on even the hottest days, and will also have efficient visor design, for good visibility and eye protection.

This high-end Arai RX7XX helmet is one of very few that I'll trust on my own head. It may have cost as much as a handful of cheap helmets, but it protects something irreplaceable to me.

(Photo courtesy of Simon Green)

Safety First

All helmets have to meet minimum safety standards set by the Department of Transportation (DOT); look for a sticker on the outside and a permanent label on the inside. Two other organizations, the American National Standards Institute (ANSI) and the Snell Memorial Foundation, also certify helmets. A Snell certification is something I look for on a helmet. Snell won't certify a half- or open-face helmet, as the DOT will, and it also has more exacting standards for the retention system than the DOT.

Getting a Good Fit

Once you get used to wearing a helmet, you won't feel comfortable riding without one. Of course, that assumes you've picked a helmet that fits you correctly. A helmet that is too loose will move around in an accident, potentially causing neck injury, and a helmet that is too tight will give you a splitting headache every day you wear it.

A helmet should be comfortably tight, though that's harder to find than you'd expect. You can't afford to have your heart set on a specific brand, as often you'll find that certain brands fit a particular head shape better than others. What you're looking for is a helmet that won't slide around your head, that is hard to pull off with the strap undone, but one that doesn't create a pressure spot anywhere on your head.

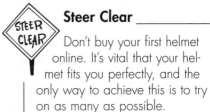

Steer Clear

Don't buy your first helmet online. It's vital that your helmet fits you perfectly, and the only way to achieve this is to try on as many as possible.

When you try on a helmet, wear it around the store for a while, and when you take it off, note any soreness or red spots. Wearing a helmet that exerts pressure on your head can turn into a brutal form of torture after an extended period; improperly fitted helmets have permanently turned many riders against helmet use. The right helmet is a revelation, something you can wear for hours on end, and something you'll learn to love wearing. Just remember, it won't work if you don't do the strap up.

Steer Clear

Never buy or wear a used motorcycle helmet. Helmets protect your head in an accident by destroying themselves. In a spill the outer shell will flex and the inner shell will crumple, often leaving no visible damage to the exterior. Hitting the damaged area a second time will result in zero head protection.

In Style: What to Wear

In a car you're surrounded by a steel shell, on a bike your only protection is what you wear. I'll give you enough information here to make an informed decision about what that should consist of. The following list describes the bare-minimum amount of protective gear you need to wear when riding:

- ◆ Leather boots, with at least ankle coverage
- ◆ Leather, full-fingered riding gloves
- ◆ Long pants
- ◆ A riding jacket

This list defines the absolute minimal amount of clothing you can wear to ride safely. You may have seen people riding in shorts, tennis shoes, and nothing else. What are they thinking?! My advice is to not become attached to these people because, should they survive even the most minor spill, they will not emerge from the experience as people you'd want to look at on a regular basis.

If you're unfortunate enough to be involved in a bike accident, good gear can make the difference between a quick recovery and a new lifestyle. Take a look at motorcycle racers: they're looking for the ultimate protection, and we can all learn a lot from their hard-earned experience.

Cycle Babble

Body armor is found within good-quality motorcycle clothing. It is often made from an impact-absorbing closed-cell foam, and can be repositioned within the jacket, pants, or race suit for comfort and effectiveness.

In the worst-case scenario, you could hit something, or slide along the concrete. So you need two different kinds of protection, *body armor* will absorb impact (from anything you may hit), and the material that your clothing is constructed from should provide you with excellent abrasion resistance.

In Europe there is a test standard for motorcycle clothing called the CE approval mark. It is similar to the Snell approval system in the United States. The CE approval process rigorously checks all aspects of bike clothing—things like armor effectiveness, the outer materials abrasion resistance, seam strength, etc. If you see a CE-approved garment that you like, then you can buy it with complete confidence, just like buying a Snell-approved helmet.

Body armor like this will give you very good protection, should you come off your bike and land hard.

(Photo courtesy of Simon Green)

Looking Good in Leather

Competition-weight cowhide leather (leather from a cow, that is at least 1.3mm thick) provides the best crash protection of any material, period. That's why it's still the material of choice for racing suits. I can guarantee you (from personal experience) that buying a new jacket is much less painful than getting road rash, which is what riders call the abrasions from a crash. Having grit picked from an open wound is unforgettable.

Racers wear a one-piece suit made from leather, which is pre-curved for comfort while positioned on their bike. The suit will have double-thickness leather reinforcing the areas on which they'll typically slide. This means the butt, back, knees, elbows, and shoulders. The guys with the top-of-the-line race suits will have a total thickness of 3mm of hide in those prone areas, and if you've ever watched bike racing, then you'll have seen them slide at 100 mph, get up, and walk away. That's how good cowhide is.

Most Europeans wear race suits on the road for that exact same reason, but not in America. I see people ride every day in shorts, jeans, or chaps. When you consider that race suits have double-thickness leather in the butt, and chaps have none … well, you can see the downside to chaps.

If you can't bear to wear a full suit, then at least wear a cowhide jacket with the same reinforced areas as a race suit. Unfortunately, fashion leather is usually made from cheaper hide, often sheepskin, and while this may initially look the same, it offers next to no abrasion protection.

If you can't even bring yourself to wear a leather jacket, then there are some other good options.

The plain black leather biker jacket comes in many styles now; you don't have to look like something from an old biker movie.

(Photo courtesy of Simon Green)

Synthetic Riding Suits: Ties Optional

While leather is still the optimum material for crash protection, an increasing number of riders choose synthetic riding suits made from materials such as Cordura and Kevlar. The advantages of leather are most apparent at extremely high speeds (which is why racers choose leather), but at speeds under triple-digit velocities, synthetic jackets and pants can provide enough protection.

Synthetics have certain advantages over leather. Most of them are machine-washable, unlike leather, which must be sent to a cleaner. And many of them are waterproof or water-resistant, eliminating the need for special rain gear. Plus, these synthetic suits can easily be worn over regular clothing, a tremendous advantage for people who use their motorcycles to commute to work. Many synthetic suits are constructed with removable liners, allowing the rider to use them over a broad range of weather conditions. In hot weather, riders can wear light clothing beneath their suits, and as the temperatures drop, riders can put in the thermal liners and wear extra layers of clothing. A company called Aerostich even offers an electric liner for its Darien jacket.

Aerostich's Darien Gore-Tex-lined jacket and pants, which feature body armor in all of the right places, combine safety and outstanding protection from the elements.

(Photo courtesy of Aerostitch)

Gloves: How Much Blood Can You Lose Through the Palm of Your Hand?

Whenever I fall off anything, my first instinct is to put my hands out to ease my fall. It is one thing to fall off a bicycle, but fall off a motorcycle traveling at highway speed and you will lose some skin. Always wearing a pair of leather riding gloves, preferably a pair that extend over your wrist bones, will make a difference. A good pair of motorcycle gloves will have extra leather on the palms, knuckles, and fingers. This provides additional protection against abrasion in case of an accident.

A good pair of gloves also will have some small amount of armor built inside the palm and knuckle areas. Your hands will often stick out further than the rest of your bike,

Motorcycle Moments

One of the bloodiest accidents I've ever seen involved a rider who went down at more than 70 mph without gloves. He had a helmet on and wasn't seriously injured, except that he completely peeled off the skin from the palms of his hands. He lost more than a pint of blood through just the wounds on his hands.

so having some impact protection is a good idea. Good gloves will even stop your hands from going numb on a long ride.

Riders trying to look tough often wear fingerless gloves. While these will provide some palm protection in the event of a crash, they don't really offer anything else. If you aren't getting enough "feel" through a regular pair of bike gloves, then search out a pair of kangaroo skin gloves. These will offer you phenomenal protection, from an ultra-thin hide, giving you the ultimate feedback from your fingertips.

A good pair of riding gloves, like these kangaroo skin race gloves, will provide comfort, feedback, and protection.

(Photo courtesy of Simon Green)

Fancy Footwear

Even choosing footwear for riding requires some thoughtful consideration. You need to wear a pair of tall leather boots to protect your ankles from being burned by the exhaust pipes and from stones and other debris. You also need to take other factors into account when selecting a pair of boots.

On a motorcycle, your feet are an important part of your motorcycle's chassis: they are what hold up the motorcycle when you are at rest. In effect, when you aren't moving, the soles of your shoes are like an extra set of tires. Because of this, you'll want to wear a pair of boots with grippy soles. While fashion boots or cowboy boots provide adequate ankle protection, their leather soles are far too slippery for them to be useful riding shoes. If you wear fashion boots, make certain they are the work-style with grippy rubber soles.

I prefer a boot with Velcro or latches to a lace-up boot, and not just because they take less time to put on. Laces come loose and get caught in moving parts like your drive chain. It really doesn't look good rolling to a stop, trying to put your left foot down, then realizing your lace is caught in the chain, as the whole bike slowly falls over and takes you with it. Not cool.

Extreme Riding Gear

Nothing surpasses the pleasure of seeing the world on a motorcycle because, on a bike, you are right there, in the thick of it. That means you get to smell the freshly cut hay alongside the road you're riding down. The morning sun recharges you, just as it recharges the flora.

The downside of all this nature worship is that you will experience the world in its entirety, and you must take the bad with the good. That means being prepared for any kind of weather.

Rain Gear

Ride long enough, and your rain suit will become as much of a part of your everyday riding gear as your helmet: you won't leave home without it. A good rain suit can turn a miserable, wet ride into a tolerable or even fun one.

 Motorcycology _____

When selecting a rain suit, choose as brightly colored a suit as possible. Visibility is especially important when it comes to gear you will wear in low-visibility situations, such as rain. Don't buy a black rain suit. Face it: you're not going to look cool while riding a motorcycle in the rain, regardless of how tough your rain suit looks. Since being cool is out of the question, you might as well be safe.

Rain suits are either one- or two-piece suits, made of polyvinyl chloride (PVC) or coated nylon. I prefer the one-piece suits because rain always manages to seep in between the pants and the jacket on two-piece suits.

PVC provides better rain protection than most coated nylon suits, but PVC doesn't breathe so it makes you sweat. Because it can get so sticky to the touch, it can be difficult to get on and off. To get around this, the best PVC suits have a nylon mesh lining that slides against your leather riding gear. Look for a suit that has such lining in both the upper and lower portions.

In my experience, the best rain gear is a waterproof riding suit, such as the Aerostich Darien jacket and pants, which are made of Gore-Tex Cordura material. With these, you don't have to bother putting a rain suit on when foul weather approaches and taking it off when it passes. Even the best rain suits are a hassle to put on by the side of the road on a windy day, and when they get wet, they can be real buggers to get off over leather.

You can get a bare-bones two-piece rain suit for well under $50. Expect to spend more than $100 for a top-quality one-piece suit.

As backward as it may seem, I've encountered a lot of bikers who refuse to wear rain gear. This strikes me as so odd. I know from long years of experience that few things in this world are as miserable as spending an entire day in drenched leather waiting for hypothermia to set in.

Are you starting to realize how many posers there are in motorcycling?

Ride long enough, and your rain suit will become part of your everyday riding gear: you won't leave home without it.

(Photo © 1998 Darwin Holmstrom)

Freezing to Death: Beating the Cold

Motorcyclists tend to get cold more often than they get hot. Even on a relatively mild day—say, 65°F—the wind-chill on a motorcycle traveling at 65 mph can approach freezing. Hypothermia (a condition in which your body temperature drops to dangerously low levels) is a very real danger on a bike. As I said earlier, in cold weather, a synthetic motorcycle suit can be a real lifesaver, but even those who can't afford such a suit can throw together the proper gear for riding on a cool day.

On really cold days, I wear jeans and a turtleneck sweater over my thermal underwear. I like to wear a sweatshirt over that, along with riding pants. When the temperatures get too cold, the summer leather riding suits usually go into hibernation.

Even if you can't afford a Darien jacket with an electric liner, you can still benefit from electrically heated clothing on a budget. Vanson and several other companies make electrically heated vests that you can wear under your jacket. These vests can keep you toasty on even the coldest ride. On super-cold days, I've worn an electric vest under my rain gear, even though it wasn't raining. The vest warmed up the entire inside of the suit and kept me as warm as if I'd been driving a car.

Motorcycology

I've found that a one-piece pair of thermal underwear (a union suit) is preferable to the traditional two-piece set. When you dress in bulky layers, your clothes tend to ride up, creating a gap of bare skin between the top and bottom pieces of a two-piece suit. You can avoid this with a union suit.

Keeping your hands warm can go a long way toward keeping your whole body warm. Several companies offer electrically heated handgrip kits, and BMW offers them as an option on its bikes. You can also purchase something called Hippo Hands, sheaths that attach to your handlebars and surround your controls. These devices may look odd, but they provide exceptional protection against the elements.

Baked, Boiled, or Fried: Beating the Heat

All motorcyclists have to deal with the heat. Riding all day under the hot sun takes a lot out of your body. You can become dangerously dehydrated and even suffer heatstroke. At the very least, you may become tired, and your judgment and riding skills will suffer.

One of my most dangerous riding experiences occurred because of dehydration. I got a mild case of food poisoning in Las Vegas, but I didn't realize it until I was headed across the Arizona desert. At the worst possible moment I could imagine, I realized I couldn't keep down water. I spent a difficult (and dangerous) day making my way from gas station to gas station, until I finally had the sense to call it quits and get a motel room.

Since that episode, I've learned a lot about riding in heat. The most important thing to remember is to keep hydrated. Always drink plenty of fluids, and on really hot days, drink fluids especially designed to rehydrate your cells, such as sports drinks. Remember that caffeine is a diuretic and will deplete your body's store of water rather than replenish it. If you feel thirsty, you have already gone too long without a drink. If you ride much in hot climates, you should really invest in a CamelBak or some other brand of water reservoir. Fill these with ice, and in addition to providing you with refreshing water to drink, they will keep you cool during the day.

Another method for keeping cool is to soak your shirt under your riding gear. This works especially well with a heavily ventilated jacket, such as Vanson's ProPerf gear, which is made from fully perforated leather, allowing the wind to circulate around your whole body. The right gear is crucial for hot-weather riding. Most leather makers now offer perforated leather riding gear, which lets air flow through the garment. A few companies even offer mesh jackets with protective armor, sort of like the gear worn by off-road riders. These help you keep cool but still provide reasonable abrasion protection. Joe Rocket's Alter Ego jacket is a very popular jacket of this type.

Lightweight, ventilated jackets like this one offer excellent, controllable ventilation, which can be closed up when the temperature drops. Any good jacket should also provide you with some serious accident protection.

(Photo courtesy of Simon Green)

Again, synthetic riding suits make excellent hot-weather riding gear. You can remove the lining from most of these and just use the outer shell, which retains all the armor and protective qualities. The suits themselves have many zippered vents, allowing you to control airflow. Aerostich recommends wearing long pants and a long-sleeve shirt under its suits because, theoretically, its Cordura can melt under extremely high temperatures (but in all the years of manufacturing, examining, and repairing suits that have been through crashes, they have yet to find one case of this happening). While I can't condone this practice, your risks would probably be minimal if you chose to wear just shorts and a T-shirt under your Aerostich suit on an extremely hot day. You would still have far more abrasion protection than someone riding in jeans and a light jacket.

Accessories: All the Extras

A good part of the fun of owning a motorcycle is getting all the accessories that go along with it. Motorcyclists may try to convince you otherwise, but they lie. They love modifying their bikes and collecting gadgets.

A huge array of accessories is available for every type of bike and every type of biker, from cruiser windshields to travel trailers, to global positioning units (computers that use satellites to tell you where you are) and bike-to-bike communicators. Some are mere novelties, things mainly used to amuse your friends when you stop for a cup of coffee. Other accessories come closer to necessities.

Motorcycology

If you choose to mount a windshield to your bike, select one that you can see over without the top of the windshield cutting across your line of vision. The airflow over a well-designed windshield will go over your face, directing wind, bugs, and debris to the top of your helmet or over it. Most Plexiglas windshields aren't optically clear enough to provide an undistorted view of the road if you look directly through them. This is especially problematic at night.

On the more frivolous side are the purely cosmetic items, things that serve no purpose except to alter a bike's looks.

Most accessories available today are harmless. That wasn't always true, especially during the chopper craze of the 1960s and 1970s. Some of the popular accessories of the day, such as high "sissybar" backrests and high handlebars, could induce high-speed wobbles in some bikes' handling. Some accessories, such as extended forks and after-market frames with steep rakes, actually made a motorcycle downright dangerous to ride.

Today's accessories can still have unintended side effects. A while back, I bought a Yamaha Venture, an ultimate behemoth type of touring bike, on which the previous owner had installed a pair of chrome covers over the vents in the side panel. While he probably found these covers attractive, they trapped heat in the engine compartment and made the bike run hot, so I removed them.

The owner had also installed a strange set of 1950s-era taillights around the license plate frame. At first, I didn't care for the way these Elvis lights, as I call them, looked; but after a while they grew on me, so I kept them. Besides, anything that makes you more visible to traffic is a functional accessory.

Windshields

On the closer-to-necessity side are windshields. While a bike with a sporty, forward-leaning riding position can get by without a windshield because the rider is naturally braced against the wind, on more laid-back bikes (such as cruisers), an effective windshield can make the difference between a comfortable ride and a trip to the chiropractor.

Saddlebags

Saddlebags are probably the most useful accessory you can add to your bike, turning it from a pretty plaything into a practical form of transportation. Hard bags, which are more or less suitcases mounted to the bike, are the most useful because they offer better weather protection, plus most of them can be locked. Unfortunately, few motorcycles offer them as options (although the number is growing). You can purchase them for many bikes from aftermarket manufacturers, such as GIVI. These tend to be expensive, but if you can afford a set, it is money well spent.

You'll probably end up buying a pair of soft saddlebags that you mount over your seat. These are usually made of vinyl, leather, or Cordura.

Tankbags

Tankbags also add much to a motorcycle's usefulness. These are similar to soft saddlebags, usually constructed of nylon, but they mount on top of the fuel tank. These can be mounted by adjustable straps or by using magnetic mounts that consist of strong magnets in the base of the bags that stick to the tank. Of course, this requires that your tank be constructed of metal; such a system won't work on plastic tanks or tank covers.

Tankbags are great for traveling, not only because they offer extra storage, but because most of them also have a clear map pocket on top. If you've ever tried to unfold a map and read it at the side of a road on a windy day, you'll appreciate this feature.

> **Steer Clear** _____
>
> Be careful of what you pack in a tankbag. I once crashed, and my motorcycle did a cartwheel, ejecting me from the saddle. In my tankbag I had a metal toolkit. When I went off the bike, I landed with the tankbag under my chest. I was uninjured except for several broken ribs from the tankbag containing the toolkit. Moral of the story? Never carry anything in your tankbag you wouldn't want to use for a pillow.

The major drawback of using a tankbag is that the straps can scratch the paint on your gas tank.

The variety of accessories available could fill its own book, and since they reflect an owner's individual taste, only you can decide which ones are right for your bike.

Magazines

Some of the most useful accessories are things that you neither wear nor mount on your motorcycles. Magazines—or, more precisely, the valuable information contained in magazines—can help you become a much better motorcyclist. That information might even save your life some day. This is as true of online magazines as it is of print magazines.

Not that I'm biased or anything, but the magazines in Primedia's Motorcycle Group, magazines such as *Motorcyclist*™, *Motorcycle Cruiser*, *Sport Rider*, *Super Streetbike*, and *Dirt Rider*, contain some of the best information found anywhere.

Where to Buy Accessories

Where you buy those accessories is up to you, too. You can buy your gear from a local dealer, or you can buy from one of several mail-order firms that sell just about every accessory available, usually at discount prices. Both methods have drawbacks, and both have benefits.

When you buy from a local dealer, you see what you're getting: you can try on a helmet or a garment, or see if a windshield fits your bike without obstructing your view.

Motorcycology

Often the price difference between buying local and ordering from a discount company is not all that great, especially after figuring in shipping and handling charges. Chances are, your local dealer can come reasonably close to those prices, if given the chance.

And if you do buy something that won't fit you or your bike (although the chances of that happening are slim because the staff can help you select the correct item in the first place), you can always bring it back. Another advantage of buying local is that you don't have to wait for it to be shipped.

On the other hand, the mail-order places usually have a much wider variety of items than any local shop could afford to carry. Plus, they usually sell those items for less than the shops. The drawbacks are that you don't get to check the fit of the items before purchasing them, and returning them can be a hassle.

One other drawback of buying from a mail-order company is that you won't be supporting your local shops. A lot of smaller shops operate on a slim profit margin, and it wouldn't take much to put many of them out of business. When you buy from some company in a distant location, you could help put your local dealer out of business. This might not seem like it would concern you in any practical way, but it does. If an emergency arises and you need to repair your bike right now, that local dealer is awfully nice to have.

For a comprehensive list of companies that provide motorcycle accessories, see Appendix C.

The Least You Need to Know

- Although some states allow you to choose whether you wear a helmet, if you have a functioning brain, there is no real choice.

- Wear competition-weight leather to protect your body from the elements and in case of a crash.

- Not wearing gloves can turn a minor mishap into a visit to the emergency room.

- Rain suits can take the misery out of rain.

- Although mail-order companies may offer a wide range of motorcycle accessories, your local dealer can help you choose the right accessories and avoid the need to return items.

Part

On the Road

Starting up your bike and hitting the road: this is what motorcycling is all about. All the rest of the motorcycling experience pales when compared to actually riding.

Riding is fun, but it's also serious business, with grave consequences if you make a mistake. Because of the serious nature of riding, you need to be prepared.

This part of the book covers a variety of survival strategies for the street, as well as the basics of how to ride. I also discuss hazards that you might encounter and what to do in case of an emergency. So get your helmet and riding gear, and make sure your bike is ready to roll, because we're going riding.

Chapter 10

Preparing to Hit the Road

In This Chapter

- How to get in the right frame of mind for riding

- Understanding the licensing procedure

- How the Motorcycle Safety Foundation can help you learn to ride

- What switches and levers do

- Mastering the pre-ride inspection

You're just about ready to hit the road (hopefully not literally), but first you need to learn how to ride. You need to learn what the controls on a bike do and how you make them do that. You'll need to learn how to prepare your motorcycle for the road, and you'll also need to prepare yourself mentally.

Before you can even ride a bike, you have to get an instructional (learner's) permit. After you learn to ride, you'll want to get your motorcycle endorsement. Not only will this keep you out of trouble with the law, but it will also statistically lower your chances of getting taken out on your bike.

If you haven't ridden before, you'll need to start from scratch. Unfortunately, most of the things you learned when you started to drive a car don't apply to motorcycles—you're a newbie!

Every day you ride, you will encounter unexpected challenges, such as all kinds of distracted car drivers. In any encounter between a car and a motorcycle, the car has the advantage.

In this chapter, I explain what you need to do to get your permit and motorcycle endorsement. I also show you how to use the controls on your bike, how to prepare your bike for each ride, and how to mentally prepare yourself for each ride.

Getting in Your Right Mind: Mental Motorcycling

Riding a bike requires your undivided attention. If you preoccupy yourself thinking about polishing the silverware on the way home, then you probably won't make it home. Before you head out onto the public roads, you have to make sure your mind is right. As Strother Martin (the overseer in the film *Cool Hand Luke*) might have said, motorcyclists whose minds ain't right get to spend the rest of eternity in the box.

Steer Clear _____

Nothing gets your mind less right for riding than messing it up with alcohol or drugs. You have to be able to balance to ride, and just one beer can upset your balance in ways you can't perceive, and that can have fatal consequences. According to the Motorcycle Safety Foundation, 50 percent of all people killed on motorcycles had alcohol in their blood—and of that 50 percent, two thirds had had only one or two drinks before their accidents.

You need to clear your mind of distractions before you get on your bike. Do whatever it takes to get your mind cleared (including going to the bathroom—you'd be surprised at how your concentration can suffer when you're twitching around with your legs crossed).

Another great distraction is anger at other drivers. Anger on the road is dangerous; it will cloud your judgment, and you need that to make the split-second decisions required to survive in traffic. You need to remain calm and collected in every situation, regardless of whether you are right or wrong. While you may have the right of way, the person in the car has your life in his or her hands. Don't develop road rage against someone who can hurt you simply by turning a steering wheel. Instead, calmly remove yourself from such situations. Use your bike to get as far away from the other vehicle as possible.

Getting Licensed

Every state in the union requires riders to obtain a special endorsement on their driver's license before operating a motorcycle. While this may seem like just another hoop to jump through, these states are probably doing you a favor. According to the Motorcycle Safety Foundation, unlicensed riders account for the majority of accident victims; by getting a license, you vastly increase your odds of not becoming a statistic. Licensing programs help get a safer, more knowledgeable population of motorcyclists out on the street.

Motorcycle tests, both written and riding, have improved a great deal since I first got my license. I'd have to say my first experience with the licensing procedure was useless. Whoever compiled the test obviously didn't ride a bike, and the questions had no relevance to the knowledge needed to survive on a motorcycle.

I had a nice surprise when I retook the written test in the early 1990s; it actually asked useful questions. You had to know things about real-world motorcycling to pass.

Each state has a different written test with different questions. The most useful tests are those devised in conjunction with the Motorcycle Safety Foundation. To obtain a study guide for your state's test, call your local Department of Motor Vehicles.

Getting Your Learner's Permit

The first step in getting licensed is to get your permit, which you receive upon successfully completing your written test. The purpose of the permit is to allow you to get out and practice in the real world before taking your test. You should get your permit even before you actually learn to ride so that you can legally practice your riding.

In most states, getting your permit will allow you to ride during daylight hours without a passenger. Most states have extra requirements for permitted riders, such as not allowing them to ride after dark or allowing them to ride on limited-access highways only. You will be required to wear a helmet if you have just a permit—but that shouldn't matter to you because you're reading this book, therefore you have a brain, so you want to wear your helmet all the time anyway. Right?

Getting Your Endorsement

You'll get your endorsement, the notation on your driver's license officially designating you as a motorcyclist, after you complete the riding portion of your test. For this, you'll be required to demonstrate your riding skills on either a closed course or public streets.

When I took my test, I just rode around a city block, did a U-turn in the street without putting my foot down, and basically didn't kill myself (or anyone else if I remember correctly). A tester watched from the sidewalk, and when I returned, he gave me my license, along with a speech informing me of the reasons why I should become an organ donor. This portion of the test has improved somewhat since then, but it still teaches you very little about the skills you'll need to survive on the mean streets. In contrast, getting a motorcycle license in Europe requires you to participate in three to five long days of training, most of which takes place on congested public roads. Currently in the United States, your best bet is to take a Motorcycle Safety Foundation RiderCourse.

The Motorcycle Safety Foundation

A nationwide not-for-profit organization established in March 1973, the Motorcycle Safety Foundation (MSF) works to make motorcycling a safer activity and has developed programs recognized around the world for their excellence and effectiveness. The MSF does the following:

◆ It works to make high-quality rider-training programs, designed for both new and experienced riders, available to as wide a population as possible.

◆ It works with state and national governments and organizations to promote motorcycle safety and to help adopt effective motorcycle-operator licensing practices.

◆ It collects data and information on motorcycle safety and works to get that information out to the public.

Motorcycology

Another advantage of completing an MSF RiderCourse is that many insurance companies give you a break on your premiums if you successfully complete the course. It is the single best thing you can do to ensure that you have a long and healthy career as a motorcyclist.

There is nothing better you can do to prepare yourself for the challenges of motorcycling than to take an MSF RiderCourse. That applies to experienced riders as well as novices. The MSF has worked to make such courses available across the entire United States. Even if you have to drive a few miles to reach the RiderCourse nearest you, you can find no better use of your time if you're serious about motorcycling. To find the RiderCourse nearest you, call the Motorcycle Safety Foundation at 1-800-446-9227 or check out www.msf-usa.org on the web.

In addition to possibly saving your butt somewhere down the line, taking an MSF RiderCourse has immediate practical value. At least 20 states will grant you your motorcycle endorsement on the spot, upon successfully completing a RiderCourse, saving you the trouble of going to a busy Department of Motor Vehicles office and taking a test. Even if the state still makes you take the test, many states give you extra credit for completing an approved RiderCourse.

And for off-road enthusiasts, the MSF even offers a Dirt Bike School. It's a one-day course that emphasizes the mental and physical skills required for dirtbike riding, and, of course, safety is paramount. Class sizes are kept small to ensure plenty of individual attention from the MSF-certified coaches, and students can be assured of getting the proper fundamentals to have big fun off-road. For more information, check out www.dirtbikeschool.com on the web; you also can enroll with a single phone call to 1-877-288-7093.

Control Freaks: How to Ride a Motorcycle

Driving a car is downright clumsy compared to riding a motorcycle. In a car you're moving your arms all over the place, steering and using the gear shifter. By contrast a motorcycle is all about finesse, every movement is small and precise. The controls are all immediately at hand, so no big movements are necessary. The bike reacts to every tiny thing you do, even an accidental shuffle will make the bike quickly change course.

Primary Controls

You use six major controls to operate just about every motorcycle made since World War II (with the exception of a couple of oddball bikes that use automatic transmissions). The location of these controls has been standardized on all motorcycles manufactured after the mid-1970s (although the location of the shifter and rear brake may be reversed on vintage European and American motorcycles). The following figures illustrate the standard places where you'll find controls on all but a few rare, classic bikes.

The six primary controls you'll use to ride your bike.

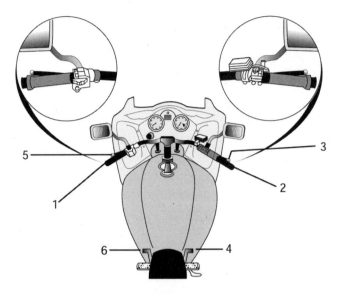

1. The **handlebars** are the bars attached to the top of the front-suspension forks, that you use to control the bike's direction. (Note that I didn't say *steer* the bike: remember, at anything higher than parking-lot speeds, you *countersteer* the bike, using the handlebars to lever the bike over, not steer it.)

2. The **throttle** is a twist grip located on the right end of the handlebar. This controls your speed. You twist the grip toward you to speed the engine up, and twist it away to slow the engine down. All properly functioning modern throttles have springs that automatically return them to the closed position.

3. The **front brake lever** is the lever mounted to the right side of the handlebar, in front of the throttle, that controls the front brake.

4. The **rear brake lever** is the lever in front of the right footpeg that controls the rear brake (some models have a weird linked braking system, so it would partially apply the front brake, too).

5. The **clutch lever** is located on the left end of the handlebar (mirror image of the front brake lever). It controls the clutch and is used to disengage the drive from the engine to help shift gears.

6. The **shift lever** (or gear lever) is located in front of the left footpeg. You operate it with the front of your foot, from above or below to shift the transmission's gears up or down.

By using these controls with your hands and feet, you can make the motorcycle stop and go, and you can control the bike's direction. While you are riding, you constantly use these controls—often using all of them at the same time. Driving a car will never be the same.

Secondary Controls

In addition to the six primary controls, you'll need to use a variety of other controls to ride a bike effectively. The most important of these are illustrated in the following figure.

1. The **ignition switch** is similar to the ignition switch in cars, except that it usually locks the forks in place (thus disabling the steering as a theft deterrent). It also operates a parking light, and it is separate from the starter. You don't turn the key to start a bike like you do a car.

2. The **electric-starter button** is on the right end of the handlebar near the throttle. Nearly every motorcycle made today comes with an electric starter, which you operate by pressing this button.

3. The **kick-start lever** is rare on most bikes made today, except for some smaller dual-sports and off-road bikes, but you may encounter it on certain used bikes. It's usually located near the right footpeg (although it's located on the left side on certain European bikes). To work this device, you need to fold it out, kick the lever in a downward motion with your foot, and then fold it back out of the way.

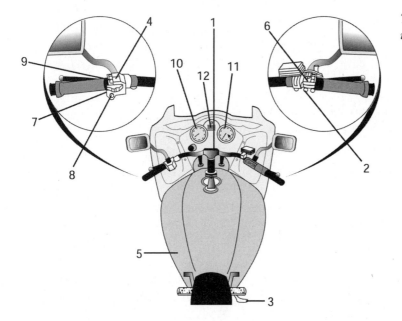

The secondary controls you'll use to ride your bike.

4. The **choke** (or enrichment control) is a lever or a knob that is located in various positions but is usually found on the handlebars; you use it to help start your bike when it's cold.

5. The **fuel petcock** (or fuel tap) is a valve that controls the flow of fuel from the gas tank to the induction system; it usually has positions for On, Off, Reserve, and Prime. Prime is used only after the engine has not been run for an extended period of time; it fills the float bowls with fuel before starting the engine.

6. The **engine cut-off switch** (or kill switch) turns off the engine. If you can't start your bike, the first thing you should check is whether the kill switch was accidentally left in the "off" position.

7. All street-legal motorcycles manufactured in the past 25 years are equipped with **turn signals.**

Motorcycology

Fuel petcocks are much less important on modern bikes than on older bikes; many modern bikes with fuel pumps don't even use traditional petcocks. Even on those that do have one, you'll seldom need to bother with it. On older bikes, you'll need to turn this switch off each time you park the bike and remember to turn it on when you restart it. The one big advantage of petcocks is their Reserve feature, which saves a small amount of fuel in the bottom of the tank, in case you run out.

Unlike cars, many bikes don't have a self-canceling feature built into their turn-signal switches. On most modern bikes, you operate the turn signals by pushing the switch left or right for your turn, and then you push it straight in to cancel the turn signal.

8. Your **horn** can save your life, so don't be timid about using it. You operate most horns by pushing a button located next to the turn-signal switch.

Motorcycology

You'll use your idiot lights more on a bike than you do on a car, especially the neutral light and the turn-signal indicator. Because most bikes don't have self-canceling turn signals, it's easy to forget that they're on.

9. The **headlight dimmer switch** switches the headlight between high- and low-beam modes. On most modern bikes, you can't turn off the lights, so this switch just changes beams.

10. The **speedometer** stops you getting tickets from traffic cops.

11. The **tachometer** indicates the number of revolutions your engine is turning each minute (rpms).

12. The **indicator lights** (sometimes known as idiot lights) are primarily the same as the indicator lights on your car, with the addition of a neutral indicator light (usually green) that indicates when the transmission is in neutral (i.e., not in gear).

Although these are all peripheral system controls used to augment riding rather than directly to ride the bike, you will need to use most of them every time you ride.

The Pre-ride Inspection

Motorcycles require more upkeep than cars. This has always been the case, and it is still a fact of motorcycling life, even with the technological advances you learned about in earlier chapters. The consequences of a systems failure on a bike are much more severe than they are if something goes wrong with your car. Take a blown tire, for example. When a tire blows on your car, you can have difficulty controlling it. When the same thing happens on a bike, it's like a fairground ride from hell.

The best way to avoid a catastrophic failure is to inspect your motorcycle on a regular basis. Some items need to be checked more often than others; some should be checked each time you go out for a ride.

The Motorcycle Safety Foundation uses the *T-CLOCK method* to help remember what to check during the pre-ride inspection:

T Tires and wheels

C Controls

L Lights and electrics

O Oils and fluids

C Chassis and chain

K Kickstand

This method is useful, but I'm going to present a simpler one because I've found that if the pre-ride inspection is too complicated, most riders just ignore the whole thing.

I try to check all the items on the T-CLOCK list fairly regularly, but to be honest, I don't check them all every time I ride. A lot depends on the bike I'm riding; for example, if I know that a bike doesn't use oil, I might check the oil only once a week. If the bike is a nasty oil burner, I might check it in the morning and then check it a couple more times as the day progresses.

I've found that the cables and other controls on modern bikes seem to need less attention than those on older bikes; I might go a couple of weeks without attending to my cables and controls, depending on the conditions I've been riding under. As for the drive chain, it'll need regular attention. You need to lubricate your drive chain for every ride, and make sure it's adjusted right, too; that way when it's finally stretched too much, it'll be the only thing you replace. If you neglect it, once loose it'll distort the teeth on both sprockets, making the chain replacement four times as expensive. We'll cover chain maintenance fully in Chapter 16.

While I'm looking around my bike I also check for loose bolts in the chassis and make certain the spring is attached to the kickstand each time I ride. The main things I consider absolutely essential to check before each ride are the tires, lights, and chain.

Checking the Tires

I check the air pressure in my tires each morning before I start my bike. I keep an air-pressure gauge in my jacket pocket, and I check the tires when they are cold (when you ride, the air inside them warms up, and the pressure reads higher). Not only is riding with the proper air pressure in your tires safer, but it also makes your tires last longer. Check your owner's manual to find the proper air-pressure level for your motorcycle.

Whenever I check my tire pressures, I also look over the tires themselves to check their wear and to look for any abnormalities, such as bulges, damage to the carcass, and cracking in the sidewalls. I also make sure I haven't picked up a nail or a chunk of glass. I will not ride on a tire I have any questions about. Neither should you.

Keep a plastic air-pressure gauge in your jacket (any metal objects in your pocket have injury potential in an accident) or on your bike so you can check the air pressure each morning.

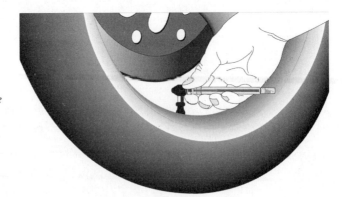

The best way to avoid a blowout is to keep a close eye on your tires and to make certain they are free of debris, such as nails or other objects that could puncture the tire. Change your tires as soon as they wear down to an unacceptable level.

While I'm on the floor checking my tires, I make certain that the bolts holding the axles in place are tight. Probably the one thing worse than having a flat tire would be having a wheel assembly fall off completely. I'm not good enough on a unicycle to get through that mess.

Motorcycle Moments _____

A friend of mine once lost the front tire on his Harley chopper while we were riding to a rally together because his axle bolts vibrated loose. He went end over end and landed in a ditch about 50 feet from his bike. Although he wasn't wearing a helmet, he seemed to be unhurt, except for a few cuts and bruises. We loaded his bike into a friend's truck and continued to the rally. My friend appeared to be none the worse for wear and tear, but later we learned he'd suffered a severe concussion, and to this day he doesn't remember a thing about that rally.

Looking at Lights

Your lighting system is fairly easy to overlook, but it can get you into a lot of trouble.

If your brake lights aren't working, you can end up with an unwelcome Chevy enema before you even get out of town. Motorcycles have awesome stopping power, and most car drivers don't give themselves enough room to stop when they're following you. Brake lights are not much protection to keep tailgaters from embedding themselves into your privates, but they are all you have (at least until someone designs an anti-tailgating device that uses a 70-mm cannon mounted on your tail section).

Motorcycology _____

Motorcycle headlights usually have two elements: one for high beam and one for low beam. Only one element burns out at a time in a properly functioning system, so you should still have a low-beam element if your high-beam burns out, and vice versa. However, be warned that the remaining element will burn out soon after the first, leaving you in the dark. It's a good idea to always pack a spare headlight bulb and tail lamp bulb in your gear.

Motorcycle headlights and taillights seem to fail more frequently than their automotive counterparts, because there's increased vibration. Some motorcycles have only one headlight, so if it burns out, you will be up the creek when the sun goes down. It's a good idea to check both the high beam and low beam of your headlight when you check your taillight and brake light.

This might seem like a lot of preparation before you can ride, and it is. But the consequences of being unprepared on a bike are just too great.

Learn the controls of your motorcycle. Memorize them and test yourself on them. In an emergency situation, your life can depend on your split-second reactions. You can't afford to lose any time in reacting because you had to think about where a control was: that microsecond can cost you your life.

Try to internalize the habit of giving your bike a pre-ride inspection. You might feel tempted to skip it when you're late for work or are trying to get to a movie on time, but the possible consequences of some sort of failure of your motorcycle could be so severe that you might never see a movie or be able to work again. Take a few minutes to check over your machine before you take your life in your hands. Those minutes may add years to your life.

The Least You Need to Know

- Unlicensed riders account for the majority of all motorcycle fatalities.
- There is no better way to learn to ride than to take a RiderCourse from the Motorcycle Safety Foundation.
- The controls on a bike are completely different from the controls on a car.
- You'll need to use both your hands and both your feet, often all at the same time, to ride a motorcycle.
- Because the consequences of equipment failure on a bike are so much greater than on a car, you need to take a few minutes before each ride to inspect certain key components.

11

Learning to Ride

In This Chapter

- ◆ How to control your bike
- ◆ The basic skills you need to start and stop a motorcycle
- ◆ Applying the brakes or throttle
- ◆ How to turn and change lanes

You're finally ready to hit the road. Everything you've learned so far has been to help prepare you for this moment. For some of you, what comes next will seem natural, and much of what I discuss may seem obvious. Others will find mastering your motorcycle a bit more challenging.

Back when I was instructing, the first question I would ask a new student was "Have you ever ridden before?" If the answer was "No," then I knew exactly what I needed to teach them. If the answer was "Yes," then my follow-up was "What model of bike was it, and when did you ride last?" Years of experience taught me that if I was given a vague, nonspecific answer about their grandpa's uncle's son who had a dirtbike, then it was a lie coming from someone who couldn't bear to admit they'd never ridden. These were always the worst students; they knew it all already. As a result, they would always be overtaken by the others (in terms of skill) very quickly. I've found that people who have to put more thought into learning to ride a bike eventually become safer and more skilled motorcyclists. Having to think about all the things they need to do seems to make them mentally more involved in riding, thus helping them develop good habits from the beginning.

In this chapter, I provide you with the basic skills you need to ride a motorcycle. Be a sponge and soak it all up; you'll be all the better for it. In Chapter 12, I'll go into more advanced techniques. You should read both chapters before doing any serious riding.

Steering Clear

Some people seem to intuitively understand how to operate a motorcycle, while others need to consciously learn to do so. Neither group has any kind of initial advantage. The latter group simply has to put a bit more mental energy into learning to ride.

While instructing, I saw many people from both groups, but every one of them loved to learn about *countersteering*. I've read so many overcomplicated explanations on countersteering that confuse the reader, sometimes the only effect they have is to turn a novice rider into a rigid, petrified mess.

Cycle Babble

Countersteering refers to turning the handlebars on a motorcycle in the opposite direction than the direction in which you want to turn. Countersteering is the only way to get a motorcycle to change directions at speeds of more than 10 to 15 mph.

Let's make it easy. You can ride a bike around slowly, sitting dead upright and turning the handlebars to point you in whatever direction you're heading. Once you start going faster on a bike, you lean. I'm sure you've watched people on bikes and seen it happen.

When you're riding your bike at higher speeds and you lean, you're putting some of your upper body weight on the handlebars. Those handlebars will move a bit with the weight of your torso. Try this: sit on your bike in the garage and lean it slightly to the right—watch the handlebars. They actually turned a little to the left, didn't they? That's countersteering.

I used to find that many of the riders who took to motorcycling in an intuitive way just knew to lean. The ones who didn't needed to be taught. But don't worry, it's easy. Let's say you're riding down a nice straight street on your shiny new bike, the sun's out, and the world's a great place, but ahead you see a right-hand curve; don't think about countersteering, just chill out and put a bit of pressure onto the palm of your right hand, and the bike will do the rest.

That's all there is to it. Push right to go right, push left to go left. Leaning the bike will have exactly the same effect; the benefit to using your hands to do this is razor-sharp accuracy. If you don't instinctively lean, then don't worry, you'll actually take to countersteering more easily using this simple technique. Countersteering leans the bike for you.

For practice you can ride down a straight, wide, empty street and experiment by ever-so-gently nudging your handlebars with the palms of your left hand and then right hand, one at a time.

Now that I've hammered that point into your head, it's time to crank up your bike's engine and go riding.

Parking-Lot Practice

Before you begin learning to ride, you need to find a safe place to practice, such as an empty parking lot, where there are no other vehicles. Practice basic starting, turning, and stopping procedures until you are comfortable with your ability before venturing out into traffic. Just mastering the basics of riding a motorcycle will prove challenging enough; you don't need to compound these challenges by adding the risks posed by other drivers. Better yet, take a Motorcycle Safety Foundation RiderCourse, in which you'll learn these skills in a controlled environment under the guidance of a trained instructor (see Chapter 10 for details).

Starting the Beast

Just getting on a bike requires a little knowledge. To begin, you always mount a motorcycle from the left side because the kickstand is located on that side, so it already will be leaning in that direction (provided it is not on the *centerstand*). Hold both handgrips on the handlebar to prevent the bike from moving, squeeze the front brake lever with the fingers of your right hand, and swing your leg over the seat. When you're standing securely over the bike, straighten it with the handlebars. After you've comfortably balanced the bike, rest your weight on the seat.

Cycle Babble

A **centerstand** is a supporting stand located just in front of a motorcycle's rear wheel that supports the bike in an upright position.

Never forget to raise the kickstand when you get on a bike. If you ride off with it still down, it'll dig into the floor and take you off the bike at the first left-hand corner—hysterical for spectators, not for you. To do this, use your left heel to kick the kickstand into the up position after you have balanced the bike.

If the bike is supported on the centerstand, the technique is a little different and requires some practice, ideally with a friend standing on the opposite side of the bike. The most common problem new riders experience when taking their bikes off their centerstand happens when the bike falls away from the rider onto the ground (hence the friend to catch it on the other side).

When a big, heavy motorcycle is rolled off its centerstand, it's an unstable rolling lump, so here's a foolproof removal technique. Stand on the left side of your bike and take a look at the centerstand. It has an arm (or operating lever) sticking out toward you. This is to give you leverage and control. Don't ever take your bike off its stand without your foot firmly in place on that arm—we'll call it your centerstand *tang*.

Now it's time to practice. Put your left hand on the left handlebar grip, and your right hand on the passenger *grab rail* (some motorcycles even have a special handle mounted under the passenger seat for this job). Put your right foot on the centerstand tang. Now rock the bike forward using your right hand, and as the bike rolls off the stand, make sure you maintain firm pressure on the tang with your right foot. The bike cannot fall over, as the centerstand's feet are now pressed to the floor (if your foot is doing its job). Next, transfer your right hand to the front brake lever so the bike can't roll, and lean the bike toward your body while simultaneously lifting your foot off the tang. Finally, mount the motorcycle just like before, holding the brake all the time.

There are thousands of people out there who don't use the centerstand on their bike, as it "doesn't feel safe." Don't become one of them; practice, and I guarantee it'll become easy-peezy lemon-squeezy.

Cycle Babble

The **tang** is an arm or lever welded onto a motorcycle's centerstand. It allows the rider to use their body weight for leverage in order to make it easy to put their bike on, or to take it off, its centerstand.

Grab rails are mounted to the back of a motorcycle. They are the handles that a motorcycle passenger holds while on the bike, so as to not accidentally fall off.

The starting procedure varies with each motorcycle. For example, if you have an older motorcycle (anything manufactured before the late 1970s), you'll probably have to turn on the fuel petcock before starting the bike (see Chapter 10). Otherwise, the bike won't start. Or if it does, it will begin to sputter and then die, as float bowls empty. This inevitably happens at precisely the wrong moment. Most modern bikes have vacuum-operated petcocks that open as soon as the starter button is pushed and close when the engine is shut down.

Start Your Ignition

The next step is to turn on the ignition switch and make sure that the kill switch is not in the "off" position. Even the most experienced motorcyclist sometimes bumps the kill switch into the "off" position and then wears his or her battery down trying to start the beast. You can save yourself a lot of grief by getting into the habit of automatically turning the switch to the "on" position each time you turn on the ignition switch.

The ignition switch is usually located on the dash, up near the instrument panel, but a recent trend is to locate the switch in some odd position under the seat or fuel tank, (where the switches were located on motorcycles manufactured before about 1970). This retro touch, which emulates the switch location on some Harley-Davidson models, appears on many of the newer Japanese cruisers.

Next, make certain your transmission is in neutral. Even though most current bikes won't start if you're in gear, there are some old ones that might start and then head off down the street on their own (I wonder how the cops would write that one up). This is why the neutral light is so important on a motorcycle; but you can't always trust the light, they can be funky from time to time.

To be sure you're in neutral, rock the bike back and forth. If the bike is in gear, you won't be able to move it more than a few inches before the rear wheel refuses to turn. If this happens, gently move the shift lever up or down until you can roll the motorcycle freely. If you have a bike that consistently gives you a false neutral reading, you may have transmission or clutch problems.

After you've switched on the ignition, you'll more than likely need to set your choke, especially if the engine is cold. How much choke you have to use varies from bike to bike. This is almost a mystical procedure, and you'll need to use every one of your senses to learn the exact combination of choke and throttle required. You'll need to listen to the engine turning over, feel it catch and begin to fire, smell the exhaust to see if you are giving it too much throttle and flooding the carburetors, watch the tachometer once the engine starts, and adjust the choke accordingly. A properly running motorcycle with perfectly adjusted controls usually needs very little throttle to start when cold, although it may need a bit more when warm. Unfortunately, we seldom achieve absolute perfection in tuning our engines, causing the procedure to vary widely.

Now pull in the clutch lever. Even though you've shifted to neutral, the light is shining brightly, and you've checked to make certain the transmission is in neutral, you can never be too careful on a motorcycle.

Motorcycology

Different manufacturers use a variety of safety devices to ensure that you don't start a bike while it is in gear, such as starters that operate only when the clutch lever is pulled in or when the transmission is in neutral. Unfortunately, there is no standard, agreed-upon procedure.

Here the procedure for starting a bike with an electric starter differs from the procedure for starting one with a kick starter. On electrically starting bikes, you start the engine with the press of a button. With the clutch lever pulled in, push the starter button; the bike should fire up. It will make a brief grinding sound as the starter spins the flywheel in the engine. Then when the engine starts running, release the starter button immediately.

If the engine doesn't fire immediately, don't hold the button down for an extended period of time because this will drain the battery, burn out the starter, and cause other damage. Usually, if the engine doesn't fire immediately, the problem will be something as simple as your forgetting to turn on the fuel petcock or accidentally bumping the kill switch to the off position.

Kick-Starting Your Bike

Kick-starting is pretty much the same, except that instead of just pushing a button, you'll need to use the kick-starting lever.

First, fold out the lever, or the peg at the top of the lever. If the lever is located on the right side of the bike (as it will be on all but a few European bikes), lean the bike slightly to the left to give your hands more leverage against the force of your kick. This supports the bike during the starting procedure.

Quickly and forcefully kick the lever downward. The inertia of the engine will want to make the lever slam back up again on many bikes, slapping it against your shin or ankle with tremendous force if your foot slips off the peg; make certain that you have a firm footing on the peg before kicking. Repeat this procedure until the bike starts. You'll soon understand the appeal of electric starters.

If all this sounds like a lot of bother, just be glad you're riding a modern bike. This procedure is simple compared to starting a tuned old BSA Gold Star.

Taking Off: The Biting Point

Taking off on a motorcycle is a lot like taking off in a car with a manual transmission, except that you have to balance the bike at the same time.

It's possible that you've never driven a car with a manual transmission; maybe you've never driven anything motorized at all. Either way, don't worry—we can still make it easy.

Think of a motorcycle as a bicycle that won't stop pedaling. You can slow it down by using the brakes, but it'll just keep going as soon as you let go of the brake lever, because it never stops pedaling. Now think of the clutch as the lever that stops it pedaling.

Let's talk about taking off, while sitting on your bike: you need to use the ball of your right foot to click the gear lever down into first gear. You should lean the bike ever so slightly to the left before you pick up your right foot, as you don't want to lose your balance. So lean left, pull the clutch lever in with the fingers on your left hand (remember, we've gotta stop that thing pedaling), and then click it down into gear with your right foot.

Now you're sitting on the bike with the engine running, in gear, the only thing stopping you from moving is the clutch. We're in no rush here; I've learned that good clutch control is one of the most important skills in motorcycling. Clutches are not just in or out, they're not like a light switch with just an on or off position; a clutch releases the engine's power gradually. Unlike some riders ….

At this point you can't just let go of the clutch lever like it's hot, you need to use some finesse. Bad clutch control will make the engine accidentally stall, or make the bike *wheelie*—you don't want either.

So here's the trick: don't twist the throttle, you are going to let all this happen while the engine is just ticking over on its own. You're now going to gradually release the clutch lever with your fingers, all the while listening to the engine note. When you hear the engine note change, that's called

Cycle Babble

When a motorcycle is ridden aggressively enough to lift the front wheel off the ground, it's called a **wheelie**.

the biting point. It means something is finally happening; motorcycle movement is next. A good practice technique is to pull the clutch lever straight back in and then find the biting point all over again. If you can find the biting point easily, then you're getting really good at this, so pat yourself on the back—with your right hand.

You want to get going? Okay, sorry, so now you're at the biting point, you need to give the bike a bit more gas by twisting the throttle toward you. The problem is that as a novice it's really easy to be clumsy and use too much gas, or to let go of the clutch too quickly, have the bike lunge forward, and then accidentally twist the throttle wide open—while you try to hold on to a runaway bike.

So position your hand carefully. You have to hold the throttle with your right hand. If you hold it ready to twist it and give it loads of gas, you'll notice it positions the wrist on your right hand very high. So we're going to intentionally position your wrist low. It's harder to give it loads of gas, but that's what we're after, at least until you're used to taking off.

Now feed the clutch out to the biting point one more time, and this time look up, as you'll need to watch where you're going. Listen to the engine and continue feeding the clutch out (what you're doing now is called *slipping the clutch*). If the engine noise drops, then twist the throttle carefully, just enough to get the engine humming again. Continue feeding out the clutch and you'll find yourself moving. At this point many novices think all the hard work is done, and let the clutch straight out in a millisecond. Don't, you'll stall the engine; you need to keep slipping the clutch. On a little bike you might need to gradually feed out that clutch for the first 20 or 30 feet; on a big bike you might need to slip it for 60 feet for an impressively smooth takeoff.

Don't actually start this practice until you've read at least the next section, how to stop!

Cycle Babble

Slipping the clutch is the term used to describe the slow release of the clutch lever on a bike, essential for a smooth takeoff. Unlike a car, most motorcycles have multiple clutch plates running in oil, preventing them from overheating or burning.

Although the biting point varies slightly from bike to bike, depending on such factors as clutch wear and adjustment, it falls near the middle of a clutch lever's travel on a properly functioning bike.

Motorcycology _____

All motorcycles now sold in the United States use a standard shifting pattern, described as one-down, four-up (they can be three-up, four-up, or five-up, depending on the number of gears). This means that you push the lever down to engage first gear and up to engage the remaining gears, with neutral found between first and second gears. This may vary on classic American and European motorcycles.

Stopping What You've Started

I've noticed one common mistake people tend to make when they teach others how to ride: they show their students how to start without showing them how to stop. You'll see these people running around parking lots, chasing their students, shrieking, "Pull in the clutch! Pull in the clutch!" It's easy to forget that stopping is as important as starting, and for the beginner, it can be nearly as difficult a skill to master.

For the first few times, keep it as simple as possible and pretend you're on a bicycle. Just pull in both handlebar levers smoothly and put both feet down. In fact, for the first half hour I would strongly recommend that you do nothing more than take off and stop this way, again and again until it's second nature.

When you've got that down, then you'll want to come to a complete stop using all of the controls. You'll need to operate your hands and your feet all at the same time. In one motion, you pull in the clutch lever with your left hand and squeeze the front brake lever with your right, while shifting down to first gear with your left foot and pressing down on the rear brake pedal with your right. Remember, just before you come to a stop, lower your left foot to the floor to take the weight of the bike.

Motorcycology _____

As silly as it is, the myth that you'll flip and go over the handlebars if you use the front brake persists among certain groups of motorcyclists (usually the same folks who don't wear helmets). The front brake provides three quarters of your stopping power and should be considered your primary brake. Some bikes even have linked brake systems to assist front brake application.

Using the brakes on a bike is much more challenging than using the brakes on a car. For starters, you'll have to use both your right hand and your right foot to brake, rather than just using your right foot as in a car. Plus, riding a two-wheeled vehicle introduces all kinds of weird chassis dynamics into the situation. I'll discuss these dynamics at greater length in Chapter 12.

Your front brake is the most important of the two brakes. An average motorcycle relies on the front brake for 70 to 80 percent of its stopping power. Unfortunately, as most new riders have been driving cars for many years before they learn to ride a bike, they're in the habit of braking only with their foot, a habit that must be changed to stop a bike safely.

Cycle Babble

There are two basic types of motorcycle crashes: **low-siding,** when you slide down, falling toward the inside of the corner, and **high-siding,** which happens when you start to slide in one direction and then as your tires regain their grip, you flip over in the opposite direction.

You don't want to hit either of the brakes hard, or you'll lock up your tires and skid, especially the rear tire, which locks up more easily than the front tire. According to the California Highway Patrol, a rider locking up his or her rear brake is a factor in the majority of crashes. If your rear tire starts to skid, there's a good chance you'll either *low-side* or *high-side.* When you high-side, you cause it by inadvertently releasing the brake while skidding, thereby allowing the rear tire to regain traction and jerking the motorcycle in the opposite direction.

Braking Practice

To know how to brake effectively on your motorcycle, you need to get your head around weight distribution.

When you're riding along normally on your motorcycle, you've got pretty even weight distribution between the two wheels. In fact, most bike manufacturers try to design a 50/50 (or close to) weight distribution into their machines.

When you accelerate very hard, the weight distribution is thrown off center to the back of the bike, making the front-end light. If you watch drag racing you can see it happen; it's also what makes a bike wheelie.

The flip side is that when you brake hard, a lot of the weight is thrown forward, onto the front wheel and tire. If there's a lot of weight pressing down on the front tire, it means the back tire's barely carrying any load. And if it's not got much weight on it, then it doesn't have much grip.

This is why under heavy braking you cannot rely on your back brake to stop you. It's far too likely to slide considering all of the weight (and therefore grip) is on the front one. I hope you now understand why your front brake is your best friend when you need to shave off some speed.

Now you can probably also understand why motorcycle manufacturers put the big brakes up front and the itty-bitty little ones in the back.

Practically, it comes down to this: good braking technique requires you to start by squeezing the front brake lever (never, ever grab), then follow with a little less rear brake as you continue squeezing the front one. Practice this, a lot. If you ever feel a tire start to slide, then release that brake and re-apply.

It's a lot to take in, which is why it's smarter to practice it before it's a real emergency. The plan is that when it finally happens for real, you'll be confident and relaxed as you deal with it.

Parking the Bike

Once your bike is stopped, turn the engine off (use the key, that way you won't forget the kill switch was left in the off position), extend the kickstand to the down position, and then gently lean the bike to the left until it rests securely on the stand. If your bike has one, it's a good idea to park the bike on its centerstand if the ground is fairly level. A centerstand provides a more secure perch than the kickstand.

If you've ever watched someone struggle to put a bike on its centerstand, you've probably watched him or her doing it wrong. Just like taking them off, there's a trick to putting most bikes on their centerstands:

1. First, get off the bike on the left-hand side, keeping a hold on the front brake, and leaning the bike slightly onto your leg.

2. Take your right foot and, using the tang again, lower the centerstand until you feel both of its feet resting securely on the ground.

3. Increase the pressure through the ball of your right foot, so that the machine rests perfectly upright on the feet of the centerstand.

4. Next, move one hand down and grasp the motorcycle frame under the rider's portion of the saddle (this gives you more leverage).

5. Position the ball of your foot on the centerstand tang, and keep your heel up in the air, so that you don't waste any of the energy coming down from your leg. Then, in one final movement, put all of your weight down through your leg onto your foot and lift upward with your right hand. The bike will make the backward movement all on its own.

Some bikes require more strength than others to lift onto their centerstands, but if you practice and do it right, you should be able to make it look easy, as you raise any bike up onto the centerstand by yourself.

Make certain that the ball of your foot is firmly planted on the centerstand tang before you lift the bike up on its centerstand.

(Photo courtesy of Simon Green)

Shifting Gears

As with any manual transmission, you'll need to shift your motorcycle's gears as engine speeds increase and decrease. Shifting up allows you to ride faster, and shifting down allows you to ride slower.

You shift up when your rpms increase to a certain point: upshift too late, and you'll rev your engine excessively; upshift too early, and you'll lug your engine (lugging refers to the chugging sound an engine makes when it is in danger of stalling). The idea is to keep the engine in its powerband (the rpm range in which the engine happily generates most of its power).

You want to keep the engine in its powerband for safety reasons as well as mechanical and performance reasons. Technically, when an engine is in its powerband, it is operating at its peak efficiency, which is good for the mechanical components in the engine and allows the motorcycle to accelerate quickly. If the engine is not in its powerband because it is running at too many rpms, it causes excessive wear on its mechanical parts; if it is not in the powerband because the revs are too low, it can cause detonation in the cylinders (tiny, uncontrolled explosions that can damage components), buildup of unburned hydrocarbons, and lack of power.

It's the lack of power that poses a safety problem. In the real world, you will regularly encounter situations in which you'll need to accelerate quickly to avoid an accident. If you don't have the engine in its powerband, you'll need to waste precious split seconds downshifting, and a split second can mean the difference between a near miss and a tragic accident.

To shift up, roll off the throttle at the same time that you squeeze in the clutch lever. When the throttle is fully closed and the clutch lever is in, move the shift lever up with your toe in a firm, smooth movement until the lever stops. Don't worry, the gearbox can only move up one gear at a time; you're not going to accidentally go up too far.

You're more likely to cause a problem by not changing up firmly: you might not get it into the next gear. This is called finding a *false neutral* and can be potentially danger-ous (because you're free-wheeling). When you have engaged the next gear (you can hear this happen and feel it with your foot), ease the clutch lever back out and slowly roll the throttle back up to speed. You change up through the gears one at a time as you feel necessary while speeding up.

When you start to slow down, you'll need to downshift. You need to do this with the same finesse as you upshift because, by downshifting when the engine is revving too high, you can lock up your rear tire just as if you had applied too much brake, caus-ing you to lose control and crash. So the key here is to change down one gear at a time, and only when the engine is running at slower rpms.

Cycle Babble

The transmission's inabil-ity to engage gears is called finding a **false neutral**, because although the transmis-sion is not in neutral, it behaves as though it is.

To downshift, roll off the throttle and squeeze the clutch. Firmly press down on the shift lever, and then apply a small amount of throttle as you ease out the clutch lever. When coming to a complete stop, you may shift all the way down to neutral without releasing the clutch, but again, you'll want to do this gradually. Many motorcycle transmissions can be damaged by shifting to a lower gear at too high a speed, even if the clutch lever is pulled in.

The easiest way to remember the direction in which to change your gears is this: change up to speed up, go down to slow down.

Motorcycology _____

You can slow your progress by carefully downshifting, a process that causes *engine braking*. To do this, you shift down one gear at a time, releasing the clutch after each downshift. But be careful not to do this too aggressively, or you can lock up the rear wheel and lose control. This is an especially useful technique when navigating mountain roads, helping you keep your brakes cooler so they remain near their peak efficiency.

Throttle Control

When I get into more advanced riding techniques in Chapter 12, I'll discuss things such as chassis dynamics and throttle control in more detail, but even when you're first starting out in a deserted parking lot, smooth use of the throttle can make the difference between successfully learning to ride and making a trip to the emergency room.

Depending on the drive system used (shaft versus belt or chain—see Chapter 5), motorcycles react differently to throttle input. The rear ends of shaft-driven bikes tend to move up when the throttle is applied, while chain-driven bikes tend to squat down a bit under acceleration. Either way, you're going to encounter some moving around back there when you ride. Jerky use of the throttle exacerbates whatever tendency a bike has to move around under acceleration, while smooth throttle use minimizes these effects.

And the more power a bike has, the more the rear end tends to jerk around under acceleration. That is one of the main reasons why smaller, less powerful bikes are easier to learn to ride—they jerk around less when you apply the throttle.

But even a smaller bike is going to have more than enough power to get you into serious trouble if you get ham-fisted with the throttle, especially when you consider that even a small bike has enough acceleration to leave a super-car sitting at a green stop light. Make certain you can accelerate and decelerate smoothly before venturing into traffic.

Taking Turns

As I mentioned earlier, you countersteer a bike, a process you'll just have to practice and learn. But turning a bike involves more than just countersteering. Because motorcyclists are less visible to other motorists while riding a bike, and because our potential for injury in an accident is so much greater, we need to take extra care when changing directions or changing lanes.

The first thing to remember is to reduce your speed before turning. Motorcycles can corner incredibly quickly, but our balance can be upset by many more things than a car driver has to contend with. Also, overly hard and poorly coordinated braking can upset a motorcycle's chassis more than a car's, causing all sorts of strange dynamics. These antics can be especially dangerous while leaning over in a corner, so brake and reduce your speed before entering a curve in the road.

Before turning or changing lanes, you should check your mirrors and make a sideways check into your *blind spot*, to make sure the lane you want to occupy is clear. Never rely just on your mirrors, which on most bikes give you a better view of your elbows and shoulders than they do of the traffic behind you.

On the other hand, you shouldn't look completely over your shoulder because many riders inadvertently turn their handlebars as they turn their head, changing their bike's course. Also, an over-the-shoulder observation takes too much of your attention away from the traffic in front of you. There is a fine line between looking too long behind you and insufficiently checking to make certain your lane

Cycle Babble

Mirrors on a motorcycle never show the whole road behind and to the side of you. The area not covered by your mirror is known as your **blind spot**. The only way to check it is with a sideward glance.

is clear, but you will have to straddle that line every time you ride. Making certain a lane is clear every time you change lanes is a vital way to avoid having an accident.

When you are certain the coast is clear and are ready to turn, apply your turn signal well in advance to let other drivers know what you intend to do. Then lean the motorcycle into the turn by applying slight pressure to the inside of the handlebar in the direction you want to turn. As I discussed earlier, this causes the motorcycle to lean in the direction you want to turn. The faster you are moving, the more you'll have to lean the motorcycle to negotiate the turn. At normal highway speeds, you should lean with the bike. When negotiating tight turns that require you to ride more slowly, just lean the motorcycle while you remain in an upright position.

Once you have settled into a turn (I'll discuss the lines you follow through a corner in Chapter 12), roll on the throttle to maintain a steady speed or accelerate slightly. This helps keep the bike stable through the turn. Rapid acceleration or deceleration in a corner can cause you to lose control of the bike.

Taking the Test

When you have mastered these basic skills and feel confident in your ability, take your test and get your motorcycle endorsement as soon as possible. This will allow you more freedom as a motorcyclist, as well as save you from potential legal hassles. Getting a license also lowers your odds of getting hurt on your bike. To find out what is required for you to obtain your motorcycle endorsement, contact your local Department of Motor Vehicles.

The Least You Need to Know

- Countersteering is the only way to turn a motorcycle traveling at speeds higher than about 10 to 15 mph.

- Before going out into traffic, find a deserted parking lot or some other place you can practice the basic skills of riding.

- The front brake provides 70 to 80 percent of a motorcycle's stopping power—use it.

- Practice being able to stop as quickly as possible, without locking up the tire. Most accidents involve locking the rear tire under emergency braking.

- Smoothness is the key to successful throttle and brake use.

- Always look to make certain a lane is clear before turning or changing lanes—don't trust your mirror.

Chapter 12

Rules of the Road

In This Chapter

- ◆ The importance of awareness and visibility in motorcycle survival
- ◆ Avoiding other drivers' blind spots
- ◆ Why trucks and motorcycles don't mix
- ◆ Using other traffic to your advantage
- ◆ Creating a safety zone

You've practiced riding your bike until the procedures discussed in Chapter 11 are instinctive. Now that you have the hang of riding and have received your motorcycle endorsement, you're ready to venture out on public roads. You're about to move up to a higher level of fun, but you're also about to move up to a higher level of risk.

The key to surviving on your motorcycle is awareness. Not only do you need to be aware of what you are doing and what others are up to, you also have to try to make all of those other drivers aware of you. Much of it boils down to visibility. By being aware and making yourself visible, you are trying to accomplish two things:

- ◆ You are trying to avoid potentially dangerous situations. The best way to survive an accident is to not get into one in the first place.

◆ You are trying to give yourself time to react to an unexpected situation as quickly as possible. Being aware shortens your reaction time in an emergency, dramatically increasing your chances of avoiding an accident.

In this chapter, I show you different strategies to help you be more aware of what's going on around you, and how to make yourself more visible to others. I also show you how to avoid potentially dangerous situations and ways to use other vehicles to your advantage.

Driving in the U.S.A.

When riding a motorcycle, the safest attitude to adopt is to view every driver as unfit to be behind the wheel of a motor vehicle. Do this, and you'll be prepared for anything that might happen on the road.

Always treat other drivers like they are an overenthusiastic extra from the *Mad Max* movies. Many of them are too busy to notice something as small as a motorcycle. The number-one thing car drivers who hit motorcyclists tell police officers is, "I didn't see the motorcycle."

Unfortunately, you can't control other drivers' habits. But you can control your own.

Be Aware

Always be conscious of what's going on around you. You need to focus on what's ahead of you because that is the direction in which a dangerous situation will most likely arise. But you also need to be aware of what's going on in your periphery and what's going on behind you.

In a study published at the University of Southern California (the Hurt Report, 1981), researchers studied 900 motorcycle accidents and identified the directions from which cars most often struck motorcyclists in collisions at intersections. According to the study, 77 percent of the collisions occurred from the front of the motorcycle, with nearly half (43.4 percent) occurring from the rider's front and left.

If the region around a motorcyclist were illustrated as the face of a clock, the area a rider needs to most focus on is the area from 10 o'clock to 2 o'clock, especially watching the area between 11 and 1.

But just because a scant 5.5 percent of accidents occur in a motorcyclist's 5- to 7-o'clock range doesn't mean you can ignore that area. Percentages mean nothing if another driver creams you from the rear.

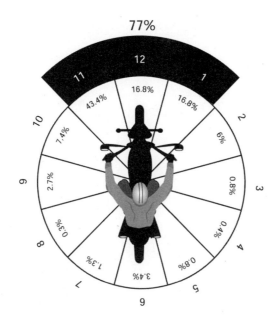

77%

12

11   1

16.8%

43.4%   16.8%

10   2

7.4%   6%

9   3

2.7%   0.8%

8   0.3%   0.4%   4

1.3%   0.8%

7   3.4%   5

6

This diagram shows the direction in which most motorcycle crashes occur. As you can see, 77 percent of a motorcyclist's danger comes from the front of a motor- cycle, and 43.4 percent comes from the front/left.

Active Scanning

To be aware while you are riding, you need to constantly provide your brain with input. Because your surroundings are always changing while you ride, you need to continuously update the information you transmit to your brain.

Because your eyes are your primary brain-input devices, you acquire the vast major- ity of the information you need to survive by seeing. But surviving on a motorcycle requires a very active form of seeing. You need to actively scan your surroundings while you ride.

While keeping the area in front of you foremost in your mind, you need to constantly scan all other areas around you for possible danger. Don't let your eyes fix on any one object for more than a fraction of a second. Scan all aspects of your surroundings, and don't just focus on other traffic. Watch the condition of the road surface. Stay alert for potholes, loose gravel, or piles of wet leaves, which can be as slippery as ice. Watch for traffic entering the road, especially at intersections. Remember that drive- ways, parking lots, and crossings are small intersections, too.

And watch for animals or pedestrians. If you hit a pedestrian or an animal on your motorcycle, you're both in trouble.

Make certain to include the rearview mirror in your scanning, but also turn your head slightly to check your blind spots, especially when turning, changing lanes, or stopping. Remember not to turn your head any farther than you have to in order to make certain your lane is clear, so that you don't steer off course or lose focus on the action in front of you.

Motorcycology

A good way to become aware of potentially dangerous situations when you ride is to play the "What If?" game. While you ride and scan your surroundings, think about those elements that could quickly turn dangerous. Imagine what would happen if a piece of the sheet metal on the flat-bed truck up ahead came loose and flew off. What would you do? Do you have enough space to maneuver out of the way in a hurry? And what if the driver of that slow-moving car in the oncoming lane suddenly decided to make a left turn into a driveway right in front of you? Are you prepared? Imagining such situations is good preparation because, sooner or later, they will happen.

To aid the scanning process, you can develop some techniques for using your eyes that help you constantly monitor the most dangerous area in front of you but also let you scan your entire surroundings:

◆ Focus on your intended path. Because you are moving rapidly through your surroundings, you need to concentrate on an area about 12 to 14 seconds ahead of your bike—that will give you enough time to react to an emergency situation.

◆ Keep your eyes up because that will aim your vision ahead, where the greatest danger resides.

◆ Move your eyes around, forcing them to move frequently and not become fixed on any one thing. This will widen your field of perception.

You need to constantly scan your surroundings for potentially dangerous situations. That car in the oncoming lane making a left turn in front of you is most likely to get you in this scenario, but any of the other elements in this picture could end your motorcycling career, too—from that woman on the sidewalk to that oil spot in the lane ahead of you.

◆ Learn to recognize potentially dangerous situations. A vague movement out of the corner of your eye may be a deer preparing to leap in front of your bike or a car backing out of a hidden driveway. That shadow on the road ahead may be oil, fresh tar, or some other slippery surface that could cause you to lose traction and crash.

◆ Constantly monitor your rearview mirrors. The region in front of your bike is the area you should primarily concern yourself with, but you constantly need to be aware of your entire surroundings, especially the area behind you.

Make awareness a required condition for riding a motorcycle; like your helmet, don't leave home without it. This is the surest way to have a long, healthy motorcycling career. As you get into the habit of being aware, you'll notice that your ability to process information will speed up, and before you know it you'll also find your automobile-driving skills have improved.

Avoiding Blind Spots

When car drivers say they didn't see a motorcyclist, they are probably telling the truth. Motorcycles are much smaller than other vehicles and are harder to see. Often other drivers don't see a bike simply because they don't expect to see a bike. Or the bike was hidden in the driver's blind spot.

 Motorcycology _____

One thing to keep in mind when scanning your surroundings and looking ahead is that your motorcycle goes where your eyes go. This is called *target fixation*. If you spot an object or some debris on the road, *don't look at it*. If you look at it, you will hit it because your bike will follow your eyes. Once you've detected something you want to avoid, look at where you want to go instead of at that object. A good way to practice this is to identify a spot on a road and make a conscious effort to avoid it.

To avoid riding in other drivers' blind spots, you need to know where those blind spots are. There's a simple way to figure this out. While you are following a car, take in look in their mirror. If you can see a pair of eyes in it, then they'll be able to see you. If all you can see is an ear, or the top of the driver's head, then you may as well be invisible to that driver.

Jockeying for Position: Lane Positioning

You need to monitor the road ahead for debris that can cause you to lose traction and crash. You especially need to watch for oncoming traffic turning left in front of you—the number-one hazard a motorcyclist will encounter at an intersection. You can count on at least one car making a left turn in front of you every single time you ride your bike in a congested area. I'll discuss this scenario more specifically in the next chapter, but for now, the important thing for you to understand is that you need to be aware of other vehicles so that you can react as quickly as possible to any situation.

Your mind needs to be up there, ahead of the bike, processing every small bit of information available. The faster you ride, the farther ahead you'll need to look. You can maximize your forward visibility by properly positioning yourself in your lane of traffic.

Keep Your Forward View Clear

Always place your bike in a position that gives you the best view of what is ahead of you. You can see best when there is no traffic in front of you, blocking your view. If at all possible, you should choose a lane in which there are no cars in front of you. If traffic is too heavy and no clear lanes are available, try to stay to the left of your chosen lane so that you have a strong dominant road position and you can see past the vehicles in front.

Avoid riding in the center of the lane, down the *oil line*, because that's usually the most slippery part of the road. Car engines, transmissions, and radiators are located between the car's wheels, and most of the slippery goop that cars drip on the highway comes from these parts and lands splat in the center of the lane. Your best traction, and your best view of the road ahead, is from the tire tracks in a lane, so ride there.

Cycle Babble _____

The **oil line** is a dark-colored area running down the very center of almost every lane of every road in the world. Any older car that leaks oil will drip this slippery stuff onto the center of their lane as they drive. Over the years it can build up considerably, becoming a slippery danger for anyone riding along it, especially when the road is wet.

Make certain that you don't follow any vehicle too closely. Stay back far enough that you can see any debris, such as a rock or a chunk of a tire, far enough in advance and can avoid it.

 Motorcycle Moments _____

Following cars too closely is the surest way to end up hitting something. One day while riding to work on my bike, I came up behind a truck traveling slower than the speed limit. As the road was empty, I moved to overtake, but unfortunately the truck was braking. The truck wasn't in great working order and had a broken brake light switch, so it had no brake lights to warn me, and I hit the back of it. The truck left the scene of the accident and the police became involved. It would have been a lot easier if I had stayed back a good distance. Once you're hurt it doesn't really matter who is right or wrong.

Tricks and Trucks

The worst position you can place your motorcycle in is behind a truck. Trucks (and large vans, sport-utility vehicles, and buses) completely block your forward vision and cause a variety of other problems as well. Because of their poor aerodynamics, trucks disrupt the air in ways that mess with your bike. The turbulent air coming off the back of a truck can move your motorcycle all over the road. Not only do trucks leave a rough wake in the air behind them, but they also leave a lot of debris. Trucks are usually filled with stuff, which often gets blown out of the back or leaks out on the road. Many of you have probably had to replace a windshield on a car because a stone flew out of a truck and hit your car. Imagine what that stone could do to your face without a helmet on to protect it.

Other things fall out of trucks besides rocks. Many trucks haul petroleum products or other chemicals. This can be nasty if it gets on you or your bike. I've been sprayed with stuff that has ruined all of my expensive bike gear. Trucks and motorcycles do not mix. As a general rule, you should just stay away from trucks entirely.

Because of the turbulent air surrounding a truck, passing one is a dangerous and difficult procedure, but there will be times, especially on multilane highways, when passing a truck will be your safest course of action. The worst thing you can do when passing a truck is to tense up and try to fight the turbulent air. Instead relax, learn what to expect, and let the turbulence work for you.

When you pass through the initial turbulent air coming off the back of the truck, a steady stream of air will either try to pull you toward the truck or push you away from it. This depends on the direction of the wind. If the wind is coming from the side of the truck opposite your motorcycle, it will create a vacuum alongside the truck, pulling you toward it. If the wind is from your side of the truck, it will bounce off the truck and blow you away from the truck.

Just relax and lean the bike toward the truck if the wind is trying to push you away, or lean the bike away from the truck if a vacuum is trying to pull you toward the truck. You want to do this smoothly, leaning your bike just enough to make it go straight down the road. As you get toward the front of the truck, you will encounter a blast of wind, perhaps the most intense turbulence of the entire passing experience. You'll need to lean into this wind to keep going straight as you pass in front of the truck. The quicker you perform your overtaking maneuver, the easier it is, so don't be afraid to use your bike's power.

Use Other Traffic as Protection

After you become familiar with traffic patterns and get into the habit of automatically positioning your bike in the area that affords you the best visibility, you can begin to use other traffic as a shield. On multilane highways, you can position yourself so that other drivers going in your direction block you from being struck by left-turning drivers in the oncoming lane. This is a skill that requires you to instantly read and assess a situation, and no two situations will be exactly the same. But if you master it, you will be able to move through crowded streets much more safely.

Doing this effectively sometimes requires you to ride a bit aggressively to keep up with traffic. Sometimes riding a bit aggressively can be a good defensive strategy. Some studies indicate that riders who go just a bit faster than traffic have statistically better odds of avoiding an accident than motorcyclists who ride at the same speed as other drivers or ride slower than traffic. My own experience backs up these studies. By moving slightly faster than other vehicles, I seem to have less trouble with drivers menacing me from behind, allowing me to concentrate more on what's going on ahead of me.

This doesn't mean that if you go out and ride as fast as your motorcycle will go you will be safer than if you travel at the speed limit. The key words here are *slightly faster* than traffic. And if you ride beyond your ability, you are not doing yourself or anyone else any favors. If you are uncomfortable riding faster than traffic, you shouldn't do so.

Be Seen

Part of your job as a motorcyclist is to make yourself visible. It helps to wear brightly colored clothing and helmets, and to wear fluorescent vests or riding suits that incorporate reflective material. This will make you more visible, especially in low-light conditions.

Realistically, I'm aware that many of you are quite unlikely to wear a fluorescent vest. I had to wear one while instructing, but freely admit that I always took it off for my ride home. Thankfully there are other ways to be seen, ways that anybody should be happy to use. When you buy your bike helmet, pick a brightly colored one. No matter what bike you ride, your helmet is visible—it will even stick out above a touring bike's fairing, and a helmet is something you should automatically put on. I've known people who own brightly colored vests, then forget to wear them. It's much harder to forget to wear your helmet, so it may as well be visible.

Consider your other motorcycle gear, too. If you've bought a red bike, then go and buy a bike jacket with some bright red panels, on the shoulders or arms, this will help you to be spotted. You don't have to look like a dork to be visible!

Use the high beam on your headlight during the daytime, when you won't blind oncoming traffic. In some states, it may be legal to mount a modulator on your headlight so that it pulses during daylight hours. Some studies indicate that such devices may be effective.

Lane position is important enough to either help you be seen, or hurt you. Most car drivers will pull up to a stop sign and take a lightning-quick glance where they expect to see a car, then move on. If you're riding in a good dominant position within your lane, just to the left of the oil line, then chances are they'll spot you. If you're riding your bike to the right of your lane, bouncing through the potholes, well, you probably won't get noticed; it's simply not where people look.

Another problem with riding your bike over to the right of your lane is that you'll you have less physical presence, subconsciously encouraging cars to overtake you, usually not very safely. Don't be a timid mouse on your bike, ride in a good strong position within your lane. You've got rights, too!

Steer Clear _____

Never trust the turn signals of other vehicles. Often other drivers will drive down the road for miles with their turn signals flashing for no good reason, but usually they just turn whenever the mood strikes them, with no warning whatsoever.

Always keep in your mind that when viewed from dead in front or directly behind, you are roughly a third or a quarter of the width of a car or truck. It's your responsibility to still be seen.

Signaling your intention to turn or change lanes early will give other drivers time to notice you and prepare for you to move. Once you've determined that the lane you want to enter is clear, activate your turn signal and check your mirrors to see if the vehicles behind you slow down to let you turn. Sometimes I've felt it necessary to accentuate my turn signal with a hand signal, just to get the attention of the dodgy driver behind me. Unfortunately, most drivers don't have a clue what hand signals mean, but at least it helps to alert them that I'm there.

If the driver in the car is still coming at you full speed after you've signaled, you may want to speed up and wait until the next turn. Always remember to cancel your turn signal, especially in a situation like this. Never leave your turn signal blinking away; it's very common for motorcyclists to do this (as our signals usually don't self-cancel). Unfortunately, you'll make the car drivers think you are turning, so they'll pull straight out in front of you.

Another trick to get the attention of other drivers is to tap your brake pedal (or lever) just enough to activate your brake light. Sometimes the flashing of your brake light can be enough to wake car drivers from whatever stupor they are in. And use your horn if you have to, but don't rely on it. The horns on most motorcycles are often quieter than squeaking polystyrene.

Even if you think you have a car driver's attention, don't assume that you do. You may think you've made eye contact with other drivers, but maybe they still don't notice you. Do what you can to make yourself more visible, but always act as if you are invisible.

The Three R's: Riding, Reading, and Reacting

Learn to read traffic while you are riding your motorcycle. After a while, certain clues will alert you to potentially dangerous situations. For example, when you are riding down a street lined with parked cars, if there are kids playing on the sidewalk you should watch for kids or dogs darting out from between cars. Look for people getting out of parked cars and opening their door in front of you. Even worse, a rushed driver could pull their car away from its parking spot and into your lane.

You can almost count on at least one driver doing something stupid in certain situations. For example, when you pull up in a lane alongside a line of cars stuck behind someone making a left turn, expect at least one of them to pull into your lane, right in front of you, to get around the turning vehicle. When you see this situation, slow down to give yourself time to react, move over to the far-right side of your lane to give yourself room to escape, and get ready, because it's going to happen.

Identify Hazards

To read potentially dangerous situations, you need to learn to identify the types of hazards you are most likely to encounter. These hazards can be divided into three main groups:

- ◆ **Cars, trucks, and other vehicles.** Other traffic has the most potential to do you bodily harm while you're riding a bike, and every driver on the road has the potential to be your executioner. Never trust any of them, but learn to identify those most likely to try to take you out.

- ◆ **Pedestrians and animals.** Although they are slower moving than vehicles, pedestrians (especially kids) and animals are more unpredictable because they can change direction much more quickly, and their movements don't follow the usual patterns of traffic.

- ◆ **Stationary objects.** These can be anything from a piece of junk on the road to potholes, signposts, trees, or guardrails. These won't cut you off like other vehicles or dart in front of you like an animal, but they do limit where you can move to avoid a dangerous situation.

The most dangerous places to ride are intersections, partly because they often contain all of the hazards mentioned here. Any place where other traffic may cross your path poses a potentially dangerous situation.

> **Steer Clear**
>
> Watch out for the paint on the road, which can be quite slippery. This includes the bars marking the crosswalk, the directional arrows, and words such as "Stop Ahead" that are painted in the lane. Never stop on the paint, and make certain that you put your feet down on unpainted pavement when you stop.

Watch the Front Tires

Watching the front tires of a car will give you some clue about what that car will do next. The front tire of a car has to turn before the car turns. When I'm riding in heavy traffic, I constantly monitor the front tires of cars around me. Seeing the front tire turn will give you an extra split second to react in an emergency situation. So will watching drivers' heads. If they're planning on pulling away from a curb or changing lanes on a freeway, they'll most likely be turning their heads to look for oncoming traffic.

Watching the front tire can alert you to a left-turning driver about to cross your path. If someone in an oncoming lane slows down, be aware of what his front tire is doing and prepare to react accordingly. Even if you're not in an intersection, the person could be preparing to turn in front of you to enter a driveway or a parking lot, or even just to make an illegal U-turn. It can happen anywhere—and often does. Watch for people who appear to be pulling into a parking space and then do a U-turn right in front of you.

Learning to read traffic helps a great deal, but it doesn't make you invulnerable. You could become the world's foremost traffic-reading expert and still be taken by surprise. Always expect the unexpected. Look both ways, even when crossing a one-way street, because fools can come from anywhere, and the world is filled with fools.

The Safety Zone

When you are on a bike, your fenders are your own flesh and blood, and you don't want to challenge thousands of pounds of metal with them. Because of your vulnerability, you want to keep as much free space around your motorcycle as possible. I've already discussed not getting boxed in, not following traffic too closely, and trying to ride in lanes with no traffic in front of you. But there's more you can do to increase the safety zone around you and your bike.

When you're riding, always try to find a spot in traffic that provides you with the most room possible. Sometimes that will mean moving over into a safer lane. Always try to be in the lane that gives you the most free space to ride in.

How you change lanes can increase your margin of safety. Make certain that you don't change lanes while you are in another driver's blind spot. And make certain that a driver from the lane on the other side of the one you intend to occupy doesn't have the same intention. If the people right next to you have a hard time seeing you, imagine how hard it is for the person two lanes over.

Do whatever you have to in order to get out of a situation in which another motorist is following you too closely. Unfortunately, you'll have to rely on evasive actions, such as changing lanes or speeding up, to extricate yourself from this very dangerous situation.

Again, never follow other vehicles too closely. At the very least, give yourself two seconds of space between you and the car ahead of you. This will give you the minimum space you'll need to swerve, brake, or perform a combination of both actions if an emergency situation arises.

Poor road conditions will increase the space you'll need to have in order to stop. If there is oil, gravel, wet leaves, or any other debris on the road, that will increase your stopping distance, too. Factor the condition of the road into the equation, and allow extra space between you and the vehicle in front of you.

Motorcycology

Being prepared to brake at any time is essential on a motorcycle, though even being ready on your brakes can be problematic. If you accidentally rest your foot (even lightly) on your rear brake, you'll activate your brake light. The problem comes when you actually brake and the driver behind you gets no warning as your brake light was already on. Most people who rest their foot on their brake pedals never realize that it's the reason why they have so many near-miss situations.

Following too closely can get you killed even when doing something that seems relatively safe, such as pulling into a parking lot. The person in front of you may suddenly stop or slow way down as he or she enters the parking lot, leaving you stuck and unable to get out of the way of oncoming traffic.

Steer Clear

Many riders will operate their front brake with just one or two fingers. For most nonemergency situations this is fine. However, when you need to brake in a real emergency, using two fingers on the lever means that the other two fingers are behind the lever—which will get crushed during heavy braking. Those two stray fingers can also prevent the brake lever from being able to travel its full distance. For these reasons, develop the good habit of always braking with all four fingers.

You even need to be aware of your safety zone in the parking lot itself. Parking lots are especially dangerous places because people are looking for parking spaces and are not watching where they are going.

It's difficult to discuss all the dangerous situations you may encounter without sounding like an alarmist or giving you a negative view of the sport of motorcycling, but it's not as bad as it sounds. Practice the procedures I've outlined in this chapter, and soon they'll be as much a part of your routine as countersteering and shifting gears. You always need to remain conscious of these dangerous situations, because that is the best way to avoid them. As you practice and internalize these procedures, you'll become more at ease with your ability to cope with any situation that comes your way.

The Least You Need to Know

- Awareness is the key to surviving on a motorcycle. Always be aware of your surroundings, and actively scan your surroundings at all times.

- Do everything in your power to make yourself visible to other drivers, but never assume that they see you. Avoid riding in other drivers' blind spots.

- Stay as far away from trucks as possible.

- Use other traffic to shield you from left-turning drivers.

- Don't let yourself get boxed in by other traffic. Always leave yourself room to get out of a dangerous situation. Keep as much free space around you and your motorcycle as possible.

13

Street Survivors: Steering Through Sticky Situations

In This Chapter

- ◆ Riding safely through intersections
- ◆ Techniques for freeway riding
- ◆ Controlling your motorcycle around corners
- ◆ The importance of remaining calm

In Chapter 12, I stressed how important it is for you to constantly scan your surroundings so that you can identify potentially dangerous situations. Now it's time for you to learn more about those dangers and how to deal with them. In this chapter, I'm going to explain how to ride in specific situations.

The problem with discussing specific situations is that every situation differs. For every bit of advice I provide in this chapter, I can think of possible situations in which that advice doesn't apply. So keep in mind that the principles in this chapter are general templates. In the end, you have to rely on the information you gather through your own diligent observations to ultimately guide your actions.

Intersection Encounters

As I said in Chapter 12, the most dangerous situation you'll encounter on a bike is a driver turning left in front of you, and most often that happens in some sort of intersection. That makes intersections the most dangerous places to ride. You can do a lot to minimize that danger by following certain procedures when approaching and passing through an intersection.

When you ride through any intersection—that is, any area where traffic can possibly cross your lane of traffic, always consider the following:

◆ Slow down. This puts you in control of the situation. It gives you more time to scan the intersection for potential dangers. The earlier you can detect a dangerous situation, the quicker you can react to avoid it. Slowing by just 10 mph reduces your necessary stopping distance by almost half.

◆ Cover both your front-brake lever and your rear-brake pedal when riding through an intersection. This reduces your reaction time.

◆ Position your bike away from other cars. This gives you room to maneuver out of the way if an errant car jockey fails to see you and moves toward you.

◆ Watch the front tires of other vehicles. I discussed this in Chapter 12, but it's doubly important at an intersection. An oncoming vehicle with its tires turned toward your lane can pull in front of you nearly half a second quicker than can a vehicle with its wheels pointing straight ahead. In this situation, half a second is literally worth a lifetime.

◆ Make absolutely certain that an intersection is clear of other traffic before you proceed. Watch for drivers stopped in other lanes waiting to turn—they may not see you and may turn in front of you. Slow down enough to allow yourself room to stop.

Memorize the preceding rules, internalize them, and make them part of your riding technique. By doing this, you'll significantly reduce your chances of getting in an accident.

Types of Intersections

When riding, consider any area where something might cross your path an intersection. This includes the usual places, like crossings and where two roads meet, but it includes a lot of places you might not think of as intersections.

For example, turnouts are intersections. Turnouts are often located at scenic points, and people pulling into and out of them tend to pay more attention to the scenery than to traffic. This applies to any spot where people congregate alongside a road, like a beach, a bridge people fish off of, or a park-and-ride parking lot (parking lots along roads where commuters leave their cars and get on buses). Always slow down when passing such a place, and move away from the side of the road the turnout is located on, giving yourself more room to maneuver.

Steer Clear _____

In some ways, alleys are similar to intersections because you have to watch for traffic crossing your path in an alley. Alleys are filled with blind driveways, and people often back out their cars without looking. Even a diligent driver who looks before backing up might not be able to see you because of some obstruction, such as a fence or a dumpster. And kids and animals like to hang out in alleys, too. Slow down when you ride through an alley, and watch for kids, dogs, cats, and cars.

The most dangerous intersections are the intricate ones, where several roads converge at once. Traffic doesn't follow usual patterns at such intersections, and vehicles enter the road at unexpected angles. Often there are frontage roads (roads running parallel to main roads) merging at such intersections, too, further confusing everybody. When riding through these intersections, slow down even more than you normally do because you have more activity to monitor.

Moving Through Intersections

When passing through an intersection while you're following a vehicle that blocks your view, such as a bus, watch for left-turning vehicles that are unable to see you behind the bus. Again, leave plenty of space between you and the vehicle in front of you so that you have room to get out of the way. And position yourself in the part of the lane that allows you to see and be seen.

When you are following large vehicles in traffic, you might not be able to decide where to position your bike. If you can see oncoming vehicles clearly, it's best to ride on the far-right side of the lane, positioning yourself as far away as possible from a left-turning driver. But if you're following a bus or a truck, you may be better off riding in the far-left part of the lane, where you can best be seen, and where you can scan for possible left-turning drivers.

Stopping at an Intersection

When approaching an intersection where you need to stop, pay extra attention to the vehicles behind you. Be especially careful when stopping on a yellow light, in case the driver behind you thinks yellow means *put the accelerator to the floor and drive like crazy.*

Because of the danger of drivers rear-ending you at intersections, you need to scan for a possible escape route whenever you approach an intersection. Always position yourself toward one edge of the lane or the other, to provide the quickest escape route if you need one. Choose the side of the lane that gives you the most free space to maneuver out of the way, which will usually be the side of the lane farthest away from oncoming traffic.

When you stop behind a vehicle, don't pull up close behind it. If you do so, you'll block yourself in. You won't have room to move out of the way if the vehicle in front backs up or rolls back accidentally, and you won't have room to get around the vehicle in front if the vehicle behind you doesn't stop. Remember that even a slow-speed nudge will be enough to knock you and your bike over. Always leave enough room between you and the vehicle in front of you so that you can move around it in an emergency situation.

Leaving yourself enough room to maneuver is important any time you have to stop, whether or not you're at an intersection. The main advantage of a motorcycle is its nimble nature, so be ready to use this to your advantage to escape any situation that turns bad. Even on the freeway, expect trouble from behind and monitor the traffic behind you. If you see a vehicle behind you that's not stopping, look for a clear spot and rapidly accelerate toward it.

To do this, your bike will have to be ready to go. When you sit at an intersection, or anytime you have to stop when there is traffic around, keep your bike in first gear, with the clutch lever pulled in. That way, if you need to get out of someone's way in a hurry, you won't have to waste time putting the bike in gear.

When you stop at an intersection, look for the best traction for putting your feet down. Avoid putting your feet down on any damp, shiny, or dark spot. The spot may be oil, antifreeze, or diesel—the latter is one of the most slippery fluids you'll encounter.

Also be careful not to put your feet down on any painted lines or marks in an intersection. Painted spots will be slippery, and just a small slip of your foot when you are stopping can cause you to fall over. And remember, if you fall down because of something slippery on the road, there's a pretty good chance that whoever is following you will also hit the slippery stuff and possibly lose traction, too.

The safest part of the lane to put your foot down in is the tire track. As I said in Chapter 12, the slippery goop that drips off cars builds up in the center of the lane creating an oil line. When you put your foot down, place it at the edge of the tire track farthest away from this oil line.

Steer Clear _____

Some people consider the first part of a red light just an extension of the yellow. The only way to protect yourself from red-light runners is to slow down when you ride through an intersection. Always make certain the path is clear before entering an intersection, even if you have the right-of-way.

Leaving an Intersection

When leaving an intersection, the number-one thing to remember is to not proceed until you're absolutely certain that the path is clear.

When the light turns green, wait until things settle before entering the intersection. Most car drivers see green and go; years of riding has made me paranoid enough to flick my eyes each way searching for unwanted movement before I take off on my bike.

When starting through an intersection from a standing stop, it is especially important not to trust eye contact as a means of determining whether another driver has seen you. Even if other drivers do see you, they might not register your motorcycle as traffic.

Turning in Intersections

The same rules that apply to passing through an intersection apply to turning at an intersection. Make certain that all lanes are clear before making a turn.

Often other traffic will block your view at an intersection, especially if a turning lane is present. If you find your view blocked, slowly ease ahead until you can see past the offending vehicle. Remember, when you do this, your tire will enter traffic before your view clears, so be extra cautious. Lean forward and stretch your neck ahead as far as is comfortable, being careful to remain stable and in control of the bike, to see around the vehicle blocking your view. This will help make certain that you don't roll your bike out in front of an oncoming vehicle when you ease ahead to clear your view.

When making a turn at an intersection, be extra careful when trucks are present. Trucks with long trailers make wide turns, and they often need more than one lane to negotiate a turn in an intersection. If you pull up beside a truck, thinking the truck is going straight, and the truck turns in your direction, you could be trapped.

You may be able to power ahead and get out of the situation, but then you run the risk of being struck by an oncoming vehicle hidden from your view by the truck. If you're lucky, there will be a shoulder instead of a curb at the side of the road, allowing you space to get away from the trailer. Personally, I'd carefully take my bike onto the sidewalk (and risk a ticket) rather than risk an injury, but then again I wouldn't let myself get into that situation in the first place.

Your best course of action is to avoid squeezing between a truck and something else at all costs, even if it means not entering a turning lane and having to use a different route.

Drivers turning left in front of you are the number-one hazard you will encounter on a bike.

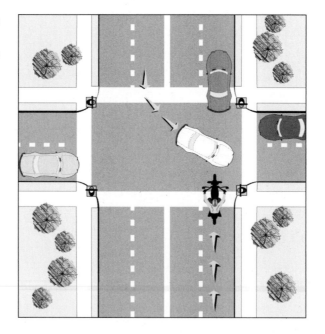

Avoiding Dangerous Intersections

Some intersections are deathtraps for motorcyclists. You will encounter intersections with electromagnetic stoplight sensors (which trigger a change in the traffic light by detecting large masses of metal over them) that might not be able to detect an object as small and light as your motorcycle. At such intersections, you can find yourself faced with the choice of running a red light or waiting until a car pulls up behind you, neither of which is an acceptable option.

Other intersections may have too many obstructions—such as signs, light posts, and buildings—for you to make certain all lanes are clear before you enter them.

If you know of an intersection like this, one that makes you uncomfortable, just avoid it. Even if you have to ride a few extra miles, if you can select a safer route, your chances of arriving are improved by avoiding dangerous intersections.

Motorcycology

If you stop at an intersection with an electromagnetic sensor, the placement of your motorcycle can determine whether the sensor will recognize your bike. Electromagnetic sensors are usually located under the pavement toward the end of a lane. You can often see them by looking for a cut in the pavement, usually square in shape, that extends from nearly one side of the lane to the other. The sensor itself is located beneath this cut, and if you stop your motorcycle directly over the part of the cut that runs parallel with your lane, you can trigger the light to change.

Steer Clear

Watch for cars trying to pass you when you are negotiating an on-ramp. This may seem insane, but some drivers actually do it. The combination of a slippery surface and a tight curve may limit your speed on an on-ramp, but that won't matter to some car jockeys. If a driver does try to pass you on an on-ramp, all you can do is move over and let the driver by.

The Lifesaver

We've talked a lot about how people can put you at risk by turning across your path at an intersection. There is another very common intersection danger, which we'll cover here in some more detail. It is the danger posed by people you haven't seen, while you are making your turn.

The Blind Spot

The first thing you need to understand is where your *blind spot* is located, and the easiest way to do this is to enlist the help of a friend or loved one.

Cycle Babble _____

The **blind spot** is an area located somewhere between the edge of your mirrors and the beginning of your peripheral (sideward) vision. It's a gap in your visibility that is big enough to easily hide a car.

You need to roll your bike out of the garage or storage shed, and take a seat on it. It's better to wear your helmet too, as we're going to be taking a look at your peripheral vision. Ask your friend to stand behind you and stay about a car length away. Position her in a location where you can easily see her in your mirror.

Now she needs to start slowly moving around your motorcycle, in a circle, while maintaining the same distance from you. You need to keep your main focus ahead of you, where it usually is while you're riding (no turning your head around). You'll notice that she soon disappears from your mirror but she doesn't immediately reappear in your peripheral vision.

She just walked right through your blind spot. Ask her to do it once more, only this time you need to stop her once she's in your blind spot. Now that she is standing in your blind spot, slowly turn your head until you can see her.

Once you can see her there, freeze your position. That's how far you need to turn your head in order to see your blind spot, no farther. Remember that, as you don't want to turn it any farther than necessary.

There is a risk to turning your head too far; actually there are a couple of risks. The first one is that you're spending a long time looking behind you when everything is still happening in front. The other risk has to do with how this glance affects your machine control.

Let's do another fun experiment. Put your arms out in front of you now, nice and straight as if they're holding your handlebars. You're now going to turn your head all the way around to look behind you, and as you do it, concentrate on what your arms just did. Do it a few times, and you'll start to notice that they move as you crane your neck. If you can't see it, get your friend to watch, or even watch your friend while they do it. Most people will move their hand about four or five inches while they look backwards.

If you're riding your bike at 40 mph and you turn around like that, inadvertently moving the steering four inches, you'll probably become a leather-encased bug on some Mack truck's windshield.

That's why after checking my mirror, I only look to my blind spot, rather than perform a full rearward observation. I call this blind-spot check the _lifesaver_, quite simply because that's exactly what it is.

Take note, it's also worth relaxing your elbows as you ride; you'll have much finer control over your motorcycle than you would with rigid outstretched arms.

Turning Left

Making a left-hand turn is more dangerous than making a right-hand turn, because you must cross the lane (or lanes) of oncoming traffic.

I've been making a lifesaver glance over my shoulder for as many years as I can remember. It doesn't upset my balance, it doesn't change the direction of my bike, and it takes just a split-second to do, but I've lost count of how many times I've seen something surprising while doing it.

> **Cycle Babble**
>
> The **lifesaver** is the observation you make just before committing yourself to making a left- or right-hand turn. It is the final check into your blind spot, which isn't otherwise covered by your mirrors.

I've had nut jobs in cars trying to pass me, or merge in (on the wrong side of the road) while I'm about to make a left-hand turn. I've seen emergency vehicles passing lines of traffic, and even other bikes racing past me while I'm signaling left. In every one of those situations, I would have turned my handlebars and hit those other vehicles if I hadn't done the lifesaver over my left shoulder first.

The idea is to check, have time to react, and then make your turn *if* the coast is clear. The point is to have reaction time. It's common, but useless, for people to look *as* they turn—all you will see is what you hit. To be effective, it needs to be lifesaver, pause, maneuver.

Turning Right

While turning right typically poses less danger than turning left (in any left-hand-drive country at least), there are still reasons to make a lifesaver. The perfect right-hand turn would involve checking your mirrors, using your turn signal, moving your bike over to the right side of your lane, and then slowing down, making your lifesaver over your right shoulder, then finally making the turn.

Moving to the right side of your lane will get you out of the way of the following cars before you start braking, it will make it very obvious to them that you're turning right, and finally it shouldn't leave room for anybody to pass you on the inside, in theory.

Using that logic, lifesavers before turning right won't show you anything. In practice I've still been surprised to see bicycles come flying up the inside. Considering the minimal amount of effort required to perform a lifesaver, it's something you should never skip. Make it a part of every turning maneuver.

Freeway Riding

Although it might not seem likely, limited-access multilane freeways are statistically much safer than city streets and highways with intersections. There are two reasons for this:

- ◆ Traffic moves in only one direction on freeways.

- ◆ Freeways remove your number-one hazard: vehicles in oncoming lanes turning left in front of you.

But riding on a freeway presents a new set of challenges. Traffic moves faster on freeways, meaning that things happen faster. You have to look even farther ahead on a freeway to give yourself more time to react to an emergency. The faster traffic moves, the farther ahead you need to look.

On a freeway, you have to be careful not to ride too fast. Motorcycles can cut through freeway traffic more quickly than cars, making it easier to speed on a bike. But riding much faster than traffic puts you at risk because, if you're riding too fast, you won't be able to react if a car moves into your lane.

And even though you don't have intersections on a freeway, you have on-ramps and off-ramps, both of which create challenges for a motorcyclist.

On-ramps are especially tricky on a bike. These often consist of tight turns, forcing you to lean hard to turn your motorcycle. This in itself wouldn't be that problematic, but on-ramps usually have extra-slippery surfaces, forcing you to negotiate the ramp more slowly than you would in a car. The cars, of course, won't slow down for you and will tailgate you or even try to pass you.

Having to negotiate the curve on an on-ramp is the first challenge. The second one is adjusting your speed once you have negotiated the curve so that you can enter traffic safely. This is where a motorcycle's capability to accelerate quickly comes into play.

As you round the curve of an on-ramp, monitor the traffic in the lane you will merge into and locate a safe space to enter that lane. Once you have finished negotiating the curve and the motorcycle is upright, accelerate toward the safe spot you've identified, adjusting your speed so that you can safely merge with traffic.

When passing an on-ramp where other traffic is merging onto the freeway, move over to a lane as far away from the on-ramp as possible. Drivers merging into your lane may not see your motorcycle and may mistake the space you're occupying as a free spot to enter traffic. And other drivers in your lane may be watching the merging traffic and may not see you. If they move over to let the merging traffic enter, they may hit you.

This is also a problem at off-ramps. If you are driving in the lane closest to the off-ramp, you risk getting cut off by a driver who doesn't see you and thinks he or she has a clear shot at the off-ramp. As with an on-ramp, your safest location is as far away from the ramp as possible.

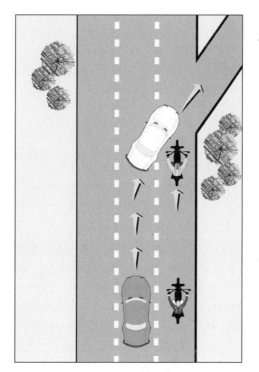

Watch for drivers who don't see you as they cut across traffic to get on an off-ramp.

Lane Positioning

You can do a lot to increase your safety on crowded multilane roads by always being conscious of your lane positioning. Always think of where your bike is in relation to the other vehicles on the road. Try not to ride in people's blind spots, and try not to ride beside vehicles. If you position yourself so that there are no people driving next to you, no one can make a sudden lane change and hit you.

It's especially important to keep a safe distance between your motorcycle and trucks. Remember, the larger the vehicle, the larger its blind spot. Sport-utility vehicles are especially bad. If you find yourself beside any vehicle, especially a truck, speed up, if you have room, until you are well in front of the vehicle. If you don't have room to speed up, you are probably following the vehicle in front of you too closely. If that is the case, you should slow down just a bit, until the vehicle in the lane beside you is clearly in your field of vision; then wait until there is adequate room ahead of you to pass.

Changing Lanes

Because traffic moves so quickly on a freeway, changing lanes requires extra caution on your part, especially on freeways with more than two lanes of traffic. On such multiple-lane freeways, not only do you need to make certain that the lane is clear before you enter it, but you also need to check to see if someone from another lane is moving into the free spot you have identified.

Steer Clear _____

Getting cut off by the vehicle behind you while you change lanes on a freeway illustrates the importance of avoiding tailgaters. When other vehicles follow you too closely, carefully get out of their way and let them pass. Remember to signal early and make definite moves so that the driver behind you is aware of what you are doing.

The speed of traffic also makes the vehicles behind you more of a threat when changing lanes on a freeway. You always need to let the vehicles behind you know what you intend to do. Once you have made certain that a lane is clear, slow down and use your turn signal early. Do everything possible to communicate your intentions to other drivers. Watch to make certain the car behind you is slowing down.

And remember not to trust that other drivers see you just because they slow down. Even if they see you slow down, they might not see your turn signal. Motorcycle turn signals are small and not very bright, so they can be hard for other drivers to see, especially in bright sunlight. Before you change lanes, make certain that the driver behind you isn't planning to change lanes, too.

As I said in Chapter 12, when you change lanes, don't do so in other drivers' blind spots. This is another situation in which the speed of your motorcycle comes in handy. You can use that speed to accelerate out of other drivers' blind spots, moving into a position where they can see you.

Always make sure you're riding in the correct gear for a given speed. To accelerate quickly, you need to keep your revs in the powerband. Remember, your motorcycle was designed to operate most efficiently at certain rpm; when you ride with your tachometer in the most efficient rev zone, you can instantly accelerate if you need to.

Make certain that the vehicle beside you doesn't attempt to change lanes at the same time you do.

Rain Grooves

Some roads have grooves cut into their surface to facilitate water runoff in a rainstorm. These *rain grooves* are especially common on freeways. They can cause your bike to feel unstable—a disconcerting experience, even for expert motorcyclists. But don't worry; even though your bike may feel like it is moving all over the place, it is a relatively harmless situation—that is, unless you panic.

When you hit rain grooves, the best thing to do is relax your grip on the bars and just ride it out. If you tense up and try to fight it, your bike will only move around more.

Cycle Babble

Rain grooves are channels cut into a road's surface to help water run off the road in a rainstorm. These can make your bike feel squirrelly when you ride over them, but if you relax and don't fight it, you'll be fine.

Splitting Lanes

In some American states and most European countries, it is legal for a motorcycle to ride between lanes of traffic. This is known as *splitting lanes* or *filtering*. Doing this when traffic is moving at normal speeds is, of course, a bad idea. When traffic is fast-moving, remain in your normal lane of traffic.

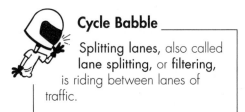

Cycle Babble

Splitting lanes, also called lane splitting, or filtering, is riding between lanes of traffic.

Lane splitting is not a task for a beginning rider. But for an experienced motorcyclist, splitting lanes when traffic is moving very slowly or is stopped can be as safe as or safer than just sitting there, if for no other reason than it gets you out of traffic more quickly and reduces the amount of time you're exposed to danger.

The ability to filter through traffic is actually one of the biggest advantages to being a motorcyclist. Personally, if I couldn't filter through city traffic I would stop riding a bike; it's really something you should learn to do well.

Some general rules help make lane splitting safer:

◆ Ride only about 10 or 15 mph faster than traffic is moving. If traffic is moving at 15 mph, ride no faster than 25 or 30 mph between lanes. If traffic is stopped, keep your speed under 15 mph. If you ride any faster, you won't have time to react if someone pulls out in front of you.

◆ If traffic slows, don't immediately hop between lanes and start lane splitting. Traffic may be slowing for just a moment and will speed up again. Make certain that traffic is slowing or stopping before lane splitting.

◆ Watch for other motorcyclists who might be lane splitting before pulling between the lanes. If traffic is stopping, odds are some other motorcyclist has the same idea that you do. Focus primarily on what's in front of you, but always be aware of what's behind you.

◆ Watch for people changing lanes. If you see an open spot in traffic, you can almost count on someone crossing from another lane to take that spot. It's best to try to keep a car on either side of you, which will block other vehicles from crossing your lane.

◆ If freeway traffic is stopped or moving very slowly, it's best to move over to the fastest (farthest left) lane before lane splitting. This decreases your odds of encountering merging traffic or drivers making sudden lane changes.

♦ When traffic stops, watch for people opening their car doors. It happens more often than you might think. Some drivers are mad at us for being able to move when they're stationary, so instead of buying a bike and joining us, it's been known for them to try and take us out with their car door. Nice, huh?

Riding in the Twisties

Although motorcycles are more maneuverable than cars, not all bikes can go around corners as quickly. Most motorcycles are capable of cornering quite rapidly if you ride them correctly—though as you learned earlier, certain types of bikes are built for higher-speed cornering, while some others are not. Hopefully you will have chosen the right type of bike for your riding style.

Steer Clear _____

Motorcycle tires are designed to operate within a certain temperature range; they need to heat up a bit before they can provide proper traction. Professional road racers use expensive tire-warmers before going out on the track. But even then they wait until they have heated up their tires before they get on the throttle. You probably won't require racing levels of adhesion from your tires, but applying too much throttle in a curve before your tires are warm is a quick way to slide off and crash.

Traction: A Sticky Matter

A variety of factors contribute to your bike's traction. The material your tire is made of plays a role. Softer, stickier rubber grips better than harder rubber. Tire temperature affects traction, too: the colder the tire, the harder the rubber. A tire that has been heated up through use has more gripping power than a cold tire. The shape and depth of your tread contribute to traction. The surface of the road also plays a role.

When cornering, the *contact patch* of your tire is crucial to traction. The contact patch is the part of the tire that actually touches the road. A big, wide sportbike tire will have a larger contact patch than a classic motorcycle with skinny tires.

The relatively small amount of rubber in the contact patch is the main reason motorcycle tires can't corner as effortlessly as cars. Plus, unlike cars, motorcycles lean when they turn. As your motorcycle leans,

Cycle Babble _____

The **contact patch** of your tire is the area of your tire that actually contacts the road while you ride.

the contact patch of its tires decreases, meaning that you have less traction available in a turn.

To further complicate matters, if you don't accelerate, decelerate, and brake *smoothly*, you'll upset the chassis, causing the motorcycle to move around. Such gyrations can cause the size of the tires' contact patches to vary, which affects traction and handling.

A final note on tire traction: brand-new tires have very little grip. After fitting a new front or rear tire to your motorcycle, you will need to scrub it in. This means riding a little more smoothly and carefully than normal for the first few miles, until the tire loses its new polished appearance.

Motorcycology

Smooth throttle control is one of the primary reasons for choosing a smaller, less powerful motorcycle for your first bike. The more power that is available when you twist the throttle, the harder it will be for you to develop smooth throttle control. Motorcycles that have abrupt throttle response, a characteristic of bikes with narrow powerbands, are more difficult to control; bikes with broader powerbands deliver smoother, more controllable power.

Gravity Is Your Friend

I've made taking a curve on a motorcycle sound like going on a ride at a carnival, and there are similarities. But on a bike, you're in control. By practicing proper cornering techniques, you can actually make all this commotion work for you instead of against you.

Get your braking done before you turn. Apply the brakes when the motorcycle is upright, before you lean over to turn. If you brake when you're leaning over, you're much more likely to slide off than you are if you brake when the motorcycle is upright. Remember, when you're leaning over, you already have less traction available.

Because of that lack of traction, you must use the throttle smoothly in a corner. Maintaining a steady engine speed keeps your bike settled in a curve, while jerky use of the throttle upsets your bike. The smoother you are with your throttle, the more control you have over your bike.

Don't accelerate or shift during a corner, because this will upset your chassis. Wait until you've finished the turn and your bike is once again upright to accelerate. As you develop your technique and become more proficient at taking curves, you will be able to apply power slightly earlier as you exit a corner. When you do this, you make the motorcycle's dynamics work for you: when you accelerate, you place more weight on the rear of the motorcycle, thus increasing your traction. As you become more familiar with your bike's reactions to throttle input, you can use that increased traction as you exit a corner.

Dangerous Debris

You always need to scan the surface of the road for debris, such as leaves, sand, fluids, and gravel buildup, but the situation in which these conditions will most often lead to a crash is when you encounter them in a curve. These materials tend to accumulate on the outside edge of a curve, so pay close attention to that part of the road when scanning a corner.

If there is debris on a curve, slow down to give yourself time to maneuver around the debris. If you are unable to avoid it, don't panic and hit the brakes; that will make you more likely to lose traction and crash than if you maintain a steady speed through the corner. If you've slowed down to a safe speed before entering the corner, you should be all right.

> **Steer Clear**
>
> Approach areas where shade covers the road with extra caution, especially in the morning, when shaded areas can be slippery from dew or frost. You may not be able to see debris like sand or oil in a shaded area. When you are unsure of the condition of the road, slow down.

If you are going too fast and need to slow down in a corner, stand up the bike for a brief moment, brake, and then immediately lean back into the curve. If you do this for more than a split second, you will run off the road, which sort of defeats your purpose.

Don't Panic

If you find yourself going into a curve too fast on dry pavement, don't panic. Just countersteer more to lean harder into the curve. The more you lean, the sharper you turn. You need to trust the capability of your tires (remember this when you're next considering buying cheap and nasty tires). Although motorcycles have less traction than cars, they have more traction than you might imagine. Just watch a Moto GP racer go through a curve leaned over so far that it looks like he's riding sideways. That should give you an idea of just how much traction a motorcycle can have.

The funniest part is that while leaning we all think we are being more heroic than we really are. Usually you'll feel like the bike is nearly touching the floor, when you're only actually a couple of degrees from vertical; so again, don't panic. Even if you feel the toe of your boot drag the ground, it's okay; most bikes still have the capability to go even lower.

Leaning harder actually slows you down. By leaning harder, you can scrub off excess speed with your tires. The most important thing is to keep a cool head. Unless you are going at a ridiculous speed, if you don't panic you should be able to make just about any corner—that is, as long as you have sufficient cornering clearance, a quantity many cruisers do not have in abundance.

Your safest bet is to make certain you're not going too fast when you enter the corner in the first place. If you're in doubt, slow down even more. You can get in a lot less trouble by going too slow through a corner than you can by going too fast. If you're riding within your abilities, you should be able to stop a bike at any time, as well as maneuver around any obstacle, whether you are going straight or around a corner.

Cornering Lines

The path you take through a corner plays an important role in both safety and speed (the safest line through a curve is also the fastest). By selecting the right route, you improve your view and make yourself more obvious to oncoming traffic.

The most important thing is to stay in your lane. One of the leading causes of fatalities among people who treat public highways like racetracks—hotshots who ride at unsafe speeds on twisting public roads—is straying over the centerline and getting hit by oncoming traffic.

When going around a corner, treat your lane like it's the only part of the road that exists. The oncoming lane might as well be a cliff or a solid wall of rock, because under no circumstance can you ride there when going around a curve.

When approaching a corner, move to the outside of the lane before entering the turn. This lets you see farther around the corner, and it also makes you visible to oncoming traffic earlier. As you enter the corner, countersteer the bike to the turn's apex—the point in the corner where you can begin straightening up the bike—and start smoothly accelerating. Racers take this line through a curve because it is the fastest way to do so, but you do it on the street because it affords you the best visibility of oncoming traffic and any hazards that might be on the road ahead.

The Vanishing Point

A great way to learn how to ride corners efficiently is to use the *vanishing point*. Using this technique will encourage you to position your bike safely, it will help you to use appropriate speed, and finally it will force you to keep looking where you want to go.

If you look at any curve in the road, there is a point where the curb for your side of the road visually meets the curb from the opposite side of the road. On a tight corner that point will appear close; on a long sweeping curve that point will appear farther away. That farthest point where your eyes see the two sides (or edges) of the road "meet" is your vanishing point.

Cycle Babble

The **vanishing point** is the furthest point around a curve that our eyes can see. It will appear to close in on us or pull away from us depending on how appropriate our speed is within that corner.

You can use the vanishing point to gauge your speed as you ride through the twisties. Riding toward a curve, the vanishing point will look like it's coming flying toward you, so you bring the bike down in speed. As you ride around the curve, the vanishing point will appear to maintain the same distance ahead of you. Once the vanishing point starts to disappear off into the distance, the curve has opened up once more and you can gradually accelerate away.

Good road position will allow you to see further around a curve, giving you earlier warning of any potential danger.

(Photo courtesy of Simon Green)

When I was instructing advanced classes, I would teach my experienced students to position themselves to the left-hand side of their lane when approaching a right-hand curve. This would give them the best view of what was around that corner. They would then use the vanishing point to control their speed (in fact, they weren't even allowed to look at their speedometers while under tuition; that was my concern). If the vanishing point was coming toward them, they were going in too fast. If it was getting farther away from them, they could safely use a little more speed. If their speed were perfect, then that vanishing point would look like it was matching their pace all the way around the curve. Though I must clarify, this was only ever taught to experienced riders on a quiet open road.

But even for you, the novice, by constantly looking at the vanishing point, you are looking as far ahead as visibility allows. This will give you the earliest possible warning of any danger around the corner, thus allowing you the maximum time to react.

Also by looking ahead, your eyes will guide the bike to where you want to go. Remember we talked about target fixation earlier? It's all too common for a novice rider to look at a tree on a curve, as the idea of hitting it worries them; but remember if you look there, you'll go there. The vanishing point forces your eyes to focus on the positive (the way out of the corner), not the negative (the tree or other obstacle).

As far as the use of speed goes, I would certainly stress the importance of slowing down if ever a vanishing point appears to be coming toward you. Once your skill levels are higher, you'll also find yourself accelerating out of corners as the vanishing point appears to move away; but let's wait until you've got some serious bike miles under your belt first.

Using the vanishing point demands total concentration, and is very, very rewarding. If this appeals to you, track days should be next on your motorcycling to-do list.

The Least You Need to Know

- Slowing down when going through an intersection or taking a turn puts you in control of the situation.

- When stopping at an intersection, always leave enough room between you and the vehicle in front of you to allow you to maneuver around it in an emergency.

- Never enter an intersection until you are absolutely certain that all lanes of traffic are clear.

- Riding too fast on a freeway puts you at risk because it decreases the time you have available to react if another vehicle moves into your lane.

- Never cross over into the oncoming lane of traffic while negotiating a curve.

Chapter **14**

Staying Alive: Special Situations and Emergencies

In This Chapter

- ◆ Motorcycling in bad weather
- ◆ Riding at night
- ◆ Riding with a passenger or in a group
- ◆ What to do in an emergency
- ◆ Raising a fallen bike

In this chapter, I explain the techniques required to ride in special situations that require you to modify your normal riding procedures and in emergencies. Regardless of how well you master safe-riding techniques, sooner or later you will be faced with an emergency situation. Like anything in life, some things are out of your control. There's always that one deer running out from behind a shrub just feet in front of your bike, or that one drunk driver who happens to fall asleep at the wheel and veer into your lane. If you go down, it may not be your fault, but you will be the one who feels the pain.

Riders on the Storm

Riding in the rain challenges your riding skills, because on wet pavement, you have less traction available than you normally do. Because of this, you can't …

 ◆ Lean as hard. As I said in Chapter 13, leaning decreases the size of the contact patch of your tire, which, in turn, decreases your available traction.

 ◆ Stop as quickly. You need to use your brakes with caution in the rain.

Motorcycology _____

You should always wear bright, reflective clothing when riding a motorcycle, but because of the reduced visibility during a rainstorm, brightly colored rain gear is crucial. Not only is visibility decreased during a rainstorm, but when it's raining, other drivers are even more unlikely to be watching for motorcycles than they normally are. You need to do everything you can to help other drivers see you.

 ◆ See (or be seen by other drivers) as well. The rain is especially problematic for a motorcyclist because you have no windshield wipers on a bike. The rain covering your visor, goggles, or windshield can be removed only by you or the wind.

Even though it is more challenging, riding in the rain can be relatively safe, provided that you use extra caution. The most important thing to do is slow down. The combination of decreased traction and decreased visibility drastically reduces your acceptable margin of error in the rain.

Smooth handling is even more important on wet pavement than on dry pavement. Jerky steering or throttle input that you wouldn't normally notice on dry pavement can cause you to lose traction and crash in the rain. This means any kind of aggressive riding is simply not an option.

You also need to take extra care to ride in the tire tracks in the rain because the oil line in the center of the lane rises to the surface during a rainstorm, especially just after the rain starts. This goop always limits traction, but just after rain begins to fall, the stuff is especially slippery. Plus, you can't see it as well because the pavement is covered with water.

You might not notice a worn tire in dry conditions, but when the road gets wet, a bald tire becomes extra deadly. Part of the reason tires have grooves cut into them is to help move water away from under the tire's contact patch. These grooves are too shallow on worn tires to allow the water to move, causing the tire to hydroplane—that is, to ride atop the surface of the water. As you might guess, a hydroplaning tire is an extremely low-traction (sometimes even no-traction) situation. This is one of the primary reasons you should always make certain that your tires are in good condition.

Motorcycology

Some motorcycle gloves have a chamois strip, or even a tiny rubber wiper blade on the back of the index finger, so that you can wipe the rain from your visor. It might be a good idea to buy such a pair.

Have you ever wondered where all of the rubber goes as your tires wear out? Well, as tires grip they're constantly shedding rubber particles. These particles sit on the road surface and when the rain finally comes, it creates a super-slippery paste, until there's enough water to wash it all away. That means that if you're on your bike and it starts to spot with rain for the first time in a couple of weeks, prepare yourself for an evil road surface. The first rain in a while always creates a unique smell; now you know what that smell is caused by—all that discarded tire rubber.

Night Rider

Reduced visibility is your primary challenge when riding at night. And at night, there are even more dangers you need to see than during the day because many animals roam around at night. Plus, a higher percentage of other drivers are drunk at night than during the day. This is especially true on the weekends.

Motorcycology

Sometimes an animal's eyes will shine in your headlights like a glass reflector. Seeing them alongside the road should serve as a warning to you that an animal is present. Slow down upon seeing the slightest twinkle, and monitor the edges of the road with added diligence. Remember that many animals, such as deer, travel in groups—so if you see one, there are probably more in the immediate area.

Here's how to practice proper night-riding techniques:

1. Don't ride too fast. When riding at night, always slow down compared to how you'd ride in the daytime.

2. Don't ride "out of your headlights." The lights on a motorcycle illuminate only a small part of the road, making some obstacles and debris invisible. If you can't see a hazard, you can't avoid it. When you do see an obstacle, you have much

less time to avoid it than you do during daylight hours. Adjust your speed so that you are able to stop or swerve as soon as you spot any potentially dangerous situation.

Motorcycle headlights have improved immensely in recent years, but they still don't illuminate the road the way a car's headlights can. Adding driving lights can help increase your field of vision.

To get the maximum visibility from your headlight, you need to make certain that it's properly adjusted. The high beam should touch the road at its maximum range, yet the low beam should be below the eye level of approaching motorists. The procedure for adjusting the headlight varies from bike to bike. Consult your owner's manual to find the procedure for your particular bike.

When riding at night, learn to read the headlights of the car in front of you. You may be able to follow another vehicle (remembering to allow even more space between you and that vehicle than you do during daylight hours) and use its headlights to help increase your field of vision. If the headlights of the vehicle ahead bounce, you can expect a bump in the road. If the vehicle swerves, the driver may be trying to avoid something.

Two for the Road

Part of the fun of motorcycling is sharing it with another person (or riding two-up). Bringing a passenger (also known as a pillion rider) along can make the experience of riding more rewarding, but it also requires extra care on your part.

Adding a passenger changes the weight distribution on your bike. It's obviously much heavier overall, but it's a weight that is unfortunately placed not only very high up, but right at the back of the bike, too. The most obvious difference will be a light-feeling front end and a much less stable bike than usual.

This dramatically changes the handling dynamics. The bike will turn differently with a passenger on board and will need more distance to stop. You can compensate for this somewhat by adjusting your suspension and increasing the air pressure of your tires. Suspension adjustments vary from bike to bike, but most modern motor-cycles at least have a preload adjustment on the rear shocks that you can adjust to a firmer setting for carrying a passenger. Again, consult your owner's manual for the exact procedure for your bike.

It's not just the bike, though; you'll need to adjust your riding, too. If you accelerate flat-out with 200 pounds of passenger perched over the back wheel, your front will start getting very light, very quickly—light enough to lift a few feet off the ground. If you don't want to ride a wheelie, or even more importantly don't know how to lower an accidental wheelie, then things can get ugly real quick, for both of you.

Before riding with a passenger, go over some rules of the road with him or her. Explain the following concepts:

- The passenger should not get on the bike until you have taken it off the stand and are secure in an upright position, using the front brake lever to prevent it from rolling.

- The passenger must wear the same protective clothing as the rest of us—a helmet is essential. If you don't have two helmets, then it looks like you're buying a second one.

- The passenger should hold on to you by the waist or hips while riding. Some riders prefer to grasp the passenger's grab rail (on bikes so equipped), but holding on to your waist or hips is a good idea as it will subconsciously encourage the passenger to lean into corners with your body.

- The passenger should keep his or her feet on the footpegs at all times, even while the bike is stopped.

- The passenger should keep his or her feet away from all hot parts, especially the exhaust pipes.

- The passenger must sit behind you, on the passenger portion of the seat. If there is no passenger seat, there should be no passenger. And never seat a child on the gas tank in front of you: basically, if a kid can't reach the pillion footpegs, they shouldn't be on the bike. Finally, the maximum capacity of a bike is two people.

While giving someone a ride, have him relax and lean with you. A passenger who has never ridden on the back of a bike before will often try and stay upright, even in corners. This greatly reduces your ability to negotiate a corner. You may find yourself leaning further and harder, wondering why the bike isn't doing what you expect of it, all because your pillion is sitting bolt upright, with an inane grin on his face, while you desperately struggle not to crash.

Above all, don't try to impress your passenger with your riding ability. An old friend of mine swore he would never go on a bike again, because as a child he'd been taken on the ride from hell. The rider was actually just trying to impress my friend with the bike's power, but all he actually did was to scare him off a bike for seven years.

Motorcycology _____

Always go over the rules with your passenger before riding. The other person may not be aware of things that seem obvious to you. Once I gave a ride to a stranded motorist on the back of a sport-touring bike. I helped the young man put my spare helmet on and gave him an extra pair of gloves I had in my saddlebag, and then I took him to the nearest gas station for help. I thought I'd done a good job preparing the kid, but after I dropped him off, my wife, who had followed on her motorcycle, said he'd ridden the entire way with his feet sticking out in the air—I'd forgotten to tell him to put his feet on the footpegs.

Eventually I persuaded my friend to ride on the back of my bike. I rode like a grandma for less than a mile and then let him off. He looked very confused, but a few days later asked to go on again. I never used the bike's power until he asked me to. The last time I heard from him, he was the proud owner of his very own sportbike.

Oddball Corners

In Chapter 13, I discussed cornering techniques. These techniques apply to normal turns with a *constant radius* (the curve follows a constant arc). Sometimes the shape of a curve can change in midcorner, forcing you to alter your technique.

A change in the shape of a road can take you by surprise, forcing you to change direction in midcorner. Like everything else in motorcycling, the key to dealing with these situations is awareness. If you are riding on an unfamiliar road, slow down and expect anything. What looks like a smooth, fast corner upon entry may be a sneaky *decreasing-radius* curve that will cause you to run off the road.

Cycle Babble _____

A **constant-radius** turn is a turn with a steady, unchanging arc. In a **decreasing-radius** corner, the arc gets sharper as you progress through the curve, while in an **increasing-radius** corner, the arc becomes less sharp.

Increasing-Radius Curves

An *increasing-radius* curve is a curve that gets less sharp as it progresses. In a way, these corners are less dangerous than a normal corner, but they may require you to alter your course in midcurve. If you are prepared, you can use the extra room you will have in an increasing-radius curve as bonus safe space.

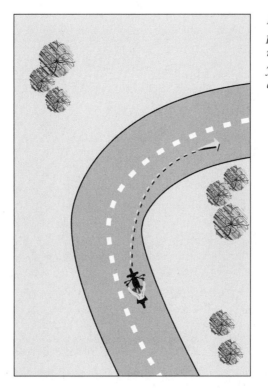

If you're prepared, you can pass through an increasing-radius curve more safely than you can a constant-radius curve.

Decreasing-Radius Curves

The most challenging type of corner you will encounter is the decreasing-radius curve—a curve that gets sharper as you progress through it, forcing you to turn more sharply as you go. And as I told you in Chapter 13, you don't want to make sudden movements in a corner.

Your best bet is to always expect a decreasing-radius corner: first be prepared to lean a bit more to successfully negotiate a turn and second always be in the right gear. If you feel that it's absolutely essential, then it's a whole lot safer to throttle off very gently (letting the engine slow you down) than it is to brake halfway round a corner.

If you're doing everything right and the radius of the corner doesn't decrease, that just means you'll have more room to maneuver. If it does decrease, you'll be ready.

When riding on an unfamiliar road, always expect a curve to get sharper as you progress, and be prepared to lean harder to complete the turn.

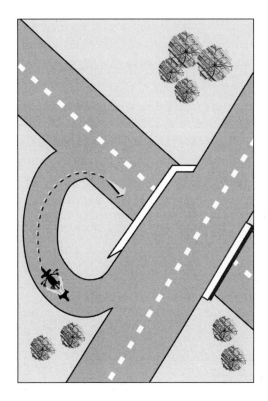

Multiple Curves

The technique for riding through a single curve may not be the best technique for riding through multiple curves. By starting in the part of the lane away from the direction you are turning, as you do on a single curve, you may find it difficult to negotiate the second curve. When you get to a snaky section of road like this, first slow down more than you would for a single curve. Then position yourself in the first curve so that you'll be best able to negotiate the following curves. Always position yourself so that you have the maximum visibility of whatever's ahead.

Riding through multiple curves will test your ability to countersteer your bike. Successfully negotiating such curves will require you to get physical with your machine. You'll need to be able to go from leaning hard in one direction to leaning hard in another direction in an instant. If you remember to push the handlebars to guide you, it can actually be a load of fun.

Crowned Roads

Some roads are shaped with a pronounced peak in the middle, to facilitate water run-off. These roads change the angle of your tires' contact patches, limiting your lean angle and causing your bike to steer differently. When you are riding on irregularly shaped pavement, slow down.

Surface Hazards

In a perfect world, there would be nothing on our roads but good, grippy pavement or tarmac. But we live in a world that is far from perfect, and the conditions of some of our public roads are the polar opposite of perfect. In metro areas, the most common surface hazards you will come across are automotive fluids of some sort, whether that is condensation from air conditioners, expelled coolant, or petroleum products such as engine oil or gasoline or diesel fuel. Often you won't even see these fluids, but they are there, and you need to be aware of them because often they are as slippery as ice. Avoid any wet spot you do see, and try to ride in the tire tracks in your lane to help avoid those fluids you don't see.

Another common metro surface hazard is broken pavement. Often you will ride on stretches of road that are in atrocious condition. Be very careful when traveling through extremely rough stretches, because hitting a sharp, deep bump can cause your tire to lose traction, leading to you getting tossed down for a close-up look at that broken pavement.

A type of hazard you're more likely to run across in rural areas than urban areas is gravel and other traction-breaking substances on the road. You can almost count on finding gravel in corners where there is a driveway or unpaved road meeting the pavement, and you'll find gravel in corners where you would never expect to find gravel. You'll find other things on the road in rural areas, too, such as hay, grain, and tire treads. Once a friend and I even hit a pool of milk left behind by a leaking milk truck. Be on the lookout for signs that you might encounter some sort of debris on the road. For example, if you are driving by a hay field where a farmer is loading hay on a wagon or truck, your odds of finding a section of nearby road covered with hay are high. Sometimes there will even be literal signs, as in road signs that say, "Cattle Crossing." Even if you don't see cattle on the road, you may encounter a very slippery by-product because cattle tend to leave behind funky-smelling calling cards when they cross a road.

Cycle Babble

A **low-side** crash occurs when the front tire, rear tire, or both lose traction, and the motorcycle tips over toward the inside of the corner.

When you encounter such surface hazards, don't panic. If you are in a corner, slow down and weight the outside footpeg with your foot. This will put your motorcycle in a more upright position—giving you a larger tire contact patch and, thus, more traction—without significantly altering your line. Remember, if you stand it up too much, you may go off the road, causing a much worse accident than if you *low-sided*

your bike because you lost traction in a corner. The most important thing to do in such situations is to ride in the tire track area within your lane. This is the area that is likely to be most clean, because tires push debris toward the outer edge of a curve.

Group Riding

Motorcyclists tend to be social creatures and, as such, often ride in groups. For many people, riding with friends is the most enjoyable aspect of motorcycling. Sometimes it's fun to ride in a large group of bikes just to see the looks on people's faces as you ride by. Going out for a ride with your friends can be a blast, but it will require extra effort on everyone's part to do it safely. You'll be riding with people whose riding skills vary, along with their temperaments.

Group Riding Techniques

When riding in a group, you can ride in one of three formations:

- **Staggered formation.** In this formation, the motorcycles line up on both sides of the lane, with one bike on the left side, the next bike on the right side, the following bike back on the left side, and so on, with each bike maintaining a two-second interval between the next bike. This formation keeps the group close together while maintaining the maximum amount of safe space around each bike.

- **Single-file formation.** When you are out riding with your friends on a winding road, you will all need to use your entire lane to safely negotiate each corner. On such roads, ride in a single-file formation. Remember not to follow each other too closely, or if one person goes down, he or she might take down other riders, too.

- **Side-by-side formation.** When bikes ride side by side, they reduce the amount of safe space between each bike, so this type of formation should be discouraged. Sometimes an escort may require you to ride in such a formation to make the group as compact as possible, but otherwise, avoid riding two motorcycles abreast.

Sure, They're Your Buddies, but Can You Trust Them with Your Life?

When riding with your friends, watch out for group mentality taking over. This is when everyone tries to outride everyone else. Many otherwise sane riders crash when group mentality takes over.

When riding in a group, ride for yourself and no one else. Be aware of who you're riding with, where they are, and how fast they're going. Above all, don't ride above your own ability. It's a lot more embarrassing to slide down the road in front of your friends than it is to arrive a few seconds later than them for coffee.

SOS: Emergency Situations

Nobody is perfect. Ride long enough, and you will go down, regardless of how careful you are, how diligent you are, or how skilled you are. Even if you always ride within your ability, not everything is under your control.

The types of emergency situations you can encounter are infinite, but they can be classified into two general categories: losing traction, and impact.

Cycle Babble

According to the Hurt report (which I mentioned in Chapter 12), 94.5 percent of motorcycle accidents happen within *the first hour* after putting the kickstand up. Often when you first get on your bike, your mind isn't completely engaged in the business of riding. You may be wondering if you put your change in your wallet at the fast-food restaurant you just visited, or you may be thinking about work. Sometimes it just takes a few miles to get into a groove. Thinking about what could happen in that first hour of a ride is likely to help you avoid having an accident, because you may be more careful when you first get on your bike.

Losing Traction

The most common and usually least consequential emergency you will encounter is losing traction and falling down.

Remember, don't panic. If you remain calm and use smooth throttle control, you can often regain control after you have lost traction. If your back tire starts to slide at speed, don't snap shut the throttle: if you suddenly quit supplying power to the back tire, it will violently regain traction, jerking your motorcycle in the opposite direction. Your best bet is to ride the slide through. Go watch some flat-track racing to see just how far a back wheel can slide without the rider crashing.

If it's too late and you know you're going down, just relax and let go of the bike. If you're wearing your protective gear—and you should *always* be wearing your gear—chances are, you're going to be okay. Try to slide on your back. Keep your arms and legs stretched out, and try not to let them dig into the ground, which can cause you to flip through the air. Stay relaxed. Stay low to the ground, and try to move away from the motorcycle. Don't stand up until you're sure you've stopped, then check out the cool battle scars on your bike leathers.

Impact: Hitting or Being Hit

If you strike a small object, it is possible to prevent yourself from crashing by following the proper technique.

If you find yourself in the position of being unable to avoid a small object or piece of debris, don't slam on the front brake. This will cause your motorcycle to pitch forward, forcing your front tire into the object rather than over it. It may even cause your front wheel to lock up, and if ever you needed traction from your front tire, now is the time.

Motorcycology _____

Many motorcyclists learn how to crash by riding dirtbikes. You are much more likely to fall down on the rough surfaces found off-road than you are on smooth pavement, so dirtbike riders crash much more often than streetbike riders. Learning how to react in a crash is probably the most important off-road skill that transfers to the street.

Try to hit the object as straight on as possible. Apply a bit of throttle to take some weight off the front tire, and as you strike the object, pull back on the handlebars. If you remain calm, you can ride over the object without crashing.

Being struck by another vehicle is probably the most serious type of accident you can have, followed by you striking another vehicle. Both situations are extremely dangerous, but if you strike another vehicle, at least you have a split second to react. When you are struck by another vehicle, you usually don't know what hit you.

The only way to deal with such situations is to avoid them—remember to be aware of your complete surroundings, ride at a speed that is slow enough to allow you time to react, and never, ever ride without a good helmet and the rest of your bike gear.

What to Do After an Emergency

If you do have a crash, you need to remain calm. If you are still on the road, you need to move off the road, if at all possible. No matter how badly you're hurt, you will be hurt worse if somebody then runs you over. It's wild to watch motorcycle racers crash, and then get up and run, but they know from experience that getting out of the way is vital.

Once you're out of harm's way, you need to take stock of your injuries, particularly to your spine. Check to see if you can move your fingers. Don't move any more than necessary until you're absolutely certain you haven't damaged your spine. Above all, don't remove your helmet until you have made certain that you have no spinal damage because that can cause even worse damage. Even if you have damaged your spine, you may be okay and suffer no paralysis if you don't further damage your spinal column.

Motorcycology

Always carry a first-aid kit on your bike. At the very least, your kit should have bandages, tape, something for bee stings, and some form of antibiotic ointment. In an emergency situation, a cellular phone can be the most crucial piece of first-aid equipment you can carry.

If you are able to walk away from a crash, you can treat it like an automobile accident; exchange insurance information if other drivers are involved, and remove your motorcycle from the roadway, if it is safe to do so. If there is any chance of spinal injury, all you can do is wait for help.

How to Raise a Fallen Bike

Once you've determined you're all right, you need to turn your attention to your fallen bike. If you're lucky, it will be safe to ride. But be careful because incorrectly raising even a small bike can injure your back. You've just survived a crash; wouldn't it be embarrassing to injure yourself when you pick up your bike? "Okay Doc, this is how it happened …."

When I was growing up, there was a strong belief among every one of my peers that if you couldn't pick the bike up, you shouldn't be riding it. It meant that if you were in the middle of nowhere, completely alone, you'd still be able to cope.

If, however, you own a bike that's way too big to pick up alone, then wherever possible, find someone to help you lift the bike. If you have to lift it by yourself, there are procedures to help prevent you from injuring your back.

When picking up your bike, the first thing is to stand on the side of the bike where you can most easily grab the handlebars. You want to try and lift the bike holding the handlebars and something at the back, like the grab rail. Don't even attempt to pull it from the other side, you'll never get enough leverage. Bend your knees and use your legs, not your back, to lift the machine upright. Get the bike back onto its stand as soon as you can. If your motorcycle is down on its right side, you might want to extend your sidestand before you even start lifting, in case you get the bike upright and it falls over in the opposite direction. Then you'd be really mad!

Don't smoke anywhere near the fallen bike because gas most likely will have dripped out. Battery acid might also be leaking. This can burn holes in your riding gear and even your skin, as well as corrode metal parts on your bike. You'll want to check the level of the fluid in your battery after a fall.

Once you've gotten the bike upright, check for other damage, too. Brake, clutch, and shift levers can get bent or broken in a fall. Riding a bike with a broken clutch or brake lever is difficult and dangerous. You may be in a situation in which you have to ride away from your crash site with a broken or bent lever, but replace it as soon as possible.

Also check your wheels and tires after a crash. Make certain that a fender or chain guard isn't rubbing on your tire. Make certain that your handlebars are firmly attached to your fork. If your handlebars break loose, you're going to crash again.

The Least You Need to Know

- The oil line between the tire tracks on a highway lane is at its most slippery just after rain begins.

- Don't "ride out of your headlights" at night.

- You need more room to stop when riding with a passenger.

- The safest method of group riding is usually in a staggered formation.

- The most important thing to do in an emergency situation is to not panic.

Doing It in the Dirt: Riding Off-Road

In This Chapter

◆ Using off-road skills to improve your on-road performance

◆ Riding up and down hills

◆ Advanced techniques for riding over ledges and obstacles

◆ Riding on a variety of surfaces

Learning to ride off-road has some advantages. When you ride off-road, you remove the number-one hazard you'll face on public highways and streets: other drivers. And the dirt generally is more forgiving than the pavement if you fall down, which you will do more often off-road, simply because you'll be riding over more rugged terrain than the relatively flat surfaces covering most roads. There are a lot more rocks, ruts, holes, and trees in most off-road riding areas than on your average city street.

Quite a few road racers practice riding off-road during their off seasons. They claim that riding off-road hones their skills and makes them better racers. Off-road riding is a fun way for all of us to sharpen our riding skills, whether we race or not. In this chapter, I'm going to give you a brief description of the challenges you'll encounter off-road and show you how to adapt to those challenges.

Form Is Function: Posture

Balance is crucial to successful dirt riding, and to achieve good balance, you need good posture—that is, correct body positioning on the motorcycle. Because most dirtbikes are so light, you use body movement to steer them more than you do on a streetbike. In the dirt, you need to get physical with your motorcycle.

A neutral, centered body position and proper throttle control are the two most important things to learn about riding off-road. They'll also make the difference between successfully climbing a hill and crashing. And the proper posture for going up a hill isn't the same as the proper posture for going down.

Generally, you want to keep your weight centered over the motorcycle. To accomplish this, you'll use one technique when going uphill and another when going downhill.

Going Uphill

Climbing a hill on a motorcycle can be one of the most fun aspects of off-road riding, but it can also be one of the scariest. That makes it scary fun, and believe me that's good!

You need to use some common sense when deciding whether to climb any hill. You might not have the skill needed to climb some hills. Even if you do, your motorcycle might not be able to make it.

Make certain that you know what is on the other side of a hill before you climb it. If you are riding up a hill that you can't see over, slow down until you can see what's on the other side. Finding that the other side is a cliff face might not be as much fun as you'd think.

The problem with slowing down to see what's on the other side of a hill is that you need your momentum to carry you to the top. On a steep hill, if you lose momentum, you lose the battle, especially on a two-stroke. If you're unfamiliar with the terrain you're riding in, take some time to explore your surroundings, and check out the hills (and what's on the other side of those hills) before attempting to climb them.

When approaching a hill, keep both feet firmly on the pegs. Shift into a low gear and accelerate before ascending. If the hill isn't too challenging, you can remain seated. Just shift your weight forward by sliding forward on the seat. If the hill is steep, stand up on the footpegs and lean as far forward as you can while still remaining in control of the bike. The more weight you can put over the front wheel, the less your chance of flipping over backward—which, I'm guessing, you don't want to do. But hey, I could be wrong ….

Motorcycle Moments

When I was growing up, my friends and I loved to climb hills on our dirtbikes. One friend could ride up hills the rest of us could never get over—he had a natural talent for hill climbing. Unfortunately, he was a bit short on common sense and often went riding over hills before he knew what was on the other side. Once, while I was following him through unfamiliar territory, he climbed a hill, but I went around it, preferring to see what was on the other side before attempting the climb. I rounded the hill just in time to see him and his motorcycle plunge into a 25-foot ravine. He was unhurt, but his motorcycle was toast.

If the hill is too steep and your bike begins to stall, you'll have to downshift, if you can. Shift smoothly and quickly, being smooth on the throttle to avoid doing a wheelie and flipping over backward. That's really the key to getting up the hill: if you see a steep spot, immediately pick the smoothest path, and give the bike some more throttle before you reach this new challenge. It's about reading the changes and reacting as quickly as you can. It's mentally and physically draining, which is probably why it's so wonderfully addictive.

When going over the crest of a steep hill, move as far back as possible to place as much weight over the rear wheel as you can.

If you don't have enough power to make it, but you're still moving ahead and have enough space to turn around, you can turn around and ride back down. If you stop, or if you can't continue and don't have enough room to turn around, you have a problem. If you have good enough footing to maneuver the bike once you've stopped, apply the front brake and remain stopped until you are stable.

If you don't have a solid footing, you're going to fall down. Usually this will hurt only your pride, but if you're on an extremely steep hill, you and your bike may fall back down the hill. If this happens, all you can do is try to get out of the way of the falling bike, and then chastise yourself for being foolish enough to try a hill so far beyond your ability.

Steer Clear

Getting stuck on the side of a steep hill with your bike is both dangerous and hard physical work. Wrestling a bike around while trying not to fall down a hill is usually enough to make most sane people think twice the next time they're tempted to climb a hill that is too steep.

If you've managed to avoid falling and you're sitting there squeezing the front brake, wondering what to do next, you can use gravity to help get you turned around. Turn your wheel toward whichever direction is most clear behind you, and then gently ease off the front brake—not enough to get yourself rolling, but just enough to slowly move to the side. Keep the bike leaning toward the top of the hill, because the upward side is the only side on which you'll have a firm footing. Lean away from the top, and you're going down the hill the hard way. When you're sideways, ease ahead and turn down the hill, following the trail you took up.

If you've fallen, follow this same procedure, except remain off the bike, standing on the downside of the machine as you turn it around. Remember to use the hand brake as you maneuver the bike, or you could run yourself over.

Going Downhill

You might not think so, but descending a hill can be just as challenging as climbing a hill. In fact, if you don't know what you are doing, you can fall even more spectacularly going downhill.

Point the motorcycle directly down the hill before descending. The more straight on you are when going down, the less your chances are of falling. Slide your butt back on the seat as far as you can, while still maintaining a firm grip on the handlebars, to transfer weight to the rear. Shift into a low gear, and don't open the throttle as you go down. Let the engine assist in your braking. Use the rear brake liberally, but be careful about locking up the tire. Be very cautious when using the front brake, especially in low-traction situations. When going downhill, your front end will want to dig into the ground if the terrain is soft or loose. Using your front brake will increase this tendency and can send you flying over your handlebars.

Just like ascending, the key to getting down a hill in one piece is reacting quickly to all the changes in the terrain. Bumps and ruts will pitch the bike sideways (as if downward momentum isn't enough to deal with). The trick is to think fast. If your bike starts going to the side, find something you can put your foot on temporarily to keep your balance. One dab of your foot onto something solid can save the bike from going over. A dropped bike will often stall, and being on a 40-degree incline trying to kick-start a stalled dirtbike is kind of tricky. Any way you can keep it upright is a very good thing.

Steer Clear _____

Gravity can be your friend when going downhill, but it also makes crashes happen more quickly and more violently. When you fall down while climbing a hill, it seems to happen in slow motion because your momentum is carrying you up, away from the ground. When your bike pitches you off while going downhill, it happens pretty quickly because your momentum is already carrying you down, toward the ground.

Ledges and Embankments

As your hill-climbing skills improve, you may want to seek out more challenging terrain. Riding up and down sharp ledges and embankments can provide those challenges, but you really need to use your head here. There is a fine line between a ledge and a cliff, and if you purposely go plunging off a cliff, chances are, you won't get much sympathy while you recuperate in the intensive-care ward.

Use the same basic technique for climbing ledges and embankments that you use to climb other hills, only more of it. You'll need to shift your weight farther forward, apply more throttle, and gain more momentum. Again, be aware of what's at the top of the embankment. If you successfully climb the embankment, you'll be going at a pretty good clip as you crest the top. As you get over the top, let off the throttle and prepare to deal with what you find at the top.

When going down a short, steep hill, you may need to give the bike a little gas as your front tire goes over the edge, to keep the bike from getting hung up on the ledge. Otherwise, follow the normal downhill procedure.

Things That Go Bump in the Road

Even on the worst paved road you can find, you won't encounter obstacles such as stumps, logs, boulders, and roots. When riding off-road, these obstacles are part of the package, and you'll need to know how to deal with them. If you hit such obstacles when you are unprepared, they can deflect your front tire, causing you to crash.

To avoid these obstacles, concentrate on the trail ahead of you, scanning for objects in your path. Adjust your speed for conditions. If you are riding through dense foliage, slow down until you can determine what's ahead of you.

Even if you avoid hitting an obstacle with your bike, if you don't maintain a proper riding position, you can hit it with your toes or feet, especially on a narrow trail. To avoid this, ride with the balls of your feet on the footpegs so that your toes don't hang below your motorcycle's frame. This prevents you from catching your toes on obstacles, which, more often than not, will lead to a bunch of broken bones in your feet. And having to ride 20 or 30 miles to the nearest emergency room with a bunch of broken bones in your feet is no fun. You'll have to trust me on that.

If you hit an obstacle that deflects your bike, resist the urge to stick out your leg. This will upset your center of gravity, making you more likely to go down, and it also creates the risk of knee injury. As bad as breaking a bunch of bones in your foot sounds, it's actually a pleasant experience compared to suffering a knee injury. Instead of sticking out your foot, keep your feet on the pegs and shift your weight around to correct your bike's course.

Riding over an obstacle is a maneuver best left only to an experienced rider. It requires precise throttle control, along with the ability to bring the front wheel up in the air at will. This is known as doing a wheelie, and when riding off-road, being able to do a wheelie can spare you many painful crashes.

If you have to ride over an obstacle, approach it as directly as possible, trying to hit it straight on (at a 90-degree angle). As your front wheel is about to strike the obstacle, apply some throttle to unload the front wheel and pull back on the handlebars, being careful not to give the bike too much gas so that you don't flip over backward. You are now doing a wheelie, with your back tire rapidly approaching the obstacle. If the obstacle is reasonably small, close the throttle before the rear wheel hits it. This will bring your front end down, and you can drive over the obstacle with your back wheel. Your front wheel is always the trickiest wheel, simply because it has the ability to steer.

If the obstacle is too large for your back wheel to go over without your bike getting hung up, you shouldn't be attempting to go over it in the first place. If you're in the middle of the attempt when you realize you're in trouble, that observation won't help you much. At the exact moment your rear tire catches the obstacle, apply a bit more throttle. This should launch you over the obstacle. To do this, you should be experienced at jumping and should be able to land on your back wheel, which is, theoretically, what should happen (either that, or you will fly into the brush). As I said, this is a procedure best left to an expert rider. Before attempting it, you should know your bike and your riding techniques so well that the entire procedure comes to you naturally.

Make certain that you know what you are doing before attempting to ride over an obstacle.

Surface Conditions

The defining characteristic of a road—even a lousy, decomposing road—is a relatively level surface. The surfaces found off-road vary as much as the flora and fauna, but they can be broken down into three general categories:

- ◆ Sand
- ◆ Water and mud
- ◆ Rocks

The one thing these surfaces have in common is that they're all low-traction situations. Learning to cope with low-traction riding can greatly improve your street-riding skills. When the rear tire loses traction at speed on the street, your greatest danger comes when you suddenly regain traction, because this violently pitches your motorcycle in the opposite direction (called a high side). You need to learn how to control a slide by using smooth throttle control rather than abruptly releasing the throttle, which will cause you to regain traction too quickly.

Because the dirt is more forgiving (you won't regain traction so abruptly when you release the throttle), you can practice sliding off-road without as much danger of high-siding the bike. Sliding on the pavement will always require a more delicate use of the throttle, and your off-road skills won't translate directly to the street, but at least you'll know how to slide and control the bike in a slide. This knowledge can save your life in an emergency.

While the three categories of off-road surfaces all have low traction in common, each will require a slightly different riding technique.

Motorcycology _____

Learning to ride under the low-traction conditions encountered off-road is the most important skill you can transfer to street riding. Learning how a motorcycle reacts in low-traction conditions and how to control it in such conditions can be invaluable information on the street. But remember one important difference: on pavement, you generally have more grip, and the speeds are often higher. As a result, when you lose the rear end at speed and then close the throttle, the rear tire tends to bite hard, and the bike tries to throw you over the high side much more violently and quickly than it does when riding off-road.

Sliding Through Sand

When riding in sand, the front end of your bike will feel as if it is moving through a thick fluid. You'll never quite feel like your front end is planted, yet the snaky movements it makes won't be as abrupt as in rocks, water, or mud.

The key to riding in sand is to remain relaxed. Keep your feet on the pegs and your head up, with your eyes focused ahead. Your bike will move around (undulate might be a better description), but this is normal.

Throughout this book, I've always told you to slow down when encountering a potentially dangerous situation. But that advice doesn't apply to riding in sand. Here, you'll want to speed up, going fast enough for your tires to rise to the top of the sand. When riding on sand, you want to re-create the condition of hydroplaning on water, as discussed in Chapter 14. There, you wanted to avoid hydroplaning. Here, it's a good thing. If you slow down in the sand, your bike will sink in, which could cause either your front wheel to knife in and veer to one side, or your back wheel to spin, losing all traction.

When turning in sand, you have to be especially careful to keep your front end from knifing in. You need to get as much weight as possible off the front tire. Shift your weight to the rear of the bike, and apply the throttle to unload some weight from the front end. When you master the technique, you'll find that you use your throttle to slide the rear end around to turn in sand more than you actually steer the bike.

A general tip to keep in mind when riding in sand is that you should accelerate sooner and brake later than you would when riding on surfaces that provide better traction. The drag created by pushing your wheels through sand means it takes your bike longer to accelerate and takes it less time to slow down than when you're riding on higher-traction surfaces.

Wheeling in Water

Riding in water and mud will provide you with skills that translate directly to street riding, because you may encounter such conditions on-road as well as off-road.

Surfaces underwater are especially slick. This applies to riding over low-water crossings on public roads as well as riding through streams and swamps. If there is debris present, such as fallen leaves or pine needles, the surfaces become even more slippery. Again, this is true of the water on a road as well as the water encountered while riding off-road.

Steer Clear

If you encounter a low-water bridge on a paved road (a place where the road descends into a creek or river), follow the procedures outlined here, and be extra cautious. If the water is moving quickly, it may actually pull your wheels downstream. You must remain calm when this happens. Keep your weight centered so that neither the front nor the rear wheel washes out from under you, and proceed at a slow but steady pace, keeping your eyes focused on the road ahead, where it rises out of the water.

When riding through water, ride slowly and be prepared for whatever your front tire may encounter because you won't be able to visually scan submerged surfaces. I've stressed the importance of using smooth throttle and brake control in all situations, but no other situation requires you to accelerate and brake more smoothly than riding in water.

When riding through water, you should …

- Beware of surface irregularities, such as rocks and holes that are hidden by the water.

- Learn to read different water surfaces. You can get some idea about how deep the water is by the way it moves. If you see shallow ripples, the water is probably being disturbed by the surface underneath, meaning that it is not too deep. If the water is slow moving and calm, it is probably deeper.

- Maintain your momentum, and focus on the opposite bank or where the road emerges from the water at a low-water crossing.

- Keep speeds relatively low. In addition to minimizing the damage if you fall down, this keeps water from splashing up onto your engine.

After riding through water, your brakes may be wet and ineffective. Dry them by applying light braking pressure while riding until they return to normal power.

If you have submerged your bike's engine, you'll want to change your oil as soon as possible.

Motorcycology

Nothing has caused me to crash more often than ruts. Ruts that are hidden in tall grass are the worst because you can't see them. But trying to turn out of a rut I could see has to rank as the second most common cause of the crashes I've had. These usually have been quite spectacular, of the end-over-end variety. Moral of the story? Don't fight a rut.

Water and mud go together because where there's water, there's mud, and where there's mud, there's water. But riding in mud requires you to modify your technique a bit. The biggest difference is that, when riding in mud, you'll usually encounter ruts. When you do, stay relaxed and let your tires follow the ruts. Don't fight the front wheel or try to turn out of a rut. It is a fight the rut will win. Again, I know this from firsthand experience. Look ahead to where you want to go rather than down at the rut.

If you're riding through heavy mud and your bike begins to bog down, don't open the throttle abruptly. Doing so will only cause your tire to dig down deeper, getting you even more stuck in the mud. You wouldn't believe how heavy a 250-pound motorcycle can feel when it is stuck in the mud. Your best bet is to gradually open the throttle and try to keep your momentum.

Riding in Rocks

Riding in rocks differs from riding in mud or sand in many ways. The most important difference is that sand and mud are, by nature, very soft, while rocks tend to be very hard.

The technique for riding on a surface composed of small rocks is similar to the technique for riding on sand: maintain a steady speed, using smooth throttle and brake control. It differs in that you don't need to go as fast. Your tires won't plow in quite as deeply as in sand. You must still maintain a steady pace, but it just doesn't have to be as quick a pace.

Another difference between small rocks and sand is that the movements of your front end caused by the rocks will be jerkier and less fluid than the undulation caused by the sand. Again, your best way of dealing with this is to remain relaxed and ride at a moderate, steady pace. If you tense up and grip the handlebars too tightly, the front-end movements caused by the rocks will increase in intensity.

School

The Motorcycle Safety Foundation offers a DirtBike School, a half-day course in a controlled environment. This fun, low-pressure course teaches the basics of off-road riding and then progresses to more advanced off-road riding techniques. Classes last from four to six hours, depending on weather, class size, and rider ability. The courses are offered in a variety of riding areas around the country, and though each area is different, the quality of the hands-on instruction provided by trained MSF staff doesn't vary. For more information, contact the Motorcycle Safety Foundation at 1-877-288-7093, or go to www.dirtbikeschool.com on the web.

Many riders go their entire lives without venturing off pavement. By doing so, they miss one of the most enjoyable aspects of motorcycling. If it is at all possible, I recommend that each of you pick up an inexpensive trailbike in addition to your streetbike, and hit the trails every chance you get. You won't regret it.

Just make sure that you do this kind of riding with a buddy. Dirt riding is like scuba diving, it's not really a solo thing. Imagine riding into the middle of nowhere and inadvertently dumping your bike on the floor while climbing some steep incline, cracking the engine case on a rock. With a buddy around, it's a major problem, if you're on your own … well, you could be vulture meat.

Preserving Your Off-Road Access

For those of you who *do* want to get down 'n' dirty, you'll learn something special about your sport right off the bat: access to your riding areas is under attack 24/7. Fortunately, you've got some superb organizations out there doing yeoman's service on your behalf, and they deserve your support. Of course, the American Motorcyclist Association (AMA) is in the thick of the fight, with the tireless efforts of its Government Relations Department. The department keeps a weather eye out for legislation—state or federal—that might discriminate against motorcyclists. Help them out by becoming an AMA member: just call 1-800-AMA-JOIN. (I'll talk more about the AMA in Chapter 19.)

Then there's the National Off-Highway Vehicle Conservation Council (NOHVCC), an educational foundation that's industry funded and that provides assistance at a grass-roots level. The NOHVCC helps local OHV/ATV clubs become active in the land-closure battle with a host of resources. To find out more, go to www.nohvcc.org on the web. Similarly, the activist BlueRibbon Coalition (BRC) uses the voices of its members in ongoing land-use issues. The BRC's motto is "Preserving our precious natural resources *for* the public instead of *from* the public," and they do so by promoting cooperation between off-road enthusiasts and other types of public land users. To find out how you can help, call 1-800-BLUE-RIB, or go online at www.sharetrails.org.

The Least You Need to Know

- Proper posture and careful throttle control are the two most important skills to learn when riding your bike off-road.

- The skills learned by riding off-road transfer to riding on-road indirectly, not directly. The increased traction on-road will require some modification of off-road emergency techniques.

- Riding off-road teaches you important techniques for dealing with low-traction situations.

Part 4

Living with a Motorcycle

In Part 1, I told you just how far motorcycle technology has advanced in the past few decades. Today's motorcycle requires a fraction of the effort needed to keep a pre-1960 model running.

But motorcycles still need more maintenance than any modern car. There are still routine procedures you'll need to perform, not just to keep your bike in top condition, but to ensure your own safety. You can't afford an equipment failure on a bike.

By buying the simplest bike that meets your needs, performing routine maintenance, and not running the bike into the ground, you can get the most out of your motorcycle.

THE EVOLUTION OF THE HUMAN RACE

BARR

Recommended—Beginner, Tourer. *BMW filled a gap in the tourer market when they made the F 800 ST. This lightweight touring motorcycle is the perfect long-distance mount for the new motorcyclist.*

(Photo courtesy of BMW AG)

Recommended—Intermediate, Tourer. *BMW is definitely the leader within the touring category. This boxer-engined R 1200 RT is another truly great mile-muncher.*

(Photo courtesy of BMW AG)

Recommended—Experienced, Tourer. *The Honda Gold Wing is one of the ultimate touring motorcycles for the experienced rider. It's also extremely popular with passengers.*

(Photo courtesy of Honda USA)

Recommended—Beginner, Cruiser. *Most cruisers are gargantuan monsters, so thank you Yamaha for making the friendly, zippy, light and compact 250 Virago for the new folk.*

(Photo courtesy of Yamaha USA)

Recommended—Intermediate, Cruiser. *One of the best-looking and most fun Harleys ever made. The Street Rod is also quite accessible—in terms of both price and rideability.*

(Photo courtesy of Motorcyclist™ magazine)

Recommended—
Experienced,
Cruiser. *With its
whopping 2300cc
engine it's not for
the inexperienced,
but Triumph's
Rocket 3 mega-
cruiser is a legend
in the making.*

*(Photo courtesy of
Triumph Motorcycles)*

Recommended—
Beginner, Sport-
Tourer. *Many
sport-tourers are
modified sportbikes,
machines capable of
making long jour-
neys comfortably.
Kawasaki's 500cc
Ninja is one of the
most manageable of the
breed.*

*(Photo courtesy of Kawasaki
USA)*

Recommended—Intermediate, Sport-Tourer. *If you like riding twisty roads but also want a bike that's capable of long journeys in comfort, then the Honda VFR is calling out your name.*

(Photo courtesy of Honda USA)

Recommended—Experienced, Sport-Tourer. *Just like the Kawasaki Concours ad says: "Supersport performance with long-distance touring comfort." Think of it as a bike version of a big European sports sedan.*

(Photo courtesy of Kawasaki USA)

Recommended—Beginner, Supersport. *Suzuki's SV650S is just about the only machine within this category that won't get the novice into a load of trouble. Fun, fast enough, and thoroughly recommended.*

(Photo courtesy of Suzuki USA)

Recommended—Intermediate, Supersport. *Honda's CBR600F4i is the slightly more "sane" version of their sporty 600 duo—not great for a novice, but a whole lot of fun for everyone else.*

(Photo courtesy of Honda USA)

Recommended—Experienced, Supersport. *Nuts. That's the best description of Yamaha's YZF-R6, light as a feather and faster than the 1000cc bikes from a few years ago. It's completely and utterly nuts.*

(Photo courtesy of Yamaha USA)

Recommended—Intermediate, Superbike. *It's just not possible to recommend any 1000cc Superbike to a novice rider—this incredible Suzuki GSX-R750 is already a handful for riders with some experience.*

(Photo courtesy of Suzuki USA)

Recommended—Experienced, Superbike. *Kawasaki's ZX-10R is brutally fast, extremely light, and amazingly well mannered, especially considering the lunacy that it's capable of.*

(Photo courtesy of Kawasaki USA)

Recommended—Beginner, Standard/Naked. *Great bikes for novice riders were never this cool (or this beautiful) in the past. Ducati's Monster 695 appeals just as much to the old hands as to the new folk.*

(Photo courtesy of Ducati USA)

Recommended—Intermediate, Standard/Naked. *Buell engineers their bikes like no others, meaning this XB-9SX is one of the most distinctive streetbikes in current production.*

(Photo courtesy of Motorcyclist™ magazine)

Recommended—Experienced, Standard/Naked. *With the 1000cc engine from their Superbike World Championship–winning motorcycle, Aprilia's Tuono-Factory is not for the fainthearted. The experienced rider will find it so addictive it should be illegal.*

(Photo courtesy of Piaggio Group USA)

Recommended—Beginner, Retro. *Royal Enfield's Bullet is like nothing in current production, mainly because it's been almost unchanged since 1955. It's not just trying to be old and cool, it's the real thing.*

(Photo courtesy of Classic Motorworks Ltd)

Recommended— Intermediate, Retro. *Triumph made such beautiful Bonnevilles back in the '60s that people still want them now. Bikes like their stunning Thruxton 900 feed this insatiable appetite.*

(Photo courtesy of Triumph Motorcycles)

Recommended—Experienced, Retro. *Ducati designs bikes like this Sport 1000 to look like old café racers, but then builds them with thoroughly modern mechanics. It's a faultless combination of old style and new performance.*

(Photo courtesy of Ducati USA)

Recommended—Beginner, Dual-Sport. *Yamaha has been building XTs for years and years, and it's not because they're out of touch. It's actually because bikes like this XT225 are still so very, very good to use.*

(Photo courtesy of Yamaha USA)

Recommended—Intermediate, Dual-Sport. *KTM is the king of the off-road world but this 640 Adventure is designed for some on-road action, too. It's a truly great machine, excelling in both environments.*

(Photo courtesy of Mitterbauer H.)

Recommended—Experienced, Dual-Sport. *This huge BMW R1200GS would scare the life out of a novice, especially if taken off-road. In capable hands, though, it's almost unbelievable how competent this giant can be.*

(Photo courtesy of BMW AG)

Recommended—Beginner, Enduro. *As most off-road bikes get more and more focused on being race capable, it's great that Suzuki still values the importance of a tough, simple trail bike like the DR-Z250.*

(Photo courtesy of Suzuki USA)

Recommended—Intermediate, Enduro. *Honda's CRF450X is as light as some 250s, it's got flexible four-stroke power, and is built as solid as any other Honda. It's hard not to buy one, they're just too good.*

(Photo courtesy of Honda USA)

Recommended— Experienced, Enduro. *Just big enough and lairy enough to be a little dangerous in novice hands. But for people who know their stuff, these Husqvarna TE510s are just something else. Well worth the price increase over the Japanese competition.*

(Photo courtesy of Cagiva USA/MV Agusta Motor S.p.A.)

Chapter 16

Zen and the Art of Motorcycle Maintenance

In This Chapter

◆ Tools you need to maintain your bike

◆ Spotting potentially dangerous tire and brake problems

◆ Changing oil and why you need to do it

◆ Maintaining your chain

People either love performing maintenance on their motorcycles or they hate it. In his book *Zen and the Art of Motorcycle Maintenance*, Robert M. Pirsig writes that the reason some people hate motorcycle maintenance is that it is part of the "inhuman language" of technology. "Anything to do with valves and shafts and wrenches is a part of that dehumanized world," he writes. Pirsig is from the other group, the tinkerers and fiddlers who think nothing of tearing apart their engines and adjusting their valves. He finds working on his bike a form of therapy, a communion with something greater than himself. "The Buddha, the Godhead, resides quite as comfortably in the circuits of a digital computer or the gears of a cycle transmission as he does at the top of a mountain or in the petals of a flower," he writes.

I didn't used to, but somewhere along the line I started to enjoy the mechanical aspect of owning a bike. Now I perform most of my own maintenance, and I've always managed to keep my bikes running. Believe me, if I can do it, you can do it. Whether you are a mechanical savant like Pirsig or a ham-fisted doofus like me, with a little patience, a little knowledge, a lot of practice, and, of course, some tools, you can do most of the things required to keep your bike on the road. In this chapter, I tell you how.

This chapter deals with routine maintenance, while Chapter 17 deals with repairing your bike if it breaks down. Many of the procedures used in routine maintenance are the same as those used to repair your bike, so use the two chapters together.

Tools of the Trade

Unless you own a Harley-Davidson, your bike will most likely come with a toolkit. This may be located under the seat, behind a side cover, or in a special compartment.

Most Harleys don't come with standard toolkits. Although BMW equips its bikes with high-quality toolkits, standard toolkits are usually poor, most often made of something that looks like metal, but is in fact more like cheese. These are best left for emergency situations, or left completely unused for resale value considerations. When you do maintenance at home, you'll want to equip yourself with a real set of tools. At the very least, you'll want to have these tools:

◆ **Air-pressure gauge.** Buy a gauge of good quality, and keep it clean so that it provides you with an accurate reading.

◆ **Wrench set.** Buy the highest-quality set of wrenches you can possibly afford—cheap ones will bend, crack, and break. The most versatile wrenches are combination wrenches. These have an open-end and a box-end (fully enclosed) spanner at either end. Harleys use SAE standard fasteners (the type of fasteners used by most American manufacturing firms, measured in inches rather than millimeters), so get a standard set of wrenches if you buy a Harley. All other bikes use metric fasteners.

◆ **Allen wrench set.** Many fasteners on motorcycles use Allen-head bolts instead of traditional hex-head bolts. This means the bolts are turned by an Allen wrench—a wrench you insert in the center of the bolt instead of around the edges. As with regular wrenches, get a standard set for a Harley and a metric set for everything else.

◆ **Screwdrivers.** You will need flat-blade and Phillips screwdrivers in a variety of sizes. As with all your tools, you will find that your work goes much better if you buy high-quality screwdrivers.

◆ **Ratchet and sockets.** These will become your most used tools, so, once again, get the best set you can afford. For motorcycles, get a set with a $\frac{3}{8}$-inch drive ratchet, with as many different size sockets as you can. Again, Harley takes standard; everything else takes metric. Make sure that your new socket set includes a spark plug socket.

Motorcycology _____

The tips of screwdrivers are called blades. Like knife blades, they get dull and rounded off over time. When that happens, you're likely to strip screws. When the tips of your screwdrivers get dull, replace them.

◆ **Pliers.** It's useful to have several types of pliers. Basic pliers work in a variety of situations, but you'll also need to get a pair of needle-nose pliers—the kind that look like they're made from a hummingbird's beak. These are useful when working in tight places (motorcycles are covered in them) and with small objects (those too). I also like to have a pair of Channellock or adjustable pliers. I use these for everything from holding odd-size large bolts to removing oil filters when my filter wrench won't fit.

◆ **Oil-filter wrench.** These wrenches come in several varieties. Get one that best fits around your particular oil filter—that is, if your motorcycle _has_ a spin-on filter.

◆ **Soft-face mallet.** You will sometimes need it to convince an obstinate part to move. The soft face will prevent you from damaging the obstinate part, even though you may want to damage it in the heat of the moment.

◆ **Lubricants.** You'll need to have some kind of penetrating spray lubricant on hand to loosen tight bolts. If you have a chain-driven motorcycle, you'll also need special cleaners and lubricants for your chain.

◆ **Funnels.** You're going to need at least a few different-size funnels on hand. Get one small funnel for filling electrolyte in your battery, a larger one with a longer spout for filling oil, and a fairly large one with a screen in the spout for filling gasoline.

◆ **Containers.** You'll need to get a gas can and some sort of pan to catch oil in when you change your oil and filter. This container should be large enough to hold at least five quarts of oil, yet be shallow enough to fit under your bike when it is on its centerstand.

◆ **Stool.** More than one weekend mechanic has suffered debilitating nerve damage from squatting in one position for too long while working on a bike.

Steer Clear _____

Before you change your oil, make certain that you know where you can dispose of the used oil. It's illegal and unsafe to dump the oil or spread it on a road. Some areas provide certified oil-recycling stations. Usually, service stations or drive-in oil-change places have large waste-oil storage capabilities. If you ask nicely down at the local Kwiki Lube, they may let you dump your waste oil in with theirs. Just remember not to make a mess and to clean up afterward, or you won't be welcome back.

Finally, you'll want a repair manual. A new bike will come with an owner's manual; used bikes may or may not come with one.

If you're serious about performing your own maintenance, your best bet is to buy an actual shop manual for your bike. These manuals, designed as guides for authorized dealer mechanics, are specific to your bike and generally tell you the best way to perform each procedure. These manuals are expensive, but they will save you money in the long run.

If you buy a used bike that is no longer in production, you might not be able to find a shop manual. In such cases, your best bet is to buy one of the aftermarket manuals from publishers such as Clymer, Haynes, or Helm, Inc., these are readily available on the Internet. If you can't find a manual for your exact model, you should be able to find one for another bike using the same family of engine. This isn't an ideal solution, but it's better than nothing.

Keeping the Shiny Side Up: Supporting the Bike

Before doing any work on your bike, make certain it's securely positioned. If your bike has a centerstand, use it for procedures that don't require you to remove any heavy parts from the bike, such as changing oil and tightening the chain.

If you need to remove heavy parts, such as wheels and tires, you'll need to find another method of supporting the bike because when you remove the parts, you'll change the weight distribution of the bike, upsetting the balance on the center-stand. You'll also need to use an alternative method of supporting the bike if it's not equipped with a centerstand.

I use a variety of materials to support my bikes, depending on the bike. I've created stable stands by using cinderblocks with two-by-fours as buffers to keep from damaging the parts under my bike. The key is to make certain that your blocking is stable.

Some companies sell special motorcycle lifts. While these are expensive, a good lift is your safest, most secure method of supporting your bike while you work on it.

Some companies sell rear-end stands that prop a bike up by the swingarm, just like the racers use. These are great and fairly affordable.

> **Steer Clear** _____
>
> If your bike has a fairing that extends around the bottom of the engine, remove this before placing your bike on any kind of support. The plastic cowling isn't strong enough to support the bike and will break under the machine's weight.

Oil: Your Bike's Blood

Oil serves three purposes in your bike's engine:

- ◆ Oil reduces friction and wear, making all internal parts move more smoothly and efficiently.

- ◆ Oil dissipates heat. It carries heat away from the moving parts of an engine as it flows over them. On some bikes, oil is sprayed on the hottest parts of an engine, such as the underside of the piston domes, to enhance heat dissipation.

- ◆ Oil cleans the inside of your engine. The inside of your engine is filled with metal parts that rub together at tremendous speeds, causing microscopic particles of metal to shear off. These particles are suspended in the oil and then finally trapped in your oil filter.

Two-stroke engines use oil differently than four-stroke engines (see Chapter 6). In a two-stroke, the oil enters the engine with the air/fuel charge and is burned up and eliminated with the exhaust, causing the characteristic blue smoke coming from the exhaust pipe. This is why the EPA isn't very fond of two-strokes.

Four-strokes circulate their oil, using either a *dry-sump system*, in which the oil is stored in an external container, or a *wet-sump system*, in which the oil is contained in the engine's crankcase. Most bikes use wet-sump systems.

> **Cycle Babble** _____
>
> In a **wet-sump system**, oil is stored in the engine's crankcase. In a **dry-sump system**, oil is stored in an external tank; the motorcycle's hollow frame may even double as an oil tank.

Checking the Oil Level

On a two-stroke, you'll need to check the oil level every day because two-strokes are designed to burn oil. On a modern, properly running four-stroke, though, you need to check the oil level only two or three times a week. If you have a bike that uses lots of oil, check more often.

On two-strokes and dry-sump four-strokes, you'll check the oil level in the external tank, usually located either beneath the seat or within the frame itself (although on some late-model Harleys, the tank is down by the transmission). On a wet-sump four-stroke, you'll check the oil level at the bottom of the engine.

In all cases, you'll either check by looking at the level on the dipstick (a flat blade connected to the filler cap), or you'll simply look into a sight glass (a window into the tank). The sight-glass method is much easier and less messy. Just make sure that the motorcycle is positioned properly before checking your oil. Most bikes need to be positioned vertically for an accurate oil level reading, so if you take your reading on the side stand, you'll be miles off.

Motorcycology

When you are checking oil, your bike should be in an upright position (unless otherwise stated in the owner's manual). On bikes without centerstands, this means you need two people: one to support the bike and the other to check the oil.

Another thing to keep in mind is that most bikes require you to simply rest the cap in the hole to get an accurate reading on the dipstick, rather than requiring that you screw the cap down. Your owner's manual will tell you which method to use.

If the oil level gets down near the add mark, fill the tank back up to the full mark, but be careful. It usually takes much less oil than you might imagine to fill the tank to the full mark, and overfilling your tank can cause as many problems as running it too low. Pour in a small amount and then recheck the level. Keep doing this until you reach the full mark.

Changin' Oil

The single most important thing you can do to ensure a long engine life for your motorcycle is to perform regular oil changes. As you ride your bike, two things happen to your oil:

- The molecules in the oil break apart, causing the oil to lose its lubricating properties.

- The oil gets contaminated with the microscopic particles that wear away from the parts inside your engine, causing the oil to become more abrasive.

Motorcycology _____

Recent friction-modifying additives used in some automotive oils may seriously damage your bike, so you should use motorcycle-specific oil. I use an automotive synthetic oil (Mobil 1), which so far has not incorporated the offending additives. It's much less expensive than motorcycle-specific oil and performs well. However, if Mobil begins putting friction-modifying additives in Mobil 1, I'll switch to a motorcycle-specific oil.

Here's how to change your oil:

1. Drain the oil. Locate the drain plug, which is somewhere on the bottom of the engine on wet-sump systems (the location varies with dry sumps), and place your pan-shape container under the plug. When you remove the plug (usually a hex-head bolt), the oil will come out with some force, so take that into account when placing the pan.

2. Remove the filter. Change the filter every time you change the oil. There are two types of filters—the canister type, which has a replaceable filter element located in a canister attached to the engine, and the spin-on type, which spins on and off like an automotive oil filter.

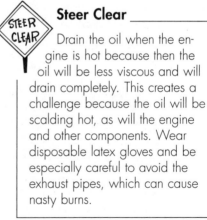

Steer Clear _____

Drain the oil when the engine is hot because then the oil will be less viscous and will drain completely. This creates a challenge because the oil will be scalding hot, as will the engine and other components. Wear disposable latex gloves and be especially careful to avoid the exhaust pipes, which can cause nasty burns.

When removing a canister-type filter, be extremely careful not to strip the fastener(s) holding the canister on, and thoroughly clean the area around the canister before removal. There will be a spring and some metal washers inside the canister to hold the filter in place. Note their location for when you install the new filter; after you remove the old filter, wipe out the inside of the canister with a clean rag. Be careful not to lose the spring or the washers.

3. Clean and replace the drain plug when the engine is done draining. Some drain plugs have a magnetic tip to collect metal shavings from inside the engine. Thoroughly clean the tip before replacing the plug. Most drain plugs have an aluminum crush washer to enhance the plug's seal. Make certain that you don't lose this washer when removing the plug. Also make certain that the surface of the engine is clean before you replace the plug/washer combo.

A spin-on oil filter is much more convenient to change than a canister-type filter.

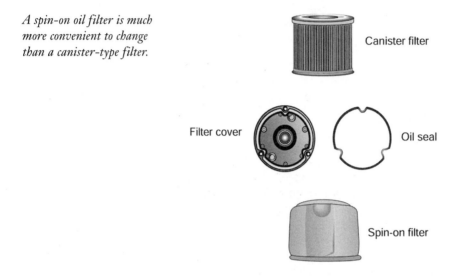

Canister filter

Filter cover

Oil seal

Spin-on filter

4. Replace the filter. With a spin-on filter, lightly smear a drop or two of clean oil around the rubber seal attached to the new filter before mounting it, to create an oil-tight seal between the filter and engine. Do not overtighten.

    A canister-type filter will come with a rubber O-ring seal for the canister. Make certain to use a new O-ring with each change. When you have the seal in place, lightly smear it with a drop or two of clean oil, making sure you don't get any foreign material on the O-ring, before replacing the canister. Mount the new filter inside the canister, making certain to assemble the spring and washers correctly. And when tightening the fastener(s), be extra careful not to strip the threads. Because of the spring holding the filter in place within the canister, it is easy to get the canister slightly askew when mounting it, which could lead to thread misalignment. If you encounter the slightest resistance when replacing the fastener(s), make certain that everything is aligned before proceeding.

5. Fill with fresh, clean oil, using the recommendations in your owner's manual for the type of oil and the amount. Next, restart your engine to pump oil into the filter. Be extra careful when doing this, and don't rev the throttle any more than is necessary because your engine will not be properly lubricated upon startup. Let the engine idle for about a minute; then shut it off and recheck the oil level.

It will have gone down because of the oil pumped into the filter, so refill to the full mark on the dipstick.

After you have changed the oil, keep a close watch on the oil level, and visually check for leaks around the drain plug and filter. An oil leak on your motorcycle is much worse than an oil leak on a car. If you've got an oil drip, it'll be flung straight onto your back tire as you ride. Not surprisingly, oil does not improve a tire's traction, so nobody with any sense lets their bike continuously leak oil.

The most likely source for an oil leak is around the filter in a canister-type unit. If you get even a small particle of foreign material between the rubber seal and the engine, you might notice leakage from the canister. This will only get worse. If this happens, you need to get a new rubber seal and do the whole thing over again.

Air Filters: Clearing the Sinuses

Air filters prevent dust and dirt from getting sucked into your engine, but over time they become plugged up with all that dust and dirt. When this happens, your bike doesn't get enough air to properly mix with the fuel charge entering your engine, leading to poor performance and increased gas consumption. Air filters are made of paper or foam. Foam filters must be soaked in special oil. They're located in a bike's airbox, a chamber connected to the carburetors. When a filter becomes clogged, you have to replace it (if it is a paper type) or clean it (if it is made of foam).

First, you need to remove the filter. On modern bikes, the airbox is usually located under the gas tank or under the seat. See your owner's manual for the removal procedure, because it varies with each model of bike.

Next, replace a paper filter, or clean and re-oil a foam filter according to your owner's manual's instructions. Afterward, replace the filter.

Motorcycology

Replacing a stock paper air filter with a quality aftermarket filter can noticeably improve your bike's performance if it has a fuel-injection system that can compensate for the increased airflow. If your bike has carbs, though, a freer-flowing aftermarket filter can cause some problems. To meet EPA emissions requirements, many bikes have carburetors that mix more air with the fuel charge than is optimal for combustion. This reduces emissions, but it also decreases performance and causes the engine to run hotter than before. By using an aftermarket filter, you increase the airflow even more, which can raise engine temperatures to dangerous levels, especially on an air-cooled bike. Because of this, it might be a good idea to have a qualified mechanic rejet (insert new parts that increase the flow of gasoline) your carburetors if you install an aftermarket air filter.

Batteries: An Electrifying Experience

Batteries are one area in which motorcycle technology has more than kept pace with automotive technology. Motorcycle batteries need far less attention. Indeed, many bikes these days come with sealed batteries that need no—as in none, zero—maintenance.

Now, locating the battery might very well be a problem. Batteries used to be located under a bike's seat, but now you can find them anywhere, from up by the headlight to back by the swingarm. Consult your manual.

Once you've found the battery, check the electrolyte level by looking at the side of the battery. The battery case is made of translucent plastic, allowing you to see the level of the fluid inside. If the level is slightly low, add distilled water.

Several things can cause extremely low electrolyte levels. Your battery may have cracked or in some way come apart and is leaking, in which case you'll need to replace it immediately. Or you may have tipped the bike over or leaned it far enough for the electrolyte to drip out the overflow tube at the top of the battery. Or your charging system may be malfunctioning, overcharging your battery and evaporating the fluid. If you suspect charging-system problems and you're not a skilled mechanic, it's probably time to take the bike in for professional help.

Keeping Cool

Today most bikes use some sort of supplemental cooling system. Some bikes spray cooling oil from the engine's sump on internal hot spots. Other bikes use a liquid-cooling system similar to that found in most cars. The liquid-cooling system is the most common on today's streetbikes and requires some maintenance on your part.

> **Steer Clear**
>
> Be extra careful about what kind of antifreeze you use in your motorcycle. Automotive antifreeze contains silica, an abrasive designed to keep the cooling system polished inside. This abrasive can damage a motorcycle's water pump, leading to engine failure and expensive repairs.

At least once a week, you should check your coolant level. Usually, you do this by checking your overflow tank, a white plastic tank located in a position remote from the radiator. When you do this, you should also give your radiator hoses a visual inspection, looking for cracks and leaks. If you need to fill the system with coolant, use a mixture of motorcycle-specific antifreeze and distilled water, as recommended in your owner's manual. Every couple of years, you should replace the coolant.

Chain Maintenance

If you have a chain-driven motorcycle, maintaining your chain will become your most frequently performed chore. You'll probably need to adjust the tension of the chain, clean it, and lubricate it roughly twice a month (more often if you put a lot of miles on your bike).

Checking the Tension

To check the tension, grasp the lower run of the chain (not the upper one hidden by the chainguard) about halfway between the front and rear sprockets, and move the chain up and down. As they don't wear evenly, check several spots on the chain by rolling the bike ahead and rechecking the tension. If the amount the chain moves varies from spot to spot, the chain may have a tight spot. If the chain moves up and down more than about an inch in the tightest spot, it needs to be tightened. If the tight spot is severe enough, you may need to replace the chain. I'll tell you how to do that in Chapter 17.

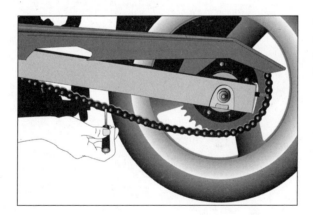

Check the tension along the chain's lower run, about halfway between the front and rear sprockets.

Adjusting the Chain

To adjust the chain, place the bike on the centerstand (rest it on its side stand if you have no centerstand) and recheck the chain's tension. Once on the centerstand, your chain's tension may vary from when you first checked it because the bike's weight is now off the suspension. Take this difference into account when adjusting the chain. If you adjust the chain to its proper tension on the centerstand, it may become too tight when off the centerstand, and a too-tight chain can break and shoot off your bike like a slinky missile.

Loosen the axle nut(s). You will have to remove a security pin on most bikes when undoing the axle nut(s). Once the nut(s) are loose, you can adjust the chain. You do this by adjusting some bolts on the very end of the swingarm, one on either side of the wheel. Usually, there will be two hex-heads on each bolt—an inner nut to move the axle, and an outer nut to lock the other in place when finished. Loosen the outer nuts and then carefully adjust the inner nuts, moving the nuts on either side of the wheel an equal amount. It is vital that you adjust the adjuster nut on the left as much as the nut on the right side; otherwise you'll be making your back wheel sit completely wonky.

When you have tightened your chain by the desired amount, tighten down the outside nuts. Retighten the axle, and insert a new security pin.

Loosen but don't remove the axle bolt.

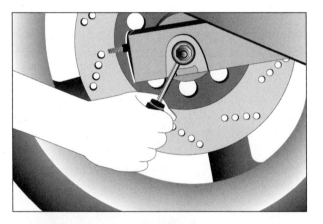

Make certain to adjust the bolts on each side of the wheel the exact same amount. Don't overtighten the chain.

The procedure for adjusting your chain varies from bike to bike, but most bikes use something similar to this method. Some bikes have a bolt on the back of the swing-arm, with the locking nut between the bolt and the swingarm. A few bikes, especially modern sportbikes with single-sided swingarms, use an eccentric cam on the axles to adjust chain tension. See your owner's manual for the procedure for adjusting these types of chains.

Cleaning and Lubricating Your Chain

To get the most use out of a chain, you'll need to keep it clean and lubricated. Most bikes now use longer-lasting O-ring chains (chains with internal lubricant kept in place by tiny rubber seals), but these still need surface lubrication. The problem with O-ring chains is that many substances degrade rubber O-rings, including common lubricants and cleaning solvents. Use only cleaners and lubricants approved for use on O-ring chains.

You may clean your chain every few rides, but you should be lubricating it after every single ride. It's best to lube it after a ride, not before, because after a ride the chain is nice and hot, meaning the lube will penetrate into the links more deeply.

To clean a chain, put on some old clothes, and place an O-ring-approved cleaner on a soft brush. Use that to clean the grime off the chain. When you've got all the crud off, wipe the chain dry before applying fresh lubricant. This is a messy, dirty, frustrating job, but it greatly increases chain life, and chains and sprockets are extremely expensive.

To lubricate your chain, aim the spray from the can of lubricant at the inside of the chain while rotating the wheel to evenly coat the chain's entire length. Like all motorcycle maintenance, this is infinitely easier if you have a centerstand. As lubricant and tires don't make a good combination (you could lube yourself right off the back of your bike) it's wise to protect the back tire while you spray on the chain lube. Holding a newspaper between the chain and the tire works fine.

Motorcycle drive chains last much longer than they did just a few years ago, but they also cost a lot more than they used to. And they still wear out. Add in the cost of replacing drive sprockets (which are usually replaced at the same time as the chain), and you're looking at spending $200 to $300.

With good chain adjustment and lubrication, I've regularly gone through two chains before my sprockets needed replacement. That's a good incentive to look after your chain! You can also minimize wear on your chain by not beating on your bike. The harder you accelerate, the more you stretch your chain.

Shaft Maintenance

Although shaft drive systems require much less maintenance than chain drives, you will need to change the oil in the rear gearcase assembly on the back wheel once or twice a year. This is a simple process. Drain the old oil by removing the drain plug at the bottom of the housing, replace the plug, and refill the housing back to the recommended level by removing a plug at the top of the housing and pouring the correct gear oil in there. Gear oil is extremely heavy oil (usually 80W) that you can buy at nearly all motorcycle dealerships. To check the oil level, remove the filler plug and visually check the level.

Filling oil in the gearcase a couple of times a year is far easier than cleaning, lubing, and adjusting your chain.

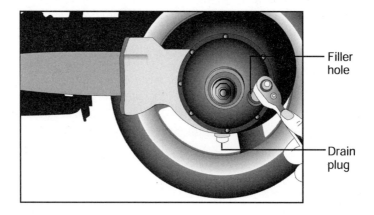

Filler hole

Drain plug

Cleaning Up

Some of us clean our bikes obsessively, while others prefer to let the grime accumulate. Sooner or later, though, even the grubbiest motorcycle needs a bath. Even if you like your bike grubby, it's a good idea to clean it once in a while, if for no other reason than that cleaning allows you to inspect the bike thoroughly, checking for fluid leaks, loose bolts, and other problems.

Don't use pressure washers on your bike, because many delicate parts are more exposed on a motorcycle than on a car. A pressure washer can force dirt and grime between seals, causing bearing failures and other problems. Instead, get a large bucket of warm, soapy water; a sponge; a soft brush; a chamois; and a bunch of soft towels and rags, and wash your bike by hand. It's not that hard if you follow the proper procedure:

1. Degrease the bike. Apply degreaser to the grimiest parts of the bike, such as the engine, wheels, and swingarm, with a soft brush. A hard brush may scratch painted surfaces.

2. Wash the bike with soap and water. Wash the bike from top to bottom with the sponge, making certain that you wash off all the degreaser. Use a small brush (such as a toothbrush) to get in those hard-to-reach places. Wipe the bike dry with the chamois cloth.

> **Steer Clear** _____
>
> When washing your bike, use a special low-salt detergent like the many wash-and-wax shampoos on the market. Normal household detergents have a high alkali content and can cause erosion.

3. Polish the bike. Use chrome polish on chromed metal surfaces (but not chromed plastic surfaces because the polish may melt the plastic). Every so often, use a light polish to buff out the paint, but don't use this every time you wash because it takes off a thin layer of paint with every use.

4. When you are done, apply a hard wax to the painted bodywork and buff it out until it shines. This is especially important after polishing the paint because the polish softens the paint and the wax protects it. Apply a light coat of lubricant, like WD-40 (though again, keep it away from your tires) to unpainted metal surfaces to prevent erosion.

On Ice: Storing Your Bike

Winter storage is the worst part of owning a bike. It's not difficult, but it means you won't be able to ride until spring. First, clean the bike so that it doesn't corrode over the winter. Make certain that the bike is dry before storing it. Change the engine oil and replace the oil filter just as you normally would.

Drain the carburetor float bowls by turning off the fuel petcock and running the bike until the engine dies. You can also drain the float bowls by opening their drain screws, which are located at the bottom of each carb's float bowl, but be careful not to let gas drip onto hot surfaces. Fill the fuel tank to the very top; this prevents corrosion from forming on the inner surfaces of the gas tank. Finally, add a fuel-stabilizing additive to the tank. Alternatively, you could completely empty the fuel tank and then spray the inside of the fuel tank with a rust inhibitor.

Unscrew the spark plugs and pour in a single tablespoon of clean engine oil. Using either the electric starter or the kick-starter, spin the engine over a few times to spread the oil around. Inflate the tires to their recommended pressures, and, if possible, place the motorcycle on blocks so the tires are off the ground. Finally, remove the battery and store it in a warm place, and your bike is ready for winter.

In the spring, you'll need to replace the battery, refill the float bowls by turning the fuel petcock to the Prime position, and again change the oil. If you've done everything right, your bike should start right up.

The Least You Need to Know

♦ Buy quality tools—it's less expensive in the long run than buying cheap tools.

♦ Before working on your bike, make certain it's properly supported so that it doesn't fall on you.

♦ Don't use automotive antifreeze in a motorcycle.

♦ Overtightening your chain can cause as many problems as not tightening it at all.

♦ Clean your bike regularly and store it carefully.

Chapter 17

Rx: Repair

In This Chapter

- ◆ Should you take your bike in or fix it yourself?
- ◆ Saving money by removing your own wheels
- ◆ Fixing potentially dangerous brake problems
- ◆ Replacing your chain and sprockets

In this chapter, I'm going to tell you about more in-depth repair procedures than I went over in Chapter 16. I'm going to explain how to perform the most common repairs you will encounter, such as changing tires, replacing brake pads, bleeding brake lines, and replacing chains and sprockets. On most bikes, the procedures generally follow those I outline here. There will be minor differences, which is why you'll also need a repair manual. For more specific repairs, you're going to have to rely solely on your repair manual.

If you can master working on your own bike, you will attain new levels of freedom and autonomy. And you'll save a pile of money. But mastering these procedures will take much time and effort on your part. You'll need to invest in the proper tools. You'll need patience.

Take It In or Do It Yourself?

Should you take your bike in to have someone else work on it, or should you do the work yourself?

A lot of that decision depends on whether you can find a shop you trust. (As I mentioned in Chapter 7, you should have done your research on this before you bought your bike.) A good, trustworthy shop will have trained mechanics with the right tools for every situation. But a bad shop can bung up your bike worse than you could yourself—and then charge you a lot of money for it.

Motorcycology

Remember that properly supporting your bike is even more important when performing the repairs in this chapter than it was when performing the maintenance procedures in Chapter 16.

If you learn to do the work yourself, you'll never be at the mercy of some shop's schedule for getting your bike fixed. And you'll develop skills that could prove valuable in an emergency. But you'll also have to buy a lot of expensive equipment.

There are benefits to both methods of repair. Ultimately, you'll be the only person who can decide which method is best for you.

Where the Rubber Meets the Road: Tires

Tires are one of the items you need to inspect each time you ride. Look over your tires each morning, checking for cracks, cuts, irregular swelling, and objects such as shards of glass or nails embedded in the tread. Check tire wear—a tire that looks okay one morning can be noticeably worn the next, especially if you've been riding hard or the air temperature has been high (tires wear faster when the pavement is hot).

Worn tires impair your bike's handling, especially in the rain, and are more likely to suffer catastrophic failure than newer tires. Your tires should have wear bars that appear as the tires age, but chances are, your tires' performance and safety will have begun to deteriorate long before the wear bars appear. Tires wear down the middle first, and as much as many of us love to corner, the reality is that modern roads require us to ride straight, a lot. When they're really worn in the center, they'll start to resist when you try and lean the bike over.

Get in the habit of checking the air pressure in your cold tires before each ride. A sudden loss of air indicates a potentially serious problem. Minor fluctuations in air pressure are normal and are often caused by changes in the air temperature. If your air pressure is a little low, inflate the tire until it reaches the pressure recommended in your owner's manual. If it is drastically low, examine the tread for a hidden nail or some other object that may have punctured the tire.

If a tire is punctured, repair is possible. You can patch a tube or put a plug in a tubeless tire, but I don't recommend either maneuver, except as a way to get your bike to a repair shop. The consequences of a blowout are too great. Replacing a tire or an inner tube is much cheaper than undergoing months of painful rehab therapy.

Removing the Rear Wheel

If you need a tire replaced, you should let a repair shop with the proper equipment do the job. That equipment is too specialized and too expensive for most amateur mechanics to have in their own shops, and the consequences of incorrectly mounting a modern tire are too great. But when you need to change a tire, you can save a lot of money by removing the wheels yourself and bringing the wheel assembly into a shop.

Motorcycology _____

When removing the axle, make certain that you are passing the axle through the swingarm in the correct direction. Many axles have a big end on one side and a securing bolt on the other. If the axle won't move in the direction you are tapping, or if it stops moving abruptly, make certain that you're not trying to push it through the swingarm in the wrong direction.

The method for removing motorcycle wheels differs with each bike, depending on the method of securing the axle, the drive system, and the brake system. Some bikes require the disassembly of suspension components or bodywork. The method described here is for a chain-driven motorcycle with disc brakes. Consult your repair manual for specific details.

1. First, remove the axle. To do this, remove the split keys securing the axle nut(s) in place, and then undo the nut(s). Some axles may have additional pinch bolts securing them in place that aren't obvious upon first inspection of the assembly. Make certain that you have loosened or removed all bolts holding the axle in place, and gently tap the axle through the swingarm with a soft-face mallet.

Be gentle when tapping the axle through the swingarm. If it takes more than a light tap, chances are, something has not been properly loosened.

2. Once you have the axle past one side of the swingarm, it should move freely through the wheel. A couple of things may hinder its progress. If the chain is too tight, it may pull the wheel forward, causing the axle to bind. If this is the case, loosen the axle adjustment bolts, being careful to adjust the bolts on both sides an equal amount. If the wheel falls down a bit after you move the axle through one side of the swingarm, it will also cause the axle to bind. You may have to support the wheel with your knee while removing the axle to prevent this.

   Some bikes will require you to unhook the rear shocks from the swingarm, allowing it to drop low enough for the axle to clear the exhaust pipes. In extreme cases, you may have to remove the exhaust pipes entirely.

3. Next, remove the wheel. Remove the spacers between the wheel and the swingarm, making notes of their location. To help remember their locations for reassembly, I lay them out on a rag, along with the axle, in the exact order they go on the bike. Push the wheel forward and unhook the chain when there is enough slack. Move the chain away from the wheel. You may need to remove the chain guard to allow you to move the chain free of the wheel.

You may have to remove some items to get the tire to clear the swingarm.

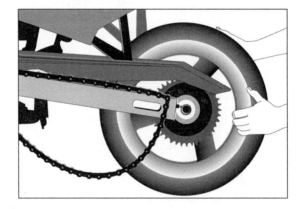

On shaft-drive bikes, wheel removal is usually easier than on chain-driven bikes. The main difference is that you pull the wheel away from the pinion housing to unhook it from the drive system rather than pushing it forward and removing the chain.

You may have to undo the brake caliper to make room to remove the wheel. If you have to do so, hold the caliper while you remove the wheel, and then make certain that it is securely supported until reassembly. Don't let the caliper hang by its hose.

4. When you have had the tire changed and the wheel balanced, reassemble by reversing the process. Don't forget to install a new split key to lock the axle bolt in place. Make certain that everything is properly assembled before riding, and stop to check all the bolts frequently the first few times you go riding.

Steer Clear

Never ride hard just after you have mounted new tires. New tires are horribly slippery for the first few dozen miles, so ride with extra caution while breaking them in. At first, they may have less traction than the ones you just replaced.

Removing the Front Wheel

Removing the front wheel is similar to removing the rear wheel, except that it's a bit easier because you don't have a drive system to deal with or a swingarm to work around. You may have to remove a speedometer cable, though.

Because you won't have to work around a swingarm or drive system, the front wheel is easier to remove than the rear wheel on most bikes.

To remove the wheel, first unhook the speedometer cable, if necessary. Then remove the axle. On many bikes, the easiest way to do this is to undo the end caps at the bottom of the fork, allowing the axle along with the entire wheel-tire assembly to drop out the bottom. If it works that way, simply roll the tire ahead, remove the axle bolts, and pull the axle out. Other bikes require you to remove the axle bolt(s) and push the axle through the wheel to remove the assembly, much as I discussed doing with the rear wheel. Either way, note the location of any spacers between the wheel and the fork.

You may have to remove the brake calipers to remove the front wheel. If so, make certain that you don't let them hang by their hoses. While your front wheel is off, don't operate the front brake lever; if you do, the brake pads will close in on each other, making it very hard when you reassemble to align the brake rotors between the brake pads.

To reassemble, just reverse the procedure.

Tires can prove to be major wallet drainers. Motorcycle tires cost much more than their automotive counterparts, running as high as $300 apiece for premium sport radials. And they won't last nearly as long as a car tire. A person who logs a lot of miles can easily expect to run through at least one set of tires per year.

A Screeching Halt: Brakes

In all my years of riding, I've seen only two people get killed in motorcycle accidents, both on a racetrack. One of them was killed when his front brake lever came off. This illustrates just how important your brakes are. If even the least complicated part of the system fails, it could cost you your life.

There are two kinds of brakes: *disc brakes* and *drum brakes*. Most modern bikes use disc brakes in front. Many also use disc brakes in back, but some still use drum rear brakes. Disc brakes slow your motorcycle by squeezing pistons inside a caliper, which is attached to your frame or fork and doesn't rotate, against a disc attached to your wheel, slowing both the disc and the wheel it is attached to. Drum brakes work by expanding the brake shoes—stationary, horseshoe-shape devices inside your wheel hub—against the inner surface of the hub, which is part of the rotating wheel.

Cycle Babble

Many bikes use a combination of **disc brakes** on the front and **drum brakes** on the rear. You will find this combination especially common on cruisers. Disc brakes use stationary calipers that squeeze pads against discs that rotate with the wheel, while drum brakes use horseshoe-shape brake shoes that expand against the inner surface of the wheel hub.

With disc brakes, you will need to periodically change the brake pads—metal-backed fiber pads located at the ends of the pistons in the calipers. These pads are the surfaces that actually contact the brake disc, and they wear down over time.

With drum brakes, you will need to replace the shoes as they wear down.

Checking Brake Pads

The procedure for checking pad wear varies according to the design of the caliper. Some allow you to simply look between the caliper and the disc, but many designs have a cover on top of the caliper that can be pried off with a screwdriver. This gives you a clear view of the pads. Some designs require you to remove the caliper entirely to inspect the pads.

If the brake-pad material is wearing thin, it is time to replace the pads. Sometimes the material will change in texture over time, especially if the pads have been subjected to extreme heat or some contaminant. If you notice a decrease in your brakes' performance, you should replace the pads, even if they appear to have enough material on them.

On many calipers, you can visually inspect the pads by popping off a cover on the top of the caliper with a screwdriver.

Replacing Brake Pads

Again, the procedure for replacing brake pads varies from caliper to caliper, so the instructions presented here are *just a general guide.*

On some designs, the correct procedure doesn't require you to remove the calipers. Others require you to do so. This is usually accomplished by removing the two bolts holding the caliper to its carrier or to a fork leg. However you do it, make sure you keep all the parts scrupulously, surgically clean, including the brake pads themselves, the

Steer Clear

When the caliper is removed from the disc, or when you remove the pads from the caliper, do not squeeze the brake lever. Also be careful not to contaminate the caliper or pads with brake fluid, oil, or dirt because this can cause your brakes to malfunction.

master cylinder caps, and the caps' rubber diaphragms. Most manufacturers sell their own brand of aerosol cleaners and lubricants, usually including something for cleaning ignition contact points or brake parts. Use it as freely as you would water.

The pads are held in place by pins that pass through the caliper body. The pins are retained by some sort of clip or by a split key. First remove the clip or key, being careful not to lose any pieces; they don't come with the new pads. When you are unfamiliar with the procedure, it helps to take notes or digital pictures to remind you of the order in which you removed parts.

Remove the pads with a pair of pliers, and insert the new pads. Because your new pads will be thicker than the old, worn pads, you may have to ease the piston back into the caliper. This should require little force. If you need to use something to push the piston back in the caliper, use something soft, such as a wooden stick, instead of a metal object, such as a screwdriver, because the metal can damage seals and the surface of the piston.

While the pads are out, visually inspect the pistons' dust seals for any tears.

Because the old pads were worn, you may have to move pistons back in their calipers when replacing brake pads.

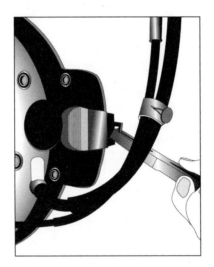

Motorcycology

A certain amount of grooving in the disc surface is natural, but if it becomes too grooved, braking performance can diminish and pad wear can accelerate. The only repair for a grooved disc on a bike is replacement, an expensive proposition.

After you have inserted the pads, simply reverse this procedure, referring to your notes or photos for the correct order of assembly. If your brake uses clips to retain the pad pins, you can reuse those. If you have a split key retaining the pins, use new split keys instead of reusing the old ones.

When you check your brake pads, you should also check your discs (these are the metal rotors the caliper presses the pads against). If you replace your pads before they become too worn, your discs should last a long time. But if your pads wear down too far, they can damage the discs. You can check your disc by looking at it and feeling its surface for irregularities.

Checking Shoes

The only way to check the brake shoes is to remove the wheel from the bike, which I explained earlier in this chapter. After you remove the wheel, pull the backing plate from the brake drum. This should be so loose that it will fall off on its own if you tip the wheel upside down—but don't do that, because the fall could damage the brakes.

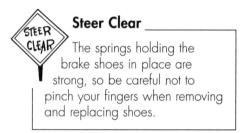

Steer Clear _____

The springs holding the brake shoes in place are strong, so be careful not to pinch your fingers when removing and replacing shoes.

It's difficult to judge the wear of the brake shoes by visual inspection, because you really don't know what they are supposed to look like. Rely on your manual to provide you with information on acceptable shoe-wear limits.

Replacing Shoes

The brake shoes are held in place by strong springs as well as clips on some designs. Remove the clip, and squeeze the brakes together to release the tension on the springs. Remove the springs and lift the shoes out. Install the new brake shoes by reversing the procedure. Just as with replacing disc-brake pads, keep everything frighteningly clean.

Two strong springs hold the brake shoes in place.

Adjusting your brake levers can decrease your reaction time in an emergency, saving your life.

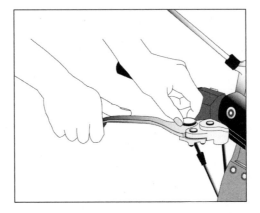

Motorcycology

The distance between the rear wheel and the engine varies slightly as the bike moves up and down on its suspension. The rear-wheel assembly is sprung—that is, it moves with the suspension. This is why you need to leave some free play in components connected to both the rear wheel and the frame or engine, like the rear drum-brake lever and the drive chain.

Brake-Lever Adjustment

Many bikes come with adjustable brake and clutch levers, items that improve both comfort and safety because they allow you to react more quickly in an emergency. Most handlebar levers adjust by rotating a numbered dial located at the lever pivot.

The pedal angle on your foot brake often is also adjustable, and finding the proper angle can make a huge difference in your reaction time and your riding comfort. On drum rear brakes, the angle is usually adjusted by a movable stop, a bolt located near the rear of the pedal. This bolt usually has a lock nut similar to that used on the rear-axle adjusting bolt. On disc rear brakes, the adjusting bolt will be part of the lever connecting the brake pedal to the master cylinder, and it works in much the same way as a drum-brake lever adjuster.

On drum brakes, you will have an adjustment for free play located on the lever that actuates the brake shoes. You will need to tighten the nut on the end of the connecting rod as the brake shoes wear. Be careful not to overtighten the free play, or suspension motion might accidentally activate the brake. You need to keep enough free play to allow the bike to move up and down on its suspension without activating the brake.

A Bloody Mess: Bleeding the Brake Lines

Disc brakes operate by moving hydraulic fluid from the master cylinder—the reservoir to which the brake lever is connected—and the calipers. The fluid, which comes in several varieties that can't be intermixed (the variety your bike needs is stamped on its master-cylinder reservoir cover), is one of the nastiest substances you will ever encounter. It melts plastic, disintegrates paint, and does nasty things to the human body.

It also absorbs water, meaning that if you have a leak in your system, you have to fix it immediately because water makes the fluid mushy and decreases your braking power. Even if you don't have a leak, atmospheric moisture will condense in your brake system over time, so you'll need to replace the fluid every couple of years anyway.

Steer Clear _____

Never use brake fluid from a container that has been opened—it may contain fluid absorbed from the atmosphere. Always use a fresh container. And make certain that you're using the correct type for your brake system. The cover of your master cylinder will be marked DOT 3, DOT 4, DOT 5, or DOT 5.1, referring to the type of fluid needed. Use *only* that type of fluid.

After you replace the fluid, you'll need to bleed the air out of the braking system. (Sometimes you'll need to do this even when you don't change the fluid, just to get air out of the system.) This is a messy job that can do damage to both you and your bike, so take your time when performing this procedure. To bleed the brakes, follow these steps:

1. Remove the reservoir cap at the top of your master cylinder by unscrewing the screws holding it in. This cap has a rubber diaphragm underneath it. Remove this to expose the fluid. You may want to wrap a cloth around the bottom of the master cylinder to capture leaked fluid before it reaches any painted metal or plastic parts. Keep the reservoir cap and its rubber diaphragm fetishistically clean.

2. Fill the reservoir with fluid. Use only fluid from a sealed container (old cans of fluid absorb water from the atmosphere), and use only the fluid your braking system was designed for. Be careful not to spill because the fluid will wreak havoc on the bike's finish. Then replace the diaphragm.

3. Bleed the brakes. There will be an odd-looking nipple on your caliper. Put one end of a clear plastic tube over the nipple, and put the other end of the tube

in a jar with some hydraulic fluid inside. Loosen the nipple approximately one turn, and squeeze the brake lever gently, causing fluid to flow through the tube. Tighten the nipple and release the lever. If you see bubbles in the tube, repeat the process until they disappear. Refill the reservoir and refit the rubber diaphragm before squeezing the brake lever. Repeat this procedure for each caliper.

Each motorcycle uses a slightly different procedure for removing and reinstalling brake pads. It's a good idea to have a shop manual for your specific model of motorcycle before attempting to replace brake pads. And it's a bad idea to poke around inside the caliper with a metal tool such as the screwdriver shown in this illustration. Use a wooden stick to pry apart the pads after installation, to avoid damaging the pad material.

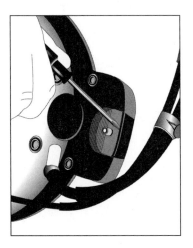

You'll need to have a length of clear plastic tubing on hand to bleed your brakes without making a mess.

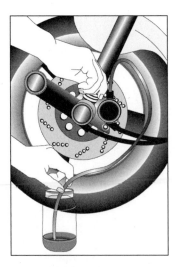

Chain and Sprocket Replacement

As mentioned in Chapter 16, modern O-ring chains last much longer than the conventional roller chains used in the past, but they also cost much more to replace. Proper maintenance—keeping the chain clean, well lubricated, and properly adjusted—can significantly increase the life of your chain, but sooner or later, you'll need to replace it. And when you do, you'll often need to replace the sprockets to which the chain is connected.

Chains have a repair link, also known as a master link or a split-link—a link that can be disassembled for chain repair—or they are of the continuous-loop variety. Replacing a continuous-loop chain requires special tools and is best left to a professional. The procedure here applies to chains with split links:

1. Clean the chain and sprocket area. This is the dirtiest, grimiest area on your bike. Cleaning the area will make your job much easier.

2. Remove anything that blocks access to your sprockets. You will have to remove the rear wheel and the casing covering the front sprocket. You may also have to remove your chain guard and other items.

3. Disassemble the chain's repair link. Using your pliers, squeeze the spring clip off of its pins. Then you can remove the side plate and push the link out the other side. You can now remove the chain.

4. Remove the sprockets. The bolts holding the sprockets on will be tight and difficult to remove. It might be easier to loosen the bolts on the rear sprocket when the wheel is still mounted on the bike. To do this, have someone hold the rear brake and help stabilize the bike, and break the bolts loose before removing the wheel. Once the bolts holding the sprockets on are removed, you should be able to lift off the sprockets.

The instructions for assembling your chain's split repair link will be provided with the chain.

It might be easier to break loose the bolts on the rear sprocket before removing the rear wheel.

5. Replace the sprockets and coat the bolt threads with a locking compound, such as blue Loctite. Then tighten the bolts to the torque specs in your owner's manual or shop manual. Finally, reinstall the rear wheel assembly.

6. Put on the new chain. The new chain will be slightly shorter than the old one (which stretched over time), so you'll need to adjust your rear axle accordingly, remembering to turn the bolts on either side of the wheel evenly to maintain wheel alignment. Place a newspaper under the chain so that it doesn't get dirty if you drop it, and then feed the chain over the rear sprocket, along the top of the swingarm, and then over the front sprocket. This will allow you to connect the chain on the bottom of the swingarm, where you'll have more room to work.

You'll need to loosen the chain adjusters to connect the chain because the new chain will be shorter than the old one. Make certain to move both adjusting bolts the same distance, to retain wheel alignment.

7. Assemble the split/master link with the rubber O-rings. (The chain's manufacturer will include instructions for doing this with the chain.) Then insert the split link through the two ends of the chain, connecting the chain. Place an O-ring over each exposed pin, put the side plate over the pins, and push the retaining clip over the pins, making certain that the closed end of the clip

faces toward the chain's direction of travel. This means that the closed end will be facing the rear sprocket if you're working on the part of the chain that lies under the swingarm.

8. Adjust the chain to the proper tension, as described in Chapter 16, and then make certain that all bolts are tight. The chain might require readjusting quite a bit when it is new, so check the tension more often than normal.

Steer Clear _____

Make certain that you replace the split/master link retaining clip's round, closed end facing the direction the chain travels. In that position, the split-link retaining clip has its open end facing away from the chain's direction of travel. If the split end is facing the direction in which the chain moves, road debris could wedge between the clip, causing it to come loose and leading to the loss of your chain.

As you perform these procedures, you will get a better idea of your mechanical abilities. You may find that you have a knack for doing your own repair. If so, cautiously branch out, performing more of your own repairs.

Even if you can afford to have someone else do all this work, if you learn to perform your own maintenance and repair, you'll derive more satisfaction from the motorcycle ownership experience.

The Least You Need to Know

- Check your tire pressure before every ride.

- New tires are slippery and need some time to be broken in properly before they provide all their potential traction.

- Always use the brake fluid your brake system was designed to use, and use only brake fluid from a sealed container.

- When replacing the split link in a drive chain, make certain that the round, closed end of the retainer clip points in the direction in which the chain moves.

Chapter 18

Creative Customizing and Collecting

In This Chapter

◆ Why customize your bike?

◆ Types of custom motorcycles

◆ Setting goals for customizing your bike

◆ What to look for when collecting motorcycles

In 1885, Gottlieb Daimler cobbled together the Einspur, the first gasoline-powered, purpose-built motorcycle. The vehicle was just a test bed for his engine, and as soon as he had a motor strong enough to power a four-wheeled vehicle, he abandoned his Einspur. History is a bit unclear about what happened to the vehicle after that. My guess is that it fell into the hands of the first motorcycle enthusiast, who promptly customized the thing.

Motorcyclists have been customizing their machines since the beginning of the sport. Whether we ride a mass-produced Universal Japanese Motorcycle (UJM) or a priceless collectible bike, we can't resist personalizing our machines.

Motorcyclists also like to collect motorcycles. People collect bikes for different reasons. Some collect bikes as investments, although the value of such investments has not been proven. Most of us collect bikes just because we like them. (Motorcycles seem to follow you home sometimes.)

In this chapter, I'm going to help you decide whether you should customize your bike and how to get started. I'm also going to explain the basics of collecting bikes. I'll offer advice on which bikes may be good investments, but mostly I'm going to try to help you find motorcycles that make you happy. Ask any serious collector, and he or she will tell you that's what it's all about.

Why Customize?

Originally, people modified their motorcycles to improve them in some way. In the early years of the sport, for example, many motorcyclists added a windshield, some saddlebags, or perhaps a sidecar to their bikes.

After World War II, customization in the United States focused on improving performance. Young American men and women had been exposed to lightweight, high-performance European motorcycles during the war. When they came home, the old domestic bikes just didn't cut it. Most motorcycle riders had to figure out alternative methods to get higher performance out of their bikes.

How'd they do it? They simply lightened their bikes. They unbolted every nonessential part they could unbolt or torch. This became the pattern for customization in this country, and to this day, the *bobbers*, as the original chopped customs were called, set the pattern for American-style custom bikes.

Cycle Babble

The custom bikes American riders built after World War II were called **bobbers** because owners cut off, or "bobbed," much of the bodywork.

As the performance levels of stock motorcycles climbed, it became less necessary to customize a bike to attain more speed. But people now customize for other reasons, too.

Many people customize for style. In the cruiser world, modifications such as lowering a bike's suspension, altering its steering geometry, and adding *ape-hanger* (tall) handlebars, have come to define the terms *custom* or *chopper* for many people. Ironically, most of the common modifications actually detract from a bike's performance, but scores of people do these things to their bikes anyway.

Recently there has been a big growth in the custom scene for sportbikes. The typically younger riders of such bikes have been watching the chopper custom scene and thinking that they can do it just as well. These bikes obviously have a whole new twist on custom style, and can be very innovative. However, they can be just as hard to ride as the customs from the cruiser scene.

Cycle Babble _____

The term **ape hangers** was coined at the height of the custom-bike movement to describe tall handlebars that forced the rider to reach skyward to grasp the controls, making the rider adopt an apelike posture. Harley-Davidson recently copyrighted this term, but it has been around since at least the 1960s.

But there's an alternate movement in the realm of motorcycle customization. Many people still modify their bikes to increase their usefulness. People add aftermarket suspension components to improve a bike's handling. They mount windshields, more comfortable seats, and hard luggage to make a motorcycle a better long-distance tourer. They add aftermarket air filters and rejet their carburetors, not only to make their bikes faster, but also to make them more efficient.

Comparing Customs

Ask a typical American to describe a custom bike, and he or she will most likely describe the radical chopper-type bike. Such bikes account for the largest segment of customization in the United States, but elsewhere in the world, other types of customs have been more prevalent. In the past few years, some of the other styles of customs have been gaining in popularity in the United States, including *streetfighters* (also known as hooligan bikes), which have long been popular in Europe.

Cycle Babble _____

Streetfighters are usually sportbikes that have had their plastic fairings removed. Originally this was done by owners who had crashed their bikes and stripped off all the broken plastics (it was cheaper than replacing them). Now they have become cool, so people remove perfectly good bodywork for the look. Streetfighters are very popular in Europe where they originated.

Choppers

Choppers define American motorcycle style. The original bobbers were American hot rods, stripped-down Harleys, and Indians built for speed. As other, faster motorcycles became available, custom Harleys evolved from the bobbers of the 1940s into the choppers of the 1960s. By then, chopper style had become carved in stone: extended forks; high handlebars; a low, fat tire on the back; a tall, skinny tire up front; and a tall backrest or sissybar.

Steer Clear

I don't recommend building a chopper-type custom yourself. Such bikes tend to be so foul-handling that they are unsafe. Riding a motorcycle is challenging enough on a bike you can steer. If you want to own such a machine, I recommend buying one from an established customizer who knows what he or she is doing when building the bike.

In the 1970s and 1980s, choppers evolved into low riders, becoming longer and lower. Now low-rider customs are more common than traditional choppers, although the original choppers' style has made a strong comeback in the past few years.

The original bobbers were either Harleys or Indians. When the British began exporting large numbers of bikes to the United States in the 1950s, these, too, became popular bikes to chop. Initially, customizers also chopped Japanese bikes, but by the early 1980s, Harleys once again ruled the custom-bike market in the United States. But due to the difficulty of obtaining new Harleys, along with their soaring prices, Japanese bikes have become a force of their own in the custom scene. You can now buy aftermarket customizing parts for a variety of Japanese cruisers.

Although typical choppers with extended forks looked pretty groovy, the bikes handled so poorly that they were unsafe to ride.

(Photo © 1998 Darwin Holmstrom)

Harley-Davidsons have long been the motorcycles of choice for customizing projects, but in recent years, Japanese bikes, such as this Honda Shadow, have become more popular among customizers.

(Photo © 1998 Darwin Holmstrom)

Café Racers

While Americans were busy chopping their Harleys, the Europeans took a different approach to customization. For many postwar Europeans, motorcycles were the only form of transportation to which they had access. In Europe, motorcycles were (and still are) used more frequently as practical daily transportation than in the United States.

Thus, customization tended to be more heavily focused on practical improvements. That, combined with the more liberal attitude toward riding fast in many European countries, meant that Europeans were more interested in building faster, better-handling customs than they were in adding higher ape-hanger handlebars and taller sissybars.

In the 1950s and early 1960s, a discernible European style of custom began to emerge. These bikes were inspired by European race bikes. Owners moved their foot-pegs toward the rear and lowered their handlebars, often using handlebars that bolted directly onto the fork legs. This placed the rider in a crouched, forward-leaning position. Some owners adapted small fairings to their bikes to mimic the fairings used by racers.

These bikes became known as *café racers*, supposedly because their owners hung out in cafés and raced each other from café to café. Such bikes have always had a cult following in the United States, a following that continues to grow over time. There are probably more café racers in the United States right now than at any time in history. In some cities, such as Minneapolis and San Francisco, the popularity of café racers rivals that of custom Harleys.

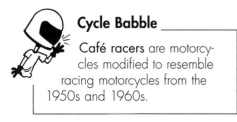

When taken to the extreme, café racers can be as uncomfortable to ride as choppers. But when modified correctly, café racers handle much better than choppers. Another benefit of building a café racer instead of building a chopper is that it's much cheaper. To build a respectable chopper, you'll need to start with either a Harley-Davidson or one of the big Japanese cruisers—an expensive proposition either way.

You can do a very nice café custom job on just about any older Japanese motorcycle—bikes you can pick up for less money than you'd spend on tax and a license for a big new cruiser. Though if you want to build the ultimate café racer, you should go and find a British classic bike to begin with.

Café racers, such as this Rickman-frame Honda 750 from the mid-1970s, have long been popular in Europe and are gaining popularity in the United States as well.

(Photo © 1998 Darwin Holmstrom)

Streetfighters

While Yankees progressed from choppers to low riders, in Europe, café bikes evolved into streetfighters: stripped-down, hopped-up road warriors of the type the original postwar customizers in this country might have devised if they had had access to modern technology.

Streetfighters are all about function, and the first ones had no bodywork, no fancy paint, and no chrome.

As sportbikes became increasingly complex, they also became increasingly expensive to buy and more expensive to repair after minor crashes. Insurance companies began writing off perfectly functional sportbikes rather than replacing expensive bodywork.

European motorcyclists started rescuing those damaged bikes, but instead of replacing expensive bodywork, they just trash-canned all the plastic. Like American customizers in the 1940s, they chopped off all the extraneous parts, replacing only what was needed, such as the headlight. In fact, they often bolted on a couple of headlights. When the whole thing was ready, they applied a coat of flat-black paint (to protect the surfaces of the exposed metal, not for any cosmetic reasons) and then went out and rode the wheels off these streetfighters.

These bikes proved to be so popular that the manufacturers got into the act. A variety of companies began marketing sporting bikes without any bodywork, but no one got the streetfighter look down as well as Triumph. The latest Speed Triple embodies the streetfighter look.

Triumph nailed the streetfighter look with its latest Speed Triple.

(Photo courtesy Motorcyclist™ *magazine)*

Custom Sportbikes

The biggest growth scene in recent years has been in the world of sportbikes. The scene started with young guys buying Japanese supersport machines, and riding them into the ground, often damaging them while riding wheelies and other stunts.

Ultimately, this was so antisocial that it started to burn itself out, though something positive grew out of the ashes. Young people had finally started getting into motorcycles. Right now the motorcycle world is rejuvenated with young blood, and most of the newer riders don't want to just blend in.

Mixing the fast-and-furious import car scene with all the Biker Build Off chopper customs they'd seen on television, they created custom sportbikes. Go to any bike night around the country and you'll see Gixxers (Suzuki GSXR's), Busas (Suzuki HayaBusas), and a wide array of other sportbikes, all customized beyond recognition. The most common modifications are lowered suspension and a stretched swingarm, to make the bike look long and low—plus custom paint and massive back wheels and tires. In this scene, the wilder, the better.

Builders like Ricks Motorcycles shape the custom sportbike scene with bikes like this radical Suzuki HayaBusa.

(Photo courtesy Simon Green)

So You Want to Customize Your Bike ...

If you are interested in customizing your bike, you need to ask yourself a few questions:

1. What do I want from my bike? Do I want to improve some functional aspect, such as comfort or handling? Do I want to improve my bike's performance? Do I just want to change my bike's appearance? What you want from your bike will guide you when deciding what changes to make.

2. What compromises am I willing to make to get what I want? A motorcycle represents a series of compromises made by the designers and engineers who

created it. They made those compromises for a reason. Altering one aspect of your bike can cause unintended consequences in some other aspect. Honestly assess what you are willing to sacrifice before making any changes.

3. How much am I willing to spend? There are many small, inexpensive alterations you can make to your bike that will improve its comfort, handling, appearance, and performance. But making any of the popular major alterations usually costs a lot, and there's no guarantee you'll achieve your desired results. Before embarking on a major modification of your motorcycle, make certain that you know what you want, that your intended modification will achieve that goal, and that the results will be worth what they'll cost you.

Only after you've answered these questions should you make any major modifications to your bike.

By nature, customizing is a personal process. Only you know what you want and need from your bike. Part of your task as a new motorcyclist will be to learn as much as possible about your bike. As you become more familiar with your machine, you'll have a better idea of how to modify it to suit you.

> **Steer Clear**
>
> Don't make drastic modifications to your bike until you are certain of your goals. Making a radical alteration that turns out to make the bike less appealing can be an expensive misstep.

I would start out small. Identify an aspect of your bike you'd like to improve, such as style. Perhaps you can add a colored windshield or chrome parts. Make incremental changes when possible. That will help you avoid making serious mistakes that will be difficult (and expensive) to correct.

Discussing various methods for modifying your bike will fill a book in itself. Fortunately, there are many fine books available on the subject. You can order most of these from Whitehorse Press or Motorbooks International (see Appendix C).

Classic, Collectible, or Just Old? Collecting Motorcycles

Ride long enough, and you'll notice something about motorcycles: no one can own just one. Becoming a motorcycle collector is an insidious process. It starts when you buy a better bike but can't quite bring yourself to sell your trusty old one. Then you'll decide to explore a different aspect of riding, such as off-road riding or touring, so you'll buy a bike suited for that purpose. But you still won't be able to part with the other two. Then you'll run across a pristine example of a classic bike you've always wanted, and you'll just happen to have enough money to buy it, so ....

Steer Clear _____

Don't collect motorcycles because you think you'll make money. You won't. Even if you pick a winner, you'll be lucky to recoup the money you spend on upkeep and maintenance. If you want to get rich, try the stock market. If you want to collect motorcycles, collect bikes you like.

By this time, you're too far gone to turn back. Like it or not, you're a collector. But it could be worse. Peter Egan, who writes for *Cycle World* magazine, once wrote that everyone needs at least four motorcycles: one for touring, one for sport riding, one for riding off-road, and one classic bike to keep it all in perspective. So go ahead and indulge yourself. Motorcycles have gotten much more expensive in the past 15 years, but they are still cheap compared to cars. And they take up a lot less space. You'll make your other half proud when you park six bikes in the space of one car—with some careful packing, of course.

Collector's Choice

In the late 1980s and early 1990s, some investors decided British motorcycles were going to rapidly appreciate in value, and overnight, the price of Triumphs, Nortons, and BSAs skyrocketed. Many of the people buying these bikes were not motorcyclists: they were investors out to get rich.

Some people did get rich off of the entire debacle, but for the most part, it wasn't the investors—it was the people who sold the motorcycles at inflated prices. The Brit-bike boom lasted a few years, and then prices declined. British bikes still cost more than they used to, even when their prices are adjusted for inflation and appreciation, but they're back down to somewhat reasonable levels.

The lesson to be learned from all this is that you shouldn't buy a bike solely as a financial investment. It's a risky proposition, at best. Even if you get lucky and buy a bike that does increase in value, it probably won't increase enough to cover the expenses you incur while you own it.

If you're interested in a particular type or brand of bike, you can look for a particular model or year that may someday be worth more than other models or years, but that is a secondary consideration. When deciding what to collect, it's a whole lot more fun to just buy bikes that you really like.

What Do You Like?

Nobody else can tell you this! Before you start collecting bikes, ask yourself what you like. Do you like classic Japanese bikes? Do you like the brutal efficiency of BMWs? How about the fluid style of Italian sportbikes? Or the simple elegance of British bikes? Perhaps you like classic American motorcycles. Whatever your style, your individual preferences are of key importance when you begin collecting bikes.

What's Your Mechanical Skill Level?

How much time and energy are you willing to devote to the upkeep of your bikes? An American or British bike will require a lot more work to keep running than a Japanese bike or a BMW. Italian bikes will fall somewhere in between. Know your abilities before you start buying bikes with maintenance requirements that you are unprepared to deal with.

What's Your Budget?

You also need to ask yourself how much you're willing to spend. With the exception of Japanese bikes, any of the motorcycles mentioned in this chapter will take a serious bite out of your bank account. You can still pick up a decent British bike or a BMW for under $4,000, but if your taste runs toward Italian or American bikes, you'd better have considerably more cash available.

You can still find nice, older Japanese bikes for fairly low prices, though. The prices of a few early models, such as Honda's Benly Super Sport 125, have shot through the roof. But you can still pick up a very nice mid-1970s CB750 for under $1,500, and you can find clean examples of other Japanese bikes for less than that. Few of these bikes will ever have any serious investment value, but they're fun to ride and easy to maintain, and they make great projects for café chops.

What Constitutes a Classic?

Classifying a bike as a classic is an almost mystical process. To be a true classic, a bike needs to have just the right combination of rarity, competence, and charisma to tickle collectors right in their reptilian stems.

Some bikes are firmly established as classics. No one questions the status of bikes such as Moto Guzzi's V7 Sport, Ducati's Round Case 750SS, Mike Hailwood Replicas, Harley's Knuckleheads and Panheads, Indian's Chiefs and Fours, any Brough or

Vincent, BMW's R60s, Ariel's Square Fours, Norton's Commandos, or BSA's Gold Stars. But to get one of these bikes, be prepared to shell out some serious cash. And be prepared to wait because there are only a handful of some of these bikes on U.S. soil, and most of those are owned by collectors who have little interest in selling them.

If you decide to fork over the big bucks to buy a classic, make certain that you're getting the real thing. For example, earlier Triumph Bonnevilles are much sought after by collectors, while collectors tend to show little interest in the later models with dry-sump oil reservoirs in their frames. And if you invest your life savings in a Round Case Ducati SS, make certain that you're getting the real thing, because other Ducati models can be converted into convincing SS replicas.

One way to tell a true Round Case Ducati 750SS from a fake is to check the frame. Most SS models didn't have provisions for mounting a centerstand, and on most fakes, the mounting lugs will have been grounded off. But some very early race bikes did have some mounting lugs, and these are the most collectible of all Ducatis. Compounding this confusion is the historically shoddy record-keeping of the Ducati factory. Given the complexity involved, your best bet is to hire a recognized expert to authenticate the bike. Such a service won't come cheap, but if you have enough money to purchase this particular bike, you can certainly afford to authenticate your investment.

How can you tell whether a bike is for real? Read all you can about a particular bike before buying one. If a bike's really a classic, there will be a plethora of books about it. Appendix C lists the names and addresses of a couple of publishers who specialize in motorcycle books. Call and get their catalogs, and you'll find books on every classic bike made.

Steer Clear

When shopping for a classic bike, make certain you're getting the real thing. Buying a fake can be one of the most expensive mistakes you'll ever make.

If you're interested in collecting classic bikes, get in touch with your local antique motorcycle club. Members of such organizations can provide you with more knowledge about classic motorcycles than any other source. And these people love motorcycles. You'll find no shortage of advice, and you may even be able to find someone who can help you locate the exact bike you're looking for.

Future Classics?

Given the scarcity and cost of true classics, collecting might seem out of most people's reach. And it can be a real gamble. Your odds of losing money are much greater than your odds of making money. That's why I recommend buying only bikes you like and bikes you will use.

That doesn't mean you can't have a lot of fun and possibly even make some money someday. There are useful bikes that qualify as great buys right now that might become classics sometime in the future.

Say, for example, that after you've become a proficient rider, you decide to buy a hard-core sportbike. You can buy any of the Japanese sportbikes.

Or, for about the same price as a 600cc Japanese sportbike, you can buy a used Ducati 900SS. The 600cc might be a bit faster than the Ducati, but the Ducati is faster than you'll ever be able to ride on public roads. And it's easier to ride fast than most 600cc. In other words, it's more sportbike than you'll ever be able to use in the real world. It will require more maintenance, and you'll need to know a mechanic skilled in adjusting its valve gear, but down the road, it may be worth the bother.

Hang on to the Ducati for 10 or 20 years, and then compare its value to the value of a 20-year-old run-of-the-mill Japanese 600. While the 600 will be worth far less, the Ducati will be worth what you paid for it, provided that you've taken good care of it. And if that particular model of Ducati appreciates, as some people speculate it might, you could come out ahead. If you factor in your maintenance costs and inflation, you still would have done better to invest in the stock market, but a Ducati is much more fun to ride than a few thousand shares of Martha Stewart's stock.

By nature of their rarity or oddity, other bikes may someday become collectibles—bikes such as Yamaha's GTS, a sport-tourer with an automotive-style front suspension instead of traditional forks, and Honda's six-cylinder CBX. But if you buy one of these, do so because you want the bike. That way, you'll have more fun, and you won't be disappointed if you don't make a fortune.

The Least You Need to Know

- Some modifications can make a motorcycle dangerous to ride.

- Get to know your bike and what you want from it before modifying it.

- If you want to get rich, invest in the stock market, not in classic motorcycles.

- When shopping for a classic, make certain you're getting the real thing.

Part 5

The Motorcycling Community

So far, I've concentrated on you and your motorcycle. From a safety perspective, that's the most important part of riding, because when you're out on the road, you're all you have to depend on.

But there's much more to motorcycling than just solitary riding. You have now become part of an extended family: the motorcycle community. In this part, I'll tell you about different aspects of that community and what it has to offer you.

Join the Club: Motorcycle Clubs

In This Chapter

- What motorcycle clubs can offer you

- The different types of motorcycle clubs

- The importance of the American Motorcyclist Association

- Finding a motorcycle club that's right for you

Motorcycles and motorcycling have fascinated me for as long as I can remember. When I was six years old, I was already figuring out a way to get a motorcycle for myself. Not long after I finally got my first bike, I discovered an aspect of motorcycling I hadn't even considered before: the motorcycling community. I started to hang out with other kids who had motorcycles, and we began riding together.

The main benefit of joining a motorcycle club is camaraderie. Motorcyclists often feel out of place around non-motorcyclists, like the odd gearhead in the crowd. Motorcycle clubs provide social outlets for motorcyclists, a place we can get together with our own kind and talk about riding and bikes without having to worry about boring each other. A club is a nexus where the motorcycling community comes together.

Whatever your interests, you'll find a motorcycle club with members who share those interests. In this chapter, I'll discuss different types of clubs. I'll also tell you what these organizations have to offer you.

How Motorcycle Clubs Were Born

A lot of the disaffected young people returning to America from World War II—people unable or unwilling to assimilate into mainstream American society—banded together to form the infamous outlaw motorcycle clubs. One such club, the Booze Fighters, became the model for Johnny's Black Rebels Motorcycle Club in the film *The Wild One.* Another of the postwar outlaw motorcycle clubs to gain some notoriety was the Hell's Angels.

Steer Clear _____

I have personal experience with some of the clubs listed in this chapter, while others I've just heard of or read about. Not all clubs will have your best interests at heart. Some groups may be more interested in collecting dues than offering anything of value to members. I haven't run across any that fit that description (all the groups I have experience with have been worthwhile), but like anything else in motorcycling, use your head when joining a club.

The Japanese invasion led to another development in the motorcycle club scene. With all those nice people out riding around on their Hondas, it was only natural that some would form clubs. Which they did, by the thousands. Today you'll find clubs devoted to every make of bike ever built, from ATK to Zundap, along with hundreds of clubs for specific models.

Today there's a motorcycle club for just about every segment of society. You'll find motorcycle clubs for members of different ethnic groups, motorcycle clubs for computer geeks, and motorcycle clubs for gay and lesbian riders. Along with the traditional outlaw motorcycle clubs, you'll find law-abiding clubs for police officers and firefighters. There are clubs for recovering alcoholics and clubs for people who like to get falling-down drunk.

Structured clubs allow motorcyclists to pool resources and achieve things individual bikers could not. In the early years of motorcycling, clubs often centered on competition. Racing clubs were able to maintain racetracks and organize events much more efficiently than individual motorcyclists. That's still the case today, and race-promoting organizations tend to maintain clublike atmospheres.

Types of Clubs

Categorizing clubs is as difficult as categorizing human beings, always a tricky and dangerous endeavor. When you divide people into groups, you end up placing people in the wrong category as often as you place them in the correct category. At best, that's confusing; at worst, it can be hazardous to your health. Placing members of the Bandidos Motorcycle Club in the same category as the Hell's Angels Motorcycle Club might seem logical to an outsider, but certain humorless members of the two groups might not find it amusing. With that in mind, I'll attempt to describe the general categories of motorcycle clubs. (Note that you'll find contact information for many of the clubs mentioned in this chapter in Appendix C.)

Off-Road and Trail-Riding Clubs

A major challenge faced by off-road riders is finding a place to ride. Very little land remains open to trail riders. Off-road and trail-riding clubs often maintain trail systems for members. Even clubs that don't maintain their own trail systems will be able to help you find public or private land where you can ride. Off-road clubs usually conduct organized rides for members and often organize competitive events.

Off-road clubs exist in most areas of the country. For example, the Panhandle Trail Riders Association (PANTRA) maintains a trail network that extends from Washington State to Montana, with trails across the Idaho panhandle for members to use.

Other off-road clubs focus on organizing competitive events. Without clubs such as the Polka Dots Motorcycle Club, for example, which puts on three races each year near Sacramento, California, few off-road events would take place.

Off-road clubs may have higher dues than some other types of clubs, but maintaining trails is an expensive business. If you like to ride off-road, membership dues in a good club can be the least expensive way to gain access to a good trail system.

Racing and Sportbike Clubs

Sportbike clubs are similar to off-road clubs in function, but tend to be less labor-intensive, because sportbike club rides usually take place on public roads, so there are no trails to maintain. Sportbike clubs often organize sport tours for members, and some clubs arrange access to regional racetracks. The only way many riders can afford access to a closed-course racetrack where they can practice high-performance riding is through a club that arranges the rental of track time.

Motorcycology _____

Make certain that you have mastered your riding skills before joining a club dedicated to sport riding. Such clubs tend to place a premium on safe riding and have little tolerance for motorcyclists who ride beyond their skills. Club members are experienced riders who don't appreciate some poorly skilled hotshot endangering their lives.

Antique-Motorcycle Clubs

If you collect and restore antique motorcycles, you'll find membership in one of the many antique-motorcycle clubs around the country essential. When restoring a bike, you can search for years for just the right carburetor you need to get your bike running or for the exact fender or tail lamp for your specific model and year. By using the extensive network of experts found in antique-bike clubs, you can make that process considerably easier. And if you can't locate a part through contacts made in an antique-bike club, club members can probably help you find someone who can make the part for you.

Many antique clubs are organized under the umbrella of the Antique Motorcycle Club of America (A.M.C.A.), a not-for-profit organization founded in 1954. World-wide membership in the A.M.C.A. is now more than 7,500; many members attend A.M.C.A. national meets held around the country each year. The club also publishes its own magazine, which comes out four times annually.

Woody Carson, national director of the Antique Motorcycle Club of America, and his one-of-a-kind 1925 Indian Prince LX2.

(Photo © 1998 Darwin Holmstrom)

Make- or Model-Specific Clubs

Many clubs were formed by fans of a particular brand or model of motorcycle. Some of these clubs, such as the Norton Owners Club, are organized around a brand or model of motorcycle that is no longer produced and could be classified as antique clubs as easily as make-specific clubs. Other make-specific clubs, such as the Harley Owners Group (HOG), tend to have a heavy ratio of people who own new bikes in their ranks. New bikes need less technical support than older bikes, so clubs such as HOG serve more as social outlets than as practical sources of parts and information.

HOG, a factory-sponsored club with 300 affiliates worldwide and nearly 1 million members, is one of the best-known motorcycle clubs in the world. HOG has helped fuel Harley's spectacular comeback as much as technological improvements to the bikes themselves. HOG helped Harley-Davidson foster a tight-knit community among its customers that, in turn, helped foster customer loyalty that borders on fanaticism.

BMW owners form another tightly knit community of riders. And these folks take their riding seriously. Many Beemer owners put tens of thousands of miles on their bikes every year and often rack up more than 100,000 miles on their machines. Some owners have been known to put 200,000 miles, 300,000 miles, or even more on a single motorcycle. Serious motorcyclists like this deserve a serious club, and the BMW Motorcycle Owners of America (BMWMOA) is indeed a serious organization. It puts on some of the finest rallies in North America and produces a monthly magazine that rivals any motorcycle journal you'll find on the newsstands.

Similarly, American Honda's Honda Rider's Club of America is home to an enthusiastic group of—naturally—Honda riders of every stripe, be they motorcyclists, ATV riders, or captains of Honda's lineup of personal watercraft. The HRCA also has its own magazines, one each for motorcyclists and for ATV enthusiasts. What's more, Honda's club offers its own annual rally, but the HRCA sets itself apart by being an all-brands rally. That's right—no matter what you ride, you're welcome at the yearly blast in Knoxville, Tennessee.

Often clubs devoted to a single popular model will emerge, like the Shadow Club USA, a club for fans of Honda's Shadow cruisers. Sometimes clubs will organize around a particular type of engine used by a company, such as the *Airheads* Beemer Club, a club for owners of BMW motorcycles powered by air-cooled Boxer motors. This group was organized in response to the increasing complexity and cost that accompanied BMW's recent technological advances.

Cycle Babble _____

Older air-cooled BMW Boxer twins are called **Airheads,** while newer air-and-oil-cooled Beemers are called **Oilheads.** There are motorcycle clubs organized by and devoted to the interests of owners of Airheads and Oilheads.

Then there are make-specific clubs that could just as easily be categorized as sport-riding clubs, organizations like the Crazed Ducati Riders of Massachusetts. Some might argue that there is no difference between a Ducati rider and a sport rider. (Some might also argue that Crazed Ducati Riders is redundant, but that's another story.)

The most useful make- or model-specific clubs are clubs devoted to _orphan bikes_—rare bikes that are no longer in production. Such clubs can be invaluable sources of parts and technical information.

A group that fits this category is the Turbo Motorcycle International Owners Association (TMIOA). The TMIOA was started in 1987 originally for owners of Honda's CX Turbo motorcycles, but in December 1988, it broadened its focus to include coverage of all the factory turbocharged motorcycles. Turbo bikes were built by all the Japanese manufacturers in the early 1980s, but they all suffered from mechanical problems, to some degree, and never became popular. Now these bikes are sought after by collectors, but parts availability is a serious problem, especially given the history of mechanical troubles in such bikes. Clubs devoted to turbo bikes can save a turbo owner a lot of time and money when it comes to keeping his or her bike on the road.

Touring Clubs

Joining a touring club is a great way to get travel tips and advice from motorcyclists who have actually been there (regardless of where "there" is). You'll learn things from members of touring clubs that you won't learn anywhere else, such as where to find good restaurants and hotels, how to find the best roads, the locations of speed traps, and roads to avoid.

Motorcycology _____

When getting traveling advice from another rider who belongs to a touring-oriented club, take that rider's riding habits and personality into account when deciding whether to act on that advice. Some touring riders might consider a ride down the Alaska Highway a nice weekend jaunt.

Sometimes touring-oriented clubs center on a particular model of touring bike, such as Honda's Gold Wing or Yamaha's Venture. One such group, the Gold Wing Road Riders Association (GWRRA), is the world's largest club devoted to a single model of motorcycle. GWRRA members organize some of the most extravagant club gatherings in the United States.

Locale-Specific Clubs

Often clubs form with no common denominator other than location. Motorcyclists just want to get together with other people from their area who ride, regardless of what they ride or how they ride. Such clubs can provide you with information on riding in an area you won't find anywhere else, an especially valuable service for new riders. The WetLeather motorcycle club, for example, exists so members can get together and discuss the challenges faced by motorcyclists in the Pacific Northwest.

Female Motorcyclist Clubs

Women have been riding motorcycles as long as men, although never in as great numbers. And women have had their own motorcycle clubs almost as long as men. Organizations such as the Motor Maids have long been a part of the motorcycling scene.

But in recent years, the number of women who ride has grown, and now more women ride their own motorcycles than ever before. As more women enter the sport, the number and variety of women's motorcycle clubs has grown.

One of the largest women's groups is Women On Wheels (WOW). When WOW was founded in 1982, women who rode their own bikes were still exceptions, oddities in the motorcycling community. WOW provided an outlet for these women, a place where they could get together with other female riders. Today there are WOW chapters all across the United States.

In the past few years, more specialized women's motorcycling clubs have emerged, such as the Ebony Queens Motorcycle Club, a club for African American women.

Age-Specific Clubs

A trend that has gained momentum as the baby boomers age is the rise of age-specific clubs, organizations composed of motorcyclists who have reached a certain age. For example, the Retreads Motorcycle Club consists of riders who are at least 40 years old.

Lately, a few clubs composed of riders under a certain age have sprouted. In Oregon, for example, there's an organization called the Mudrats, a club for people 15 years old and younger who like to ride dirtbikes and all-terrain vehicles.

A group of Retreads kicking back at a local watering hole after a long ride.

(Photo © 1998 Darwin Holmstrom)

Spiritually Oriented Clubs

During the past 20 years, Christian motorcycling clubs have multiplied prolifically. The Christian Motorcyclists Association (CMA), one of the largest of these organizations, can be found at rallies and events around the United States.

Christian motorcyclist groups do a great deal to promote a positive image of motorcycling to the general public. If you are so inclined, joining such a club would be an ideal way to combine your spirituality and passion for motorcycling.

Christians aren't the only group to combine their spiritual beliefs with motorcycling. There are Taoist and Buddhist motorcycle clubs, and there are pagan motorcycle clubs. There is even one group, the Bavarian Illuminati Motorcycle Club, which quotes the Western mystic Aleister Crowley in its club bylaws. The club has very little of what could be called structure, but members do receive a suggested reading list that includes *The Illuminatus! Trilogy*, by Robert Anton Wilson, and *Heart of Darkness*, by Joseph Conrad, as well as an eclectic collection of books on motorcycling and mysticism.

Activity-Oriented Clubs

A variety of clubs combine other interests with motorcycling. Sometimes these clubs combine motorcycle-related interests. If you're interested in motorcycling and camping, for example, you can join the International Brotherhood of Motorcycle Campers, a group dedicated to riders who camp out rather than stay in motels when they tour on their motorcycles.

Other clubs combine motorcycling with unrelated interests, such as the Motorcycling Amateur Radio Club (MARC), composed of motorcyclists who are also ham radio operators.

Motorcycle Moments _____

A man who lived in the town where I attended college once mounted a small refrigerator on the back of his motorcycle and rode the bike like that for an entire summer. Years later, I met the guy and asked him about the fridge. It turned out he was a member of the Motorcycling Amateur Radio Club, and he mounted his ham radio in the fridge to protect it from the elements. He gave up that system because the weight disrupted his motorcycle's handling, and now he tows his radio in a special trailer.

Motorcyclists who have access to a computer can even join virtual motorcycle clubs, organizations such as Cyber-Bikers On The Web. These are clubs for people who love to ride but also like to surf the Internet.

Socially Active Clubs

Many motorcycle groups form to support certain causes and hold poker runs and other events to raise funds for charity. One such group, Friends of Children with Cerebral Palsy, located in Regina, Saskatchewan (Canada), organizes an annual Ride for Dreams to raise money to help children with Cerebral Palsy.

Another club that raises a lot of money for a specific charity is the Women's Motorcyclist Foundation (WMF). In 1996, the WMF organized the National Pony Express Tour, a 14,537-mile motorcycle relay around the perimeter of the United States, to raise awareness of breast cancer and to raise research funds for the Susan G. Komen Foundation in Dallas, Texas. Female motorcyclists who participated in the ride (and their supporters) raised $317,000.

Profession-Related Clubs

Often motorcyclists in certain professions form motorcycle clubs with other members of their profession. One of the most famous clubs of this type is the Blue Knights, a club composed of law-enforcement officials. Chapters of the Blue Knights are located in all 50 states, as well as 12 other countries.

Creative Clubs

People are getting more creative when forming motorcycle clubs. Often these are just groups dedicated to having fun, such as the Good Vibrations Cycle Riders, located in Florida. Good Vibrations holds no meetings, collects no dues, and has just one bylaw in its charter: have fun.

Other groups solely devoted to having fun have appeared around the country. The Hell's Rice Burners Motorcycle Club from the Delaware area was formed for people who ride ratty old Japanese bikes. Ideally, members should pay no more than $25 when they buy their bikes. Little is known of the ominous Death's Head Motorcycle Club, located deep in Appalachia, except that members have a proclivity for body modification, such as piercing, tattooing, scarification (making shallow cuts in the skin), and branding.

There are clubs for curmudgeon motorcyclists, and there are clubs for vampires who ride, such as the Santa Cruz Vampires Motorcycle and Scooter Club. There is even a club for riders who don't like to bathe. Biker Scum is an organization dedicated to the pursuit of happiness through riding and the neglect of personal hygiene. Believe it or not, this club is quite popular. Originally formed in central Texas, the club now has chapters in Pennsylvania; Virginia; California; Indiana; Ontario, Canada; and Okinawa, Japan.

The American Motorcyclist Association

No single group plays a more influential role in motorcycling in the United States than the American Motorcyclist Association (AMA), a 220,000-member organization founded in 1924.

The world's largest motorsports-sanctioning body, the AMA oversees more than 80 national-level racing events all over the United States. These events encompass the entire motorcycle-racing spectrum and include events as diverse as the Superbike races at Daytona, Supercross and Arenacross racing, dirt-track racing, and hill climbing. The AMA's Member Activities Department coordinates thousands of amateur races across the country, with dozens of competition classes for everyone from grade-school kids to senior riders. Through its 1,200 chartered clubs, the AMA oversees more than 3,700 road-riding and competition events each year. If there's motorcycle racing taking place in the United States, the AMA is probably involved.

Perhaps even more important than its promotion of racing is the work of the AMA Government Relations Department, which works harder than any single organization to make riders aware of bad laws and anti-motorcycling discrimination at the local, state, federal, and corporate levels. You'd be amazed at some of the anti-motorcycle legislation proposed at all levels of government, as well as the discrimination to be found in the workplace. Fortunately for all of us, during its 80 years of existence, the AMA has developed successful methods for dealing with discrimination against motorcyclists. Even if you join no other motorcycle organization, I highly recommend joining the AMA.

Motorcycology

There is no more effective way to protect your rights as a motorcyclist than to join the AMA. Write to:

American Motorcyclist Association
13515 Yarmouth Dr.
Pickering, Ohio 43147

You can call the AMA at 1-800-AMA-JOIN (1-800-262-5646), or e-mail it at ama@ama-cycle.org.

Finding a Club

One of the best ways to locate a club in your area is to contact the AMA and get a list of AMA-chartered clubs in your area.

If you know of a local place (such as a bar, café, or motorcycle shop) where motorcyclists hang out, you can ask if the folks there know of any local clubs. The Internet is also a terrific resource for finding motorcycle clubs, especially some of the more off-the-wall organizations.

You can also check Appendix C for contact information for some of the national motorcycle groups that may be able to put you in touch with local groups in your area.

After you've found a club, look into it before joining. Attend a couple of meetings and visit with members. Perhaps you might even go for a ride with them. If you enjoy the time you spend with members, chances are you'll enjoy being a member.

Joining a club may not be a necessity for enjoying the sport of motorcycling—motorcycling is, in the end, a solitary activity—but it can greatly enhance the experience. The enthusiasm club members have for riding is infectious and can motivate you to explore new areas of the sport. And if you live in a climate where you can't ride for long periods of time each year, meeting with your motorcycle club can help you make it through the long winter months.

The Least You Need to Know

♦ Club memberships can be practical as well as fun.

♦ Clubs can be great sources of hard-to-locate parts and information.

♦ Many clubs do a great deal of work supporting causes other than motorcycling, such as breast cancer research.

♦ Joining the AMA is the best way you can ensure the future of motorcycling.

Chapter 20

The Open Road: Touring and Rallies

In This Chapter

- ◆ Preparing your bike for a trip
- ◆ Planning your trip
- ◆ Packing gear on your bike safely
- ◆ Learning about motorcycle rallies around the country

I enjoy all aspects of riding, from commuting to work to trail riding, but I enjoy touring on a bike most of all. I find nothing more thrilling than cresting a hill and seeing a new expanse of world open up before me. Whether I'm exploring the Sand Hill region of Nebraska, the High Desert in Southern California, the lush Ozark Mountains of Arkansas, or the wheat fields of Minnesota, I never get bored when I'm traveling on a bike.

In this chapter, I'm going to share with you some of the tips I've learned over the course of my trips.

I'm also going to talk a bit about where to go on your motorcycle (as well as where not to go). And I'll discuss different motorcycle-related events you can attend, such as rallies.

Any Bike Is a Touring Bike

If you have a dependable motorcycle, you can travel on it. Ed Otto, a competitive long-distance rider, rode 11,000 miles on a Honda Helix scooter during the 1995 *Iron Butt Rally*, one of the most grueling long-distance motorcycle rallies in the world.

> **Cycle Babble**
>
> The **Iron Butt Rally** is arguably the most grueling long-distance motorcycle rally in the world. Participants ride around the perimeter of the United States, often including side trips that take them hundreds or even thousands of miles out of their way. Finishing the rally requires that you ride at least 11,000 miles in 11 days. Top-10 finishers often ride 12,000 to 13,000 miles in that time.

Of course, some motorcycles make better tourers than others. Selecting a bike to tour on is an individual choice. It doesn't matter how well a motorcycle works for other riders—what matters is how well it works for *you*. How well does your motorcycle fit you physically? Is it comfortable on day-long rides? How well do its power-delivery characteristics suit your riding style?

You also need to feel comfortable with the reliability of your bike. You don't want to get stranded in the middle of some unfamiliar urban area or isolated mountain road on a bike. Before you decide to take a bike on an extended trip, you should know its mechanical condition. If you do travel on a bike that has a tendency to break down, you should be familiar enough with the bike's mechanics to perform some basic repair work on the side of the road.

Honda's Helix scooter might not be the ideal mount for 1,000-mile-a-day rides, but at a more relaxed pace, it can make a fine traveling companion.

(Photo courtesy of Vreeke and Associates)

Planning a Trip

I have a tendency to overplan trips, marking out each gas stop on my map, along with my estimated time of arrival. But some of my best motorcycle tours have been the least planned. I once went on a meandering two-week trip through Wyoming and Colorado with a friend who is perhaps the least-organized human being I've ever met.

Once I let go and gave control to a higher power (in this case, my buddy's disorganized ways), I had the most relaxing trip of my life. And I saw more of the country I rode through than I ever had before. I discovered that the most entertaining road is the road to nowhere.

Touring Range and Fuel Stops

But even on the road to nowhere, you have to prepare at least a minimal amount. Motorcycles have small gas tanks and can travel only a short distance between fuel stops, at least when compared to cars. You need to plan your trip so that you know you'll be able to find fuel when you need it.

Some bikes have more touring range than others, depending on the size of their fuel tanks and what kind of gas mileage they get. For example, a bike with a 4.7-gallon tank that gets 36 miles per gallon on average can travel 169.2 miles before you have to start walking, while a bike with a 3.7-gallon tank that gets 54 miles per gallon on average can go almost 200 miles before refueling.

Motorcycology _____

Learn to predict whether a town will have an open gas station by checking its population. State road maps always list the names of all the towns in the state, along with their populations. A town with a population of 500 or more should have a gas station, but the station may be closed in the evenings and on Sunday. To find an open gas station after hours or on a Sunday, you'll need to find a town with a population of 1,000 or higher. Make sure you plan your course accordingly.

Touring and sport-touring motorcycles generally have big fuel tanks, but sometimes they burn so much gas that you really don't have that great a range. Cruisers tend to have smaller tanks, but some cruisers, especially the V-twins, use less fuel, so they can travel nearly as far. Some bikes with exceptionally small tanks, such as older Harley-Davidson Sportsters, can barely travel 100 miles before they start sucking air out of their tanks.

Steer Clear _____

When traveling through isolated areas such as the American West, it's better to err on the side of caution when planning your fuel stops. It's better to refuel too often than to not refuel often enough.

Not only is having to constantly refuel your bike time-consuming and annoying, it can also be dangerous. In many areas in the United States, especially in the West and Southwest, you can easily ride 150 miles between gas stations. These are isolated areas, and if you were to run out of fuel in such a place, you would probably be eaten by buzzards before someone found you.

Even if you aren't going any place in particular, keep your bike's range in mind when deciding which roads to take.

Don't push your luck when it comes to refueling. If you are getting low on fuel and pass a gas station, refill your tank. If you decide to wait until the next town, you could find that the town has no gas station.

Keep in mind that your fuel mileage can vary, depending on conditions. If you are riding fast or have a heavy load, you can count on running out of fuel sooner than if you are traveling more slowly or carrying a lighter load.

Preparing Your Bike

Throughout this book, I've tried to stress the importance of properly maintaining your motorcycle. When traveling long distances on a bike, this is especially important. If your bike were to break down in an isolated mountain pass, you could freeze to death before someone found you. Making certain your bike is in good shape before you take a trip serves an economic purpose as well. Having a breakdown far from home can be much more expensive than having your bike fall apart while commuting to work. When you break down in an isolated area, you don't have the luxury of shopping around for the best prices. You also don't have the luxury of finding a mechanic you trust.

Your best bet is to get your bike in as good shape as possible before taking a trip. Study the procedures in Chapters 16 and 17. Make certain that you perform all routine maintenance. Here's a checklist of procedures you should always perform before an extended trip:

- ◆ Change the oil.
- ◆ Top off the electrolyte in the battery.
- ◆ Check your coolant and chain tension.

- ◆ Tighten every bolt on your bike.

- ◆ Replace leaky fork seals, as well as worn bearings and bushings in the frame.

- ◆ Replace worn shocks and fork springs.

- ◆ Pay close attention to your tires. If there is the slightest possibility that your tires will wear out on your trip, replace them before you go.

What to Bring?

No matter what I tell you, you will probably overestimate the amount of clothing and gear you'll need when you take your first motorcycle trip. But here are my suggestions for all you need for a safe, comfortable ride.

The Clothes Make the Motorcyclist

On my first extended trip, which I took about 15 years ago, I brought a couple of different jackets (for riding in a variety of weather conditions), along with five or six complete changes of clothing, including some dressy clothes in case I wanted to go out to eat or on a date.

Now I bring a couple of pairs of jeans, a couple of turtlenecks, a couple of sweatshirts, and a couple of T-shirts. I may bring three T-shirts if the weather is hot or if I plan to be gone a week or more. And I bring pretty much every pair of underwear and socks I own. If I go out for a nice dinner, I wear my cleanest pair of jeans and the turtleneck with the fewest holes in it.

Motorcycology

When packing for a motorcycle trip, pack light. A lighter load will tax your motorcycle less and will not have such a pronounced effect on your bike's handling. Leave a little extra space for any souvenirs you might pick up.

Your best bet is to travel light on a bike. Bring only clothing you'll wear. And you'll always seem to wear less than you bring. As you become a more experienced motorcycle traveler, you'll find that you bring less clothing on each successive trip.

Tools You'll Use

Although I pack fewer clothes for each trip, I find that my list of must-bring gear grows each year. Every time I've needed an item I didn't have, I've included that item on following trips.

I always bring a small selection of extra tools, even when I'm on a new bike. The toolkits that come with most bikes will do in a pinch, but I always like to have an extra set of combination spanner wrenches, a couple of pliers (needle-nose pliers and channel-lock pliers), a ratchet, and a small selection of sockets. I also include a cigarette lighter, a small selection of nuts and bolts (including some for connecting my battery cables to my battery), some electrical connectors, a roll of wire, zip ties, and a couple of rolls of tape (friction and duct tape).

Safety First: First Aid

I also carry a first-aid kit with me. I make certain that the kit includes the following items:

- A selection of bandages, including gauze bandages
- Adhesive tape
- An antibiotic of some sort
- Something for bee stings

This is a list of the absolute minimum amount of items a first-aid kit should include. If you can pack a more complete kit, you should do so, even if you need to leave something else behind to make room for it.

For the Scenic Routes: Photographic Equipment

I'm a photographer and always bring my camera equipment when I travel, which presents some challenges on a bike. The greatest of these challenges is weather protection. If you have watertight hard luggage, this is not as much of an issue, but riders with soft luggage will have to come up with a way to keep the rain off their camera equipment. Before a trip on which I'll be using soft luggage, I buy a box of the most durable garbage bags I can get (the kind for bagging leaves seems to be the toughest) and then double-wrap my cameras in these bags.

Motorcycology _____

Always buy a large box of heavy-duty garbage bags before going on a motorcycle trip. You'll be amazed at the uses you'll find for them. I place my clothes in them and then put the garbage bag in my saddlebags. Not only does this protect my clothes from getting wet, but it also makes it easier to pack and unpack my saddlebags. I also wrap my sleeping bag in garbage bags. If you've ever had to spend a night in a wet sleeping bag, you'll see the value of this practice.

Another option is to use small point-and-shoot cameras when you travel. You can keep these in your vest pockets or fairing pockets, where they'll stay dry and be ready when you need them.

If you pack your camera in your luggage, whether you have soft or hard luggage, be careful not to place it in a location where it will bounce around. Just the vibration from your bike can pound expensive cameras to pieces; if they bounce around in your trunk or against your shock absorbers while in your saddlebags, you could end up with very expensive paperweights instead of cameras. To protect your equipment, pack soft items, such as towels, clothing, or pillows around it to absorb shocks and vibrations.

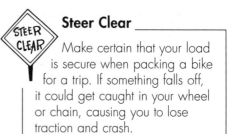

Steer Clear _____

Make certain that your load is secure when packing a bike for a trip. If something falls off, it could get caught in your wheel or chain, causing you to lose traction and crash.

Carrying your camera in a fanny pack or carrying a point-and-shoot camera in your vest pocket can eliminate much of this problem, though be aware—anything you carry that's directly attached to your body can amplify your injuries if you come off. Personally, I don't carry anything like house keys (that could pierce me) in my pockets while I'm riding.

Protective Gear

I always wear a full-face helmet with a visor when traveling. Not only does a full-face helmet provide superior protection in an accident, but it also provides superior protection from the elements and superior comfort.

The most versatile piece of protective gear you can own is a waterproof riding suit like Aerostich's Darien jacket and pants (mentioned in Chapter 9). These suits eliminate the need for rain gear, freeing up a lot of luggage space, and they provide unmatched versatility. With all liners in place, such suits provide excellent cold-weather protection; yet with the liners removed and all vents opened, they are the best hot-weather gear you can buy. This is especially important when traveling in high mountains, where temperatures can vary by 60 or 70 degrees in just a few miles.

You Can Take It with You: Packing Your Bike

Once you've decided what to bring, you'll need to figure out how to bring it with you. Packing techniques are more important than you might think. If your gear falls off your bike, the best you can hope for is that you'll just lose a few items. A more likely outcome is that your gear will get caught in your wheels or chain, causing you to crash.

Luggage

To provide enough carrying capacity for touring, you'll need to have some sort of luggage. Most bikes will accept soft saddlebags and a tankbag; these items are the easiest and most economical way to provide extra carrying capacity on your bike.

Steer Clear _____

When mounting soft luggage on your motorcycle, make certain that your luggage doesn't come into contact with your exhaust pipes, or you could lose your belongings in a fire.

Some bikes won't accept soft luggage because of the shape of their tail pieces or because their exhaust pipes ride too high. This is especially problematic on sportbikes. Some bikes won't accept tankbags, either, because of the shape of their gas tanks. If this is a problem on your bike, there are tailpacks that strap onto the passenger's portion of your seat. If you can't mount soft luggage and you don't have a passenger seat on your bike, you'll need to carry all your belongings in a backpack or choose a different bike for traveling.

A few companies, such as Givi, make hard luggage for many motorcycles. This luggage is expensive, and mounting it can prove quite a challenge, but the convenience of hard luggage makes it a worthwhile investment.

Soft luggage, such as this tankbag, tailpack, and saddlebags, all from Chase Harper, can convert just about any motorcycle into a tourer.

(Photo © 1998 Darwin Holmstrom)

If soft luggage won't fit on your motorcycle, you can carry your gear in a tailpack, such as this Supersport from Chase Harper.

(Photo courtesy of manufacturer)

Hard luggage, such as this Givi Wingrack system, can make a motorcycle significantly more useful.

(Photo courtesy of manufacturer)

In addition to soft luggage and a tankbag, I strap a duffel bag to the passenger seat of my bike. This provides all the carrying capacity I've ever needed.

Camping

If you choose to camp rather than stay in motels when you travel, you can save a lot of money, but you also need to bring a lot of extra gear. The bulkiest items you'll need to pack are your tent and sleeping bag. But if you use your head when packing, you can use these items to help make your load more secure. I'll tell you how to pack your camping gear in the next section.

Loading Up

Before attempting to pack your bike, go to your nearest bike shop and buy at least four bungee nets. Bungee nets are stretchy webs made of nylon ropes with metal hooks that attach to your bike. They are the most wonderful devices ever invented for motorcycle touring, especially if you camp out.

Use a pyramid design when packing a load on a bike—put the widest, stiffest pieces on the bottom, and put the narrower, spongier items toward the top. My own method is to lay my duffel bag crosswise on the passenger seat, so that the ends of the bag are resting on my saddlebags. Behind that, I lay my tent, also crosswise. I then place a bungee net over the two items, tightly securing it in the front and in the rear.

Steer Clear _____

Check your loads, including your soft luggage, frequently when traveling on a bike. The vibration from your bike can loosen hooks and straps. If you find a strap or a bungee hook that has worked its way loose, take the time to adjust it. The consequences of luggage flying loose can be deadly.

Then I lay my sleeping bag in the crotch created between the tent and the duffel bag. Often a single bungee net won't go all the way around my sleeping bag and still solidly attach to the bike, so I'll secure the bungee net in the front of the load and stretch it as far over the sleeping bag as it will go. Then I'll hook the rear of the bungee net to the hooks of the bungee net holding the tent and duffel bag in place. If the top net won't reach the hooks of the bottom net, I'll hook it to a place on the bottom net where the nylon cord is doubled up. Next, I firmly attach another bungee net to a secure point behind the load and hook it to the front of the bungee net covering the sleeping bag, again trying to attach it to the hooks on the other net. The fourth bungee net is a spare, since they sometimes stretch or break.

Different size loads require variations on this theme. If you're traveling two-up, you'll need more carrying capacity. Unless you are riding an ultimate-behemoth touring bike or you're pulling a trailer (neither of which I recommend until you're an experienced rider), you should probably consider not camping when traveling two-up.

First, attach the widest and stiffest items at the base of your load.

(Photo © 1998 Darwin Holmstrom)

Using a luggage rack also requires you to alter your methods of packing. A luggage rack can increase your carrying capacity and provide you with more secure points to attach bungee nets, but make certain that the rack is mounted securely, and don't overload the rack.

Next, attach narrower, softer items.

(Photo © 1998 Darwin Holmstrom)

You may have to make adjustments to the method described here, but if you structure the load so that it is solid and securely attached to the bike, using a pyramid method to keep your center of gravity as low as possible, you should be fine. Check your load frequently (including the straps attaching your soft luggage to your bike); if anything starts to loosen, take the time to adjust and tighten it.

Pacing Yourself

Traveling on a motorcycle drains you physically much more than traveling in a car. It's important that you receive proper nutrition and rest when riding.

Unfortunately, fine dining isn't easy on the road. Road food is notoriously unhealthy and doesn't provide the kind of energy you need for touring. Try to eat as many carbohydrates as you can. Have pancakes instead of an omelet for breakfast. (And eat all your toast.) Have salads for dinner instead of steaks.

Most important, make certain that you drink enough water. If you drink just soda or coffee, the caffeine in those drinks actually depletes your body's supply of water. Get in the habit of buying a bottle of water each time you stop for gas instead of buying a can of soda. Onboard water systems are increasing in popularity. Aerostich Darien jackets even have a special pocket to hold CamelBak water systems.

When riding long distances, exhaustion can creep up on you, diminishing your riding skills. You may not even be aware it is happening. This is especially problematic on hot days and can cause otherwise safe riders to make mistakes. As I've said repeatedly, you can't afford to make mistakes on a bike.

You need to be aware of your mental and physical condition. When you feel yourself getting tired, stop. Find a rest area and stretch your legs. Pull into a convenience store or gas station, buy some juice and a bag of peanuts, find a shady spot in the parking lot, and sit down for a bit. If you are out in the middle of nowhere, find a crossing or turnout where you can park your bike, and then find a shady spot to lean against a tree, or lie down in the grass and watch some clouds go by. Take a nap, if you feel like it. It may slow down your schedule, but if you continue riding when you're exhausted, you might never get where you're going.

Motorcycle Madness: Rallies

So now that your bike's all dressed up, you probably want someplace to go. Just about any place makes a good destination for a motorcycle tour—a visit to friends, to relatives, or just to nowhere in particular. If you have no particular destination in mind, you might want to attend a motorcycle rally. Rallies make a logical destination for a bike trip. While the trip is its own reward on a bike tour, rallies are hard to beat, as far as destinations go.

There are rallies for cruiser fans, rallies for tourers, rallies for sportbike riders, and rallies for antique bikes. There are Norton rallies, Moto Guzzi rallies, Ducati rallies, and BMW rallies. Whatever your interests are, you can find a rally where you'll meet hundreds, or even thousands (in some cases, hundreds of thousands) of like-minded riders. Rallies are places where you can go and revel in all aspects of motorcycle culture.

Major Rallies

Motorcycle rallies have distinct personalities. Some are mild-mannered and relaxed, while others are obnoxious and just plain rude. Most fall somewhere in between. The biggest, loudest, rudest rally of all is Bike Week at Daytona.

Bike Week: Daytona

Held during the first week of March each year in Daytona, Florida, Daytona Bike Week is the wildest party in the United States.

Daytona began as a racing-oriented event, and racing still plays an important role in the rally. The American Historic Racing Motorcycle Association (AHRMA) helps sponsor and organize some of the best historic racing in the country at Daytona, along with a variety of antique-bike shows and contests.

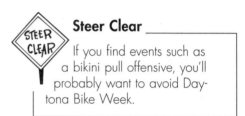

Steer Clear

If you find events such as a bikini pull offensive, you'll probably want to avoid Daytona Bike Week.

Antiques and classics aren't the only motorcycles raced at Daytona. You can catch flat-track racing, Supercross racing, and drag racing, along with the Daytona 200 Superbike race, the rally's main event.

But it's the variety of other activities that gives Daytona its unique character. All kinds of motorcycle-related events take place during Bike Week, like the American Motorcycle Institute's Brute Horsepower Shoot-Out Dyno contest, Spider's Show of World's Most Unusual Motorcycles, the Annual Alligator Road Tour, Side Car and Trike Day, the Classic and Modern Japanese Bike Rally, the European Bike Day and Show, flea markets, swap meets, and the Rat's Hole Custom Chopper Show.

The non-motorcycling activities are what really make Daytona infamous, though many of them are not exactly family-oriented. In addition to the ever-present live bands, free beer, and wet T-shirt contests, you'll be able to take in the Ugliest Old Lady contest, the Biggest Beer Belly contest, egg wrestling, the Slippery When Wet Oil Wrestling contest, his and hers tattoo contests, a celebrity bra auction, and Jesse the World Famous Human Bomb, who can blow himself up at least three times during the rally.

The Rat's Hole custom bike show and competition, the focal point of Daytona Bike Week for expensive, unique machinery.

(Photo courtesy of Simon Green)

But Daytona is not all racing and debauchery. The American Diabetes Association sponsors a charity ride, the Real Ride For The Cure, and the American Red Cross holds a blood drive each year.

Daytona is not a destination for the easily offended, nor is it a place for anyone with a low tolerance for loud Harley-Davidsons or the anti-everything-but-Harley attitude of some Harley owners. But if you're looking for the ultimate all-in-one motorcycle event, you have to check out Daytona Bike Week at least once.

Sturgis Rally & Races

Sturgis is somewhat tamer than Daytona, generally attracting an older crowd, but calling it a family event is a bit of a stretch. Held the first full week of August each year in Sturgis, South Dakota, the Sturgis Rally & Races is a Midwestern version of Daytona Bike Week.

As in Daytona, racing was the original purpose for the gathering at Sturgis, but over the years, the spectacle of the rally began to eclipse the racing. There is still a lot of racing at Sturgis, sponsored by the AMA and the Jackpine Gypsies Motorcycle

Club—everything from hill climbing to vintage racing to Grand National Flat Track racing. That alone makes the rally worth attending.

But also like Daytona, it's all the other events taking place that give Sturgis its character. Main Street during the rally becomes a sea of black leather and denim, swirling around the vendor booths lining the sidewalk.

One of the best things about the rally at Sturgis is riding in the Black Hills of South Dakota. The roads in the Black Hills offer terrific riding any time of the year, but during Bike Week, you'll be sharing those roads almost exclusively with other motorcyclists.

Sturgis gained a reputation in the 1970s as a wild party spot for outlaw bikers, but the wild days are history. Like the motorcycling public in general, Sturgis is becoming more mature.

Laconia Bike Week

Laconia, New Hampshire, hosts the last of the three major American bike weeks. Like both Daytona and Sturgis, there are race events held throughout the week: you can catch a hill climb, some flat tracking, vintage racing, and the road racing at New Hampshire International Speedway.

Also just like the others, there is a big downtown gathering of motorcycle people getting crazy. Laconia really does have the most incredible surroundings though. In almost every direction, there are twisty mountain roads, and every time you pull in for gas or some food, you'll find how great the locals are. If you've got a sportbike and like riding the curves, this is a can't-miss summer destination.

Other Rallies

As motorcycles become more popular, appealing to more diverse and ever larger numbers of riders, motorcycle rallies multiply and become more diverse. There are rallies scheduled at certain times of the year, such as Biketoberfest. There are rallies devoted to all brands, such as the Honda Hoot. There are even cultural motorcycle rallies like the Roundup, which began as a rally for African American riders but now encompasses any rider who just wants to have a good time. This is my personal favorite rally.

Most motorcycle clubs (like those mentioned in Chapter 19) hold national rallies. Women On Wheels holds its International Ride-In each summer at various locations around the country. The Christian Motorcyclists Association holds several rallies each year. The International Retreads has a big get-together each summer, as do the Harley Owners Group, the BMW Motorcycle Owners Association of America, the Moto-Guzzi National Owners Club, and just about every other group you can imagine.

The American Motorcyclist Association holds its Vintage Motorcycle Days (VMD) at the Mid-Ohio Sports Car Course in Lexington, Ohio, each July, and this event provides some of the most spectacular vintage racing in the country.

One of the more entertaining events held each year is the Davis Rally, held in New Hampton, Iowa, every September. This rally offers much the same experience as other touring-bike orientated rallies like "Americade," but with a bit more elbow room: only about 4,000 motorcyclists attend Davis each year, rather than the 40,000 at Americade. Another small rally that provides big entertainment is the Sportbike Rally in Parry Sound, Ontario. This is a great place for Yanks to go and see Canadians take on the sport.

One of the great things about all rallies is that you get to meet interesting people, many of whom you encounter again and again over the years. While the motorcycle community is growing, it's still a relatively small group, and sooner or later, you'll meet just about everybody, from Willie G. Davidson to Dennis Rodman. If you attend some rallies, you might even bump into me—I'll be the guy you don't recognize taking your photograph.

The Least You Need to Know

- ◆ Any dependable bike that you are comfortable riding can be a touring bike.
- ◆ While it's fun to be spontaneous when traveling on a bike, you should at least plan where you'll make your next fuel stop.
- ◆ Make certain that your bike is in top running condition before you take a trip, and don't take off on questionable tires.
- ◆ Sloppy packing on a motorcycle can lead to your gear falling off and getting caught in your wheels, causing you to crash.
- ◆ Attending rallies is a great way to meet other members of the motorcycling community.

Speed Racer: Motorcycle Road Racing

In This Chapter

◆ The influence of racing on the sport of motorcycling

◆ The different types and classes of racing

◆ Getting started in racing

◆ Taking a racing course

Motorcycle road racing is as old and varied as motorcycling itself. Given the historical importance of racing and the impact it has had on street motorcycles, it's surprising how many motorcyclists haven't yet discovered it.

Racing provides drama as intense as any work of fiction. Take great American racer Kenny Roberts's first two Grand Prix (GP) seasons, for example. After defying all odds and becoming the first American to win a Grand Prix World Championship in his rookie season, Roberts broke his back during practice just six weeks before the start of his second season.

It looked like the end of the line for the young racer, but fans were amazed to see Roberts back on the track by the second race of the year. The season that followed provided a tale as suspenseful as anything Hitchcock could have whipped up. The championship was not decided until the final race. Roberts's ultimate win after such a devastating accident has to rank as one of the all-time greatest triumphs in motorsports history.

In this chapter, I give you an overview of some of the more popular forms of road racing as well as tell you a bit of history about the sport and about the people and organizations that make racing possible.

A Brief History of Motorcycle Road Racing

Motorcycle competition has been around as long as motorcycles themselves. By the turn of the century, promoters and racers were already working to organize racing, whether that racing took place on racetracks (as it tended to do in the United States) or on closed sections of public roads (as it often did in Europe).

Fédération Internationale de Motocyclisme (FIM)

In 1904, the Fédération Internationale des Clubs Motocyclistes (FICM) was created to develop and oversee international motorcycle racing. In 1949, the FICM became the Fédération Internationale de Motocyclisme (FIM). The FIM is the primary sanctioning body for world-championship motorcycle-racing events, and it oversees both the MotoGP/Grand Prix Championship series and the World Superbike series. The FIM also sanctions a variety of other types of motorcycle racing, including everything from motocross to sidecar racing.

The American Motorcyclist Association and Racing

Since its formation in 1924, the American Motorcyclist Association (AMA) has maintained a presence in almost all aspects of professional motorcycle racing in the United States, including road racing, motocross, speedway, flat-track, and observed trials.

Since the early 1970s, the AMA has been the American affiliate of the FIM. The AMA participates in the FIM's management and rules-making process, and has hosted many world-championship motorcycle-racing events. The AMA is also heavily involved in amateur motorcycle racing.

Types of Racing

The days of a BSA Gold Star getting you to work and then doubling as your weekend racer are long gone. Race bikes are now incredibly specialized machines. In modern professional road racing, bikes are generally divided into three main categories: Supersport, Superbike, and MotoGP/Grand Prix.

The late Joey Dunlop crosses Ballaugh Bridge on a Honda NSR 500V during the Isle of Man TT.

(Photo © 1998 Brian J. Nelson)

FIM World Championship Grand Prix Series

The World Championship Grand Prix series is the most prestigious motorcycle-racing series in the world—the pinnacle of FIM racing. Unlike Superbike and Super-sport hardware, which are based on street-going motorcycles, Grand Prix race bikes have nothing at all in common with any motorcycle you can buy. These machines are purpose-built racers wholly unsuited for public consumption.

Up until 2002, GP's most respected class, 500, was as exclusively two-stroke as the 250 and 125 classes remain. In 2002, though, the 500 class became the MotoGP class. Initially this allowed either a 500cc two-stroke or a 990cc four-stroke engine. In

2007 it was changed yet again. Maximum engine displacement was reduced to 800cc. Changes aside, catch a race and keep your eyes on modern legend Valentino Rossi, multiple championship winner.

Grand National Dirt Track: American Racing

In the United States, many early races were held on horse-racing tracks at county fairgrounds. After World War II, this type of racing began to take the form we know today, and in 1954, the AMA established the Grand National Dirt Track series. Today that series is the oldest and most traditional racing program the AMA sanctions, and dirt-track (also called flat-track) racing has a distinctly American personality.

Over the years, a number of manufacturers have had success in the Grand National series, including Triumph, BSA, Yamaha, and Honda, but this is the one racing environment where Harley-Davidsons are really in their element. Harley-Davidson XR750s have captured more Grand National Championships than any other make.

Anyone who rides their machines sideways at over 100 mph on dirt tracks has to have absolute faith in their abilities. Seeing the superhuman feats dirt-track racers perform will humble even the most arrogant street squid.

Dirt-track racers make this look easy, but if you've ever tried sliding a motorcycle sideways through a turn at 100 mph on a rutted dirt road, you'll know it ain't!

(Photo courtesy of Simon Green)

Production-Based Motorcycle Racing

By the early 1970s, it was clear that the escalating cost of racing motorcycles was going to make it increasingly difficult for people to take up the sport. To try to keep racing affordable, clubs organized new series based on production motorcycles.

Such series proved popular with fans, so it's ironic that some production-based series can now cost nearly as much to get into as Grand Prix racing. Fortunately, new series are formed every year, many with rules specifically designed to keep costs down.

World Superbike Racing (SBK)

Although the World Superbike Racing series has been around only since 1988, it has quickly become one of the top international racing series in the world. The original idea was to provide the highest-quality four-stroke racing possible, while at the same time keeping the appearance of the racing bikes as close as possible to the streetbikes on which they were based.

It worked. Motorcycle manufacturers realized the sales boost that success in such a series would give them, and they jumped in with both boots on, either fielding factory teams or giving full support to independent teams. The success of the sport led to a phrase within the industry, "win on Sunday, sell on Monday."

However, following the success of the redesigned MotoGP series, World Superbike saw its significance severely undercut. In fact, several factories chose to abandon SBK in favor of MotoGP, causing SBK to experience a steady bleeding off of resources—development, sponsorship, riders, and dollars—to MotoGP. SBK adapted to the changes thrust upon it, and is still an edge-of-your-seat racing experience.

AMA Superbike Racing

AMA Superbike racing was created in 1976 and was the prototype for the World Superbike series. It is the leading class in the AMA road race series, and without doubt your best opportunity to see top-level, heavily modified, production-based 1000cc motorcycle road racing in your local area. The series takes place at multiple racetracks around the United States.

AMA Superstock and Supersport Racing

Superstock and Supersport class racing motorcycles are lightly modified production bikes. Because of the limited modifications allowed to the bikes, building a Supersport racer (600cc class) is one of the least expensive ways to get into motorcycle road racing in the United States at the national level.

A few changes from standard are allowed but these are basically the closest motorcycles to showroom stock in the AMA superbike series.

AMA Formula Xtreme Class

Formula Xtreme (FX) gives manufacturers virtual carte blanche to create the nastiest thing on two wheels. Rules allow almost unlimited modifications to motorcycles' chassis and engines.

Vintage Racing

Even more affordable than Supersport racing is vintage racing, sponsored by organizations such as the American Historic Racing Motorcycle Association (AHRMA). Because this type of racing is accessible for so many people, it becomes more popular every year, both with fans and with racers.

Finding parts for older machines that are out of production can be a problem, forcing racers to use altered and nonstandard parts. This makes it difficult for organizers to require the use of stock items, as they do in Supersport racing.

If you want to race something a bit more modern, you can build a bike for the Classic Superbike class. Motorcycles manufactured between 1973 and 1985 are eligible for this series, provided that they have air-cooled engines and twin-shock rear suspension. Generally, there are two classes in the series: Lightweight Classic Superbike (which includes bikes up to 550cc) and Open Classic Superbike (bikes up to 1100cc).

Other Racing Series

In addition to the main national series, you can become involved in several other types of racing. I've been able to include only a few examples, but if you start looking, you will find a lot more.

Although no longer a sanctioned race (the British Grand Prix moved to Silverstone in 1976 because the Isle of Man course was deemed too dangerous), the Isle of Man TT is arguably the world's most famous motorcycle road race. The Mountain Circuit, where the race has been held since 1911, is also one of the world's most dangerous racecourses.

Back in the early years of motorsports, races were often held on public roads that were closed down for a race. England had a law against closing public roads for racing, so racing promoters worked with the government of the Isle of Man, a small hunk of land in the Irish Sea, to open a racecourse there, and the first Tourist Trophy motorcycle race was held in 1907.

Except for being interrupted by a couple of world wars, races have been held every year at the Isle of Man. The TT is one of the last old-style races in the world, and it is one of the world's deadliest races. There are no runoffs for riders to regain control on if they veer off course. Instead, riders will likely end up in trees, against a stone wall, or in a fence if they make the slightest mistake on the narrow, winding roads. Such obstacles prove much less forgiving than the hay bales lining most racecourses. When averaged over the race's 100-odd-year history, at least a couple of riders have been killed per year.

Drag Racing

I have to admit that I used to have a prejudice against drag racing. I thought it seemed crude and silly compared to motorcycle road racing. I couldn't have been more wrong, as I found out when I finally attended a motorcycle drag race.

The first motorcycle drag race I attended was an All Harley Drag Racing Association (AHDRA) event, and it forever changed my view of the sport. Watching the drag racers straddle their freaky-looking machines as they rocketed down the quarter-mile track at speeds of over 150 mph made me realize that drag racing requires every bit as much skill as road racing—just different skills.

And the entertainment provided by drag racing at least equals that provided by other forms of racing. If you ever have an opportunity to see a motorcycle drag race, do so. You won't regret it.

The noise, the smell of burning nitro, and the sheer power of the drag-racing spectacle can only be compared to a religious epiphany or a Led Zeppelin concert.

(Photo © 1998 Darwin Holmstrom)

I urge you to discover the excitement of motorcycle racing for yourself, and as some of you may want to become more than just racing fans, I'm going to tell you a little about becoming a motorcycle road racer.

It's not as difficult as it might seem. While it's not cheap, racing motorcycles is still considerably less expensive than racing automobiles. It requires more training and skill than automobile racing, but here you're in luck. In recent years, several quality road-racing schools have appeared—places where you can learn to race or just learn to be a better rider.

How to Become a Racer

Racing is not as dangerous as it might seem. It's more dangerous than a lot of activities—watching TV, for example—but less dangerous than others. Many racers feel safer on the track than they do on the street, and, statistically, they have a point. On a racetrack, the flow of traffic is controlled; everyone moves in the same direction, at roughly the same speed. And on a track, you eliminate your number-one traffic hazard: the left-turning driver.

Racing a motorcycle is safer than you might think, and you can minimize what danger there is with proper preparation.

Track Days

One way to experience firsthand the thrill of riding a motorcycle on a racetrack is to attend a track day. They've long been popular in Europe and have been gaining popularity in the United States. Usually, you are required to make a few modifications to your motorcycle. For example, you will likely have to replace the coolant in your radiator with regular water because coolant is very slippery and very difficult to clean up if you crash.

Vehicular Chess

Motorcycle road racing is a physical activity. You need to be able to wrestle your machine from a hard left turn to a hard right turn in a heartbeat. You need to be in fairly good physical condition. But racing is also a mental activity. A good racer not only rides fast, but he or she also maneuvers for position on the track much like a master chess player controls the area of a chessboard.

Club Racing

The most convenient way to get into road racing is to become involved in club racing. Although competing professionally at the national or international level can be prohibitively expensive, most areas around the United States have racing clubs that provide relatively affordable amateur racing. There are dozens of such clubs around the country.

One example is the American Federation of Motorcyclists (AFM), a California-based organization that conducts seven to nine racing events each year at Infineon Raceway in Sonoma, California; the Thunderhill Park Raceway, near Willows, California; and the Buttonwillow Raceway Park, near Buttonwillow, California.

Motorcycology

To be successful in motorcycle racing, you need to have good upper- and lower-body strength, and you need to be in good cardiovascular condition. The best riders work out on a regular basis and eat low-fat, high-carbohydrate diets.

Another is the Central Roadracing Association (CRA), located in Minnesota, which conducts club racing at Brainerd International Raceway (BIR). CRA events are wildly popular with racing fans across the upper Midwest, with events attracting fans from as far away as Montana and Colorado. Without the CRA, organized road racing would not exist in the region.

Racing Categories and Classes

Categories and classes may differ slightly from one racing organization to the next. You'll need to consult the rule books of the organization you are joining for specific details, but most more or less mirror the categories used by CRA.

CRA has three general motorcycle competition classes: Supersport, Superbike, and Grand Prix. In addition, it conducts races for a variety of amateur classes, generally divided according to engine displacement: Ultralightweight, Lightweight, Middleweight, Heavyweight, Unlimited, and Lightweight Sportsman Superbike.

Motorcycology

All road-racing clubs require you to obtain a racing license before you can compete, and all require you to complete some form of rider course before you get a novice license.

Licensing

All clubs require you to purchase a racing license, which usually costs between $45 and $125. Some clubs will accept the licenses of certain other clubs, while some organizations will require you to go through the entire process from scratch before you can race in their club.

The licensing requirements vary from organization to organization (again, you'll need to check the rule books of any organization you are thinking of joining).

Racing Schools

To go racing, you are required to attend some sort of new rider's course. You can attend these through the clubs themselves, or you can attend one of the courses offered by various high-performance riding schools.

High-Performance Riding Schools

Schools specifically for people who want to learn to race, or who just want to ride better, have appeared across the country in recent years. Many of these schools take their classes on the road, offering high-performance riding courses at racetracks around the county. Completing a course from an accepted riding school qualifies you for a novice license in most clubs. Even if you don't race, attending a course offered by one of the following schools raises your riding abilities to new heights and makes you a much safer rider.

California Superbike School (CSS)

Founded by Keith Code, former racer and trainer of such legendary racers as Eddie Lawson, Wayne Rainy, Doug Chandler, and John Kocinski, the CSS is one of the oldest and most respected high-performance riding schools.

Begun in 1980, this school set the standard for what a high-performance riding school should be. Courses are now offered at four levels: level 1 focuses on throttle control and cornering lines, level 2 focuses on overall awareness of your surroundings, level 3 concentrates on body positioning on the bike and the mental aspects of motorcycling, and level 4 focuses more tightly on the 15 specific riding techniques learned in previous levels.

For the beginner—and, in particular, for those who need structure in learning situations—the Code school is exactly the right course. You'll learn a huge amount from the first level and get rid of a host of bad habits. However, at the higher levels, it seems Code has less to teach, and there is, curiously, less track time.

Among instructor Keith Code's former pupils is racing champion John Kocinski, shown here aboard a Honda RC45 at the 1997 Laguna Seca World Superbike race.

(Photo © 1998 Brian J. Nelson)

Freddie Spencer's High-Performance Riding School

When I bought my first streetbike, Freddie Spencer was the hottest motorcycle racer in the world. During a 30-year racing career (1966–1995), the man learned a thing or two about riding. If you take this course, he'll share his secrets with you. Courses are offered at two levels: SR for street riders and SR Pro for those with racing aspirations. These courses are not cheap, but for 30 years' worth of Fast Freddie's experience, it's well worth the price.

Preparing a Race Bike

As with just about everything in racing, the details of race-bike preparation vary from club to club, but for most, you'll need to remove some of the street equipment, such as turn signals, mirrors, the license plate and brackets, passenger footpegs, the sidestand, and the centerstand. Headlights and taillights need to be removed or taped over.

Cooling systems can't contain any antifreeze because spilling that slippery substance on a track poses a serious safety hazard. You'll need to install three number plates: one on each side and one on the front. Some bikes have an area on the fairing or seat that is large and flat enough to hold a number sticker. Novice number plates are yellow with the assigned AFM number in black. As a safety precaution, certain fasteners need to be safety wired or have locking devices.

The best way to learn how to set up your bike for racing is to obtain a rule book from the club you want to race with and study it. Then go to a race to browse through the pits, look at the bikes, and talk to people about how they set up their own bikes. I've found racers to be some of the nicest, friendliest people I've ever met, and I think you'll find them very helpful to talk to when getting started in motorcycle racing.

Buying Your First Racing Bike

When buying your first racing bike, follow the recommendations I outlined for buying your first streetbike. Choose a motorcycle that will allow you to get the most racing time and fun for the least money. Select a bike that isn't so large that it intimidates you or hinders your ability to learn. Bikes such as 250cc twins (such as Kawasaki's Ninja 250), most thumpers, and 500cc or 650cc twins (like the Suzuki SV650) are good choices for beginners.

An alternative to preparing a race bike yourself is to buy a motorcycle that has already been converted into a racer. One of the best places to find such a machine is from road race–oriented want ads, like those found in the back of *Roadracing World*. You can also find race bikes for sale in the pit areas of racetracks when races are being held.

Attend a high-performance riding school and see if you are interested in becoming a racer. Even if you decide the sport is not for you, at the very least, you'll improve your riding ability immeasurably.

The Least You Need to Know

- The AMA is the primary sanctioning body for motorcycle racing in the United States, and it is involved in nearly all organized racing in the United States.

- The Isle of Man TT is one of the oldest races in the world, providing fans with a view into the past.

- Racing requires good mental and physical preparation on your part.

- All racing clubs require you to attend some sort of racing class and obtain a racing license.

- It can be cheaper to buy a race bike than it is to build one.

Biker's Buying Guide
to New Bikes

Motorcyclist™ magazine runs an annual buyer's guide in its March issue that lists all street-legal motorcycles for sale for the following year, along with technical specifications, prices, and editors' comments. This guide alone makes subscribing to *Motorcyclist*™ worth the money. I've used this guide as a general template for this appendix, but I've modified the guide to be more useful to you.

My recommendations vary from those of the *Motorcyclist*™ staff because for the sake of this book I'm judging the bikes using different criteria. The magazine publishes its guide for experienced motorcyclists; in contrast, my recommendations are geared toward helping new riders. I've evaluated each bike using the following criteria:

◆ **Ease of use.** Learning to ride is difficult enough without choosing a difficult motorcycle to learn on. In evaluating the bikes in this guide, I've placed a premium on power characteristics (because you will find smooth throttle control to be easier on bikes with a broad, smooth powerband) and on ease of handling.

Note that ease of handling is not the same as outright handling prowess. When I discuss ease of handling, I'm talking about how maneuverable a bike is in the kind of situations in which you will ride. A bike might be the best-handling machine on the racetrack but be a real handful when you practice braking and swerving in a parking lot.

Bikes that combine smooth power and easy handling earned a "Recommended—Beginner" rating.

♦ **Versatility.** You probably aren't going to go out and buy several bikes right off the bat, so your first motorcycle should be capable of serving you in a variety of situations. It should also be a bike you can grow with, rather than a machine you'll want to ditch midway through your first season of riding.

♦ **Ease of maintenance.** I don't have an unlimited expense account to maintain my fleet of bikes, so I perform most basic maintenance procedures myself and therefore take ease of maintenance into account when recommending a bike for you.

♦ **Fun.** Because the primary purpose of motorcycling is to have fun, selecting a bike based solely on its practicality would be foolish. I've also included style under the category of fun. I didn't feel that style warranted its own category because it relies so heavily on opinion, and my opinion of what looks stylish may vary from yours. If you like the way a bike looks, don't worry about what I or what anyone else thinks about it.

The descriptions of the many motorcycles within the Buying Guide are all self-explanatory, but you'll also notice that some bikes are marked as "recommended." To make this Idiot's Guide useful beyond the learning stage of your motorcycle ownership experience, I've broken the recommendations into three categories:

♦ **Recommended—Beginner.** These are bikes that should be both safe and un-intimidating to you once you've completed your initial motorcycle training.

♦ **Recommended—Intermediate.** Motorcycles in this category will be more challenging to ride than the beginner group, but will be great bikes to move up to once you've clocked up some miles on two-wheels.

♦ **Recommended—Experienced.** Finally, these are the machines that really need some skill to ride safely, but are among the best-of-the-best at what they do. They're the bikes we aspire to.

All of these recommended bikes are featured in the color section, too, as I figured you'd like to take a closer look at them. By the way, it's much easier to clean drool off the shiny colored paper, so don't hold back.

This appendix lists virtually all readily available street-legal motorcycles for sale in the United States, as well as off-road and playbikes. I've excluded competition bikes such as motocross and trials motorcycles because such focused machines aren't relevant to most people. I've divided the appendix into five sections based on the system used by *Motorcyclist*™ magazine: Cruisers and Tourers; Sportbikes, Sport-Tourers, and Standards; Dual-Sports; Cross-Country and Enduro; and Playbikes. I describe each category in more detail at the beginning of each section. Within each category, I've organized the motorcycles alphabetically by manufacturer.

Cruisers and Tourers

Since the advent of the touring cruiser (see Chapter 3), the line between touring bike and cruiser has blurred. With a couple of exceptions, most touring cruisers and touring bikes are too heavy and cumbersome for a novice rider, but the cruiser category provides ample examples of terrific first motorcycles. Most cruisers are on the heavy end of the motorcycle spectrum, but their low center of gravity (especially the V-twin-powered machines) can mask that weight, making them feel much lighter when they're moving. Also, the relaxed power output of most V-twin engines is ideal for newer riders trying to learn smooth throttle control. Generally, most motorcycles of 1000 cc or more are going to be too big, too heavy, and too powerful for novice riders. There are, of course, exceptions, and I've noted them.

BMW Cruisers and Tourers

BMW K1200LT

This big tourer is essentially a German version of Honda's legendary Gold Wing. It's loaded with an abundance of features to help eat up the miles on long journeys. Nothing comes without a price, and with this beastie it's weight. Luxurious and comfortable, but can be hard going at low speeds.

BMW R1200RT (Recommended–Intermediate)

Light and sporty when compared to the BMW mentioned above, though still pretty heavy compared to a true sport-tourer. Quite a fun bike for something so capable and practical, and previous versions have been around for decades, so reliability is well proven. A great German Bahn-stormer.

BMW F800ST (Recommended–Beginner)

BMW describes this bike as their midweight touring bike. In this company it's positively light-weight, and more of a sport-tourer than a tourer, but who am I to argue with BMW? What's not up for debate is that it's fitted with a great new engine and the overall package makes an awesome first touring bike.

Harley-Davidson Cruisers and Tourers

(Photographs in this section courtesy of Harley-Davidson Photography & Imaging. Copyright Harley-Davidson)

Harley-Davidson Ultra Classic Electra Glide

This is the really, really big Harley. For those of you that believe the old adage "Bigger is Better," this is undoubtedly best. To many people it's the ultimate; others think anything this big is missing the point of motorcycling. Either way, it's loaded with as much stuff as a Cadillac and can prove it, weighing in at 840 lbs.

Harley-Davidson Classic Electra Glide

Still the same really, really big and heavy Harley, it loses some of the "Ultra" features (like CB radio, cruise control, and about 20 lbs) but still includes the hard luggage and built-in sound system. Guaranteed to impress small children, and guaranteed to make them look even smaller.

Harley-Davidson Electra Glide Standard

The Electra Glide Harley in its most basic form. Stripping it down reduces the weight to 770 lbs, dropping it into the "really heavy" category—which is still way too heavy for a novice rider. This version isn't fitted with top-box but does include panniers and an old-school handlebar-mounted fairing.

Harley-Davidson Road Glide

This model takes us back up into the really, really heavy category, and is regarded as the sleek model in Harley-Davidson's touring range. Its fairing is frame mounted, meaning it doesn't turn with the handlebars. Still loaded, coming with such features as a stereo and cruise control.

Harley-Davidson Street Glide

Think of this model as a lighter-weight Electra Glide. It's still got the luggage, stereo, and big old-fashioned handlebar-mounted fairing but weighs in at 770 lbs, which we'll categorize as merely "really heavy" for the sake of the novice rider. These big bikes are very well suited to effortlessly cruising straight highways.

Harley-Davidson Road King Custom

"Custom" pretty much sums up the Harley specs on this Road King: it comes with many of the custom touches owners typically apply to basic models. The rear suspension is lowered, the wind-shield is replaced by a small chrome wind deflec-tor, and leather bags with hidden mounts carry your peanut butter and jelly sandwiches.

Harley-Davidson Road King

The Road King is the classic American touring V-twin, with hard saddlebags and cast wheels, plus lazy-boy cruise control on the Classic model. Rub-ber mounting quells the vibes from the old-world engine. The Classic version comes with spoked wheels and whitewall tires as well as the familiar handlebar-mounted windscreen.

Harley-Davidson Heritage Softail Classic

There are many variations on the Softail theme; this particular one comes with a massive windscreen, a backrest to help your passenger stay put, and studded leather saddlebags. Whether studded leather is very tough looking or just way too reminiscent of those guys singing "Y-M-C-A" is completely up to you.

Harley-Davidson Softail Springer Classic

In the language of Harley-Davidson, Softail means the bike has hidden suspension at the back, and Springer means it has a really old-fashioned set of exposed springs for the front. On the Springer Classic, those front springs are black. This model is unusual for Harley, having an exhaust pipe on each side of the bike.

Harley-Davidson Softail Deluxe

Another Softail variation, this time with a very low seat height, which is a good thing for shorter riders or riders with less strength (remember: a lower center of gravity always makes the weight of a heavy motorcycle much more manageable). It also has big, fat whitewall tires and a pretty useful little luggage rack.

Harley-Davidson Softail Deuce

Yet another Softail variation, this one has a longer gas tank, a matching rear fender, and a front end rich in chrome. In contrast they painted parts of the engine black, then finished it off with a long chrome panel down the gas tank. Bikes like this Harley unfortunately still fall into the category of "heavy" for the novice rider.

Harley-Davidson Softail Custom

This Softail is planted firmly in the seventies, with a gigantic King and Queen seat (as yet not endorsed by any actual monarchs) and a backrest big enough to nap on. It also has a very tall pair of ape-hanger handlebars. It's not often that you can combine Kings, Queens, and Apes in one motorcycle ….

Harley-Davidson Softail Standard

And finally we reach the "standard," the base model of the endless softail family. It comes with the same hidden rear suspension, a silver-colored motor, and a big 200mm rear tire. A little more basic than some of the others, though maybe all the better for it?

Harley-Davidson Night Train

Just when you think we're done, here's another Softail. Though Harley refers to this one simply as the Night Train, and like a train in the dark, it is indeed very black. The bike pulls off this non-color very effectively and is arguably one of the most understated Harleys in production.

Harley-Davidson Fat Boy

Without a doubt the best name in use on any Harley. Who else could get away with naming a bike the Fat Boy? The name comes from the oversized front end and solid alloy wheels, the front one being a stubby little 17 incher. Let's hope the PC crowd can never change this wonderfully evocative name to the Weight Challenged Pre-adolescent.

Harley-Davidson Dyna Wide Glide

Finally we reach an entire family of Harleys that fall into a weight class that is only "heavy" to most novice riders. The Dyna Wide Glide weighs in at 678 lbs, which ironically makes it a middleweight in the Harley family. With its raked-out front end and skinny wheel, it's a very graceful-looking motorcycle cruiser.

Harley-Davidson Dyna Low Rider

The Dyna Low Rider is a great bike for the shorter rider. The seat height is only a fraction over 25 inches. If you like the V-twin style and aren't the tallest person out there, you'll really love this grunty Harley. It also has footpegs mounted onto the frame so you can cruise the highways just like Peter Fonda, or maybe even Jane Fonda, if you think you can carry it off.

Harley-Davidson Dyna Street Bob

The third bike in Harley's Dyna series is another very low-riding bike, making it great for anyone with a shorter inseam. The Street Bob (not an abbreviation for Street Robert) is only fitted with a single seat, so it's really designed for riders with a short inseam who regularly need to get away from their spouse.

Harley-Davidson Dyna Super Glide Custom

Variation number four on the Dyna theme (are you starting to see a pattern yet?) features a silver-coated engine with chrome covers and a lower set of handlebars than those fitted to the Street Bob. The bike also has a bigger 5.1-gallon tank, not only giving longer runs between gas stops, but giving it a slightly heavier look, too.

Harley-Davidson Dyna Super Glide

The final bike in Harley's Dyna series is a little more stripped down. Budget-conscious cruiser fans can latch on to the Super Glide, Harley's least-expensive Big Twin. It's the last Harley that we're listing here with the Twin Cam 96 motor, this time finished in silver, with a single seat for you antisocial types.

Harley-Davidson V-Rod

Formerly known as just the V-Rod, this bike now comes in a multitude of different model variations, this version being the closest thing to the original model. When launched it was a super radical departure from the norm for the Harley crowd. It's still powered by a V-twin, but it was their first new motor with truly modern design touches. With the exception of a few Harley die-hards, it was an immediate success.

Harley-Davidson Night Rod

A V-Rod with an all-black appearance once more, Harley uses the word *Night* to describe any bike with a lot of black paint in its finish. This variant comes with a very low seat height of 26 inches, a tiny headlight fairing called a Nacelle, and foot-pegs mounted in a position more streetbike than cruiser.

Harley-Davidson Night Rod Special

If the previous model is called a Night Rod, then this one should be called the Lunar Eclipse Rod. It's almost all black, and comes with a wide 240mm back tire, lower drag-race style handlebars, and forward control foot pegs (an unusual combination). It also has an almost unbelievably low 25.2-inch seat height.

Harley-Davidson VRSCX

This is a tuned-up V-Rod put together with Harley-Davidson Screamin' Eagle parts. For authenticity it comes with a replica paint scheme from their NHRA Vance & Hines drag-racing team, a smoked windshield, and a wide 240mm rear tire. If you want a fast Harley, then this is definitely where you should be looking.

Harley-Davidson Street Rod (Recommended—Intermediate)

A V-Rod with a black frame, black engine, black upside-down front forks, and black everything else. The Street Rod gets more ground clearance and other subtle changes all with one thing in mind: to corner better and therefore handle street riding as well as possible. If you like Harleys *and* you like twisty roads, it's either this or a Sportster.

Harley-Davidson Sportster 1200

The Sportster is often looked down upon by the riders of the bigger Harleys, but don't worry about it, it looks great and most non-Harley riders can't tell the difference anyway. It "only" weighs 585 lbs, making it easier to ride than its heavier brothers, and it's unusually nimble along roads with twists and turns.

Harley-Davidson Sportster 883

The smallest, cheapest Harley is essentially the same as the 1200cc Sportster, but fitted with a very novice-friendly 883cc engine. An engine size of 883 may sound big, but Harleys deliver their power in a lazy way, making this baby of the Harley family an absolute breeze to ride. It's the perfect first-time cruiser.

Honda Cruisers and Tourers

Honda Valkyrie Rune

It looks like a one-off high-dollar custom bike, or a dreamlike concept machine that will never get made. Amazingly, it's a production Honda motor-cycle. Being based on the Gold Wing, it should never let you down. Just be aware, though: at 811 lbs it's another big and heavy beast of a bike.

Honda Gold Wing GL1800 (Recommended–Experienced)

Honda's huge (and hugely entertaining) maxi-tourer, it's a big machine, but has an appropriately powerful 1832cc six-cylinder motor to hustle it along. It's as efficient as tourers get and is now available with airbags. It's a little too much for most novice motorcyclists, but it's the original grand tourer and certainly something to aspire to.

Honda VTX1800T

Fancy an American cruiser but like things a little more refined? Then the VTX1800 is the bike for you: ultra-reliable Japanese engineering made in the good ol' U-S-of-A. This version carries the T suffix, meaning it's set up by the factory for tour-ing; coming as standard with saddle bags, a wind-shield, and a passenger backrest.

Honda VTX1800N

Honda also makes the VTX in a version carrying the N suffix. N seems to mean Nostalgia—with a modern touch, the bike features cast wheels, "hot-rod" fenders, and a cut-off exhaust. Just like the Harleys they're clearly competing with, these Hondas can be customized with a multitude of accessories.

Honda VTX1800F

The F version of the big Honda cruiser comes with smaller fenders, straight handlebars, and a drag-bike seating position. It also comes with a "gun-fighter" styled seat, according to Honda. Though we're unsure what makes the seat so good for gun fighting, we're sure it's mighty comfortable whilst doing it. KaBoom!

Honda VTX1800R

R is for Retro, and in typical cruiser fashion this is the fourth version of what is essentially just one bike. The R designation comes with more chrome than most, deeper fenders, cast wheels, and a staggered set of exhaust pipes.

Honda VTX1800C

The street-rod-style C model is styled to resemble the original VTX1800. It's also the base model of the 1800cc range, being finished with a two into one exhaust system and a drag-bike riding position. Thankfully, a drag-bike doesn't require you to actually wear women's clothing, though it's a common misconception.

Honda VTX1300

A smaller version of the VTX, you'll drop around 20 hp compared to the 1800, but also around 100 lbs of weight, making it a much better proposition for the less experienced. Like its bigger sibling it comes in various versions: the S, R, and C, which follow the same basic pattern as before.

Honda Shadow Sabre

The next range of bikes in Honda's cruiser range are the Shadows. Bikes like this Sabre come with a 1099cc liquid-cooled V-twin and shaft drive as standard. Weighing in at 577 lbs it's a manageable weight for the new rider, and being a Honda means that reliability is a given.

Honda Shadow Spirit

Turn back the clock, poof your hair, and reach for those big, clunky eyeglasses: the 1980s are here! Actually, in the Spirit, they never left. Despite cosmetic and technical improvements, the Spirit retains the same basic style and feel of those early Shadows. It's got the same 1099cc engine as the Sabre, but also has some pullback handlebars and a passenger backrest.

Honda Shadow Spirit 750 VT750 C2/DC

These 750cc-engined Shadows look almost identical to the bigger-engined variants, but obviously weigh significantly less. They also have a much lower seat height, making them a really safe first cruiser. Two versions are currently available, with the typical cosmetic-only differences.

Honda Shadow VLX/VLX Deluxe

Honda's entry-level cruiser is what you'd expect: relatively lightweight, short, and newbie-friendly. Still only four speeds in the wide-ratio gearbox, but what do you want for $5,500? The Deluxe model gets you extra chrome on the engine and a choice of color that isn't black, I mean night. No, I mean black.

Honda Rebel

In the promotional materials for *Rebel Without a Cause*, James Dean's character is described as a "bad boy from a good family." Honda's little 250cc Rebel would love to be bad, but it's too cute to be anything but a worthy, if tiny, entry-level bike. It's popular with the Motorcycle Safety Foundation (MSF) for its ridiculously easy handling and anvil-like reliability.

Kawasaki Cruisers and Tourers

Kawasaki Vulcan 2000

Kawasaki calls this the *King of the Cruisers*. If it's size alone that counts, it may have a point, with each cylinder displacing more than an entire ZX-10R. The pushrod, eight-valve, liquid-cooled V-Twin engine is all new, but the machine's styling is a cool mix of retro and rocket, featuring design elements such as a modern four-bulb projector-type headlight encased in an old-world chrome nacelle.

Kawasaki Vulcan 2000 Classic

Like the original Vulcan, the Classic has an engine the size of a family car, but it also comes with slightly more traditional Cruiser styling. If you're precious about your passenger's rear, then choose this model because it has a super-plush pillion seat; they'll find a way to thank you for it.

Kawasaki Vulcan 2000 Classic LT

The Classic LT variation comes with the familiar touring package as fitted to most big cruisers: big windshield, backrest, floorboards for your feet, and studded leather saddlebags. Stud fans (and we know you're out there) will be pleased to hear they continue this theme into the seat too, you lucky, lucky things.

Kawasaki Vulcan 1600 Nomad

Kawasaki's flagship 1600cc cruising tourer gets its motivation from the same basic liquid-cooled, 50-degree V-twin design used in all Vulcan 1600s. The fuel-injected Nomad includes a large adjustable touring windshield and hard bags that open conveniently to the side. As you'd expect of a 1600cc bike, it's hauling some weight, not making it the best choice for any new folk.

Kawasaki Vulcan 1600 Mean Streak

Sometimes a name is an apt descriptor; sometimes it's wishful thinking. For the Mean Streak, it's a bit of both. Although it's outgunned by other power cruisers, the 1600cc Streak can outrun almost any car. Think of it as a Black Labrador of a motorcycle—willing to go anywhere you go, and do it with a big, sloppy grin.

Kawasaki Vulcan 1600 Classic

The classically styled version of Kawasaki's 1600cc cruiser range. Features include wide pullback handlebars, slash-cut exhaust mufflers, and a long, low look. The bike is also fitted with large tires and wide fenders to give it a tough look (apparently). So don't make eye contact with those tough tires, you've been warned.

Kawasaki Vulcan 1500 Classic

This bike launched Kawasaki's successful 1500 series back in 1987, looking as Americans expected: a classic cruiser look, but with the performance and trouble-free technology for which the Japanese are so justifiably famous. Because it has been around so long, there's plenty of aftermarket stuff.

Kawasaki Vulcan 900 Custom

The smaller sibling to the 1600 Vulcans, this new custom version wears a 21" cast front wheel and a contrasting chunky 15" one at the back. The Custom has much the same running gear as the 900 Classic, including the torque-y 903cc liquid-cooled V-twin, chain drive, and five speeds.

Kawasaki Vulcan 900 Classic/Classic LT

For the price, you might assume that this mid-cruiser is short on content. But Kawasaki is feeling generous—something you can do when a model's been around approximately ... forever. The 900 Classic and Classic LT differences are much the same as on the 1600 models.

Kawasaki Vulcan 500 LTD

At one time, this bike was called the 454 LTD. (If you're old enough to remember Kawasaki's LTD cruisers, please sit down before you break a hip.) The spunky twin-cylinder cruiser pounds out pretty good power at a pretty good price and offers an unintimidating perch for smallies and newbies.

Kawasaki Eliminator 125

This is Kawasaki's version of the essential learner bike. Smart riders don't just take their MSF courses on learner bikes, they continue to ride them for a few months before trading up. If that's your plan, then it couldn't be easier than on this dinky cruiser!

Moto Guzzi Cruisers and Tourers

Moto Guzzi California Vintage

An Italian interpretation of the classic cruiser. Guzzi uses their own V-twin engine, which is essentially the one from their sporty Breva 1100 streetbike. This makes for a very unusual twist on the cruiser theme. If you like to be different, and want a bit of sport thrown in with your cruiser, then the California is all you.

Moto Guzzi Nevada Classic 750

Guzzi's entry-level cruiser is by no means a stripper. The fuel-injected, air-cooled V-twin is the same as on their other cruisers, driving a five-speed gearbox and shaft final drive. Guzzi has recently done an extensive redesign on this model, so while it still looks retro, it's packed with every modern feature imaginable.

Suzuki Cruisers and Tourers

Suzuki Boulevard M109R

The most powerful cruiser Suzuki has ever made, and make no mistake, Suzuki is a company that knows about power. This thing has gobs of it, and it's also huge. Everything about it seems utterly massive, yet it weighs 703 lbs, surprising for an 1800cc V-twin at any rate. Treat with respect, it's a whole lot of bike.

Suzuki Boulevard C90

Suzuki's range of C90 Boulevards fall into the 1500cc class. There are currently three model options: the standard C90 (think of it as a typical Classic spec cruiser), a C90 Black (which is, well … black), and finally a C90T—a Touring version complete with some nice whitewall tires, a big screen, and the obligatory studded leather bags.

Suzuki Boulevard M50

You could think of this as Suzuki's interpretation of the Softail. Like the Harley, it has hidden rear suspension, making it look like a hardtail, which is great if you think a fake hardtail is important in the twenty-first century. The 50-cu. in.-engine size falls into the 800cc class, and this particular variation is something that Suzuki describes as a muscle-cruiser.

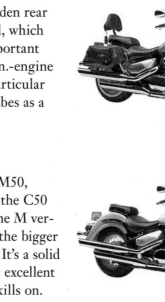

Suzuki Boulevard C50

The same basic mechanical setup as the M50, complete with the 800cc engine, though the C50 models are more classically styled than the M version, and come in the same variations as the bigger C90 series (Classic, Black, and Touring). It's a solid bike with a low seat height and should be excellent for any novice to perfect their cruising skills on.

Suzuki Boulevard S83/S50

Suzuki's last offerings in the cruiser world are the S series. The S83 has a 1360cc air/oil-cooled motor, and the S50 has the liquid-cooled 800cc power plant. Both bikes share the same basic styling and have been around for donkeys' years. Luckily that's their only similarity to a donkey: they don't bite and they ain't hairy.

Suzuki Boulevard S40

And so we come to the final Suzuki cruiser. Like the S50, this 650cc bike has been around forever. Unlike their other V-twin engined cruisers, it's a single cylinder delivering its power in a totally different way. If you like its looks, then go and invest with complete peace of mind; this 650 Boulevard was quite literally made for the newer rider.

Triumph Cruisers and Tourers

Triumph Rocket III (Recommended–Experienced)

"Wild Thing, you make my heart sing." Fitted with a humongous 2293cc 3-cylinder engine, could it be any wilder? Is it really possible? Fortunately the bike isn't just an exercise in unnecessary excess; it genuinely rocks, and does indeed make everything groovy. Wild thing, I think I love you.

Triumph Bonneville T100

Triumph steadfastly refused to remake a Bonneville when they relaunched the brand back in the '90s. Thankfully, somewhere along the way they changed their mind and now we have bikes like this. The T100 model is an upscale version of the standard Bonnie, with two-tone paint, kneepads on the tank, and hand-painted pinstripes.

Triumph Bonneville

This may be the bike that best sums up the new Triumph. Totally modern yet unabashedly retro, the Bonneville trades on decades of goodwill and pathos yet is its own, highly capable machine. It's the only modern motorcycle capable of giving you just a little bit of that Steve McQueen, cooler king, style.

Triumph Bonneville America

A longer, lower, mellowed-out, more cruiser-oriented version of the Bonneville, the America gets its own kind of Anglo/American retro styling and its own thumpy-thump, 270-degree-crank engine. Make sure to save some of your money for their super-tempting line of accessories.

Triumph Bonneville Speedmaster

Take your basic Bonneville America; rejuggle the graphics; slap on a lower, straighter handlebar; and you've got the Speedmaster. Under the slightly altered exterior beats the heart of a Bonnie, with the 270-degree-crank version of the 865cc, parallel-twin engine and five-speed box.

Victory Cruisers and Tourers

Victory Arlen Ness Signature Series

Bet the other cruiser makers are kicking themselves for not signing Arlen and son to help put their styling on the map. This is a limited-edition version of the Vegas, festooned with all kinds of gleaming Ness-spec billet goodies. You could call it a Look Ness! Monster? Okay, don't.

Victory Vegas

It's amazing what the input of the father-and-son team of Arlen and Cory Ness has done to upgrade Victory's street cred. Once known for dowdy cruisers, the "other" American streetbike company has rebounded big with the Vegas. An uprated Freedom engine makes it go—and go very well, thank you.

Victory Vegas Jackpot/8 Ball

The Jackpot is a custom variation on the Victory Vegas; think flashy paint, 250 size rear tire (translation: Big), and custom style headlight. Add that familiar fuel-injected Victory 1634cc V-twin and you've got a storming beast of a bike. The 8 Ball is another custom model, this one going down the all-black route.

Victory Kingpin Tour

Returning basically unchanged, the V92TC is Victory's touring rig: it comes complete with a tall windscreen and hard saddlebags. Hard bags are considerably more useful than the leather kind for real-world touring, something to consider when dusting off the credit card.

Victory Kingpin

The Victory Kingpin starts with the same basic engine/chassis combo as the Vegas, but then it goes its own ruggedly independent way with deeper fenders; six-spoke, 18-inch cast wheels; and a fat 180-mm rear tire. An inverted fork pushes the look even farther into performance land. Victory is on the gas now.

Victory Hammer/Hammer S

Here's another bike that's being called a muscle-cruiser. With a pair of floating brake rotors, a set of upside down front forks, and a 250mm rear tire, it's clear this bike isn't just for show. If you then consider that the Hammer puts out around 100 ft-lb of torque and weighs in at 657 lbs, muscle-cruiser it is! There's also an S version with blacked-out cycle parts and custom PM wheels.

Yamaha Cruisers and Tourers

Yamaha Royal Star Venture

The Royal Star is Yamaha's big daddy luxury tourer, though unlike many of its peers it isn't driven by a big V-twin. Instead Yamaha fitted a 1300cc V-four engine, making the bike quite unique. It's loaded with everything you need to rack up serious miles with the other half, in complete and utter comfort. It may be a bit too much for the novice, but it's one hell of a bike.

Yamaha Royal Star Tour Deluxe

This Tour Deluxe Royal Star is part tourer, part cruiser. It's capable of eating miles with you and a passenger, but also oozes cruiser charisma. Just like the Venture, it comes with a very generous and equally impressive five-year warranty from Yamaha. Now you can sit back and quit worrying while you ride, unless you have other things to worry about ....

Yamaha Stratoliner S

The Stratoliners are Yamaha's big V-twins, and at 1850cc, they're truly big. As we've already learned, big usually goes with heavy, which can ruin the fun for a novice. Anyway, the S version has all of the touring goodies: lockable luggage, a backrest, and an appropriately large windshield. It's also covered in chrome, so *S* must stand for schrome, no? Oh, then maybe it's for *shiny*.

Yamaha Stratoliner Midnight

By now you should be an expert on cruiser jargon, so considering this next bike's called the Midnight, what are you expecting? You've got it—it's all white. No, not really; it's black. It's also a very good bike, just not the best bike to choose as your very first.

Yamaha Stratoliner

The last of the Stratoliners is the base model, though it still comes pretty loaded and ready for that cross-country trip you've been postponing. Say, have you noticed that all of the other Yamahas are known as *Star*, and this one begins with *Stra?* Makes you wonder, does somebody at Yamaha type beyond their abilities?

Yamaha Roadliner

Where the Stratoliners are Yamaha's big touring-cruisers, these are their big cruisers. Take off the screen, luggage, and backrest and basically what's left is the Roadliner. Still a big machine, still a great machine. Like the Strat, it comes in the Shiny S version, the Midnight black version, and a base model.

Yamaha Road Star Midnight Silverado

The Road Stars are fitted with a slightly smaller 1670cc V-twin engine than the previously mentioned models. Being called Midnight, we all know what color it comes in, but it's also called Silverado and that means bags, backrest, and windshield. Sometimes Yamaha refers to it as the "Dark Star," thankfully not the "black hole"—as that wouldn't inspire much confidence.

Yamaha Road Star Silverado

Silverado still means the addition of soft leather bags, a medium-size windshield, and a touring seat for rider and passenger. This version also comes from the factory with whitewall tires, and you have to admit, they do look very good on these touring-cruisers.

Yamaha Road Star Midnight

This bad-boy Road Star gets the punched-out 1670cc engine, a raft of engine and drive train tweaks, and chunky wheels front and back. The Midnight also receives added blackness, as in engine, tanks, fenders, and so on. The light at the end of this dark tunnel? The chromed front end, of course.

Yamaha Road Star

Even the base Roadie gets the 1670cc engine, new cast wheels, tubeless tires, and new brakes lifted right from the SuperSports R1. The seat is wider and flatter, the drive belt is wider and lighter, and the handlebar is recurved for your pleasure. It even comes with a heel/toe gear shifter, which works perfectly with those standard footboards.

Yamaha Warrior

Have you noticed the aggressive nature of cruiser names? Where are all the Stylists and Retail Assistants? For now we'll have to go with the Warrior; it's Yamaha's last 1670cc bike and considering this bike is an AMA ProStar drag-race multiple champion, it has at least won its fair share of battles. There's an all-black Midnight version, too.

Yamaha V-Max

Introduced nearly 20 years ago, the mighty V-Max survives for the same reason crocodiles have: it simply eats anything that gets in its way. If you were raised on V-twins, you owe it to yourself to ride, if not own, this roaring, raging V-four torque monster from the past. No serious changes in years—didn't need 'em.

Yamaha V Star 1300 Tourer

The 1300s are a new addition to Yamaha's over-whelming lineup of cruisers. This new model features an all-new fuel-injected V-twin motor, which is also liquid-cooled—though you'd never know it. The boffins at Yamaha did a great job of hiding all of the pipes required to cool an engine. The Tourer spec includes bags, shield, and backrest once more.

Yamaha V Star 1300

The base version of the new 1300 V Star was "hot-rod inspired" and styled to look lighter and sportier (in a cruiser kind of way). Maybe Yamaha really hit the mark: it's one of their cleanest-looking cruiser designs, but engineered in a thoroughly modern fashion.

Yamaha V Star 1100 Silverado

The Silverado is the 1100cc version of the V Star designed for the wide-open road, with an adjustable windshield, classic leather saddlebags, a passenger backrest, and studded seats. Under it all is the time-tested V-Star 1100 motor, an air-cooled 1063cc engine, with its power transmitted through an exposed-shaft final drive.

Yamaha V Star 1100 Classic

The Classic is essentially the Silverado touring version, but without the touring-specific shield, bags, and so on. Done up in more of a traditionally American motif, it's got deeper fenders, fat 16-inch tires on cast wheels, a covered fork, lower bars, and footboards. It has the same motivation from the air-cooled V-twin.

Yamaha V Star 1100 Custom

The base model of the V Star 1100 line, the Custom uses the same 1063cc, two-valve-per-cylinder, SOHC engine; exposed-shaft final drive; steel frame suspension pieces; and triple-disc brakes as the others. The Custom differs with a lower, narrower seat; a slimmer 18-inch spoked front wheel; and a junior-petite headlight.

Yamaha V Star Silverado

If you don't need 1100cc of air-cooled V-twin to feel manly (or womanly, for that matter), check out the touring version of the smallest V Star, the 650. It's got an adjustable windshield and studded leather bags and seats—even a sissybar. Go ahead: say "sissybar" out loud.

Yamaha V Star Classic

Big, poofy fenders, a low seat height, and a chrome bill that would choke a rap star: this must be the V Star Classic. The 649cc, air-cooled V-twin is surprisingly powerful, while the single-disc front brake does the job—just. This is supposedly one of Yamaha's very best sellers—as high-value bikes usually are.

Yamaha V Star Custom

Psst. Here's the long, low chopper treatment applied to the likable and beginner-friendly V Star platform. To prevent potential owner embarrassment, Yamaha does not broadcast the displacement in the smaller V Star's moniker—only you know it's not a liter bike. Hush up, will ya?

Yamaha Virago 250 (Recommended–Beginner)

What do beginners want? Just guessing, but maybe this: Yamaha's smallest Virago has good power, a low seat, and utterly manageable dimensions. It's relatively cheap, reliable as an end-of-year budget redo, and even cute … in a tiny terror sort of way.

Sportbikes, Sport-Tourers, and Standards

Most sportbikes make poor first bikes because they tend to be hard-edged and single-mindedly focused on riding fast. But many of you reading this book will eventually end up on sportbikes, and there is some logic in learning to ride on the type of bike you intend to ride later. Fortunately, there are some very good sportbikes that also make good tools for perfecting your riding skills. Foremost among these bikes is Suzuki's pair of SV650s: the naked SV650 and the more sporting SV650S, which features a more racy riding position and a small fairing. One thing to keep in mind when considering a sportbike, however, is that most of these bikes have at least some plastic bodywork, and some bikes have extensive bodywork. That bodywork could be very expensive to replace if you have even the slightest tip-over. And you'll probably have at least one slight tip-over while learning to ride.

The sport-tourer category is something like the "Potpourri" category on the game show *Jeopardy:* it contains everything from gigantic touring bikes such as Honda's ST1300 to lighter-weight, sportier machines like their Interceptor. Most of these bikes are too bulky for a beginner, although some, such as Ducati's ST3, can do the job if necessary. Others make flat-out terrific first bikes.

The standard category is even more of a mixed bag, but it provides the most versatile bikes for a beginner. Generally, these bikes are naked or without bodywork, although more examples are now including a small fairing. Also, some naked bikes, such as Ducati's Monster 800 S2R and the previously mentioned Suzuki SV650, make terrific sportbikes. I suggest not getting hung up on labels. Forget what other people think. Decide what type of bike most appeals to you, and go for it.

Aprilia Sportbikes, Sport-Tourers, and Standards

Aprilia RSV 1000R Factory

Also known as the Mille (pronounced mee-lay), which is Italian for 1000. So obviously it's an Italian sportbike; it's also one of the best sporting motorcycles on the planet. In the Mille, Aprilia's V-twin motor shows the world what an engine of that configuration can really do. Standard on this top-of-the-line Factory model are Ohlins suspension and forged wheels. Brava!

Aprilia RSV 1000R

The more affordable Mille, and still, what a bike. In the real world, it will take most people years to be able to ride a machine like this anywhere near its limits. Surprisingly easy to ride sensibly, but becomes a race bike with a snap of the throttle. With so much instant, effortless power at the ready, you'd better train your right hand.

Aprilia Tuono 1000R Factory (Recommended–Experienced)

Take a Mille, strip off the bodywork, tidy up all of the wires and hoses, add some street handlebars and a little bug screen, and you've got a Tuono. Do you like the sound of a bike with 133hp and 75 ft-lbs of torque weighing only 400 lbs? Yeah, thought so. Lots of top-shelf goodies make up the "Factory" specs on this version.

Aprilia Tuono 1000R

Once again, this is Aprilia's slightly more affordable version. How many ways can we describe the Tuono? Fun, fast, nimble, fast, charismatic, uh … fast. It's so much fun you'll want to live on it. Your family members won't appreciate it, but hey, if you own one of these, you won't really care.

BMW Sportbikes, Sport-Tourers, and Standards

BMW K1200GT

The K1200GT is essentially a touring version of
the venerable K1200RS, with a taller fairing upper
and wind deflectors routing the air up and around.
Its four-cylinder motor kicks out 152hp, but at
more than 600 pounds, it's no racer. Not a cheap
bike either, but it's a BMW so unsurprisingly it's a
great all-weather long-distance runner.

BMW K1200R Sport

This one is a new addition to BMW's four cylinder, K series family and it's quite a looker, too.
It comes with a half fairing (upper part only), a
reasonably upright riding position, and an impressive 163hp. It definitely falls on the sporting side of
sport-tourer.

BMW K1200R

Take the K series engine, in a 163hp state of tune,
strip off the bodywork, and you've got the 1200R.
The resultant looks fall into the love 'em or hate
'em category; there's really not much room in the
middle. BMW calls this a hooligan bike, but do
hooligans really ride BMWs? Maybe they mean
nice, respectable hooligans.

BMW K1200S

An extremely competent bike for eating up the
miles, rapidly. This baby will go from stationary to
60mph in 2.8 seconds and then remain calm and
collected at the first curve in the road. If you're
considering buying one of these, choose the ESA
suspension option, as this lets you switch between
sport and normal riding modes.

BMW R1200ST

The R series of BMWs feature a horizontally opposed two-cylinder motor, commonly known as a boxer engine. This one comes in a sport-tourer package, which like most big Bee-Ems will eat up the miles very capably, and will take the twists and turns in its stride, too. The ABS is definitely an option worth having.

BMW R1200S

The dramatic, David Robb–penned R1200S is one of those bikes that's almost unimpressive on paper. If you just perused the specs, you probably wouldn't test-ride one. Well, I'm telling you: test-ride one, they're great. It's the kind of bike with which you become "as-one" very quickly.

BMW R1200R

The R1200R Roadster uses a more classical chrome headlight and chrome trim where the more extreme models tend toward flat black. Underneath is the tractable and reliable Oilhead Boxer, ready to leap tall states in a single sitting. The seat height is low, but the enjoyment is not.

BMW F800S

The F800S is fitted with the same motor as its F800ST stable mate, though this version is marketed as a sportbike. When compared directly against a Japanese four-cylinder sportbike, this little Bee-Em struggles. Viewed in its own right, it's actually a whole lot of fun. It's also an extremely good sportbike for a beginner.

Buell Sportbikes, Sport-Tourers, and Standards

Buell XB12R Firebolt

Take the Buell Firebolt XB9R, and give it some extra urge with the simple addition of a longer-stroke crank. What do you have? An all-American streetfighter, as before, but this one has the cojones to back up its enraged-alien look. Buell trickery remains: a fuel-filled frame, an oil-filled swingarm, and clever engine isolation.

Buell XB12S Lightning

The Lightning incarnation of the XB12R concept looks a little meaner with its tiny bug screen and dual headlights, but it has every bit of the original's clean-sheet design and knife-edge chassis dynamics. Also available with stretched wheelbase as the XB12S*s* and lower seat as the XB12S*cg*. If you don't give a damn about how they do it in Hamamatsu, here's a little something from Wisconsin.

Buell XB12STT Super TT Lightning

This Lightning Super TT is made with the same engineering marvels as the others. But this one also comes with its own set of styling touches, such as Super side panels, some Super handlebar protectors, and Super-duper headlight covers that emulate the enduro look. Take it for a ride and you'll agree it is Super indeed.

Buell XB9R Firebolt

A techno tour de force, this is the original Buell which attacked sportbike orthodoxy. The fuel lives in the frame, the oil sloshes in the swingarm, and the overall package features an ultra-short wheelbase akin to that of a GP race bike. It's not like anything else, except another Buell.

Buell XB9SX Lightning (Recommended–Intermediate)

Also known as the City-X, this Buell is right at home in the urban jungle. The bike is unbelievably nimble, has bucketloads of grunt, and is very cool looking with its translucent gas tank and bug screen. If you're a city dweller who's new to motorcycling, this thing needs to be at the top of your grocery list.

Buell Blast

What does the Buell Blast have to do to earn some respect? Um, I'll get back to you on that. The Blast looks built to a thin nickel (I'm too kind to say "cheap"), but it has proven to be nearly bulletproof in the hands of novice riders. You'll find modest performance here, but it's a good stepping-stone for the truly damp behind the ears.

Ducati Sportbikes, Sport-Tourers, and Standards

Ducati Desmosedici RR

Fancy your own world-class GP race bike? Willing to trade your luxury Euro sedan for it? There's no point even thinking about justifying what makes this bike worth every penny of the $70,000 ticket price, but believe me, it *is* worth it. It's being called the "ultimate Ducati experience," but maybe it's the ultimate sportbike.

Ducati 1098/1098S

Ducati's superbikes are the Ferraris of the motorcycle world, built with an obsession for performance and stunning looks. The 1098 is the latest in a long line of stunning big-bore V-twin sportbikes, and like every Ducati that came before it, this bike epitomizes great twenty-first century motorcycle design. Not for the beginner, but don't you wish it was?

Ducati ST3 S ABS

This is about as sport as sport-tourers get, complete with ABS brakes, high-end Ohlins suspension, and super-light Marchesini 5-spoke wheels. Just think, you can throw on some Ducati hard cases for your stuff and beat all of your friends to the motel. As long as the motel is on a closed-circuit track and you are a professional rider, don't attempt at home, etc., etc.

Ducati ST3

A couple of grand cheaper and essentially the same bike as the ST3 S, some of the swanky parts have been traded out for the kind used by us mere mortals. In other words it still rocks if you're in the market for a sport-tourer, especially when you consider it's roughly the same price as a common Japanese bike.

Ducati Monster S4R S Testastretta

The Monster started off life as a great town bike, a real modern café racer. Unfortunately, journalists kept wanting more power (I'm sorry); fortunately, Ducati listened and gave it the nuts engine from their 999 superbike (maybe I'm not sorry). The result is a slightly demented naked bike with a sweet Cobra/Shelby Mustang kind of paint scheme.

Ducati Monster S2R 1000

It may be a 1000cc V-twin just like the S4R, but this is a totally different motor. This time it's the air-cooled, dual-spark kind, but it's still a beaut, producing loads of torque. Trading out that motor saved you around $5,000; obviously there's more to it than that, but the point is: this Monster still provides more than enough Halloween fun.

Ducati Monster S2R 800

Somehow the 800cc Monster falls perfectly into the middle of the engine range, and I don't mean mathematically. The 800 is plenty powerful enough for hooligan fun, totally manageable, and with its single-sided swing arm—it's just as good looking as its big brothers. To complete its winning formula, it also costs a chunk less money.

Ducati Monster 695 (Recommended–Beginner)

The baby Monster might not have the rushing power of the bigger ones, but it's gorgeous, very lightweight, and has the lowest seat height of any Ducati. Why buy a cruiser just like everyone else, when you can learn your motorcycling skills on this work of art? Thoroughly recommended for the motorcycling probie.

Ducati GT1000

You'd expect a bike looking like this to fall into our Cruisers and Tourers category, but somehow Ducati always adds too much "sport" to allow that to happen. The GT was styled to look like a 1970s Ducati (retro is the new black), yet runs off the current 1000cc dual spark. No doubt it's fun, but are you ready to bust out your flares again?

Ducati SPORT 1000 Monoposto/Biposto (Recommended–Experienced)

Another take on the '70s theme, this time it's not styled after a standard bike, but after a custom of the time. The coolest modification back then was the café racer, hence this SPORT 1000 model. With this bike they got the look right on the money. Will somebody please give Ducati a medal or a cookie, or something …?

Ducati SPORT 1000S

The last of Ducati's new models looking like old ones is the SPORT 1000S, and this time its looks fall somewhere between a café racer and a vintage race bike with an old-school cockpit fairing. Fitted with the current 1000cc dual-spark motor, it's proof that vintage-looking doesn't have to mean slooow.

Ducati 1100 Multistrada

The radical Multistrada tosses the faux-adventure-tourer idea into a big Italian blender. It's really more of an upright sportbike than a dual-sport; the Multistrada is a truly wonderful do-anything sport utility bike (SUB). An S model is also available with upgrades such as top-notch Ohlins suspension front and rear.

Honda Sportbikes, Sport-Tourers, and Standards

Honda ST1300

Honda's flagship sport-tourer, designed as a halfway house between a Gold Wing and a CBR. It's smooth, quick, and amazingly light on its feet considering its weight—the bike of choice for many fast-riding European police forces. For an extra grand, the ABS version gets some no-skid stoppers.

Honda RC51

A road-legal version of the Honda that has already won both AMA and World Superbike Championships, meaning this is about as "sports" as a sportbike gets. Being a V-twin, it's capable of manic acceleration from tickover. Unfortunately this doesn't make it very forgiving in novice hands. A few steps away from the ideal first ownership experience.

Honda CBR1000RR

In the United States it's the CBR; in many other countries it's known as the FireBlade. It's a legend, pure and simple. With rock-solid Honda build quality, it will withstand merciless abuse and gain respect anywhere you park it. It's just too much bike for the novice, too much to *ride well*, at least.

Honda CBR600RR

Honda's smaller CBR/RR (sometimes nicknamed Baby-Blade) continues to fight for Honda in the manufacturers' never-ending performance war. It's a smaller bike, but remember: smaller means less weight, too. Dropping 40 lbs off the CBR1000RRs bulk means this little sportbike really flies.

Honda CBR600F4i (Recommended—Intermediate)

The F4i is the sane version of the CBR600RR, capable of keeping the smile on your face day after day in a multitude of situations. This bike is a serious contender for your money if you're new to bikes and lust after sport machinery. Fun, fast, rugged, and even forgiving of clumsiness.

Honda 919

Honda's designed-in-Europe naked bike is powered by a re-purposed CBR900RR engine, so the simplest description of this bike is a naked CBR1000RR Fireblade. Ridiculous fun around town, but like any naked bike it can be hard fighting the windblast during long stretches on the highway.

Honda 599

If the 919 is a naked CBR1000, then the 599 is a naked CBR600. In Europe it's called the Hornet 600 and is one of the most popular city bikes in existence. Highly recommended for the new rider, this one is in its element if you plan on riding short, traffic-clogged journeys to work. As fun as an F4i, and even more nimble.

Honda VFR800 V-TEC Interceptor (Recommended—Intermediate)

Another legend by Honda, the VFR has been the sport-touring motorcycles benchmark for years. Now it comes with V-Tec valve operation and an ABS option. One of the few do-it-all motorcycles, very hard to fault, and very easy to ride day after day, after day ….

Honda CB250 Nighthawk

Of Honda's extensive range, this is the bike that any intelligent new rider will use to rack up a few miles, thereby polishing riding skills. Not the coolest bike on the planet, but unintimidating and therefore excellent for learning. If your buddies laugh now, you'll laugh later as your riding rapidly improves without the hindrance of overwhelming horsepower.

Kawasaki Sportbikes, Sport-Tourers, and Standards

Kawasaki Concours (Recommended—Experienced)

This is Kawasaki's take on the big sport-tourer concept. Fitted with their warp-speed-capable 1400cc motor, it's obviously no slouch. It also comes fully loaded with all of the civilized touches you want in a mile-eater: hard cases for your gear and an electrically operated windshield, but what about a tire pressure monitoring system and an electronic keyless ignition system? I need that!

Kawasaki Ninja ZX-14

Kawasaki's biggest SuperSport mount. To understand it, look at the figures: the Fourteen produces nearly 200 horsepower (really!), 113 lb-ft of torque, and weighs in at 474 lbs. If you're a numbers person, then your mouth is already wide open. If you're not, trust me, open your mouth very wide and suck in some air. Don't you feel knowledgeable?

Kawasaki Ninja ZX-10R (Recommended—Experienced)

It's a dinky little bike, considering it's a 1000ccs; it's also super-fast and reassuringly stable. If you're buying one of these, though, your eyesight needs to be good, because whenever you snap the throttle open hard, you'll be arriving at those little dots on the horizon in seconds.

Kawasaki Ninja ZX-6R

Kawasaki's old ZX-6R was loved for its all-around goodness. Well, screw that. The new Six is deadly serious. If you want a light sportbike that you can ride to work and use for going nuts on weekend track days, well here you go. Just hold on really tight.

Kawasaki Z1000

Ooh yeah, take a look at this machine. It has the engine from Kawasaki's old ZX-9 Super-Sports bike, and brand-new bodywork that was inspired by their original 1973 Z900. While everyone else is making a retro bike that goes down the classic styling route, Kawasaki dares to be different with this gorgeous, thoroughly modern naked bruiser.

Kawasaki ZZR600

If the current ZX-6R is a little too focused on manic sports performance for you, then this should tickle your fancy. It's less racetrack, more street-orientated. The bike's really just a previous generation ZX-6 with a different name, but it's also a great choice for you Idiot's Guide readers and new riders.

Kawasaki Ninja 650R

Another 600-class sportbike from Kawasaki. If you're getting confused, then I'll clear it up for you. The ZX-6R is their SuperSports 4 cylinder, the ZZR-600 is their Sports 4-cylinder, and this Ninja 650R is their Sports 2-cylinder; and yes, it does make a difference. Manageable power delivery and light weight make the 650R effortless to ride.

Kawasaki Ninja 500R (Recommended–Beginner)

Another twin-cylinder Ninja, it's not just 150ccs smaller than the last one, it's a different bike. The styling of this twin is either old or classic, depending on your perspective. It's probably an "if it ain't broke, don't fix it" mentality coming from Kawasaki, and this old girl sure ain't broke.

Kawasaki Ninja 250R

Back in the day, we all expected the high-revving, hard-charging Ninja 250 to revive the stagnant 250 class, but, well, it's only one bike after all. It's still selling in modest numbers to smaller riders and the few (but vocal) supporters of the quarter-liter sportbike class. Fast? Not really. Fun? Absolutely.

KTM Sportbikes, Sport-Tourers, and Standards

KTM 990 Super Duke

Austrian firm KTM is best known for their off-road machines, which often set the standard the others must follow. This Super Duke is a bonkers streetfighter fitted with their ridiculously powerful 1000cc V-twin. It's not cheap, but it's certainly one of the best streetfighters in current production.

Moto Guzzi Sportbikes, Sport-Tourers, and Standards

Moto Guzzi Norge 1200

Guzzi's Norge is a charismatic sport-tourer. Apparently Moto-Guzzi invented the modern motorcycle swingarm, and tested it with a 4,000-mile journey from Italy to Norway in 1928. Apparently (once again) this bike is the "first Gran Turismo of the twenty-first century," hence the Norge (Norway) name. It had sure better have a swingarm.

Moto Guzzi Griso 1100

A slightly oddball but very cool naked bike. The Griso is the result of several million dollars' worth of Guzzi's development budget. Its styling is unique enough that it appeals as much to cruiser riders as it does to hooligan naked-bike owners. Guzzi makes solid bikes, but don't expect performance comparable with the other Italian brands.

Moto Guzzi Breva V1100

Considering Moto Guzzi's penchant for making lots of models out of not so many different pieces, the Breva 1100 seemed all but inevitable. It's the same modern styling treatment of the Breva 750, but it uses a thoroughly updated driveline.

Moto Guzzi Breva V750

Moto Guzzi cribs from its past for this entry-level model, the Breva. Based on the old V75 pushrod V-twin, the Breva's air-cooled, transverse power plant gets fuel injection and a five-speed transmission plus fresh styling, a newbie-friendly 31.1-inch-high seat, and naked simplicity. What's not to like?

MV Agusta Sportbikes, Sport-Tourers, and Standards

MV Agusta F4-1000R

Okay, so straight off the bat—this bike's not cheap, but if you've got the money, who cares? You could buy one just to look at and be happy: it's stunning. But there's a bonus—it's incredible to ride, too. The only drawback to riding it is that you can't see it. So periodically you have to get off and look at it again. Repeat as necessary.

MV Agusta Brutale 910R

For years we were promised the Brutale, and now it's here. It's a compact, frenetic piece of Italian moto-desire, with amazing looks, a high-revving engine, and suspension equally at home on the track as it is on the street. Hear the sound of an F1 grid every time you downshift, and watch the expressions of passersby as they check out your exquisite bike.

Royal Enfield Sportbikes, Sport-Tourers, and Standards

Royal Enfield 500 Bullet (Recommended–Beginner)

In 1950s Britain, the original Royal Enfield Company made the Bullet as a standard-type streetbike. The company eventually folded, but only after they had already established a second factory in India (in 1955). To this day the Indian factory still produces almost the same 1955 model of Bullet that it has been making for 50 years. Now that's real retro!

Suzuki Sportbikes, Sport-Tourers, and Standards

Suzuki GSX1300R Hayabusa

The Big Daddy, the legend, the Hayabusa. The Busa has become the ultimate symbol of speed for a new generation of riders. The looks certainly aren't to everyone's taste, but then it was created as much by wind tunnel as by a designer's pen. It's so very, very fast that it's just not a smart choice as your first motorcycle.

Suzuki GSX-R1000

Just like the Hayabusa, Suzuki's GSX-R series of bikes have grown to symbolize something special. To many owners they're more than just another superbike model: to them they are *the* superbike. Year after year, Gixxers have been the benchmark for razor-sharp handling and searing acceleration, on none more so than this 1000cc version.

Suzuki GSX-R750 (Recommended—Intermediate)

The 750 is even better than the 1000 for street use, but if you're finishing up this book for the first time and looking for that first bike, then quit looking here. Yeah, plenty of people buy them as a first bike, but you can spot them wobbling around corners from a mile away. If you're re-reading this with some experience under your belt, then go for it—this bike will not disappoint.

Suzuki GSX-R600

Contrary to what you'd think as an outsider, even the 600cc GSX-R flies. This is the only Gixxer to even contemplate—until you've racked up some miles and honed those skills. In the right hands, a GSX-R600 can blow a bigger bike into the weeds. Don't let its small capacity fool you, it's a lot of motorcycle.

Suzuki SV1000S

There's a couple of ways to look at this bike. You can either think of it as a GSX-R but with a tuned V-twin motor replacing the in-line four-cylinder (giving it a totally different style) or you could say it's Ducati fun at a Suzuki price. Either way, it's guaranteed to get you smiling.

Suzuki SV650S (Recommended—Beginner)

The original, smaller Suzuki SV is still powered by a V-twin like its 1000cc stable mate, but this one is better suited to the newer motorcyclist. In fact, you could almost say that this is the perfect bike for the newer motorcyclist. If you're drawn to the sport style, then there really isn't much out there to beat it.

Suzuki SV650

The SV650 in naked guise. It's quick, has incredible cornering capabilities, and is super-nimble at low speeds. You could climb aboard this bike the day after your motorcycle course and not be intimidated, but two years later you'd still be enjoying it doing track days. There aren't many bikes as versatile as the SV650.

Suzuki Bandit 1250S

The Bandit is neither sportbike nor sport-tourer. It's not really a naked bike either, but whatever it is, it's sold well for over a decade. Fitted with an older generation of GSX-R motor, they're basic but very strong and have proven to make great everyday bikes, often owned by people without cars who ride daily. Unglamorous, but brilliant.

Suzuki Katana 750/600

With a steel frame, and well, not the most responsive suspension, this is a throwback bike. The original Katana was a Suzuki legend; unfortunately, this bike shares only the name. It's a low-cost sport-tourer, with an engine derived from the original GSX-R. Available in two engine sizes, the Katana is at least a good candidate for cheap, reliable motorcycling.

Suzuki GS500F

It's reliable, it's nimble, and it's extremely novice friendly, but to call it a sportbike is simply wishful thinking. The GS500F is essentially a low-cost commuter bike with a GSX-R-style fairing slapped on. The naked version of this bike is hugely popular with European motorcycle training schools, which means it's about as bulletproof as they come.

Suzuki GZ250

Getting into this whole biking thing shouldn't be an exercise in intimidation, and with a GZ250, it isn't. Suzuki's bantamweight boulevardier makes sure it's fun. The bone-simple air-cooled single makes accessible power, while a low seat keeps the street accessible to short legs. Maybe most important is an accessible price tag.

Triumph Sportbikes, Sport-Tourers, and Standards

Triumph Sprint ST

Triumph's Sprint ST sport-tourer is pretty fast and handles great; it's also good-looking, comfortable and remarkably versatile. It's fitted with Triumph's wonderfully torque-y three-cylinder motor and comes as standard with good luggage. So all in all, it's one of the only true rivals to Honda's legendary VFR.

Triumph Speed Triple

The original factory-made streetfighter. The Speed Triple was an inspiration to all other bike manufacturers. It's fast, furious, excitable, and outlandish; it's also easy to live with and halfway comfortable. The Triple is a thoroughly naughty naked, with a torque-stomping three-cylinder motor and a hooligan's manner. Its bad attitude is so infectious, you'll be sneering before you know it.

Triumph Daytona 675

Triumph did it, they made a class-leading middleweight sports-bike. This little Triple has blown everyone away with its grunty motor, racetrack-ready handling, and compact size. The Daytona is a very serious alternative to the current crop of Japanese four-cylinder super-sport machines. Finally, being different doesn't involve compromise.

Triumph Thruxton 900 (Recommended—Intermediate)

The Thruxton is essentially a Bonneville that's been tweaked at the Triumph factory. This time, they're going for a 1960s racer look, with clip-on handlebars, cropped mudguards, and a seat-hump. It sure looks the part, which in this case is enough to base your buying decision on. The standard Bonneville is a great bike, so this variation shouldn't disappoint.

Yamaha Sportbikes, Sport-Tourers, and Standards

Yamaha FJR1300/FJR1300 ABS

It's big, it's comfortable, it's even quite sporty, but what it does best is gobble up the miles on fast roads. The FJR comes standard with good luggage and is as comfortable for your passenger as it is for you, and you know what life's like when your passenger's unhappy—don't you?

Yamaha YZF-R1

Yamaha's big sportbike is the YZF-R1, known more commonly as just the R1. It needs more revving than most 1000cc sporties, but absolutely flies when ridden appropriately. A very popular bike worldwide, maybe the R1 is a little more road focused than the competition; maybe it's more beautiful, too.

Yamaha FZ1

Take an R1, ditch the full-size plastics and replace them with a small upper fairing. Then re-tune the engine for more midrange power and add high comfortable handlebars and you get the FZ1, also known as the Fazer. Just as much fun as the R1, in a slightly different way, but a whole lot cheaper to insure.

Yamaha YZF-R6 (Recommended—Experienced)

Years ago none of us would have believed that a 600cc machine like this could exist. It's really a bike that was designed for racing, actually that's wrong, it was built to *dominate* World Supersport racing. Its natural environment isn't the road, so as incredible as it is, you probably don't need a bike capable of 17,500rpm for street use. Want—maybe. Need—unlikely.

Yamaha YZF-R6S

This version of the R6 has its feet planted a little more firmly on the ground. It's still very fast and ultra light, but arrives a thousand dollars cheaper than the R6. If you want a middleweight Yamaha sportbike for the road, not the track, then this is the place to dump your money.

Yamaha YZF600R

Another sporty 600cc Yamaha may seem confusing, but it needn't be. This model is more sport-tourer than sportbike, in modern terms at least. It's small money to buy, has a comfortable seat for two bums, and still manages to look good. No surprise to hear it comes recommended as a good starter motorcycle.

Yamaha FZ6

And finally we have the FZ6, the nearly naked version of Yamaha's 600cc sportbikes. Yamaha calls it a streetfighter, but with that perfect nose, it's definitely no fighter. It's more like an FZ1 that got shrunk when you washed it too hot, but somehow, being smaller, it fits the new rider better anyway.

Dual-Sports

There was a time when most riders started out with dirtbikes, moved up to dual-sports, and then graduated to streetbikes. These days, new riders often go straight for the big-inch cruiser or sportbike of their choice, ignoring the fact that they often haven't mastered the skills needed to ride such equipment. In this day and age of land closures, finding places to ride a dirtbike has become increasingly difficult, but the dual-sport category is booming. With the exception of the ultimate-behemoth class of giant trailbikes coming from Europe, just about any of these motorcycles can be a terrific first bike.

Aprilia Dual-Sports

Aprilia ETV1000 Caponord

Our first dual-sport features potential problems common to many of the breed, it's very tall and quite heavy. This particular machine is fitted with Aprilia's glorious V-twin, and is a truly wonderful bike for everyday use. Unfortunately, it's also a challenge for anyone below average height.

BMW Dual-Sports

BMW R1200GS Adventure (Recommended–Experienced)

The GS is not just a motorcycle—it's a way of life. The more adventurous Adventure is lighter, features more suspension travel, big aluminum side cases, engine guards, and other Sahara-ready goodies. The top-shelf GS also has a shorter first gear for tiptoeing through the tulips, though first gear is the *only* thing short on this bike, so be aware.

BMW R1200GS

Good roads, bad roads, or no roads; BMW's omnivorous 1200cc GS has been taking travelers farther off the beaten tracks for more than two decades now. This bike can take you to work today and to Tierra del Fuego tomorrow. Considering it has some off-road capability, it's quite amazing just how sporty it can be on-road.

BMW F650GS

Instead of the big 1200cc twin, this Bee-Em is powered by a single-cylinder 650 motor. Being smaller, lower, and lighter than the 1200s, it's an easier off-road machine. It's also a wonderful roadbike to rack up some miles on, particularly if you're new to this whole bike thing.

BMW G650 Xchallenge

It's got its roots in the F650, but this model has all of the trick lightweight goodies you want in an off-roader; air-damped suspension, a cast alloy swingarm, and a wavy front brake rotor. However, being more off-road focused does mean it's tall, too, taller than even the 1200GS.

BMW G650 Xcountry

With the same tuned-up version of the single-cylinder engine as its Challenge cousin, the Country is pretty quick. All of the G650 variations are getting the goodies fitted; the taillights are LEDs, they've got stainless-steel exhausts, and this Country model even has a catalytic converter. Figure in the $3\frac{1}{2}$-inch lower seat height, and the Country is the one to get for the novice.

BMW G650 Xmoto

As I mentioned in the body of the book, Super-Motards are a relatively new addition to the dual-sport world of bikes in America. From BMW we have this G650X Moto. It's got smaller cast wheels, grippy tires, upside down front forks, and the hotted-up version of the 650 motor, making it a real hoot to play with on city streets.

Buell Dual-Sports

Buell XB-12X Ulysses

Like most dual-sports, you won't be taking this one up the side of a wooded 45-degree mountain. It will take you along trails happily enough, though. Maybe not the best of the bunch when the going gets rough, but it is one of the finest-looking duallies on the market.

Ducati Dual-Sports

Ducati HyperMotard

Super-skinny and lightweight, powered by Ducati's legendary 1078cc V-twin, tuned for torque, torque, and more torque, it's possibly the most fun you can have on two wheels. This bike's definitely geared more for street use than most dual-sports, but at least it excels at what it's meant for.

Honda Dual-Sports

Honda XR650L

Compared to current, liquid-cooled dirt four-strokes, the air-cooled XR650L is big, fat, and old. The only problem is, it works wonderfully—the perfect motorcycle for people who want to ride everywhere and see everything. A legend from Baja to Bangor, it may be responsible for the popularity of dual-sport riding today.

Husaberg Dual-Sports

Husaberg FS650e/FS550e

Super-Motards from Sweden. The Husabergs come with White Power suspension, Brembo brakes, Behr rims, and electric start. They also weigh in at 245 lbs, so if you pull off some Wildman Super-Motard jump trick, just beware: you may never land. It could just float away in the wind like a stray feather.

Husqvarna Dual-Sports

Husqvarna SMR510/SMR450

Some dual-sports are basically road bikes in a fancy dress costume, while some are the real deal with very little in common with a regular streetbike. Husqvarnas are totally authentic: their two SMR Super-Motard models are real replicas of their world Motard championship winners. Not for the fainthearted.

Husqvarna SM610

Husqvarnas have a cult following because they're very focused and efficient off-road bikes; to most aficionados they are simply "Huskies." This 610 Husky has a 600cc engine and is built as an every-day Motard for street use. It's about as civilized as this company makes them, even having a dual seat so can you ride into the sunset with your passenger screaming all the way.

Kawasaki Dual-Sports

Kawasaki KLR650

Kawasaki's biggest dual-purpose bike has been around for an incredible 21 years, and it still sells well. That says a lot about this practical midsize motorcycle. It's not as off-road focused as some, but with a host of recent improvements it's still the perfect first duallie for anyone new to the sport.

Kawasaki KLX250S

In complete contrast to the KLR, this KLX is very off-road focused. It's road legal and Kawasaki lists it as a dual-purpose bike, but this one is pretty competent off the tarmac with good ground clearance, an engine guard, and electric start. This is another great starter bike from Kawasaki, especially if you dream about being covered in sticky brown mud.

KTM Dual-Sports

KTM 990 Adventure S

This street version of KTM's big rally racer is more fun than a bathtub full of Jell-O. The massive 1000cc V-twin engine is wonderful: compact and torque-y. The chassis reminds me just how good a streetbike can be; honestly, it's weird how good this bike is! The S version is 1.4 inches taller, with new rally graphics.

KTM 990 Adventure

Aside from less suspension travel and a lower seat, KTM's basic Adventure twin is anything but. It's actually more accessible if you're not as tall as an NBA center. Available in orange or black, it carries nearly 6 gallons of fuel for the 98-horse V-twin, and it's better behaved off-road than you'd expect a 450-pound dual-sport to be.

KTM 640 Adventure (Recommended—Intermediate)

A whole lot smaller, a whole lot lighter, and just as much fun. The 640 Adventure is powered by a single-cylinder motor, which still propels the bike rapidly on- or off-road, and this time the whole KTM package weighs only 350 lbs.

KTM 950 SuperMoto

If you've been paying attention, you'll have noticed that KTM barely had any bikes listed until we reached this dual-sports section. That should give you an idea of how focused the company is within this sector. This massive SuperMoto runs off their big V-twin, and is predictably excellent as an oversized duallie.

KTM 690 SuperMoto

KTM's next size down in the Super-Motard category is a 650cc single-cylinder that weighs only 335 lbs. Seriously, how do they do it? You could almost pick it up with one hand to oil your chain. Do you know how much fun a light, powerful bike like this is? I'm telling you it's spelled F-U-N.

Suzuki Dual-Sports

Suzuki V-Strom 1000

If you like the idea of a go-anywhere Big Twin but know you'll ride most of your miles on pavement, the big V-Strom is about right. It's lower than the Europeans and works well enough on the dirt roads you're liable to travel. With optional bags, it can do it all.

Suzuki V-Strom 650

I love the SV650 streetbike, and this adventure-tourer version should be extra-wonderful as well. With a compact yet semi-protective fairing, complete with adjustable windshield, it should make a swell middleweight sport-tourer. Less weight and a lower seat should make it even better than the 1000 on fire roads.

Suzuki DR650SE

Roost mightily on local trails, horrify the Starbucks barista with actual dirt on your face, and then ride to work all week. Powered by a steadfast electric-start 644cc single, Suzuki's DR650SE acts like a garage full of motorcycles for just $5,000. Vertically challenged types can lower the seat 1.6 inches.

Suzuki DR-Z400S

More like a dirtbike that you can take on the street, the DR-Z400S is the dual-sport for serious dirt people. The engine makes enough power for almost any off-road need, and the chassis and true long-travel suspension are easily up to the occasional enduro. Lights, license plate, action!

Suzuki DR-Z400SM

Add the letter M as a suffix to the old DR-Z400S and you've got a very different bike. SM means Super-Motard and Suzuki made a host of changes in creating this new model. New forks and swing-arm, plus brakes and wheels make for one of the best and most affordable Motards on the block.

Suzuki DR200SE

This is what Stinky Pete, the prospector from *Toy Story*, would have ridden out to his claim in the desert. Not tall, loud, or exciting, the DR200E is nonetheless perfect for small, beginning, or more casual riders. Nothing new here, but what would you change?

Triumph Dual-Sports

Triumph Tiger 1050

The Tiger is Triumph's shot at an adventure-tourer. The fuel-injected, liquid-cooled 1050cc triple is unique in the dual-sport sector, but it makes for a very fast Tiger that's more at home touring the highways than any of the other bikes in this sector.

Triumph Scrambler

The Scrambler stands out amongst this bunch of bikes. The appearance of most dual-sports is dictated by function; this one was designed the opposite way around. It's a new Bonneville, which has been styled to look like an off-roader from the '60s. There's no doubt that it's beautiful, but even with those knobby tires and high pipes, it's probably better kept on the road.

Yamaha Dual-Sports

Yamaha XT225 (Recommended—Beginner)

If the XT225 were a person, it'd be old enough to date. Why is it still around? Because it's exactly what many casual dual-purpose riders want: a relatively low, relatively lightweight machine with just enough power to make life interesting. Call this the Hugginator.

Yamaha TW200

Okay, the TW may look unusually different. But it foments a kind of silly fun all its own, with those big, floaty tires bouncing over the dunes like high-speed basketballs. Think of it not as a motorcycle, but as a street-legal ATV that lost a wheel a few years back.

Cross-Country and Enduro

For those lucky enough to have access to off-road riding trails, there is still no better way to start riding than to do it in the dirt. But the off-road class of motorcycles is bewilderingly complex, containing everything from overgrown two-stroke trials bikes to tame, off-road trailbikes and even full-boat motocross race bikes with lights. When choosing a first bike in this category, you must choose a bike you can manage, or you will never develop your off-road riding skills. Master those skills, and you will be a much better rider on the street, too.

ATK Cross-Country and Enduro

ATK Enduro

The Japanese may try, but fortunately they don't completely dominate motorcycle manufacturing. ATK motorcycles are proudly made in the USA, and they rock. This Enduro is just wicked, running off a highly tuned 450cc four-stroke and weighing a mere 248 lbs. No, that's not a typo—they really are that light.

ATK Motard

The Motard has the same storming 450 motor as the Enduro, but it's also fitted with some of its own goodies like Excel wheels, wavy brake rotors, and Brembo front brake calipers. Add Ohlins suspension, fuel injection, and even electric start and well, you want one. You really badly want one.

ATK 620/700 Intimidator

That's right, a whopping 685cc (or 616cc, for the slightly less insane) of earth-moving, horizon-seeking two-stroke power. The engines are built by Maico, the German company that made too much seem just right with the legendary Maico 501 of the 1970s. If you, like Scottie, always need more power Cap'n, ATK might just have the wild-haired weapon for you.

Honda Cross-Country and Enduro

Honda XR650R

This big dog is the king of the "B for B" category: built for Baja. If the road is long, fast, and eye-watering, this liquid-cooled aluminum-chassis bomber is just about perfect. And if the stock 649cc power plant isn't enough, your dealer can slip you a kit to crank out even more fire-road–shredding torque. ¿Un mas cerveza, señor?

Honda CRF450X (Recommended–Intermediate)

Honda's midsize dirt-devil has recently changed. Now you get the race-ready 450 motor fitted to an alloy-framed bike with enduro suspension. I guess Honda figured we should all be riding the trails much faster, so come on ... keep it moving back there.

Honda CRF250X

The 450's baby bro also gets the full go-faster treatment from Honda. If you want an Enduro bike that's fast, light, and almost certain to never go wrong, and if you prefer having a professional service facility close to home, then it's hard not to buy one of these bikes.

Husaberg Cross-Country and Enduro

Husaberg FE450e/FE550e/FE650e

Husaberg's earth-moving four-strokes come in three tasty enduro versions, from the semi-sane 450 all the way to the thoroughly excessive 650. Whether you choose mild or wild, you get the same high-quality bits: a lightweight, chrome-moly frame, WP suspension, electric start, Brembo brakes—the works. Do good things (and strong drink) come from Sweden? Fer shure!

Husqvarna Cross-Country and Enduro

Husqvarna TE250/TE450/TE510 (Recommended–Experienced)

Anders Eriksson nabbed his seventh World
Enduro Championship on the TE450 four-stroke.
If you want to win, consider one of these high-tech
flyers. They use titanium valves and exhaust pipes,
plus a trick F-1-style rocker-arm and an engine
that pumps out strong, smooth power. Lightweight
electric starting also means all your energy goes
into the race.

Husqvarna WR250/WR125

Two-stroke enduro bikes are the ultimate in lightweight, agile off-roaders, and Husqvarna's WR duo
comes complete with superb credentials, including
an amazing 67 World Championship titles. You
should test-ride a two-stroke before you buy (if
anybody will even let you), as it's way too easy to be
ejected off the back and be left sitting on your butt,
watching your pride and joy ride off without you.

Kawasaki Cross-Country and Enduro

Kawasaki KLX450R

Start with a hard-core Moto-X bike, then make
the engine's flywheel heavier to help provide a less
snappy power delivery, and you've got a Kawasaki
Enduro. A stupid fast one, but an Enduro nonetheless. It's the off-road equivalent of a 1000cc sportbike.

Kawasaki KLX300R

What does the R stand for in Team Green's KLX300R? I could be mistaken, but it just might stand for off-road legend Larry Roeseler, the man who made the KLX300 so justifiably famous. Serious power comes from the four-stroke power plant, while a KX-inspired chassis, featuring Uni-Trak suspension and an inverted fork, calms, bumps, and whoops.

KTM Cross-Country and Enduro

KTM 950 Super Enduro R

Yes, the 950 designation does mean that it's an off-roader with a 942cc V-twin engine. That's certainly a scary prospect—it would be comparable to having a 2000cc sportbike! If you buy this for your first bike, then I'll bring you some magazines and chocolates for your stay in ER.

KTM 525 EXC-G and 450 EXC-G

In KTM-speak, the EXC enduro models have lights, digital speedo/odos, and wide-ratio gearboxes. These Austrian superthumpers all come standard with six-speed transmissions and are equipped with lightweight electric starting—you push their buttons, and they push yours!

KTM Off-road Competition XC Series

The XC series is completely and utterly overwhelming, but basically it's a large group of bikes that KTM designates as cross-country machines. There are nine models, featuring different-sized motors that come in both two- and four-stroke versions. Whichever you choose, you're unlikely to be disappointed.

KTM Off-Road Competition SX Series

Equally complex is the SX series: they come as big as 450cc and as small as 105cc. The one thing they all share is that they're designed for SuperCross, Moto-X, and Arena Cross. Very focused bikes, but it's what KTM does, and they quite possibly do it better than anyone else.

Suzuki Cross-Country and Enduro

Suzuki DR-Z400E

The kick start-only DR-Z400 disappeared a while back—it looks like everybody preferred the E-model's electric starter. And why not? The E's push-button spinner added just a little weight for a whole lot of trailside convenience. One of the few trailbikes without a race-derived engine, but good for Suzuki. Many people prefer a softer, more relaxed motor.

Suzuki DR-Z250 (Recommended—Beginner)

Suzuki's DR-Z250 is what's known in the motorcycle world as a "gapper": a bike that bridges the gap between big-guy off-road thumpers and smaller, less-serious playbikes. The electric-start 250 does this by offering serious off-road performance in a smaller, lower, more user-friendly package, one perfect for everyone from full-size novices to height-challenged vets.

Yamaha Cross-Country and Enduro

Yamaha WR450F

Based on the fabulous YZ450F, the WR450F is Yamaha's take on the open-class desert or enduro machine. Powered by the YZ's liquid-cooled, titanium-valve 449cc four-stroke, the WR adds an electric starter; a wide-ratio transmission; slightly plusher suspension; an 18-inch rear wheel; and a headlight/taillight assembly. Brrrraaap!

Yamaha WR250F

As it does with the 450, Yamaha offers a desert/enduro version of its five-valve YZ250F—the quick-revving, highly maneuverable WR250F. The WR features electric starting (yeah!), upside-down forks with an antistick coating, lightweight aluminum brake pistons, a sump-guard, and a high-grip seat cover. BooYaa!

Playbikes

The playbikes category is odd because what some companies consider playbikes, others might consider to be full-fledged race bikes. Some of the off-road bikes in the cross-country and enduro categories are really just for playing off-road, although some of the bikes in the playbike category are mildly detuned race bikes. With a very few exceptions, the bikes in this class are minibikes and are best suited for very young novices.

Honda Playbikes

Honda CRF230F

All of the letters used to designate models by the various factories can be very hard to fathom. Honda's off-road machines fitted with two-stroke engines are CR, when fitted with four-strokes they become CRF. This 230cc model is a breeze to ride, making a perfect first bike for playing in the mud.

Honda CRF150F

The CRF150F is another one of Honda's low-stress, recreational off-roaders. It offers the same type of all-around, easy-to-ride performance as the 230F, but in a smaller, even more manageable package. Positioned halfway between the 230F and the 100F, the 150F has a low-maintenance nature plus a race-inspired body and graphics that are sure to please.

Honda CRF100F/80F/70F/50F

The smaller CRFs are there for the kids. The idea is that you'll start your little sprog off with the 50, assuming they're old enough to listen and balance (so leave your six-month-old in their crib, please). Then they'll gradually work their way up as they outgrow each size, waving the Honda flag all the way.

Kawasaki Playbikes

Kawasaki KLX110

The KLX110 is an entry-level recreational dirtbike that's not only easy to ride, but simple to take care of as well. Motivated by an air-cooled four-stroke engine with a three-speed transmission and automatic clutch, the smallest KLX offers big KX styling, knobby tires, a low-to-the-ground seat, and a throttle limiter that should help stop Junior from pulling acci-mental wheelies.

Kawasaki KX65/85/100

Kawasaki's little trio of two-stroke screamers should be successful at rearing your own little screamer in the ways of the motorcycle. There's no great starter bike here, they're all set up with a competition-obsessed kid in mind. Hmm, sounds just like me.

KTM Playbikes

KTM SX50/65/85

These itty bitty little KTMs are playbikes for the kind of kid who likes to play at standing on the winner's podium, holding a plastic trophy. In true KTM style, they're little flyers, so make sure the young'un is ready.

KTM 50 Mini Adventure/Senior Adventure

These are the smallest KTMs, designed to throw your baby onto. Your baby really needs to be 3 years old, but this little bike is probably the most popular steed for the microscopic racer. The senior version is for 6 to 8 year olds. So does that mean an 85cc version would be for retirees?

Suzuki Playbikes

Suzuki DR-Z 125L/DR-Z 125

These versatile playbikes thrive anywhere there's dirt. Powered by a dependable single-cylinder four-stroke engine, these first-timer mounts show their main difference in wheel size: the L-model uses a 19/16 (front/rear) combo, while the standard version uses smaller, 17/14-inch hoops for more inseam-challenged confidence.

Suzuki RM85/RM85L

Let's say that your son (or daughter) is just starting out on the dirt and is at least 9 years old but is a touch too big for Suzuki's JR50—what to do? Try the RM85, a beginner bike that's one step more advanced than the littlest JR. Like the DR-Z125, there's a standard and an L version for the larger/longer kids.

Suzuki JR50

A long-time favorite of moms and dads, not to mention kids, the JR50 is arguably one of the best kid-spec dirtbikes available. Light in weight, small in stature, and loaded with such safety conveniences as a throttle limiter, the JR50 is a near-bulletproof yellow zonker that'll teach your kids right and give them plenty of smiles in the process.

Yamaha Playbikes

Yamaha TT-R230

Sometimes a manufacturer's own words do the job perfectly: "Designed for both new and casual off-road riders … the TT-R230 is tailor-made for fun." A low seat height and electric starter further this mission, as do the reliable four-stroke engine and rugged frame. "Perfect for novice, women, and recreational riders"—I agree.

Yamaha TT-R125E/TT-R125L/TT-R125LE

Playbikes that share basic chassis and engine platforms are nothing new, and Yamaha's TT-R125E, TT-R125L, and TT-R125LE do the job surprisingly well. The differences: LE models feature electric start while the L versions are kick start only—both with a 19-inch front wheel and 16-inch rear. Finally, the TT-R125E gets electric start and smaller (17/14-inch) hoops.

Yamaha TT-R90E/TT-R50E

Yamaha's smallest four-stroke is the TT-R50, and it's one of those entry-level dirtbikes that generate miles of smiles for newer and younger riders. There's also a taller 90cc version. Both bikes feature electric start and an automatic clutch, which should give mini-you less to remember, or forget.

Yamaha PW50

Many people regard the PW50 as the "perfect" beginner bike—and a lot of them are giggling kids. Weighing just 82 pounds and carrying its seat just 19 inches above the dirt, Yamaha's Pee-Wee offers no-shifting power and a throttle limiter. Oil injection and shaft drive help keep maintenance chores simple.

Biker's Buying Guide to Used Bikes

Appendix A listed just about every new streetbike sold in the United States, some of which can honestly be called bargains. But as you may have noted, even the so-called bargains will require you to lay out some serious cash before you can park one in your garage.

If the price of a new bike is beyond your means, you needn't worry much; the used-bike market can help get you on two wheels.

While some motorcyclists trash their machines, most keep them in fairly good condition. Many of the used bikes you'll find will be in nearly the same shape as a new bike.

In Chapter 7, I told you how to make certain a used bike is in sound mechanical shape. In this appendix, I list some used bikes that will make exceptional first motorcycles.

Because used-bike prices vary according to a variety of factors, from the condition of the bike to locale, I'm not including prices in this guide. Generally, bikes that cost more new tend to cost more used. Just as a new BMW costs more than a new Kawasaki, a used BMW will cost more than a used Kawasaki.

As with the "Biker's Buying Guide to New Bikes" in Appendix A, I've listed the used bikes alphabetically, by make. I've included only bikes manufactured since 1982. However, some good, dependable motorcycles were manu- factured before that time, and if you find one that runs well and is in good shape, you shouldn't pass it up just because it's older. But be aware that you will have more mechanical trouble with older bikes than with newer bikes. In addition, technological advances from the early 1980s to the present make motorcycles manufactured since then safer and more practical.

For more information, the *AMA Official Motorcycle Value Guide* is one of the best sources we've found for accurate used-bike prices. Published monthly, the guide goes for $77 for a year's subscription, and individual copies can be purchased for $19.95 by calling Black Book National Auto Research at 1-800-554-1026, or visit www. blackbookusa.com on the web. The services of *Kelly Blue Book* can also be a big help. You can find out the typical problems of any given model and determine the bike's current value. Go to www.kbb.com on the Internet.

Aprilia

Aprilia has been selling motorcycles in the United States for a few years now. Although there aren't a ton of used Aprilias on the market, there are a few. More recent models are better.

Aprilia Pegaso

Aprilia's Pegaso makes a terrific first bike, whether you buy it new or used. While it presents itself as some sort of dual-sport, this one works best on the street. Although a few injected versions have been imported into the United States, I recommend going with the simpler carbureted version, which will be much smoother and easier for a novice to ride.

BMW

Like new BMWs, used Beemers tend to cost more than most other bikes, but they are well worth the extra money. The care with which these bikes are built means they tend to last longer than most other motorcycles.

BMW R1150R/R1100R/R850R

BMW's least expensive Oilhead bike, the R model (available in 850cc, 1100cc, and 1150cc versions), makes a terrific first bike, the kind we like to recommend. That is because it is a competent machine that will serve riders well long after they graduate from being novices to experienced riders.

R80GS/R100GS

These big Beemer dual-sports, the original leviathans of the trailbike world, might be a bit of a handful for a new rider, but their torque-y, tractable engines and overall balance make them much easier to ride than other bikes of similar engine displacement. These are expensive motorcycles, but they tend to last a long time.

R80/R80ST

This is a street-only version of the original R80GS dual-sport. The R80s are even easier for an inexperienced rider to learn on than the GS series because they have lower seats—a factor that seems to make new riders feel more secure. The R80s are relative bargains, too. These are some of the few used Beemers you'll find priced less than $3,000.

K75/K75S/K75C

These bikes use three-cylinder versions of BMW's unique flat, four-cylinder engine. They are rather large bikes for a beginner, but as with the R80 and R100 boxer twins, their power-delivery characteristics make them easy to ride. Also like the Boxers, they tend to cost more than most other used bikes.

BMW F650

We heartily recommend the original carbureted version of BMW's F650 as a first bike. In fact, we recommend it as a second, third, or forty-fifth bike because it is that good. Built on the same assembly line as Aprilia's Pegaso, this bike differs from the Aprilia in having a four-valve head rather than Aprilia's five-valve head, but BMW's version puts out even more power than the Aprilia, so apparently it gets on just fine without that extra valve.

Honda

Honda is another manufacturer that makes motorcycles of exceptional quality. You'll find a lot of nice used Hondas out there.

NX650

Back in the late 1980s, Honda decided to produce a dual-sport that didn't look like one—or like anything else the motorcycling world had seen before. The result was the unique NX650, a streetbike based on Honda's XL600R dual-sport. Honda created a rather interesting and useful street thumper, one that will cost you less than half of what the cheapest new 650 single will cost you.

XL350R/XL500R/XL600R/XR650L

These bikes are rather crude compared to the newer XR650R dual-sports, but in their day, they were the nicest trailbikes around. The dual-carburetion system of the XL600R can cause the power delivery to seem a bit abrupt, making that bike more difficult for a novice to master than some other thumpers. Considering that used XLs will cost you only between $750 and $1,500, you can probably learn to live with it.

XL600V Transalp

This V-twin dual-sport, which was imported into the United States only in 1989 and 1990, is one of the best all-around motorcycles produced those years and is easy for a beginning rider to master. This model is popular in Europe.

VTR250 Interceptor

While only a 250, this little V-twin sportbike is capable of freeway riding. It is also a fun, good-handling little bugger—and pretty, too.

CB650SC/CB700SC Nighthawks

If you're looking for a good inline-four-cylinder Japanese motorcycle, I highly recommend Honda's original Nighthawk series. In fact, I (and many motorcyclists) prefer them to the newer 750 Nighthawks simply because they have shaft drives, while the newer Nighthawks have chains. Even with shaft drives, they are some of the best-handling motorcycles of their day. Some riders take issue with their 16-inch front wheels, which make these bikes seem a bit twitchy in some circumstances, although many novices prefer the maneuverability those same wheels provide.

CB750 Nighthawk

While the newer Nighthawk hasn't won me over quite like the older version, it is still a fantastic all-around motorcycle, and a clean used example represents an even better value than a new one.

FT500/VT500 Ascots

These are two different bikes. The FT uses an air-cooled, single-cylinder engine derived from the XL500 dual-sport, while the VT uses a liquid-cooled V-twin lifted from the 500 Shadow. Both make excellent first bikes.

NT650 Hawk GT

These little V-twin sportbikes have become more popular since Honda stopped importing them to the United States. They are more fun on a twisty road than just about any motorcycle I've ever ridden, and one of my greatest regrets is not buying one. The only drawback is that they're a bit cramped for riders over 6 feet tall.

VF500C V30 Magna/VF500F Interceptor

Both these bikes use different versions of the same engine. The Magna surrounds the engine with one of history's most elegant little cruisers, while the Interceptor is the finest-handling motorcycle built in the mid-1980s.

VT500/VT600/VT700/VT750/VT800/VT1100 Shadows

The Shadow cruiser line contains some of the most reliable motorcycles manufactured in the past couple of decades. I especially recommend the 1986–1987 VT700 Shadows, which combine striking looks and genuine comfort with the low maintenance of a shaft drive and hydraulically adjusted valves. In my opinion, this model makes a better all-around motorcycle than any of the new midsize cruisers. The 1988 VT800 looks much the same as the VT700, but it comes with only a four-speed transmission, detracting from its versatility.

Kawasaki

Because Kawasaki has a reputation as a high-performance company, many Kawasaki motorcycles will have seen hard use. But they are rugged bikes that can withstand a lot of abuse.

KLR600/KLR650/KL650-B2 Tengai/KLX650

Not much has changed in the KLR line since the 600 first appeared in 1984, which is a good thing because it's such a good basic motorcycle. The Tengai is a funky rally-style version (one of the most unique-looking dual-sports to come out of Japan), and the KLX is a more off-road-worthy machine. All make fine first bikes.

EL250 Eliminator

This nifty little power cruiser shares its engine with the EX250 Ninja, meaning that it is a snappy bike. These motorcycles are easy to ride, plenty fast, and, with their small bikini fairings, just about the cutest bikes ever made.

EX250 Ninja

This is the same bike as the 250 Ninja that Kawasaki sells today, and it hasn't changed much since its introduction in 1986, except for graphics. If the new bike is a best buy, the used version is even better.

EN450 454 LTD/EN500 Vulcan 500

These ancestors to the Vulcan 500 LTD are fast little cruisers, but many people question their styling. If you don't mind the way they look, they are useful bikes.

EX500/500 Ninja

Kawasaki has made incremental improvements to its 500 Ninja over its long production run, but the original is still a good bike. A 1987 model will cost about far less than what you'll pay for a new model.

KZ550/KZ550 LTD/KZ550 GPz/KZ550 Spectre

Kawasaki's 550 four-cylinder bike was impressive when it first appeared, and it's still an impressive bike. Reliable as a claw hammer, the 550 still has enough power to get you into serious trouble with legal authorities. The best of the bunch is the GPz, which practically created the current 600cc sportbike class.

ZR550 Zephyr

Although the Zephyr is a good bike, it isn't noticeably better than its predecessor, the KZ550—and it costs more. Still, if you can find a deal on a ZR550 Zephyr, you'll have a great motorcycle.

VN700/750 Vulcan

If you can get past the styling of this one, you'll find a great motorcycle underneath.

Vulcan 800/Vulcan 800 Classic/Vulcan 800 Drifter

Kawasaki's 800cc Vulcans make great first bikes. Their hardtail-look rear ends, created by hiding the shocks, give them a low center of gravity that allows for easy handling at parking-lot speeds and stability at freeway speeds. The standard Vulcan 800 looks like a 1970s-era chopper, the Vulcan 800 Classic re-creates the look of a 1950s-era touring bike, and the Vulcan 800 Drifter recalls the classic streamlined Indians of the 1940s.

ZL600 Eliminator

This is a fun, easy-to-ride power cruiser. Its main drawback is a too-small fuel tank that can barely go 100 miles between fill-ups.

Suzuki

Suzuki has built some unique, often highly functional motorcycles, but throughout the company's history designers have occasionally created bikes that the buying public has not warmed up to. One such bike, the rotary-engine RE5, almost bankrupted the company. On the other hand, when Suzuki designers get the look of a bike right, they create some of the prettiest machines on the road.

DR350S/SE/DR650S/SE

Basically, these are the same as later versions of Suzuki's dual-sports, at lower prices.

GS500E

Everything I said about this bike in Appendix A goes for the used version, except the price. These bikes have been popular ultralight racers, so if you buy a used GS500E, make certain that it hasn't been raced.

GS550E/ES/L/M/GS650G/GL/GS650M Katana

Any of Suzuki's air-cooled four-cylinder 550s and 650s make excellent, dependable bikes, but these are older, so expect them to need small repairs more frequently than newer motorcycles. The switch gear and electrical components are the items most likely to need some attention.

GSF400 Bandit

Some people consider the smallest Bandit, built between 1991 and 1993, one of the best-handling motorcycles ever made. You have to rev the snot out of its little four-cylinder engine, but when you do, it goes like stink.

GSX600F/GSX750F Katanas

These are high-performance sportbikes that require a rider with self-control, but they are such good all-around motorcycles that if you think you can trust yourself, you might want to consider buying one.

VX800, Intruder, VZ800 Marauder

These capable motorcycles might be a bit much for most new riders, but those who feel comfortable with bikes of this size will find them best buys.

Yamaha

Yamahas are rugged, well-constructed bikes, although the fit and finish aren't always up to Honda's standards. Don't be surprised to find chrome plating peeling off older Yamahas.

XT350/XT550/XT600

These bikes trace their roots back to the original big Japanese thumper, the XT500 of the 1970s. Although it was a nice dual-sport, it wasn't competitive with the other thumpers from Japan and was discontinued in 1995.

XJ550 Seca/Maxim/XJ650 Seca/Maxim/XJ700 Maxim

Yamaha's first four-cylinder midsize engine series, which powers all these bikes, set new standards for performance when introduced in 1981 and has proven rugged and dependable over the years. The same basic engine design was still used in the 1998 Seca II.

FJ600

Although it was considered a sportbike in its day, the FJ seems like a standard now. With its frame-mounted half-fairing and sporty riding position, this bike is still striking. If you can find a clean example, buy it.

YX600 Radian

The successor to the FJ600 had all that bike's mechanical virtues but lacked the FJ's style. It's still a good bike, though.

XJ600S Seca II

If a new Seca II costing $5,300 was a best buy, then buying an older version of the exact same machine for $3,000 less should earn the buyer a place in the bargain-hunter's hall of fame.

Resources

Throughout this book, I've discussed what a wonderful community of people you will meet when you become a motorcyclist. This appendix tells you how to get in touch with that community. I list the addresses of some major clubs and organizations, and I also tell you where you can find all the books, videotapes, accessories, and other paraphernalia you'll want and need.

Motorcycle Safety Foundation (MSF)

The Motorcycle Safety Foundation is a national nonprofit organization sponsored by the U.S. distributors of BMW, Ducati, Honda, Kawasaki, Suzuki, and Yamaha motorcycles. I've tried to stress the value of taking a Motorcycle Safety Foundation RiderCourse, but in case I haven't made myself perfectly clear, taking such a course can save your life. No other action you can take will help you have a safer motorcycling career. To find a RiderCourse near you, contact:

Motorcycle Safety Foundation
2 Jenner St., Suite 150
Irvine, CA 92718–3812
1-800-446-9227
www.msf-usa.org

American Motorcyclist Association (AMA)

Taking an MSF RiderCourse is the most important thing you can do to help make you a safer rider. Joining the AMA is the most important thing you can do to safeguard your rights as a motorcyclist. Contact the AMA at:

American Motorcyclist Association
13515 Yarmouth Dr.
Pickerington, OH 43147
1-800-AMA-JOIN
www.ama-cycle.org

Clubs and Organizations

As I said in Chapter 19, joining a club can be your best way to get in touch with your local motorcycling community. The following list gives you the names and addresses of just a few of the thousands of clubs available.

Biker Scum

Biker Scum is a motorcycle group dedicated to the pursuit of happiness through riding and the neglect of personal hygiene. Their goal is to form a worldwide network of riders, connected via the Internet, who assist other motorcyclists when planning trips, specifically by giving them advice on local roads and brew pubs. So far, they have chapters in Pennsylvania; Texas; Virginia; California; Indiana; Ontario, Canada; and Okinawa, Japan. To contact Biker Scum, send e-mail to:

http://drlubell.home.mindspring.com/bscum.html

Blue Knights

The Blue Knights is a club specifically for law-enforcement officials, with chapters located in all 50 states. To find the chapter nearest you, contact:

Blue Knights International Law Enforcement Motorcycle Club, Inc.
International Headquarters
38 Alden St.
Bangor, ME 04401
1-800-BKI-LEMC (prospective members only)

BMW Motorcycle Owners of America (BMWMOA)

BMWMOA has chapters across the country and puts on some of the best rallies you'll find anywhere. Plus, it puts out an excellent monthly magazine. You can contact its national headquarters at:

BMW Motorcycle Owners of America
PO Box 3982
Ballwin, MO 63022
636-394-7277
www.bmwmoa.org

Christian Motorcyclists Association (CMA)

As I said in Chapter 1, motorcycling is a spiritual activity—so much so that some people like to formally combine it with their religion. If you would like to do the same, a great way to do so is by joining the CMA. These folks put on some terrific events and have chapters all across the country. Contact them at:

Christian Motorcyclists Association
PO Box 9
Highway 71 South
Hatfield, AR 71945
870-389-6196
www.cmausa.org

Gold Wing Road Riders Association (GWRRA)

GWRRA is the largest club in the world devoted to a single motorcycle: the Honda Gold Wing. Membership is open to owners of the ultimate behemoth, as well as Honda Valkyries. You can contact GWRRA at:

GWRRA International Headquarters
21423 N. 11th Ave.
Phoenix, AZ 85027
www.gwrra.org

Motor Maids

Motor Maids is not only one of the oldest clubs for female motorcyclists; it's one of the oldest motorcycle clubs, period. Some of the women still riding with Motor Maids were dispatch motorcyclists in World War II. Contact them at:

Motor Maids
PO Box 157
Erie, MI 48133
www.motormaids.org

Retreads Motorcycle Club International, Inc.

Retreads Motorcycle Club International boasts a membership of 5,000 motorcyclists, and all of them have at least two things in common: they have reached the age of 40, and they love to ride motorcycles. If you are interested in locating a club near you, just go to the club's home page:

http://retreads.org

Turbo Motorcycle International Owners Association (TMIOA)

The TMIOA is a club for owners of all the factory turbo-charged motorcycles. You can contact them at:

Turbo Motorcycle International Owners Association
PO Box 1653
Albrightsville, PA 18210
http://turbomotorcycles.org

Women On Wheels (WOW)

I've spent some time with members of this motorcycle club for women and have found them to be some of the most enjoyable motorcyclists I've ever ridden with. If you are a female motorcyclist, I highly recommend joining your local chapter of WOW. To find your nearest chapter, contact Women On Wheels at:

WOW International Headquarters
PO Box 14180
St. Paul, MN 55114
1-800-322-1969
www.womenonwheels.org

Ronnie Cramer's Motorcycle Web Index—Clubs/Organizations

This site has the most complete listing I've found of motorcycle clubs and organizations. If there is a club—or even a type of club—you're looking for, you should be able to find it here. Check out Ronnie Cramer's Motorcycle Web:

www.sepnet.com/cycle

Books and Videotapes

You can learn anything you've ever wanted to know about motorcycles and motorcycling by reading one of the tens of thousands of books available on the subject.

Whitehorse Press

Whitehorse Press publishes and distributes nothing but motorcycle books. It's owned and operated by Dan and Judy Kennedy, both of whom are devoted motorcyclists as well as publishers, and that devotion to the sport shows in their books. Whitehorse publishes many excellent books on motorcycling, and its catalog contains one of the most complete selections of motorcycle-related books and products you'll find anywhere. To obtain the latest catalog, contact them at:

Whitehorse Press
107 E. Conway Road
Center Conway, NH 03813-4012
1-800-531-1133
www.whitehorsepress.com

Motorbooks International

Motorbooks International publishes and distributes books on all aspects of vehicular culture, from antique tractors to airplanes. It also produces and distributes an incredibly diverse collection of motorcycle books. You can order books or a catalog at:

Motorbooks International
PO Box 1
Osceola, WI 54020-0001
1-800-826-6600
www.motorbooks.com

Web Pages

You can find literally hundreds of motorcycle-related web pages on the Internet. My favorites are the ones that update their content on a daily basis. The great thing about these webzines is that they have absolutely up-to-the-minute news. Within minutes of the finish of a national or international race, you can log on to one of the racing-oriented sites such as www.speedtv.com and get the latest points standings. If a racer is injured, you can monitor his condition by checking the Internet. When a company releases a new model of motorcycle, you don't have to wait months to see it on the cover of a magazine because it is instantaneously broadcast over the Internet.

While there is a nearly infinite number of motorcycle-related web pages on the Internet, I just want to list a few of my personal favorites, along with their addresses. Again, this is my subjective listing, so do your own research because you may find magazines that you like far better than the ones listed here.

- AMA Superbike: www.superbikeplanet.com
- American Motorcycle: www.americanmotor.com
- MotoGP: http://motogp.tiscali.com/en/motogp/index.htm
- Motoworld.com: www.motoworld.com
- Motorcycle Daily: www.motorcycledaily.com
- Motor Cycle News: www.motorcyclenews.com
- Motorcycle Online: www.motorcycle.com
- Motorcycle World: www.motorcycleworld.com
- Roadracing World: http://venus.13x.com/roadracingworld/
- Speed Channel: www.speedtv.com
- *Motorcyclist, Motorcycle Cruiser,* and others: www.primedia.com/divisions/ enthusiastmedia

Mailing Lists

To find mailing lists related to your particular motorcycling interests, start searching around on the Internet. There you will find the home pages of such lists, along with instructions on joining the group.

Suggested Reading

The following list includes some of the most important books you can read when starting out as a motorcyclist. Everyone has their own preferences and individual tastes, so any suggested reading list has to be somewhat subjective. But whatever your tastes, you will find the following books useful:

Harley-Davidson Evolution Motorcycles
Greg Field
Motorbooks International, hardbound, 2001, 192 pages
This book covers Harley history from The Motor Company's precipitous decline and near bankruptcy in the late 1970s and first half of the 1980s to its resurrection and eventual return to the number-one position in the American market. Author Greg Field has done a fantastic job researching company history and the history of the Evolution engine family, the series of engines that powered Harley's remarkable comeback. This is one of my favorite motorcycle books.

Harley-Davidson in the 1960s
Allan Girdler and Jeff Hackett
Motorbooks International, softbound, 2001, 96 pages
Author Allan Girdler and photographer Jeff Hackett document the history of the most important American motorcycle company of all time during the tumultuous 1960s. This was a time when the monolithic corporation AMF bought out the original families that had run Harley Davidson since the company's inception just after the turn of the century.

A Century of Indian
Ed Youngblood
Motorbooks International, hardbound, 2001, 156 pages
This beautifully photographed book tells the story of Indian motorcycles through the "Century of Indian" exhibit at the Motorcycle Hall of Fame Museum. Youngblood developed the book in conjunction with his work developing the exhibit and penned the informative yet entertaining text that accompanies the photography.

Honda Gold Wing
Darwin Holmstrom
Whitehorse Press, softbound, 2001, 96 pages
The story of the Gold Wing is, in many ways, the story of American motorcycling, making this a worthy read for anyone interested in the sport. Besides, I wrote it. Hey, if you've gotten this far, you can't hate my writing. Yes, this is a shameless plug.

How to Set Up Your Motorcycle Workshop: Designing, Tooling, and Stocking
Charles G. Masi
Whitehorse Press, softbound, 1996, 160 pages
This book can save you a lot of headaches (as well as a lot of aches in other places) when doing your own motorcycle maintenance. Masi even manages to make the subject entertaining, with his offbeat sense of humor.

Against the Wind—A Rider's Account of the Incredible Iron Butt Rally
Ron Ayres
Whitehorse Press, softbound, 1997, 240 pages
This book gives you an inside look at what it is like to compete in one of the most demanding motorcycle endurance events in the world. Ayres's storytelling skills make what is already a fascinating story even more fun to read.

Pictorial History of Japanese Motorcycles
Cornelis Vanderheuvel
Elmar/Bay View Books, hardbound, 1997, 168 pages
(distributed by Classic Motorbooks)
This book does an excellent job of chronicling the evolution of the Japanese motorcycle industry—an evolution that helped make motorcycling accessible to most of the people riding today. More than 375 color illustrations are included.

One Man Caravan
Robert Edison Fulton Jr.
Whitehorse Press, softbound, 1996, 288 pages
In this book, Fulton chronicles his 17-month around-the-world motorcycle trip, which he began in 1932. In this fascinating story, Fulton gives the reader an idea of what it was like to tour on a motorcycle in the days before electric starters and gas stations on every corner.

Motorcycle Owner's Manual: A Practical Guide to Keeping Your Motorcycle in Top Condition
Hugo Wilson
DK Publishing, softbound, 1997, 112 pages
(distributed by Whitehorse Press)
This book won't replace a good repair manual specifically for your bike, as the author himself admits, but it serves as an excellent additional source of information. General procedures are explained much more clearly than in most manuals, and the photos are easier to follow.

The Motorcycle Safety Foundation's Guide to Motorcycling Excellence: Skills, Knowledge, and Strategies for Riding Right
Motorcycle Safety Foundation
Whitehorse Press, softbound, 1995, 176 pages
If you can't take a RiderCourse, at least buy the Motorcycle Safety Foundation's book, which is a collection of its instructional material. If I discovered that any idea, technique, or practice I discussed in this book differed from MSF practice, I deferred to them—these folks know what they're doing, and they know how to save lives.

World Superbikes: The First Ten Years
Julian Ryder, photographs by Kel Edge
Haynes Publishing, softbound, 1997, 160 pages
(distributed by Classic Motorbooks)
When World Superbike racing first began in 1988, journalist Julian Ryder left the Grand Prix circuit to cover the new series. He's been doing so ever since, and now he's written a book chronicling the first decade of the immensely popular series. His in-depth knowledge of the racers and the sport in general make this a gripping book, and Edge's photography is superb.

Ducati Story: Racing and Production Models 1945 to the Present Day
Ian Falloon
Patrick Stephens Limited, hardbound, 1996, 160 pages
(distributed by Classic Motorbooks)
During the past decade, many books have been written about Ducati. This is one of the best of those books. *Ducati Story* is a case study in how to build the finest high-performance motorcycles in the world and how *not* to conduct a business. Motorcyclists and business types alike should find this a fascinating book.

Zen and the Art of Motorcycle Maintenance: An Inquiry into Values
Robert M. Pirsig
Bantam Books, softbound, 1974, 380 pages
(distributed by Whitehorse Press)
I try to reread Pirsig's motorcycle classic at least once a year, and each time, it is like reading a different book. It may prove a tough read for those without a philosophical bent, but it is worth the effort.

Hell's Angels: A Strange and Terrible Saga
Dr. Hunter S. Thompson
Ballantine Books, softbound, 1967, 276 pages
(distributed by Whitehorse Press)
Hunter S. Thompson may be more famous for his excessive lifestyle than for his writing, but long after everyone has forgotten about his excesses, his writing will live on. His command of the English language rivals that of any author, living or dead, and when he chooses to write about motorcycles, so much the better.

Recommended Viewing

Street Smarts: The Advanced Course in Urban Survival video series
Produced by Paul Winters and David West, distributed by Whitehorse Press
Nothing compares to taking an MSF RiderCourse, but if you choose not to do so, at least buy these three videos—they may save your life. Much of the material presented in the videos is covered in a RiderCourse, and while you won't benefit from individual instruction and instructor feedback, you'll at least be able to see how it's done. Ideally, you should take a RiderCourse and buy these videos. Considering what's at stake, the relatively low cost of these videos represents one of the best investments you can make.

Parts and Accessories

In the long run, you're better off buying as many motorcycle supplies as you can from your local dealers, but often you won't be able to find what you want locally, and you'll have to look elsewhere. The following list provides you with names, addresses, and phone numbers where you can find just about anything you need.

Aerostich

To get one of Aerostich's fantastic riding suits, you're going to have to go directly to the source and give owner Andy Goldfine a call. Even if you're not in the market for a riding suit, you should contact him and get a copy of the Aerostich catalog, which contains the most useful collection of quality riding accessories you'll find anywhere. It is also the most entertaining catalog you'll ever read.

Aero Design
8 S. 18th Ave. West
Duluth, MN 55806-2148
1-800-222-1994
www.aerostich.com

Chaparral Motorsports

Chaparral has one of the widest selections of gear and accessories for both on- and off-road riding you'll find anywhere. Contact them at:

Chaparral Motorsports
555 S. H St.
San Bernardino, CA 92410
1-800-841-2960
www.chaparral-racing.com

Dennis Kirk, Inc.

Dennis Kirk may not always have the lowest prices on all items, but they have an incredibly wide selection and they get your stuff to you fast. Besides, on some items, they will match the best price you can find elsewhere. Contact them at:

Dennis Kirk, Inc.
955 S. Field Ave.
Rush City, MN 55069
1-800-328-9280
www.denniskirk.com

Dynojet Research, Inc.

Many motorcycles come with their carburetion set too lean. Not only does this hinder performance, but it can cause your engine to run hot, especially if you install an aftermarket air filter. If your bike suffers from such problems, or if you just want to improve its overall performance, the helpful folks at Dynojet Research can set you up with just the carburetor jetting kit. Contact them at:

Dynojet Research, Inc.
2191 Mendenhall Dr.
North Las Vegas, NV 89081
1-800-992-4993 or 1-800-992-3525
www.dynojet.com

J&P Cycles

If you have a Harley-Davidson garbage wagon and want to chop it, if you have a basket-case Harley chopper and want to refurbish it, if you want to spiff up your

Harley, or if you just want to build a complete motorcycle from spare parts, you'll find everything you need to do so in the J&P Cycles catalog. Contact them at:

J&P Cycles
PO Box 138
13225 Circle Dr.
Anamosa, IA 52205
1-800-397-4844
www.j-pcycles.com
jpcycles@netins.net

JC Whitney

If you're a careful shopper, you can get some killer buys on motorcycle accessories from JC Whitney. Although inexpensive, some of the items JC Whitney carries are of surprisingly high quality. You can contact them at:

JC Whitney
1 JC Whitney Way
LaSalle, IL 61301
1-800-603-4383
www.jcwhitney.com

National Cycle, Inc.

National Cycle builds some of the finest aftermarket windshields and fairings you can buy. I've owned six of them and have found them all to be of the highest quality. You can purchase products from any shop or catalog, but if you call the folks at National Cycle and order direct, they can help you select the windshield or accessory that best fulfills your needs. It is a tremendous opportunity for you to benefit from their experience. Contact National Cycle at:

National Cycle, Inc.
2200 S. Maywood Dr. PO Box 158
Maywood, IL 60153
1-877-972-7336
www.nationalcycle.com

Sport Wheels

Ex-racer Denny Kannenberg owns more motorcycles than anybody—at least 10,000, at last count. He also owns the world's largest motorcycle-salvage operation, meaning that he has more used parts to sell than anyone else. And even though he's located in Jordan, Minnesota, he does business with motorcyclists across the country. If you ever need something—whether it is a part or a complete motorcycle—and can't find it, give Denny a call. You can contact Sport Wheels at:

1-800-821-5975
www.sportwheel.com

Tuners and Builders

As a new rider, you really don't need to make your motorcycle any faster than it is. I'm not trying to be a wet blanket; it's just that today's motorcycles are ultra-high-performance machines right out of the crate. If you do want more power, the following people can help you out.

Graves Motorsports, Inc.

Chuck Graves knows a thing or two about building fast bikes. In 1993, he won the Formula USA championship, and he's a four-time Willow Springs Formula One champion. Contact him at:

Graves Motorsports, Inc.
7645 Densmore Ave.
Van Nuys, CA 91406
818-902-1942
www.gravesports.com

Hahn Racecraft

Bill Hahn's claim to fame is building motorcycles for drag racing. For a price, he'll help you build what will without a doubt be the quickest motorcycle in town. Contact him at:

Hahn Racecraft
1981 D Wiesbrook Dr.
Oswego, IL 60543
630-801-1417
www.hahnracecraft.com

HyperCycle

If, for some reason, you want a flat-out AMA Superbike for the street, you should get hold of the folks at HyperCycle. Contact them at:

HyperCycle
15941 Arminta St.
Van Nuys, CA 91406
1-877-486-3125
www.hypercycle.com

Mr. Turbo

Mr. Turbo builds turbo kits for a variety of motorcycles, from ZX11 Ninjas to Harley dressers. Contact them at:

Mr. Turbo
4014 Hopper Road
Houston, TX 77093
281-442-7113
www.mrturbo.com

Racing Clubs

The following is a list of clubs that can help you get started in motorcycle road racing.

American Federation of Motorcyclists
6167 Jarvis Ave. #333
Newark, CA 94560
510-796-7005
www.afmracing.org

American Historic Racing Motorcycle Association
PO Box 1648
Brighton, MN 48116
810-225-6085
www.ahrma.org

Central Motorcycle Roadracing Association
PO Box 123888
Ft. Worth, TX 76121-3888
1-817-377-1599
www.cmaracing.com

Central Roadracing Association Inc.
PO Box 5385
Hopkins, MN 55343
612-332-4070

Hallett Road Racing Association
www.hallettracing.com/comma.html

Mid-Atlantic Road Racing Club
PO Box 2292
Wheaton, MD 20915
703-494-9394
http://marrc.nova.org

Motorcycle Roadracing Association
PO Box 4187
Denver, CO 80204
303-530-5678
www.mra-racing.org

Northern California Mini Road Racing Association
PO Box 2791
Citrus Heights, CA 95611-2791
916-722-5517

Oregon Motorcycle Road Racing Association
www.omrra.com

Utah Sport Bike Association
www.utahsba.com

Washington Motorcycle Road Racing Association
www.wmrra.com

Western Eastern Roadracers' Association
www.wera.com

Willow Springs Motorcycle Club
PO Box 911
http://members.aol.com/racewsmc/

High-Performance Riding Schools

Besides taking the Experienced RiderCourse from the Motorcycle Safety Foundation, the best way to improve your riding skills (and your chances of having an injury-free riding career) is to take a course in high-performance riding. Whether you are going racing or you just want to hone your street-riding skills, taking a quality high-performance riding course can teach you things that can save your life. Usually these schools are expensive, but if they can make you a better (and safer) rider, they are worth the money.

Although most of these schools have their headquarters in the American Southwest, many conduct classes at different racetracks around the country, making it easier for riders to attend. Call or write for a schedule of class dates and locations.

CLASS Motorcycle Schools
320 E. Santa Maria St., Suite M
Santa Paula, CA 93060-3800
805-933-9936
www.classrides.com

DP Safety School
PO Box 1551
Morro Bay, CA 93443
805-772-8301
www.dpsafetyschool.com/main.html

Freddie Spencer's High Performance Riding School
7055 Speedway Blvd., Suite E106
Las Vegas, NV 89115
1-888-672-7219
www.fastfreddie.com

California Superbike School
940 San Fernando Road
Los Angeles, CA 90065
323-224-2734
www.superbikeschool.com/us/index.shtml

STAR Motorcycle School
www.starmotorcycle.com

Cycle Babble Glossary

ABS (Antilock Brake System)   A system that detects when a wheel is not turning and releases pressure to the brake on that wheel, preventing a skid.

aftermarket   The sector of the market that sells parts and accessories other than original equipment manufacturers (OEMs).

airheads   A term for older, air-cooled BMW Boxer Twins.

ape hangers   A term coined at the height of the custom-bike movement to describe tall handlebars that forced the rider to reach skyward to grasp the controls, making the rider adopt an apelike posture.

bagger   A motorcycle equipped with saddlebags and other touring amenities.

belt-drive system   A final-drive system that transmits the power to the rear wheel via a drive belt.

big twins   The engines in the larger Harley-Davidson bikes.

blind spot   The area not shown in a rearview mirror.

bobbers   The custom bikes American riders built after World War II. The owners cut off, or bobbed, much of the bodywork.

body armor   The protective padding in motorcycle clothing.

bottom end   The bottom part of the engine, where the crankshaft and (usually) the transmission reside.

boxer   A two-cylinder engine with the pistons opposing each other, resembling fists flying away from each other.

brakes (disc and drum)   Disc brakes use stationary calipers that squeeze pads against the discs that rotate with the wheel. Drum brakes use horseshoe-shape brake shoes that expand against the inner surface of the wheel hub.

café chop   Converting a stock motorcycle into a café racer.

café racer   Motorcycles modified to resemble racing motorcycles from the 1950s and '60s. They are called café racers because their owners supposedly raced from café to café in London, where the bikes first appeared in the 1960s.

cam   A rod with eccentric lobes on it that opens the valves.

carbon fiber   A high-tech material favored in many motorcycle applications because it is extremely strong and light. The distinctive look of carbon fiber has become trendy.

carburetor   A device that mixes fuel with air to create the fuel charge burned in the combustion chamber.

cases   The two clamshell-like halves in the bottom end of the engine, surrounded by a metal shell.

CE approval   A European standard of certification for motorcycle clothing.

centerstand   A stand that supports the motorcycle in an upright position.

centerstand tang   A small lever attached to the centerstand.

chain-drive system   A final-drive system that transmits the power to the rear wheel via a chain.

chassis   The combined frame and suspension on a motorcycle.

chopper   Once used to describe a custom motorcycle that had all superfluous parts chopped off in order to make the bike faster, a chopper today is a type of custom bike that usually has an extended fork, no rear suspension, and high handlebars.

clip-ons   Handlebars that attach directly to the fork tubes, rather than to the top yoke, and hold the fork tubes together.

clutch   A device that disengages power from the crankshaft to the transmission, allowing a rider to change gears.

combustion chamber   The area at the top of the cylinder where the fuel charge burns and pushes the pistons down.

coming on the cam   The term used when a four-stroke reaches its powerband.

coming on the pipe   The term used when a two-stroke reaches its powerband.

connecting rods   Rods that attach the crankshaft to the pistons via the eccentric journals. The rods' up-and-down movement is converted into a circular motion through the design of the journals.

constant-radius turn   A turn with a steady, constant arc. In a decreasing-radius corner, the arc gets sharper as you progress through the curve, while in an increasing-radius corner, the arc becomes less sharp.

contact patch   The area of your tire that actually contacts the road while you ride.

cordura   A synthetic outer material used to make motorcycle clothing.

counterbalancer   A weight inside an engine that cancels some of the engine's vibration.

countersteering   The way you use the handlebar(s) to lean the bike into a turn. If you want to turn right, you push the handlebar(s) to the left, and vice versa.

cowling   A piece of bodywork that covers the engine area.

crotch rocket   A term some people use to refer to sportbikes.

crowns   The tops of the pistons.

cycle   The up-and-down motion of the piston. The terms *cycle* and *stroke* are used interchangeably when referring to engine types.

cylinder block   The hunk of aluminum with holes bored through it, inside which the pistons move up and down.

cylinders   The hollow shafts in the top end of an engine inside which internal combustion occurs.

decreasing-radius corner   A turn in which the arc gets sharper as you progress through the curve.

dirtbike   Bikes intended for off-road use that aren't legal to ride on public roads. Sometimes the term *pure-dirt* is used to distinguish a dirtbike from a dual-sport motorcycle.

discs   The metal rotors the caliper presses the pads against to brake.

double-cradle frame   A bike frame with two steel tubes circling the engine from the front and cradling it.

dresser   A motorcycle set up for long-distance touring.

dual-sport Street-legal motorcycles with varying degrees of off-road capabilities. Also called dual-purpose motorcycles.

eccentric journals Used to attach the connecting rods to the crankshaft.

ergonomics The science used to design devices, systems, and physical conditions that conform to the human body. This is a prime consideration when designing a motorcycle.

evolution (Evo) When Harley-Davidson began using aluminum to build its cylinder jugs, it called this new engine the Evolution.

fairings The devices mounted at the front of a motorcycle to protect the rider from the elements. These range from simple, Plexiglas shields to complex, encompassing body panels.

false neutral When you fail to engage gears and the transmission behaves as though it is in neutral, even though it isn't.

flat cylinders Cylinders arranged in a flat, opposing configuration, found in the flat-four- and flat-six-cylinder engines used in Honda's Gold Wings.

foot paddling The way an unskilled rider walks his or her motorcycle around at low speeds.

forks The metal tubes holding the front wheel to the rest of the motorcycle.

four-cylinder bike A motorcycle with four cylinders.

fuel-injection system A system that mixes the fuel-air charges and forcibly injects them into the combustion chambers, unlike carburetors, which rely on the vacuum created by the engine to draw the charges into the combustion chambers.

garbage wagon A scornful term used by some outlaw bikers to describe touring bikes.

gearhead A person with a strong interest in all things mechanical; a motorcyclist.

gearset A set of gears within a bike's transmission.

grab rail The handle that a passenger holds on a motorcycle.

high-siding Pitching a bike over away from the direction you are turning. This is the most dangerous kind of crash.

horsepower A measure of an engine's strength.

hydroplane When your tires start to float on top of water, causing them to lose contact with the road's surface.

increasing-radius corner   A turn in which the arc becomes less sharp as you go through the curve.

inline-four   An engine with four cylinders in a row.

inline-triple   An engine with three cylinders placed in a row.

Iron Butt Rally   The most grueling long-distance motorcycle rally in the world. The rally requires that you ride at least 11,000 miles in 11 days to finish.

kick start   The method of starting a motorcycle without an electric starting system.

knucklehead   A term for Harley-Davidson's first overhead-valve Big Twin, introduced in 1936.

L-twin engine   A V-twin engine with its cylinders splayed apart at a 90-degree angle, which creates a smoother-running engine. These engines can be placed either transversely (crosswise) or longitudinally (lengthwise) in the motorcycle frame.

lane splitting   Riding between lanes of traffic on a freeway.

laying the bike down   A crash in which you slide down on one side of the bike.

leviathan   Used to describe big, multicylinder dual-sports.

lugging the engine   Letting the rpm fall below the engine's powerband.

manual transmission   A device consisting of a set of gears (the gearset) that alter the final-drive ratio of a vehicle to enable an operator to get up to speed. Automatic transmissions do not have gearsets; they use a complex system of fluid and metal bands to vary the final-drive ratio of a vehicle.

naked bikes   Bikes without any type of fairing.

oilheads   Newer, air-and-oil-cooled BMW Boxer engines.

oil-line   The spilled trail of oil in the center of a busy road.

open-class   When referring to street-legal sportbikes, open-class designates motorcycles with engines that displace more than 800 cubic centimeters of volume.

original equipment manufacturers (OEM)   The companies that build the bikes.

orphan bikes   Rare bikes that are no longer in production.

otto cycle   Term sometimes used for the four-stroke engine, in honor of its inventor, Otto Benz.

overbore   When you overbore your engine, you drill out the cylinders and then put oversize pistons in the holes, effectively increasing your engine capacity.

overhead-cam system   A system in which the cam rides above the cylinder head. There are single-overhead-cam (SOHC) and double-overhead-cam (DOHC) designs.

panhead   A term for Harley-Davidson's second-generation overhead-valve Big Twin engine, introduced in 1948.

parallel-twin engine   A two-cylinder engine with its cylinders placed side by side in an upright position.

pistons   The slugs moving up and down within the cylinders.

pillion   The passenger who sits behind the rider on a motorcycle.

polycarbonate   The variety of plastic used to construct cheaper motorcycle helmets.

powerband   A certain rpm (revolutions per minute—how many times per minute an engine's crankshaft spins around) range in which an engine makes most of its power.

primary drive   A drive system—via gears, chain, or belt—connecting the engine's crankshaft to its clutch, and from there to its transmission.

production motorcycles   The bikes manufacturers produce to sell to the general public, rather than bikes built specifically for racers.

pushrod system   System in which the cams are generally located below the cylinder heads and push on the rocker arms by moving long rods, called the pushrods.

radial   When used to describe a tire, refers to the way the cords of a tire are constructed.

rain grooves   Channels cut into a road's surface to help water run off the road during a rainstorm.

repair link   A link in some motorcycle chains that can be disassembled for chain repair.

repli-racers   Hard-edged sportbikes. These motorcycles are characterized by riding positions that tuck the rider into an extreme crouch, forcing him or her to practically lay down on the fuel tank.

revolutions per minute (rpm)   The number of times the crankshaft spins around each minute. Often the term *revs* is used, especially in conversation.

riding two-up   Carrying a passenger on your bike.

rocker arms   Devices that work like upside-down teeter totters and push on the valve stems.

rubber-mounted   Engines that use a system of rubber cushions and/or jointed engine mounts to isolate engine vibration from the rider.

shaft-drive system   A final-drive system that transmits the power to the rear wheel via a drive shaft.

shaft jacking   Shaky or bumpy motion created by the impact of acceleration and then fed back into the bike's frame.

shovelhead   A term for Harley's third-generation overhead-valve Big Twin engine, introduced in 1966.

sidecars   Small carriages attached to the side of a motorcycle to provide extra carrying capacity.

slipping the clutch   The term used to describe only partial engine drive propelling a motorcycle.

sissybar   The backrest put behind the passenger's portion of the saddle.

snicking   The act of shifting a well-functioning transmission is often called snicking because that's the sound the action makes. A transmission that doesn't snick into gear is described as sloppy-shifting.

solid-mounted   Engine that is bolted directly to the frame tubes.

splitting the cases   The metal shell surrounding the bottom end is composed of two clamshell-like halves, called cases. Taking these apart to repair the motor is called splitting the cases. *See also* bottom end.

sport-tourer   A motorcycle that combines the comfort and carrying capacity of a touring bike with the handling and power of a sportbike, with larger fairings and hard, lockable luggage.

sportbike   A motorcycle designed for optimal speed and handling characteristics, often with extensive bodywork.

springer fork   Springer forks use large, exposed springs to dampen the impact of road irregularities.

squid   Someone who rides a sportbike on the street as if he or she were on a racetrack.

steering geometry   The geometrical relationship between the motorcycle frame, the angle of the fork, and the position of the front tire.

sticky   A term used to describe tires with very good grip.

streetfighter   A bare-bones sportbike, stripped of all extraneous body work (also called a hooligan or naked bike).

stroke   The up-and-down motion of the piston.

stunt riding   Riding wheelies and similar maneuvers on a motorcycle.

Super-Motard   A type of dirtbike with wheels and tires from a roadbike (also called a Super-Moto).

suspension   The forks, shocks, and, to a degree, tires of a motorcycle. The springs, fluids, and air in and construction of the tires in these items support the motorcycle.

tappets   Small metal slugs between the cam and the pushrod or rocker arm.

telelever system   The most successful alternate front suspension, made by BMW, which transfers the shock-absorption function of a hydraulic fork to a shock absorber located behind the steering head.

thumper   Bikes with large-displacement, single-cylinder, four-stroke engines.

top end   The upper part of the engine, which contains the pistons, cylinders, and valve gear, and the induction system, which consists of the apparatus that mixes an air-and-fuel charge and feeds it into the combustion chamber.

torque   A twisting force and, in a motorcycle, a measure of the leverage the engine exerts on the rear wheel.

touring bike   A bike equipped for longer rides with fairings and lockable saddle-bags.

track days   Organized group riding days at a race track.

traction   A tire's ability to grip the road.

travel   The distance that suspension components—the forks and shocks—move when the bike rides over bumps.

tricomposite   A mix of three materials used in helmet construction.

twin-spar frame   A bike frame with two steel or aluminum spars (flat beams) that pass around or over the engine.

two-up   A term for carrying a passenger on your motorcycle.

two-stroke engine   An engine whose power cycle consists of just two movements, or strokes: the piston moves down, drawing in the fuel-air charge, and then up, combusting the charge.

unitized transmission   A transmission (often referred to as a unit transmission) that is an integral part of the engine's bottom end.

Universal Japanese Motorcycle (UJM)   During the 1970s, the Japanese became so identified with the four-cylinder, standard-style motorcycle that this term was coined to describe them.

V-four   An engine of four cylinders, arranged in a V-shape configuration, with two cylinders on each side of the V.

V-twin   A two-cylinder engine with its cylinders placed in a V shape.

valve guides   Metal tubes that house the valves.

valve train   The system of valves that lets the fuel charges in and the exhaust gases out.

valves   Devices consisting of metal stems with flat discs on one end that open and close to let fuel charges in and exhaust gases out.

vanishing point   The furthest visible point in the road.

wheelie   Lifting the front wheel of a motorcycle whilst riding.

Index

U–V